DATE DUE	RETURNED
OCT 1 0 2012	OCT 2 6 2012

Prentice
Hall

Singapore   London   New York   Toronto   Sydney   Tokyo   Madrid
Mexico City   Munich   Paris   Capetown   Hong Kong   Montreal

Published in 2001 by
Prentice Hall
Pearson Education South Asia Pte Ltd
23/25, First Lok Yang Road, Jurong
Singapore 629733

Pearson Education offices in Asia: *Bangkok, Beijing, Hong Kong, Jakarta, Kuala Lumpur, Manila, New Delhi, Seoul, Singapore, Taipei, Tokyo*

Printed in Malaysia

8 7 6 5 4
08   07   06

ISBN 0-13-090828-2

CONTENTS

THE CAST
(In order of appearance)

Nick Cohen

John Webster

Jim Riswold

Mark Sitley

Ron Mather

Roy Grace

Steve Henry

Hugh Mackay

Jeff Goodby

Sean Cummins

Stacy Wall

Neil French

Michael Prieve

Lionel Hunt

Keith Reinhard

Scott Whybin

John Hegarty

Indra Sinha

Dion Hughes

Gary Ruskin

Ellen Oppenheim

Tim Delaney

Hal Riney

Professor John Philip Jones

Noel Delbridge

David Blackley

James Best

Paul Fishlock

Warren Brown

Hal Curtis

Warren Berger

Ted Horton

Kirk Souder

Andy Berlin

Arthur Bijur

Cliff Freeman

Adrian Holmes

Tracy Wong

Anthony Simonds-Gooding

Gee Thomson

Jon Steel

Ian Batey

Bill Oberlander

Richard Butterworth

Marcello Serpa

Lee Garfinkel

Mike Cozens

David Droga

Kes Gray

Ron Lawner

Chris O'Shea

Mary Stow

Peter Carter

Andrew Bell

Robert Gibralter

Siimon Reynolds

Nigel Dawson

Naresh Ramchandani

Jack Vaughan

David Lubars

Bruce Bildsten

John Kingsmill

Matt McGrath

David Perry

Graham Fink

Andy Bridge

Paul Malmström

Linus Karlsson

Harvey Marco

Neil Godfrey

Ken Schuldman

Michael Newman

Scott Vincent

Chuck McBride

Mike Gibbs

Antony Redman

Kash Sree

Michael Patti

Jonathan Teo

Rowan Dean

Sue Carey

Jan van Meel

Dean Hanson

Ian Macdonald

Francis Wee

Eddie Wong

Bob Giraldi

Terry Bunton

David Holmes

Steve Gray

Russell Smyth

Jeff Manning

Frank Todaro

David Denneen

Rick Dublin

Ray Lawrence

Steve Orent

Jeff Darling

Helene Nicol

Les Gock

Michael Lynch

Peter Soh

Daniel Lim

Cheryl Chong

Paul Tan

Rod Pullen

Mike Fromowitz

Ravi Deshpande

Anil Thakraney

Yasmin Ahmad

S. P. Lee

Ted Lim

Dharma Somasundram

Kamal Mustafa

Paul Loosley

Harmandar Singh

Bhanu Inkawat

Donald Gunn

FOREWORD

A FEW WORDS ABOUT JIM.

I first met Jim Aitchison judging the 4As awards in Hong Kong, about six years ago.

His sense of fun was a rare attribute at such an event. People take advertising awards far too seriously.

But then Jim also takes advertising really seriously — and so do I.

That's the contradiction at the heart of this business. We sweat over strategy and conception. We swear at anything that gets in the way of our ideas — whether it be ill-informed clients, badly-done research, or the censorship boards who live in another age.

We work unholy hours and lose precious weekends, and a lot of it is spent in the only place you know you're being creative — which is a place where you just don't know if what you're doing is going to work or not.

That's the essence of creativity. To be in a place where you're unsure.

But we do it because it's fun, and also because at one level it's very important.

What we are doing is building brands — and brands are arguably the biggest thing in the world, bigger than organised religion or politics as it is currently being played.

Because brands are what we identify with, so they are of massive importance in everybody's lives.

And nobody knows more about brands than advertising agencies.

But, at the same time, a lot of what we produce is of less importance than people's bladders — they will use our months of hard work as a cue to go to the toilet.

Each TV ad probably takes a few months of your life, and sometimes a few years OFF your life. And you do all this for something that acts as a cue for people to go to the lavatory.

Jim is perfectly equipped to see both sides of this equation. And it will be obvious that he has worked incredibly hard to produce a work of this ambition and scope.

A FEW WORDS ABOUT LENGTH.

This is an amazing book.

But there's a fine line between awesome and ominous, and the sheer scale of it may be off-putting at first sight.

Let me give you my perspective on that.

Dip into it — pick a chapter or a topic, or dip into it at random. I promise you that you will have read something to challenge and inspire you in virtually no time at all.

Most of my heroes are included in the book. And he's found out from them some amazing stuff — from dealing with research, through dealing with rejection, to why directors pick agencies.

If you care about advertising, you'll love this book.

Just don't try and read it all at one go.

It'll drive you completely bonkers.

A FEW WORDS ABOUT FUN.

If you read this book wisely, you'll get a real sense of the fun you can have in this business.

But don't buy this book because you want to win an award. Award juries aren't very good at celebrating real innovation. And innovating is the only game in town.

We owe that to our clients, and we owe that to consumers, and we owe that to ourselves as creative people.

Of course, there's no simple solution — the whole thing is subjective, it's gut instinct, it's playing games with emotion. But there's a lot of fun along the way if you keep pushing the boundaries and trying stuff that nobody has ever done before.

If you're a client who's scared of making a brave decision, a researcher who doesn't know how to interpret research intelligently, or a member of the regulatory boards who still live in Victorian times, read it and weep.

Look at all the fun you're missing out on.

Steve Henry
Creative Partner
Howell Henry Chaldecott Lury & Partners
London

WITH SPECIAL THANKS

To everyone who so generously contributed their time and talent to my search for wisdom. This is truly your book. It was a privilege to spend an hour or so with each of you. And to all those busy people who worked miracles for me, kindly supplying still frames and arranging permission to reproduce them, my very sincere thanks.

Cover design: Andrew Clarke
Cover artwork: Paul Clarke

ACKNOWLEDGEMENTS

Extracts from feature *Product Placement Takes a Digital Turn* from *New York Times Service* published in *International Herald Tribune*, 2 October 1999, reprinted with permission of International Herald Tribune and New York Times Syndicate.

Extracts from *The Cybergypsies* by Indra Sinha, Copyright © Indra Sinha, 1999, published by Scribner UK, reprinted with permission of Simon & Schuster UK Ltd.; Viking Penguin, a division of Penguin Putnam Inc.; and Scovil Chichak Galen, New York.

Extract from interview with Richard Paul Evans in *Writer's Digest*, October 1999, reprinted with kind permission of Writer's Digest, Cincinnati, Ohio.

Still frames from *Training Camp* used with permission of Little Caesar Enterprises, Inc. © 1995, Little Caesar Enterprises, Inc. All rights reserved.

Still frame from *Origami* used with permission of Little Caesar Enterprises, Inc. © 1988, Little Caesar Enterprises, Inc. All rights reserved.

Still frames from *Lenny* used with permission of Partnership for a Drug-Free America, New York. All rights reserved.

1

THE TRUTH ABOUT
TELEVISION

"A television commercial is a bit of dead air that you can use to connect with someone." According to Nick Cohen of New York agency, Mad Dogs & Englishmen, "It's almost as though if you don't fill it, the whole of the world will just see nothing."

A TV commercial can be whatever you want it to be. "Jeff Stark said, when you think of a TV commercial, think of it as thirty seconds of air time that's just blank, that you can do something with. If you think of it in that way, you'll open your mind a lot more; you'll be more likely to come up with really interesting ways of defining what a TV commercial is. People tend to look at too many of other people's commercials and if you do that, it's going to be really easy to find yourself falling into a formula of just copying."

John Webster, the legendary creative director of London's BMP DDB, describes the power of television. "The influence it has over people is huge, much more than any other medium really." Television, for Webster, has always been a wonderful opportunity, "a beautiful plaything, because you can do what you want with it. But I also think it gives you a huge responsibility," he cautions. "You're going to influence what people say, what people think. One *has* to bear that in mind. I've always tried to use it intelligently and not underestimate the intelligence of the public, or irritate them."

"While 99% of advertising underestimates the intelligence of its audience, we like to make mistakes by *over*estimating their intelligence," states Wieden & Kennedy executive creative director, Jim Riswold. "All you're trying to do in a television commercial, or any ad for that matter, is make a friend. I have never known anybody who liked anybody who thought they were stupid and treated them as such. It confounds me how a thing that simple is never realised in most advertising out there."

Somehow, the advertising industry has lost the plot. If a television commercial can be whatever you want it to be, if it can liberate creativity, presume intelligence on the part of the viewer *and* make friends for brands, then something has gone seriously wrong.

"The business has become stuck in the jungle of eye candy," laments Mark Sitley, director of broadcast at Fallon Minneapolis. "Style for style's sake, execution being the reason to be. The level of production is really high, but so what? It's all *homogenised*."

"Slickness is awful now, it's just wallpaper," agrees Ron Mather, national creative director at Australia's Campaign Palace. "You see these ads on air, and they're just ads. They look like ads, they feel like ads, they've got the tone of ads. You know nothing is going to deliver, it's just going to be another ad. You can actually make these ads now and just put different logos on the end. It's all nice people doing things in slow motion…"

Roy Grace and Helmut Krone talked about making things *raw*, taking people off-guard. Paul Arden used to ask, what can we do that's *wrong*?

When Steve Henry reviews work at London's Howell Henry Chaldecott Lury & Partners, he asks one question: "*Is this going to be the most talked-about ad of the year?* No matter what the brief is, I always have that in the back of my mind." Challenging assumptions and hijacking the break are Henry's objectives. "We're great experimenters. Everybody else is out there doing one thing, and we're coming in doing something completely different. Our work at its best does that, has that energy, and that's what gives me a kick."

But what gives the public their kicks? Television is supposedly the most formula-ridden medium of all. What is good enough for the

Three ordinary looking blokes are chatting on a street corner. One gulps his Tango. Our two commentators have spotted him.

Ralph: *Hello, Gordie, I think we might use a video replay here...*

Tony: *Super, Ralph, let's do that.*

The event is rewound and played back faster than in real time so we can see what really happens when you drink Tango.

As the bloke lifts his Tango, a big, orange, semi-naked, bald genie runs up from behind him and taps him on the shoulder.

Ralph: *Whoa! We could be in for a quintessential Tango taste sensation here!*

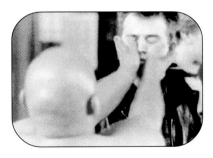

When he turns his head, the Big Orange Man gives him an enormous two-handed slap on the cheeks then runs off. The commentators call for another replay and the film is rewound again...

Tony: *Yes, Ralph, the big orange fella run in from the left and gives him a good old slapping.*

Ralph: *It just illustrates the bite and buzz of real oranges in Tango!*

Tony: *Yes, Ralph, super taste sensation, smashing drink, lovely.*

End VO and super: *You know when you've been Tango'd.*

When Steve Henry reviews work at Howell Henry Chaldecott Lury, he asks: "Is this going to be the most talked-about ad of the year?" In the case of Tango, the Orange Man *was one of the ads that defined the decade.*

programmes ought to be good enough for the commercials. If we do care to take advertising creativity to the cutting edge, will the public reciprocate?

THE VIDEO WATERFALL

"Television audiences are mostly looking for tranquillisation," asserts Australia's most respected social researcher, Hugh Mackay. "Sometimes they might look for stimulation, but the mass audience is there to be damped down by television. It is like the mass drug that Karl Marx predicted."

Have we had fifty years of television, or one year repeated fifty times? While critics wring their hands about the "dumbing-down" of content, television prospers. In America, there were 96 TV stations in 1950; by the end of the century, 1,216. The advent of cable promised greater diversity, even a chance for the masses to run the medium. The reality is, fewer than 20% of public access channels are being used; when they are, they are practically unwatchable.

Is television really a mindless medium? A mesmeriser, nothing more? Mackay has explored the roles of media. Newspapers, for example, are a source of authority, confidence and substance. Radio is the intimate companion. Magazines offer either leading edge information that will fuel the reader's self-esteem, or in the case of mass-circulation women's magazines, a mix of escape, adventure, hope and encouragement. But media distinctions are blurring. Functions overlap. And as Mackay's research shows, *all* mass media, including television, are moving in the direction of being personal, private and individual. There is less scope for advertising of the "public announcement" variety and more for messages that create personal contact between the brand and the consumer.

Real differences still exist in media usage. Reading a newspaper or magazine demands intellectual effort; watching television doesn't. The challenge for television creativity is therefore very complicated, Mackay warns. *Compatibility* is one issue. "The reason people bitterly complain about sound levels increasing for commercials, or about endless repetition of the same commercial, is that both of those things are like jagged edges in a media consumption environment that is meant to be smooth and seamless and rather soporific. In a way, there is an advantage to the advertiser to provide a bit of a jagged edge, so you do stand out, but there's a very low threshold of irritation for the audience."

Nor have we paid nearly enough attention to the question of compatibility with the actual programme context, Mackay suggests. "The idea that any commercial will work in any programme is really weird. In print, we've known for generations that you design an ad for a publication, but we're still in the Dark Ages about designing commercials for programmes. If someone's watching *Friends*, a certain kind of commercial is going to feel right; it's going to match the mood they're in, which is quite different to the mood they're in if they're watching *60 Minutes*."

"When I look at TV concepts," says Jeff Goodby of Goodby, Silverstein & Partners San Francisco, "I try to imagine what they'd feel like, stuffed into a 30-inch box amidst three needy children, someone talking in the next room, and the doorbell ringing. If they do something welcome in that atmosphere, they're starting to work..."

A great television commercial is one that lives and works in the context of the commercial break, concurs Sean Cummins of cummins&partners Melbourne. "We so often see television commercials in a rarefied atmosphere. Watching them on reels, being able to pore over them, rewind them, and look at them again and again is all well and good. But it's the ones that really stop you in-between all the other commercials that matter the most."

"If we have 60 seconds or 30 seconds of time on television, there is *no* reason that that piece of film, even though it is an advertisement, can't be *the most interesting thing that you might see on television that night*." At Wieden & Kennedy New York, Stacy Wall says we should never assume that commercials take second place to programming. Nor should we assume that because commercials have an agenda to sell, they must be pedestrian or pitched to the lowest common denominator. Wieden & Kennedy's legacy, quotes Wall, has been described as creating work that didn't pollute. "At the very least, if we have something to sell, we might as well make it *enjoyable* for people, and not shout at them or speak down to them."

"The video waterfall is like a warm waterfall," Mackay tells us, "a warm shower of audio-visual experiences in which the viewers will happily, *willingly* immerse themselves but only if, when it comes to commercials, the temperature doesn't change too much. They've got to still be comfortable with it." This doesn't mean commercials have to be bland. Mackay believes commercials must trigger "what is the universal response to all advertising, which is, hey, this is about *me*."

Is Anybody Watching?

"I always say that advertising is a bit like trying to get laid in a singles' bar," considers Neil French, worldwide creative director of Ogilvy & Mather. French explains what he calls the Three Steps to Heaven. "You wake up one evening, after your little nap for the day, and you go out. And it's a 3-point thing. First, you've got to be noticed. Secondly, you've got to get their interest. And thirdly, you might get laid. So it's Get Noticed, Get Their Interest, Get Laid. Now you can't get to number two without getting past number one. And you certainly can't get to number three without getting past number two."

Getting noticed and avoiding sameness are French's priorities for any television commercial. "At least with press," says French, "you can always flip back and have a look at the ad again, whereas on TV if you've missed it, you've missed it." French discusses a familiar creative scenario. "I've just been sent a brief for a television commercial which is a little confusing, as they usually are, with far too many bits and pieces that they want to put in. But we can negotiate our way around that. They also sent me examples of everyone else's ads in the market, as well as their own reel, and that was *very* depressing. All their ads, with which they're extremely pleased, look absolutely identical to everyone else's. And the reason they're so pleased with them is because they've got everything in them that they think ought to be in them. They've completely forgotten that the consumer is going to ignore them, *or* be confused, *or* buy a competitor's product. *Sameness is a dreadful problem.*"

In the early days of television, in order to attract attention, Mackay reminds us, they thought you had to have a knight on a white charger galloping across the screen. Other gimmicky visuals included a man in a white coat pointing to a blackboard, or an eruption or an explosion, all of which became recognised video vampires. "That was never how you attracted attention. You attract attention in television, as in any other medium, by pushing the *relevance* button."

But who said all clients really want to be noticed? Not Michael Prieve at Wieden & Kennedy New York. "A lot of clients don't want interesting advertising, there's no benefit in it for them. If you actually asked them, they wouldn't advertise. It's a necessary evil. Every time that they advertise, they're making a statement, and then they're held to it, and it would be much easier not to say anything. A lot of times the great work happens when you deal directly with the guy who owns the company. But some middle-level executive somewhere, what's the benefit for him in doing anything provocative? Nothing. Because his career is going to be based upon whether or not they're on budget, or whether or not things are done in a timely manner. But to do something really interesting or creative, which usually is something that is provocative or controversial or that people will talk about, companies just don't want that."

Arguably, one side effect of television is the reduction of the world's attention span. The implications are obvious.

"The worst sin of all is to be dull," reflects Lionel Hunt, chairman and creative director of Lowe Hunt & Partners Australia, and chairman of the Lowe Lintas Group Australasia. "The greatest commercials I've seen have all been hugely entertaining. That's not enough in itself, but it's a very good start. There are two ways of succeeding in a commercial. There's the way a lot of multinationals use; they do dull commercials, either on purpose or because they aren't able to do anything else, and then beat the consumers over the head with them. And then there are the commercials that approach you with warmth, and wit, and charm, and can be far more successful than the other type, even on a smaller budget. I've got a theory that brands are just like people. If you meet a new person, and you're struck by their warmth and their wit, and they're open and they're not pompous, you tend to like them very much. Whereas if they come in and browbeat you, they're arrogant and boring, you don't want to spend any time with them. Brands are like that; commercials are like that. No matter what they say, no one's listening."

"You can't sell a man who isn't listening." Keith Reinhard, chairman and chief executive officer of DDB Worldwide, quotes Bill Bernbach. "Today, with the proliferation of direct marketing and all the other media forms, that principle is as valid as ever, maybe more so." Reinhard looks for a combination of simplicity, surprise and a smile. "The smile doesn't have to be humour. It often is. It can be a smile of recognition, a smile of appreciation; how well you as a marketer have understood me, and how much I agree."

Even if the consumer is watching, he may not be concentrating.

"There's always a muddiness to bad commercials," says Scott Whybin of Whybin TBWA & Partners Melbourne. "They don't take propositions and make them clear to people." Nor do they help build the brand. "If you waste an opportunity to build the brand while you're selling things, it's as much a waste of money as if it doesn't sell at all."

"Never waste an opportunity to build the brand," says Scott Whybin.
The Campaign Palace Melbourne proves that retail commercials don't have to be
dull and boring. For Target Australia, knitwear bargains are unravelled and there
is no mistaking the advertiser!

TO HYPE OR HYPE NOT

The insubstantial nature of television as a medium calls for extra effort in establishing authority and credibility in the message. There is less scope for hype, according to Mackay.

John Hegarty of Britain's Bartle Bogle Hegarty, agrees. "The public have become completely aware of how marketing and advertising work, therefore they're not intrigued by it in the way they might have been twenty years ago. And because they're more aware of the process, they're more aware of things being sold to them that they find dull and boring. They're not the 'gullible consumers' they once were. If you're trying to involve them, you have to be more entertaining. You have to understand the *power of integrity* in what you're doing."

Manipulation occurs everywhere, Hegarty believes, and ad avoidance is not merely limited to advertising. "The public in general are aware of hype all around them. It's not just something about advertising. They're aware that newspapers try to inveigle them by buying up a story and pretending it's a very powerful one. They're aware of the fact that Hollywood makes *Rocky 4, 5, 6* and *7*, because it's a formula. People in general are just wary. They want things that are entertaining, involving, stimulating, because more often than not they're leading boring lives. And I think they look at advertising in the same way. They just think it's boring, which most of it is, so why am I watching it?"

Reinhard describes how consumers have empowered themselves. "With everything we see in research, people around the world are taking the decision that *I will make my own decisions*. Allegiance to fashion magazines on the part of women — on the decline. '*I will decide.*' Church attendance down — spirituality up. '*I am my own authority.*' In some categories, brands are selected based on their attitudes. Brand allegiance can become very strong because the values expressed by the brand are the values I elect for myself."

British writer Indra Sinha admits: "Occasionally I have the misfortune to catch a commercial, either the beginning or end of one, or sometimes even a whole one, and I find one sees through them with an X-ray vision, not because I've been in advertising, but because I'm a human being living in the real world."

Minneapolis-based writer Dion Hughes shares those sentiments. "We as an industry have created a species of super-media-aware people who understand that on a certain level, *all* advertising and marketing is nonsense. *If we let them know that we know that, they appreciate it.* In fact, they're so post-modern-aware of what we're up to, they know what our jobs are, they know our motives, they're totally on to us, *they no longer feel vulnerable to advertising because they believe they are immune from lies.* If we entertain them, they're willing to relax their critical faculties and take our tap-dancing for what it's worth…"

As Mackay reports, consumers make quite different judgements about advertising from the judgements they make about programme content. "Advertising is recognised as being overtly persuasive. The motives of the advertiser are transparent and the inherent biases can easily be dealt with, unlike the insidious biases of journalists which may be hidden from the viewer." Mackay's research indicates ambivalence on the part of the audience. While they believe television news footage shows them reality, they nevertheless perceive television as *quasi*-reality. Surprisingly, in the Australian market at least, the medium's credibility is no longer an issue. According to cynical viewers, it's either all unreliable and biased, or it's credible *enough*.

But when a commercial is not a commercial, where will the line be drawn? Virtual advertising can digitally insert lifelike images into programmes, making them appear real when in fact they're not. Virtual signs can be generated onto sporting venues. Virtual products, packs and shopping bags can be placed, on demand, into dramas and sitcoms. Advertising and programme content can now integrate seamlessly. What do you zap?

"People are being bombarded with ever-craftier ways of getting them to desire products," states Gary Ruskin, director of Commercial Alert, a Washington organisation founded by consumer advocate Ralph Nader. "It's another good reason they ought to be giving up their TV sets."

"As more and more media become digital, people are more aware reality is being tampered with," counters Ellen Oppenheim, a media director at the New York office of FCB Worldwide. People who have grown up with digital editing in movies, she contends, are less bothered, less likely to complain about someone messing with their reality.

So how *should* we come to grips with creating television commercials? Mackay, for one, argues it is the same as writing any advertising. Knowing what your audience already thinks and feels about the product is still your starting point. "Expand that knowledge to include the medium. What do you know about the people watching the programme? What do they know about the product category that is already part of their personal cage? And be aware that if you can't get into that cage, you won't reach them, it'll just bounce off."

Tim Delaney of Britain's Leagas Delaney offers a similar perspective: "I've never believed there's any difference between writing a print ad, a poster, a radio ad, or a television spot. There are differences in the craft, but essentially you're trying to write to somebody about a service or a product. You're sitting down to write something which is interesting, engaging, and most important of all, on strategy. You're trying to capture their imagination in some way. So as long as you start out with that as an objective, then the medium dictates things back to you. If I was to say there was one key influence on television in the post-Doyle Dane Bernbach era, it's definitely Wieden & Kennedy. They, almost alone, have shown what television can do in the modern era." He calls them commercials that defy conventional parameters; commercials that to all intents and purposes aren't even commercials. "Obviously they're ads with a swoosh on the end, but the level of intelligence, all the combination of new things and new influences on the advertising scene, have been born out of Wieden & Kennedy."

EMOTIONAL OR RATIONAL?

"In general, people react to television more emotionally than they do to the facts we may present," believes Hal Riney of Publicis & Hal Riney Advertising San Francisco. "And in my personal experience, people relate to and react to situations involving people, families, continuity of life, and other timeless things that they might imagine their own lives to have been about." Riney's ingredients are appropriate music, thoughtful writing and reality in production. Emotionally involving an audience, in Riney's words, "is what advertising, at its best, *must* do."

"Effective advertising employs rational arguments enclosed in emotional envelopes," argues Professor John Philip Jones of Syracuse University, citing the content analysis of successful campaigns. "All successful commercials are an amalgam of emotional and rational values. The emotional ones are normally the more important. However, it is vitally important for there to be a small nugget of rationality embedded in the commercial, to strike a harmony in the mind of the user of the brand, triggering a response to purchase the brand when she is next in the store. The emotional quality of the commercial gets attention," maintains Jones, "the rational nugget gets action."

Noel Delbridge, the doyen of Melbourne creative directors, inspired a generation of Australian creatives. "I was actually working in the industry when television arrived in Australia in 1956 and we didn't have a clue. What we knew about television was basically Rosser Reeves. We'd been applying the rational unique selling proposition belief. It wasn't until I went to an *Advertising Age* workshop in America, in the early 60s, that I heard people from Doyle Dane Bernbach and Burnetts, and I started to understand the emotional power of television that we'd neglected totally in Australia. Suddenly, a whole new world had opened up to me. *Humanity...*"

"I always wanted a smile..." One of the men who changed television creativity forever was Roy Grace of New York's Grace & Rothschild. When America's *TV Guide* voted the fifty best commercials of all time, Grace had three out of the top six spots: numbers two, three and five. His work for Doyle Dane Bernbach was classic in its time, and remains so today. Of "The Hundred Best Commercials of All Time", Roy Grace can boast twenty-five. Of the seventeen commercials in the Museum of Modern Art's permanent collection, four carry Roy Grace's name. Grace judges commercials on their ability to provoke a significant emotional reaction. "The real joy of the business is coming up with something that in essence has never existed before. A turn of thought, a concept, a way to make

We track around a gleaming Mercedes-Benz, only to discover the horrific damage on the other side.

VO: *This Mercedes-Benz was travelling on a highway outside Melbourne at 9 o'clock on a Tuesday evening. Inside was the Nies family — husband, wife, and two teenagers — on the way to their farm.*

As they crested a hill, another car on the wrong side of the road, and travelling at high speed in a 100-kilometre zone, speared into the Mercedes.

In all, 120 safety features are built into every Mercedes-Benz and in that split second of the accident, many of them saved the family's lives. The driver's pedals dropped to the floor, away from his feet. The electronic seat belt pre-tensioning device pressed the occupants deep into their seats. And, despite the horrifying impact, the Mercedes safety passenger cell did not collapse. Survival space remained intact.

This is the Nies family. To them, a Mercedes-Benz is not a luxury.

End super: *Engineered like no other car.*

David Blackley of Clemenger BBDO Melbourne says, "An ad should kick the door down." His 60-second Gold Lion-winning Mercedes-Benz spot did just that.

people think, that opens their minds to look at something in a fresh new way."

"There are really only two kinds of commercials that we believe in," observes David Blackley, chairman of Australia's Clemenger BBDO Melbourne. *"Ads that walk straight into your heart, or ads that kick the door down."* Blackley's Gold Lion-winning Mercedes-Benz commercial "kicked the door down" by tracking around a family's gleaming Mercedes to reveal horrific damage on the other side. *A Mercedes-Benz is not a luxury*, said the voice-over. "I don't believe in commercials that are just a number of scenes set to music. I believe in telling a story with a beginning, a middle and an end. They could be funny or dramatic, but they move the audience in an *emotional* way."

LOGICAL OR ILLOGICAL?

"We live in an illogical world," Riswold explains. "When you can make an emotional connection with somebody, it's a far stronger bond than you can get by creating a logical bond with somebody. I don't know who gets married for logical reasons."

Once, commercials were always logical, always linear, everything neatly constructed and sensible. But as the world moves from logic to ideas, communications reflect that change. Messages are more textured, more layered, less logical. Creative methodologies have become less disciplined, less defined. That said, the dichotomy remains; *advertising's job is to change behaviour.* Surely there is a more scientific, more logical, more rational way of achieving our goals?

"Everything we do, in the end, must be to do with behaviour," believes James Best, group chairman of London's BMP DDB and president of DDB Northern Europe. "But we've got this tradition of *intermediate* measures such as awareness, recall, attitude shift, so-called persuasion shift. They are meant to measure stages in human decision-making between being exposed to a message and taking action. I think the increasingly well understood reality is that people do not behave like that; there is not the old AIDA-type model of Attention, Interest, Desire, Action. We are not rational creatures and our brains simply don't work that way. Advertising just doesn't work in a 1-2-3 way, but gives us meaning in other ways." In fact, the way the information is delivered can be just as important in its own right as the information itself. Best cites his agency's famous Volkswagen Polo TV campaign. In one commercial, a woman suffering from hiccups is sitting at her kitchen table reading a newspaper. When she reaches an ad for *Polo from only £7990*, her hiccups stop. In another, a grenadier guard outside Buckingham Palace maintains his rigid stance, ignoring tourists, kids and a dog. But his gaze shifts instantly when a bus drives past with an ad reading *Polo L, only £8145*. "The way you express what could be a very rational point can say a lot about the people *behind* the price offer."

VISUAL OR VERBAL?

"Successful commercials are visual, not verbal," says Jones. "The words are simply used to underpin the pictures." As Jones warns, this does not mean sticking the words on the screen. "The connection is much more subtle than that. It embraces voice casting and the general tone of the commercial."

Despite all advice to the contrary, many copywriters continue to *over*write their scripts; and nowadays, what the voice-over can't cope with, ends up on the screen as well. Visual graffiti?

"Almost all great advertising is visual first, and verbal second," asserts Riney. "That was true even of David Ogilvy's best work; even though he was primarily verbal, even verbose, his advertising at its best reflected a style and elegance that was uniquely his own."

Perhaps, creative arrogance permits us to presume attention on the part of the audience, but not intelligence.

At Sydney's Brown Melhuish Fishlock, Paul Fishlock believes the voice-over column is often a security blanket for agencies. "A lot of strategy is actually put there because people feel they have to tick a lot of boxes along the way, and they can say, yes, we've said that, and we've said that, and we've said that. Car commercials can be some of the worst offenders; they feel they *have* to talk about the load-swallowing boot, the sumptuous leather seats…"

As his art director-agency partner Warren Brown puts it: "TV commercials are such a passive experience. No one out there is a student of advertising. No one out there is going to hang on to every word you say. No one really wants to be sold to. Consequently, if it gets too hard to listen to, or if they have to try to decipher the message, you've lost them."

John Hegarty talks about *ads-on-wheels*: "Essentially, print is an information-led medium. Information has to be at the very heart of what you do, whereas television is more emotionally driven. In a sense, all information is emotionally driven, but print tends to be more factually based. So when you're creating for television, you're creating an emotionally-driven piece of communication; the way you conceive it, the way you actually write it, the way you construct it, you *have* to understand that television is a visual medium. More often than not, I think that what happens is people try and take a print ad and put it on television. We refer to that as ads-on-wheels; it's a way of saying that you're trying to make something that works as a print ad now work in television. The two media are completely different. How often do we read a great book, but we don't see it as a great movie? Moviemakers are faced with the same problem: how do I convert this fantastic book into a fantastic film? I often say to people, one of the best books I've ever read on advertising has got nothing to do with advertising. It was written by William Goldman and called *Adventures in the Screen Trade*. Goldman is a great screenwriter and in it he talks about how you write for the screen, and I think that it really does give you quite an absolute sense of what it is."

Craft disciplines aside, Hegarty invokes a broader issue. "We are now living in a visual culture. People are *more image aware* than they've ever been before in their lives; in the way we dress, the options; in everything we do now, the places we shop, the places we eat, even the way the food is put on the plate, it's all visually driven and people are now making choices on that basis. Obviously underneath that, it's got to be good, it's got to be great, it's got to be all those things, but we're more aware of so much visual stuff around. We're also now confronted with so much information that if that information isn't, to a certain extent, depending on where it is and what it is, reduced down and communicated in a way that's very rapid and fast, we just don't have time to absorb it. That's where visual culture becomes very powerful. It's easier to absorb a picture.

You absorb a picture faster than you absorb words. That doesn't mean to say that words are not important. Words are fundamentally important, but we've got to understand how they now operate and where they operate." As an example, Hegarty points to the way words are used in print. "The day of the long copy ad is over; we have so many other things to read, why do I want to read an ad?"

How Creative Should You Be?

"Bad advertising is a pollution," charges Webster. "Advertising that's infantile, as much of it is, treating the public like idiots, and irritating them, and shoving and pushing, I find that a pollution. I find a responsibility on my shoulders not to do that. I've made my life to serving that end." Webster, one of Britain's most admired creative directors, counsels: "With anything progressive, or that breaks new ground, obviously there's a little bit of risk, but that can be taken care of quite a long way by research these days. You can put your toe in the water and test ideas with members of the public before you actually do them. But in my experience, members of the public are as desperate for good, witty, intelligent, entertaining ideas as we are. They don't want boring work to look at anymore than we do."

Goodby concurs. "If you were a new business prospect who used TV, I would hope that GS&P would offer you an honest reassessment of that use. If we decided that TV was still the way to go, I believe that our TV would be more strictly based on a real truth about your product, that it would be more rigorously discussed with potential consumers, and finally that it would treat people with *respect*." In Goodby's book, respect is key to the memorability and success of any advertising. "We think it's very important that it shoot for the *highest common denominators* rather than the lowest, that it presume attention and a real sense of humour on the part of the viewers."

Defenders of mainstream, formulaic work dismiss such thinking as indulgent. The highest common denominator equals the highest possible risk. Advertising has to sell, not be clever. Creativity should not get in the way of the message. The only people who will understand and appreciate clever work are the award judges, not the consumers. Valid enough arguments on the surface, but quickly refuted by the success of brands like Nike.

"If you write a basketball commercial for Nike, it's always best to write that commercial for the *top end* of that pyramid, to the real basketball fanatics." Riswold discusses cutting edge commercials that have a layered approach to communication. Peel off one layer of meaning, a deeper level of intelligence manifests below. "That same piece of communication can then appeal to a *wider audience*, but it does it on different levels."

"*A good commercial is like a conversation...*" Wieden & Kennedy creative director Hal Curtis talks about his work for Nike. "The brand holds so many strong voices. It can speak about the subject of sports in a way that is very personal. Brands are like people. You interact with them like another human being. When you inject something into your work that you feel strongly about, something that is very true, it resonates."

If Curtis is right, and a commercial is a conversation between a brand and a consumer, then at some point the advertiser has to stop talking. The recipient must be allowed to respond. In fact, the recipient must be *trusted* to reach his or her own conclusion about the message, which is anathema to all practitioners of formula-led advertising.

"The best work that we do," explains Riswold, "gives somebody an open-ended invitation; it points them in the right direction, but allows *them* to finish the piece of communication on their own terms, to interpret the commercial in their own way. *A good commercial should always let the viewer put the final piece of punctuation on the message.* I'm putting a period on the end of this, I'm putting a question mark on the end of this, I'm putting an exclamation mark on the end of this; or I'll put a semicolon on the end and then *I'll add more to it.*" As Riswold stresses, the viewers will interpret the work into their lives. The relationship is symbiotic. Rather than the brand speaking at you, it's the brand speaking with you. "Most advertising spells out everything; this is exactly the way you're supposed to feel at this point, and this point, etcetera, etcetera. Hollywood does the same thing." Riswold draws a parallel with Andy Warhol's art. "He would never tell you what it was about.

You would start to *think* what it was about, and interpret it. It was up to you to find out what it was about, and I think we try to do the same thing in advertising."

"Effective campaigns almost invariably offer a reward to the viewer," Jones reminds us. "A *thank you* for spending thirty seconds in the company of the advertiser. This can take the form of emotional warmth, humour, entertainment, intrigue. There is no formula, but to use the jargon of the American research industry, likeability is important."

"You can be remembered and noticed and believed, but if you're entirely unsympathetic and unlikeable, then sod it," stresses Best. "Life is busy and confusing, sometimes threatening and frightening, and very often boring. You're trying to open up some new little *'what if'* in people's minds. Humour can engage their affections, their senses, get them on side, so that one isn't in any way trying to batter at people…"

Sinha applauds the idea of using humour: "Humour, expressed through people; doing funny dialogue commercials or situations which illuminate some wry aspect of human life. I was an enormous fan of Collett Dickenson Pearce's work before I ever went there. There's a mass of wonderful dialogue commercials done from the late 60s onwards. They were engaging, witty, warm little insights into human life and they tied the products in well, and they served the products up to you with a little smile wrapped round them, and you were inclined to treat them like friends therefore."

Warren Berger, editor of The One Club's *One* magazine, discusses the trend to what he calls Oddvertising. "One of the problems with entertainment and attitude-driven ads is that you have to keep upping the ante. There is a feeling that you have to be even more wildly entertaining, with more attitude, and to achieve that you must go over the top. The stories, and the characters in them, are getting more and more bizarre. Characters in American commercials now are apt to behave in anti-social ways: attacking other people, painting their faces blue, walking around naked, dressing up in animal costumes. It's partly a reflection of the culture, in which rebel culture has become the norm. The biggest fear in society used to be that you'd be an outcast; today, the biggest insult is to be called ordinary. But once you push the envelope past a certain point," warns Berger, "it's hard to pull it back in. Of course the nature of advertising is such that people start to zig when others zag, so maybe a response to Oddvertising will be a return to quieter, more gentle commercials. We've seen a few of those already, from Volkswagen, Saturn, and others. Quiet, minimalist stuff, that actually has a point to it." Will Oddvertising continue? "The young Internet companies seem to enjoy doing this stuff to get attention," Berger muses. "But as Jeff Goodby told me, those Internet guys don't seem to realise that wild commercials don't necessarily create good feelings about your brand."

Jones, also, has a view on what the industry calls weird, wacky and bizarre work: "Creative styles are driven by fashion. The greatest influence on creative people is what other creative people are doing. There is good evidence of effectiveness from the Tango advertising in Britain, and a good deal of American advertising for brands directed at the MTV target group. In any event, the adjectives 'weird', 'wacky' and 'bizarre' have no precise meaning. As a general rule, sensible advertisers will use advertising that works. And they will take the trouble to find out whether it works or not."

Australia's Ted Horton maintains that creativity must be seen in the context of achieving behavioural change. "I know everyone believes that if you entertain people, your commercial will be more effective. I often don't actually agree with that. Sometimes we are so worried about communicating a benefit or doing something that's descriptive of the brand or what the product represents, we forget we have to go *beyond* description, *beyond* communication, *beyond* entertainment, and understand that the fundamental thing we have to do is actually create behavioural change. We often admire commercials, but what we really admire is the ingenuity of the communication." If the commercial can quickly position the product, adds Horton, so much the better. "And if the advertising is born out of a truth, it can withstand any scrutiny by cynical consumers."

How much scrutiny? French gazes into the crystal ball. "The Net has suddenly made life a lot simpler for us. Over the next half-decade, and possibly more, the most powerful medium in the world is *not* going to be television, or press, or pop-up boxes, or banners … it's going to be *viral marketing*." French defines it as the twenty-first century equivalent of the most effective medium ever: word of mouth. "It's started already. Someone sees a commercial they like a lot on TV or on some website. They download it and send it to a few pals. If they like it, they forward it to another half dozen each, and so on. Within a couple of weeks, a real killer commercial can be seen in isolation, and with 100% attention, by literally millions of punters. And because they're all in some way connected, they're probably all loosely within the target market."

As French points out, the medium is free. No media schedule is required; simply a great idea that just *one* of your audience loves. "The bottom line is that if we don't amaze, intrigue, inspire or amuse our audience, we fail. It has always been thus. All the storyboard research becomes irrelevant, which it always *has* been, of course. All that twaddle about what consumers are 'taking out' of a script doesn't count. If they *aren't* entertained and blown away, they *won't* put their name to the film and distribute it. End of story."

WHY REFLECT CULTURE WHEN WE CAN CREATE IT?

"The role of great brand advertising is not to mirror culture and therefore leave us with nothing new," advises Ground Zero's Kirk Souder. "Regrettably, that's the formula of many big agencies whose budgets allow such laziness." Souder says great brand advertising will create culture, thereby providing consumers with a reason to think about it, *guaranteeing* it a place in an already over-crowded consumer consciousness. "Consumers only accept a brand as 'for real' when they see its footprints outside of the world of advertising. Therefore, what advertising should really seek to do is create messaging that enters the cultural nomenclature. To do so, something must be inherent in the commercial that allows it to live on in the mind of the consumer way after its thirty seconds on screen. There is much talk today of things called *memes*, self-replicating ideas and entities. Great commercials are communication *memes*; ideas, words and images that self-replicate in the culture at large, or at least the culture of the audience."

Souder quotes the famous Wendy's campaign as an example. "To this day, almost weekly on national television, I hear political

Open on a man returning to his apartment from a holiday.

He unlocks the room where he keeps his precious Knowledge. Sadly, it has shrivelled up in his absence and is huddled forlornly near a water dish.

The man's monotonal voice-over is heard: *My girlfriend made me go to Cancun.*

I could not watch NHL 2night. When I got back, my Knowledge was smaller.

I hate Cancun.

The word Knowledge appears as a shadow against the wall.

Super: *NHL 2night Tuesday–Saturday at 11.30pm on ESPN2.*

Create culture, says Kirk Souder of Ground Zero. His agency's campaign for ESPN brought a sports fan's Knowledge to life. It won a Silver Pencil for the Most Outstanding Television Campaign at Britain's D&AD Awards.

reporters refer to candidates who are light on the issues with the phrase, *Where's the beef?* It has been over ten years since Wendy's used that as their campaign anthem, but it has permanently entered our cultural vocabulary."

"Usually, advertising follows trends rather than setting them, but I think it's possible to actually lead in some cases," observes Webster. "I remember a *Guardian* ad I did with a skinhead, which showed the same action from three points of view." A woman looks askance at a skinhead running past her house in a bleak inner city street. The skinhead hurls himself at an elderly man carrying a briefcase. It's only then we see a load of bricks toppling to the ground from a nearby construction site. If the skinhead hadn't seen an accident about to happen and raced in to help, the old man would have been crushed; so much for our prejudices. "It brought home to people that you've got to see all points of view before you can make up your mind about something. That commercial was used in colleges, universities, and even in court to defend people. It led a way of thinking, it illustrated a way of thinking, quite apart from selling a newspaper."

Delaney stresses why commercials and popular culture should be interchangeable. "There is now an understanding, by a few people, of the relationship between advertising and popular culture. Wieden & Kennedy and Nike made it so, and Levi's made it so in the UK. The original hypothesis that people hate advertising is completely wrong. It always was wrong. The hypothesis was that people did not like advertising, and did not *need* to like advertising. It created a television culture of comparative, rather boring advertising that yells at you about the superiority of one product over another..." Delaney cites Procter & Gamble. "They can make a case if they like for a product, it's their right, but they don't have to do it twelve times a day. Several P&G people over the years have told me that they don't care whether people like their advertising, they use it to gain an effect. What they never realised with that kind of mantra was that it wasn't whether people liked their advertising, it was whether people could engage with their advertising *more deeply* by enjoying elements of it, and still get a message out of it, which is what they wanted. Their deep mistrust of things called 'creative' created a whole culture of people who said, there's good creative advertising which is not really effective, it's indulgent, and then there's the real stuff over here which is Mars, P&G, Unilever, Kelloggs. It's taken them thirty years to realise that if you can have a blockbuster movie which is popular, and has a story in it, and makes money, there's no earthly reason you can't have a blockbuster film for Kelloggs or P&G which is popular, and is well made, and makes money. The idea of populism and entertainment and the sense of capturing people's imagination in an interesting way has finally dawned on these companies; *they've wasted billions being ordinary and there's no reason for it…*"

When Bill Bernbach died in 1982, *Harper's* magazine hailed his impact on American culture as "probably greater … than any of the distinguished writers and artists who have appeared in the pages of *Harper's* during the past 133 years."

AGENCIES: OLD TRUTHS, NEW TRUTHS

"Somehow I can't believe that there are any heights that can't be scaled by a man who knows the secrets of making dreams come true," said Walt Disney, a man who changed American culture forever.

Disney might well have been talking about advertising. And the secrets he described — curiosity, confidence, courage and constancy — are the attributes of every great advertising leader. Disney singled out confidence as the greatest of his four Cs. "When you believe in a thing, believe in it all the way, implicitly and unquestionably."

Goodby, Silverstein & Partners. Andy Berlin of New York's Berlin Cameron & Partners recalls the start of his partnership with Jeff Goodby and Rich Silverstein in San Francisco. It meant *"not being intimidated by the distance between imagination and making something into a fact."*

They were mercenaries. "It was about a group of social deviants who suddenly became useful to the centre part of society trying to sell stuff, because of their combination of business and art skills. GBS was one of the first agencies of a seminal generation of people in America who had definitely deviated from the norm in society because it was necessary, because the social norm was so stupid. GBS was one of the first voices of that generation. It was the 80s, but the voice was really born in the deviance of the 60s and 70s. That social deviance was predictive of the way society as a whole would change, and that deviance became mainstream as time went on, hence Goodby's fame and adoption by the mainstream."

The agency was able to take a kind of mercenary art quite far, notes Berlin, and still does. "Goodby's work is about emotional ambiguity, where people aren't necessarily good or necessarily bad. In fact, if you look for a consistent theme, a lot of the best work tends to be about what people are comfortable with accepting as reality. Then a layer is peeled back and you see that things are not the way that we think they are. And because they're not the way that we think they are, some aspect of character that's closer to the soul of human nature is revealed." In fact, says Berlin, a commercial might even begin with a premise just like that. "That embarrassing moment of deeper revelation is more charming. It's closer to the truth. It's like perception in regular life. You stand on the street and you notice superficial things. You notice the bodies of women, you notice the height of men, you notice displays that suggest social power, worth, or threats. But you see things quite superficially. Stand in line with one of those people as you're going to get a coffee on your way to work and exchange a bit of conversation, four or five or six deeper layers start to happen. Get caught with those people in an elevator, and it's quite a different world."

Often, Bartle Bogle Hegarty is seen as the British equivalent to Goodby's. "BBH operates in a fundamentally different way. It identifies, and sometimes creates, fashionable cultural icons, and juxtaposes those intelligently. So it's both an art director's agency, but also there's an intellect behind it. It's not just about how things seem, it's more the juxtaposition of how appearances lead you to other things."

With characteristic modesty, Berlin describes himself as a writer who became a businessman. "I started out as a writer and I still think of the world like a writer does. And because I've always been a lover of good work, I've been associated with a lot of people who are very talented."

Howell Henry Chaldecott Lury & Partners. Across the Atlantic, Steve Henry discusses his agency's new creativity. "Everybody else had a house look; but I wanted our ads to always be the ads that people said, *Where did that come from? What are they doing there?* What I love is work where you say, you can't do that, and then you think about it and you say, yes, you can. It's where people have challenged the assumptions in any marketplace."

Henry acknowledges First Direct and Tango as the agency's most radical work. "When the *Campaign* jury chose the top one hundred ads from the UK from this century, it was interesting that Orange Tango *Slap* got in at number four, which I thought was quite high, but the point about it was that it kind of defined this decade. When we launched, our whole attitude was about doing something different because if you do what everybody else is doing, by definition you'll get lost in the clutter. It was a very established marketplace we came into. The spirit of the age was what we call Second Wave, which was Lowe Howard-Spink, Abbott Mead Vickers, Gold Greenlees Trott, Wight Collins, Leagas Delaney, BBH; fantastic agencies, but they were all ruled by a presiding creative *guru* and they produced ads to the taste of, and in the house style of, that guy. Now I'm not saying that everything they did was the same, but a lot of it was." Instead, Henry and his partners drew their inspiration from a quote by Jay Chiat when he launched Chiat/Day: "We don't have a house style, we have a house *standard*."

Cliff Freeman & Partners. Another agency that defined the decade is Cliff Freeman & Partners New York. Arthur Bijur explains how the agency's repertoire is so varied, from the madness of Little Caesars and the outrageous Outpost.com campaign, to Lenny, the heroin addict, inviting us back in a year to witness his success. "It's the culture. It's our commitment to doing excellent work. Cliff and I started this agency about twelve years ago. We've always done work that we thought was a little different. We have a very clear point of view that entertainment is a key to selling; that people don't want to sit and be sold to, they want to be entertained into a proposition, into being open to a product. As a result of that, and doing some pretty high visibility work, we've attracted a lot of like-minded clients; clients who want to do work that breaks through, that gets seen.

Maybe it's a little *risqué* but always smart. Work that entertains as well as sells. So the culture has been able to maintain itself." Bijur talks about a self-fulfilling prophecy. "You do good work, you attract clients who want to do good work, you attract creative people who are really great. I always think of it as a stage that we've built, that people can come and perform on and be seen…"

Lowe Howard-Spink. "Frank Lowe is not a creative person by craft, although he causes great creativity to happen around him." Adrian Holmes, chief creative officer of Lowe Lintas & Partners Worldwide, discusses one of the most successful agency brands. "He values the quality of creative work above everything else. He was managing director at Collett Dickinson Pearce. Geoff Howard-Spink was planning director. When the two of them decided to break away from CDP in May 1981 and start Lowe Howard-Spink, Geoff said to the press, I design the circuits, Frank provides the electricity."

A very important component of the Lowe philosophy, says Holmes, is the production and traffic system, which was designed at CDP. In fact, the agency's DNA is very similar to Collett's. "The whole notion of control — of timing, the signing-off of briefs and work and the Monday morning traffic and production meetings — is very important as a trellis up which the roses of creativity may clamber. I've been in agencies where that structure doesn't exist, and you can tell. It might be a freer atmosphere, but it just leads to confusion."

WONGDOODY. Art director Tracy Wong thought he had died and gone to Heaven. He was at Goldsmith/Jeffrey in New York, one of the first nine employees. "I thought it was the last job I'd ever have. Gary was my creative idol." And even when Wong moved back west, Gary Goldsmith and Bob Jeffrey remained his role models. After a high profile stint at Goodby, Silverstein & Partners, including Chevys *Fresh Mex*, he became creative director at Livingston & Co. in Seattle, working with general manager and head account handler Pat Doody. "I am the Yin to his Yang," Wong explains. "Actually, O'Yang, Pat being a good Irish Catholic boy." When they went out on their own, their Yin-Yang logo wickedly sprouted shamrocks. "Why Seattle? That's where we lived. But from day one, we never, ever wanted to be a 'Seattle' agency. We wanted to be a national agency based in Seattle. Our Los Angeles office is now bigger than the Seattle mother ship."

Wong himself has long been an icon for young American and Asian creatives. His agency culture is sensibly unconventional. "Ben Wiener, our managing partner and head of the LA office, calls us a 'democracy of good ideas'. Anyone, from any department, has a say in the work." In the early days, when Wong and Doody employed only one account handler and one freelance writer, all the ideas were thrown in a pile in the middle of the floor and votes were cast on which ones to pursue. "Of course, there are standard departments now," says Wong, "but we still encourage anyone to contribute. That way, everyone has ownership. I have never, ever worked in an environment as open as this." Wong loves working with planners. "If planning is done by smart people, it reveals insights and truths. *Who* wouldn't want that? Creatives who are precious, pampered, overpaid brats. There, I said it."

Dissolve To...

Being different, being brave and being interesting are the war cries of cutting edge advertising men. Do clients agree, or are they averse to risktaking?

"It is crucial that the risks are calculated, and that there is a robust intellectual rationale underpinning the risk." Anthony Simonds-Gooding joined Unilever as a management trainee in marketing. He earned his stripes as marketing manager and advertising manager at Birds Eye Foods, then joined Whitbread as marketing director. As client, he signed off on two of Britain's most famous campaigns: Stella Artois' *Reassuringly Expensive* and Heineken's *Refreshes the Parts that Other Beers Cannot Reach*. Becoming UK managing director and finally group managing director, he left Whitbread and crossed to the other side of the table as worldwide chairman and chief executive officer of all Saatchi & Saatchi communication companies. He now crusades for the cause of creativity in communications as chairman of British Design & Art Direction. "To achieve something new, one has always to cross some unknown, forbidden territory. Unquestionably this will involve being brave and taking some risks. Too often one sees work that takes

foolish risks, lazy risks, self-indulgent risks with no discernible justification. The irony for me," he observes, "is the billions of pounds spent on work which runs the ultimate risk of never being noticed through its utter dullness and product overstatement."

One man who sees more commercials than most is Gee Thomson of *Shots*. Thomson estimates that only the top 5% of the world's new commercials are submitted by agencies and production houses that are thoroughly conversant with the *Shots* criteria. Of those, only 5% will be selected for inclusion on a *Shots* reel. "The audience of creatives is usually the most hardened, the most critical, in terms of the vast audience out there anyway."

So what does get into *Shots*? "Our audience has seen all the relative ploys over the past twenty or thirty years. If stuff comes in with fantastic production values but follows themes which have been done before, our audience doesn't want to see it again. They're pressed for time. They want to be stimulated." Rumour has it that Thomson reviews the work on fast forward, stopping only when something grabs his attention. "The work we show must be refreshing in some sort of way, the elements must be different in some sort of aspect. It might be humour, satire, irony, dialogue, surrealism, which is taken further. It might be shock tactics which are taken further. It might be production values which are taken further. Sometimes the elements have been used before, but they've been *disjointed* in some way, or arrived at *in a different order*. It's usually the combination of a set of values which will produce a commercial that is recognised as groundbreaking. Sometimes," he adds, "the sheer *simplicity* of a commercial will be revolutionary."

If Thomson's critical, hardened audience of *Shots* subscribers is a microcosm of the broad public television audience, then the elements he prescribes are not apparent in the majority of television commercials. Things do not bode well for what Indra Sinha has called "the weird realm that hides behind our eyelids".

2

CUTTING EDGE THINKING

A rnold Toynbee said: "The greatest enemy of any civilisation is the enemy within. Its name is not subversion or revolution, but rigidity."

And so it is with advertising.

Traditionally, agencies have developed very conventional strategies in very conventional ways. The problem is, the more ordinary your strategy, the more ordinary your advertising. In fact, many big agencies cling to structures, rules and formulae that conspire to defeat freshness and intuition.

"Most of us are more comfortable under a protective cocoon of rules, formulae, and organisational charts," speculates Jon Steel, vice chairman and director of account planning at Goodby, Silverstein & Partners and an alumnus of London's BMP DDB. "As long as we follow the rules, our asses are covered. If we adhere to the formulae, we don't have to think. And if we always remain aware of our position on the organisational chart, we can usually avoid taking responsibility for anything. This might not sound so shocking in a government department or an insurance company, but in an *advertising agency*? Aren't we supposed to be lateral thinkers? Aren't we supposed to break rules? So why don't we? Because we're whores, that's why. Because our clients like us to work that way, because *they* work that way. And because they pay us vast sums of money, we don't like to say no. At least, that's the traditional model of American advertising."

Great creative breakthroughs begin with great strategies and great briefs. In the last quarter century, crafting new cutting edge strategic models has become a science. The planning revolution had its genesis at London's Boase Massimi Pollitt. In Paris, BDDP's Disruption philosophy provided a system for overturning marketing and advertising conventions. Howell Henry Chaldecott Lury dispensed with the agency relay race; no briefs are passed from one department to the next. Instead, briefs and solutions are developed organically by dedicated account director-planner-writer-art director teams working as cells within the main agency structure.

All of these methodologies are intended to find a path through the strategic minefield, to throw a clearer light on where the best, most appropriate opportunities for advertising might reside. Without that focus, without knowing where to concentrate the advertising concept, campaigns will be generic or superficial, rather than coming to the consumer with a really fresh, startling and relevant insight.

Because we are solving business problems with communications, "advertising *has* to be strategic," insists Tim Delaney. "Deciding what the platform for the communication will be takes you eight-tenths along the way creatively."

In many agencies, though, it seems that the strategy is simply, let's run an ad. Many account handlers believe they've done their job when they write out a shopping list of features with a deadline. Somebody *has* to bite the bullet. Often, out of sheer desperation, it's the creatives. Some do it intuitively.

"Most of the best creative people already apply a lot of planning principles to their work," acknowledges Steel. "After all, the principles of planning are really broader principles of advertising. Of course, planners do add some specific skills in consumer research, which can be replicated by really smart, enthusiastic account people, or smart, enthusiastic external research people."

Is there a precise formula for developing a truly fresh strategy? Is there a system, an intellectual structure, available to jump-start your thinking? Intuition and the ability to listen are certainly critical qualities. Experience helps, too, having been there before, but as James Best cautions: "You've got to resist that, to some extent, and make sure your mind is open."

One thing, though, drives everything we do.

"Every ad is a brand ad," says Ian Batey of Singapore's Batey Ads. "As soon as you put a logo in it, the brand is talking. Which means a commitment to upholding the brand's values across everything, strategic *or* tactical."

Advertising, more often than not, must have brand building as its mission. And brand building has witnessed more fundamental change in the last decade than ever before. If you still believe a brand is a dogmatic thing that says "Buy me because", think again. Even the most functional products need personalities, as Procter & Gamble themselves have discovered.

BRAND BUILDING: IT'S ALL IN THE MIND

"A brand is the emotional relationship between yourself and a product," says Andy Berlin. "The brand is owned by the person who perceives it, not by the company that owns the brand." According to Berlin, it has always been the case. "It's just that our understanding of these things has become more acute, more insightful."

"Brands have always existed in the minds of consumers," agrees James Best. "*They're a set of values, associations and beliefs that reside only in the mind of the beholder.* In many ways, the beholder owns the brand. That's why a relationship with the brand can exist; because it's something that the user finds comforting, or comfortable, or a reflection of his or her character. In that respect, brands have increasingly become things to identify with rather than to look at or see from a distance. The nuances of what differentiates a brand have become *more to do with the personalities of the users than with the absolute presence of the brand.*"

New York agency Kirshenbaum Bond & Partners defines a brand as *a community of users.* Apple, Mercedes-Benz, Harley-Davidson and Nike are very distinct communities, with their own social codes and sharply etched loyalties. Users have clear affinities with their brands and with fellow users. "Television is the most sensational medium to get the community feeling the most passionate about their brand." Creative director Bill Oberlander advocates a less literal approach to brand building. What people do in their real life is one thing; what they fantasise to be is another. Television, he says, can afford to be "20% more fantastical than reality". A community of users not only celebrates its affinity with the brand, but also with fellow users. The brand is not merely a socio-economic badge; it serves as a means of mutual recognition. Members share what Oberlander calls *identified affinity*. One of his clients, Target, is a mid-American, mass-market community of users. "Their aisles are extra-wide because they know that mom has two kids hanging off the cart and she needs that room to manoeuvre; they call their customers 'guests', and they call their employees 'team members'." When Kirshenbaum Bond did the marketing to open Target stores in the Northeast, the agency wanted to announce the grand opening launch party with only the bull's eye logo. As Oberlander explains: "A lot of people on the East Coast were relocated West Coast and middle American people. So they identified with the bull's eye and their affinity for the brand just came gushing out. Within two hours of running the ad, we had closed down the 1-800 number because the party was full."

What's difficult now about brand work, Best tells us, is the sheer plethora of products, services and ideas in the marketplace. Consumers have more experience and more knowledge of what's out there than has ever been the case before. "A new product is something which answers a need in a new and interesting way for consumers. Initially it's a branded product, but if it's easily replicable and becomes a very ordinary part of life and anybody can make it, then any opportunity for brand presence will be eroded." Utilitarian products are most vulnerable. "We used to advertise aluminium cooking foil and washing-up cloths. At the time, those products were genuinely new. But they were very utilitarian things. Gradually the added value was squeezed out of them. Now they're no longer advertised products."

Brands do have significance in people's lives. In fact, brands themselves are like real people with their own characteristics and foibles. So much so that author Jackie Collins even uses brand names as shorthand for her characters.

As Keith Reinhard tells us, brands are not ethereal things that have no value. They are what we create. When he talks to college students, he holds up two gold-coloured necklaces. "From a distance, the students can't tell whether they are any good or whether they are junk. The point is nonetheless made that even if they were both very good, or both very poor, it is very hard for me to determine that. So when I place one in a Tiffany box, and another one in a box that says K-Mart's Finest, it's not advertising, it's *transformation*. In the case of the Tiffany box, it's the experience of buying something really good, the experience of delivering the gift, and the experience of wearing it, as opposed to labelling myself as a really smart shopper…"

But the old matrix for building a brand is broken. Brand values are no longer carved in stone. Brand building now means relationship building, and for good reason. These days, achieving a *sustainable* product advantage for more than a very short period of time is impossible, Anthony Simonds-Gooding reminds us. "Consequently, an increasingly important part of the competitive business mix is how you present your me-too product to the market, and how you develop a compelling relationship with your customer, one that differentiates you emotionally from your competitor. This means fresh, compelling and above all, creative ways of forging that link. The opposite, being dull and repetitive and boring, just won't do."

"What people want from brands these days is different," maintains Delaney. "I don't think that people necessarily want just a selling relationship; you show me something you've got and I'll buy it. It isn't a straightforward transaction. It's much more about an experience. It's much more about the brand being something I can feel the sides of. When I buy into a brand, I buy into a whole sense of what the brand actually is; not just what it stands for, but what it actually delivers *over and above* the purchase." Delaney reviews his agency's television work for a famous British brand, the BBC. "We took something that was seventy-five years old and had never really talked to anybody. They were like a shoemaker who makes the best shoes in the world but never advertises. Trouble was, the BBC started confronting the future; they could see the armies of change coming and they didn't have any tanks. What *Perfect Day* did was to turn around and remind people what the scope of the organisation is. But instead of saying, we do news, we do sports, we do this, we do that, we said even within the tightest definition — which is to do with *one song* — the way that we span different things can be a metaphor for the whole organisation. And the lesson in that really is *you can say one thing to say twelve things, if you say the one thing well.* You can focus on one aspect of the business, and use the atmosphere, the personality and the tonality of that to speak for the *entire* business. One spot can do that, and that's the power of television, which is not true of a print ad, which is a very much more rational experience." Delaney believes advertising should restate brand values in such a way that it makes them relevant and fresh to people. "*Perfect Day* transcended all the logic and went past your previous experience of what the BBC is, even though you've known this brand since you were a kid."

In Britain, brand building is hampered by the fact that the average job tenure of a marketing manager is now only eighteen months. As a result, the brand's strategic continuity resides most likely at the agency. The brand owner isn't the brand guardian; the agency is. Sadly, in today's business climate, the incoming marketing manager is more inclined to opt for conservative solutions rather than potentially interesting ones. Doing something that hasn't been seen to fail will top the personal agenda.

"If capitalism worked differently," contends Stacy Wall, "companies wouldn't advertise. They don't like doing it, they don't want to do it. It requires committing to saying something."

Oscar Wilde said: "I can resist everything except temptation." The question is, how much temptation is really palpable in today's television advertising? Are we tempting our audience to change their behaviour, or merely tempting them to zap us?

BRANDING REALITY CHECK

"Reality, two hundred years ago, was the Church," says Berlin. "Fifty years ago, it was Physics. Today, it's the Media." If that is so, and we really live in a world of *competing realities*, he argues, then the Procter & Gamble method of stating a physical and rational attribute for a product doesn't matter so much. "We know we can fix jumper cables to attitudes. We know the space between need and desire is internal and controllable; if you've given up smoking, which is supposed to be addictive, look at it in the rearview mirror: where was the addiction?" Reality, he says, has always been a series of social agreements. "A community of *beliefs*. You'll be part of that consensus, or you won't be part of that consensus. If you're not part of that consensus, you've got Columbine. If you are part of that consensus, you've got Bill Clinton, or at least some aspects of it. By managing that consensus, and standing for it, you can manage and manipulate politics. In that kind of world, the *rational* approach to features and benefits advertising doesn't do so well. So Procter hasn't done well."

Berlin believes people have become extraordinarily sophisticated in building personal worlds and feel very empowered to do so. "You would think that this anarchic capitalism of realities would create people who felt disempowered. It doesn't. It creates people who feel *em*powered. People feel that they've got more control over their values. *People use brands as furniture to decorate their realities and help make them more real, more satisfying.* Now, we grew up and did ads where we fought to sell the benefits of the product as opposed to the features because we could do better advertising that way. I think that's changing. Benefits advertising is increasingly meeting with a sophisticated consumer who says, *don't* tell me what to feel about this thing or what it means to me. Tell me what it *is* — not in the old sense, but present it to me like the way a person is presented to me, so I can make an assessment of its character. Will accommodating it in my life make things fun and interesting for me? Give me both an emotional characteristic of the thing, but also a very clear idea of whether it/he is divorced, whether it/he cheated on his wife."

Planning Creative Breakthroughs

"What used to exist," recalls Best, "were boring clients and agencies who plodded along doing the safe stuff, and exciting, off-the-wall, zappy, zany ones who didn't take much notice of marketing disciplines or research or anything else, but felt intuitively that an idea would work because it would excite or outrage or upset or make people laugh. Both were living in fool's paradises and what we did, with planning, was try to bring the two things together."

The agency helmed by Best, BMP DDB, represents the synthesis of two distinct cultures: "Stanley Pollitt's market-grounded strategic account planning and the creative revolution of Bill Bernbach, which had rejected research of any stripe." Pollitt first experimented with account planning at London's Pritchard Wood Partners in the mid-60s. When he teamed with Martin Boase, Gabe Massimi and John Webster to form BMP in 1968, planning became the agency cornerstone. As Best puts it, BMP became the birthplace of planning, as well as the nursery for planners.

But like a lot of things, planning has become part of industry jargon. Some agencies sprout planning departments to look trendy. Others decry it. In its purest, most authentic form, what is planning?

"The best job in advertising," admits Best. "It embraces art and science, the creative and the experiential. Planning is a process of discovery. Our job is to listen, and learn from that listening, and tease out strands of new understanding from it if we can. If we can hear things other people haven't heard, if we can make connections other people haven't made, then we're on the path to getting a unique communication strategy that will give us an edge. *Planning can liberate creativity by giving it a better starting point.*"

The important thing about planning as BMP DDB has always practised it, says Best, is the fact that it is tasked with making the work better. "Getting the right work out, *through a better understanding of the consumer's relationship with the brand.* The only real definition of better work is that it works better. Our belief, borne out by thirty years of doing it, is that work which is considered 'creative' — that is, it's distinctive, it's original, it grabs people, it has empathy, it has humanity, it connects with people in a new and exciting way — will be more effective, *provided it's been properly directed.*"

Best walks us through the planning methodology for a new product launch. "When things are new, you can't expect consumers to tell you a lot about them. We would always spend time understanding, from a consumer's perspective, how this new thing is going to relate to their lives; how it would be used by them; what aspects of it seem to matter the most to them or *could* become significant to them. It would be very rare if the planners didn't personally get out into the marketplace. They'd get under the skin of both the product and the consumers, *to understand how they can fit together*, how the new brand can be presented to people." This qualitative research might be individual interviews, group discussions, filming people in their homes or in shops, or just talking to them in the street. *"The planners will bring that understanding back to the agency team and the client team.* They will help work out what the strategy and communications are going to be. The planner will be the craftsperson in the best use of research, analysis and interpretation."

BMP DDB planner Richard Butterworth is assigned to Volkswagen. He works on a day-to-day basis with the account team and creatives, and is present at every client briefing. Butterworth believes that his biggest contribution to the client's communications is simplification, "the simplification of potentially very complex communications tasks. The challenge is to take an attractive self-evident product truth, look at what the competition is doing, and work out how best to get that truth across in a way which is different to how any other car advertisers are doing it." He sees himself as a creative resource, at two stages: "By referencing the consumer and trying to devise a strategy that isn't just sensible on paper, or sensible in a kind of McKinsey management consultant sense, but one which is *executable within the frame the creatives operate in.* Then, at a slightly later stage, shepherding ideas through research and making sure that the good ones don't get buffeted or stopped by bad research." Butterworth has a psychology degree. Before becoming a planner he worked as a postman, a baker and a random market researcher. A good planner should be the mouthpiece of the consumer, he contends, able to ground every debate about strategy and creative work against genuine consumer motivations.

Whether or not we subscribe to planning, one thing is more certain now than ever before: *the first creative act in any project must be committed by the account service person writing the brief.* The brief should contain an idea, or at the very least, a single insight on which the advertising can be based. If it doesn't, creative people will just start creating ideas that bear no relationship to the brand or the consumer or the product or the problem.

"The most important thing is to define what you want to say *before* you start work, and then say it in the boldest, most creative way," says Marcello Serpa, partner and creative director of Almap/BBDO, Brazil's most honoured art director and the only one to win Gold at the One Show. At Cannes alone he has carried away over thirty Lions in six years as well as the Grand Prix in 1993, and chaired the jury in 2000. "We always start out of the product, out of the service. Before we start working, we like to define what the brand stands for. Is it trust? Is it love? What are we looking for in the brand, and what should we pass? You have to have this insight *before* you start creating something." This insight, Serpa says, could come from the client, from the agency, from research, from intuition, from commonsense. But without it, the work will lack relevance and substance.

The Perfect Brief

"To my mind, a brief should be just that: brief." According to Hal Riney, the word "brief" wasn't used a lot in America before the British planners showed up; until then, people thought more in terms of strategy documents. "Perhaps I'm giving creative folks more credit than they're due, but I have found throughout my forty-some years in this business that good creative people have a unique ability to grasp and interpret a problem and its many components with relative ease and precision. That's why we have creative people working on our problems." Riney debates the trend to longer briefs. "As our client organisations have grown larger, and our clients often tend to arrive in their jobs with only a modicum of experience, there has been a tendency in this country over the past two decades or so to make the briefs or strategy documents lengthier and more complex. Essentially, they create the ad and its required elements even *before* the creative people get to work. *This limits originality and imagination, at the very least.* And predictably, results most often in the predictable." Some of Riney's best clients offered him no brief at all. In fact, Ernest Gallo refused to look at a strategy document or a chart. "He said, 'Just show me the ads. If I like them, I'll say so.' Ed

Crutchfield, our First Union Bank client and chairman, simply told me to whom he wanted to talk, and what he wanted his advertising to accomplish. That was all the time he cared to spend on the subject, and all we needed to hear," Riney recalls. "When I was asked to create President Reagan's advertising in 1984, I was presented with over fifty pounds of research and other documents. I didn't read a word. I wrote the advertising in two hours in a bar."

The best briefs are *brief*. A truism, yes, but creative brains are not jump-started by longwinded documents. A brief brief is actually a reasonable enough request; Winston Churchill demanded something similar of his generals. If the situation and strategy for an entire theatre of war could be summarised in a few paragraphs, why not an advertising brief?

The client's brief to the agency is certainly no exception.

"On one side of a single sheet of paper, if possible." Simonds-Gooding stresses brevity. A massive briefing document may appear to be a manifestation of thoroughness, but it risks blurring the issues. "I had an open book relationship with agencies, which was based on total trust; a trust *earned*, not foolishly given. A factor that helped succinct briefing was that the agency knew that the client, at all levels, had a consistent, known point of view on advertising. So, there was no need for double guessing, reading between the lines, politicking, etcetera."

Simonds-Gooding also believes agencies should assign *one* key person to an account; he or she should be from account service, and be an advertising "fanatic". "Everyone in the agency knows there is no going past him or her to the client. The client entrusts him with the task totally. His mission is to make sure that whatever talents lie within the agency, and even in the biggest emporiums there is always a very limited supply, are diverted towards his business." He would make the client's business the most challenging and fun to work on, pushing both agency and client to do new things. "This person will be particularly gifted in briefing, motivating and judging the creative product. He will be a creative man who cannot draw or write copy, but knows what is good when he sees it, and knows how to get it."

Noel Delbridge is famous for tossing away briefs and writing his own. "A lot of the evils that are perpetrated on television go back to weak briefs, where account service people have simply sopped to the client and tried to cover off everything. Really, the brief should be no more than half a paragraph, a paragraph at most: what is the central thing we have to communicate?"

If Riney, Delbridge and Simonds-Gooding are right, the strategy and briefing process has become convoluted. Or has it? Great creativity does not exist in a vacuum. Somebody has to set the objectives, decide the platform and set the tone for the work. Enter the planner.

"Generally, the best creative work, the stuff that wins prizes, is clearly based on a strong strategic idea, a strong piece of positioning, or a strong proposition," adjures Best. "You're giving a good weapon to creative people if you can get to a role for the advertising which is well-defined so they know what its task is and *which levers they're trying to pull*. On top of that, if you can find a *competitive proposition* for your brand, something that is singular, then you're giving them something to say. Very rarely is there a unique selling proposition, but there can be a unique character or brand personality, or a unique relationship between a brand and its users. There can simply be a *unique expression* and that's where the real creative genius comes into play. That expression can be made easier because you know the character you're trying to express, and you know what traits that character has, what ambitions that character has, what abilities that character has, therefore you're in a stronger position to create a great character."

OPINION is divided. Is the planner the midwife of advertising, or just someone who buys you more time?

Neil French believes briefs should contain ideas; however, "I have grown to loathe and detest planners. The proportion of good planners to really rank, bad ones is much lower than the proportion of good advertising to really rank, bad advertising men. If you find a good planner they're great, but I tell you what, I can't think of any offhand." French observes that the title of planner is a useful way of dressing up a bad suit, or putting a suit on a bad creative person. "I used to think that I was behind the times; I used to think, well, planners are everything in London so I must be wrong. But I've learned I'm right." French calls planning, an aberration of the industry. Planners, he says, are process driven. "Very rarely do they actually come up with something that the creative guy wouldn't have come up with in a tenth of the time. They work through loads of processes, describing why they're right; it's this terrible feeling that we ought to be able to prove that advertising works before we actually write it, which, of course, we can't. I've been to meetings in which a planner has held up a chart and said, the client loves this chart. And I suggested, if it's that good, let's just stick a logo on the bottom right-hand corner and go and have lunch." For French's money, the whole process is fascinating only from a purely cerebral point of view. "Actually, when it gets right down to it, a great idea has something to do with the brand and something to do with the perception of the brand by the consumer. Any idiot can work that out; a road sweeper can work that out; you don't need a planner."

French prefers to work with great suits. "The great suits are quicker than we are," attests French. "The cleverest account man can give you a brief and you *know* he knows what the answer is, and you know he's just waiting for you to come to the same conclusion. He's actually saying, I know what this ad should look like, but I'm not allowed to do it because I'm a suit, so I'll give you as many hints as possible and see if you can get to it. And he's usually dead right. He's been up to the top of the mountain, but he's come down to let you go up and put *your* flag there. And that's when you can shine, and do it in a way that's more convincing and more astounding than he could have thought of. So you find a way up the mountain, and plant a bigger flag, to make him go, I see, that's why *you* get the big bucks…"

"I look for a very simple premise that's going to guide every piece of advertising in a campaign." Lee Garfinkel, chairman and chief creative officer of Lowe Lintas & Partners US, wants some key words that he can refer back to. "I look for something that's not only short and to the point, but something I believe is true to the product and relevant to the consumer. *It doesn't have to be a unique selling point, but at least some truth in the product.* Everything should come out of some core truth in the brand. You're not going to be able to find a unique selling point in every single product you work on, but there's got to be something about the product that can separate it from everybody else's. If someone can give me a brief that's *three or four words*, that's fine. If you can get it down to *one word*, that's great. When it starts to become a sentence, or a paragraph, or a couple of pages, I start to get very nervous. It looks like people are trying to compensate for not having an idea by having a lot of words."

Indra Sinha recalls the proposition for Collett Dickenson Pearce's famous Fiat campaign was a single word: "*Brio*". The Italian word for gusto, zest, life, inspired the Fiat Strada commercial in which robots assembled the car to the exuberant strains of Rossini's *Figaro*. Another commercial captured a slice of Italian life. "It was made without words. An Italian family puts granny on the train. They're all waving to her, and as it pulls out they see that she's forgotten her suitcase. So the father has a brainwave, grabs the suitcase, shepherds the family into his Fiat. He drives like a maniac, blood up, full Italian *macho*, racing from one station to the next, trying to catch the train. And the beautiful thing about this is, it's not some sleek-looking 25-year-old male model, slightly self-conscious, seeing his girlfriend off, which is what they'd do today, I suppose. This was a middle-aged man, not particularly prepossessing, a bit sweaty in fact. He was just a real Italian, he was oozing spaghetti carbonara from every joint."

Mike Cozens also prefers a single-worded, single-minded brief. Cozens was formerly Young & Rubicam's creative director for Europe and a co-founder of Bartle Bogle Hegarty. "I remember seeing the brief on Heineken *Refreshes the Parts that Other Beers Cannot Reach*, and the word was just 'Refreshment', just one word, then obviously the copywriter comes in and adds a bit of magic to it." Cozens believes that planners should come up with *product differentiation*. "I'm not sure about an idea. Often it becomes a bit too executional. There is a danger that some planners may come up with something that could be made into a line, then it becomes a bit too clever-clever. I'd rather a much more factual brief. I'd rather supply the idea from the planner's facts." The brief is one thing, says Cozens, information is another. "Robin Wight invented Interrogating the Product. He actually made two hundred different points that differentiated one brand of washing machine from any others. I really do think you need to know as much as you can about the product."

David Droga, executive creative director of Saatchi & Saatchi London, prefers a single "nugget". "If the proposition can be honed down to one word, fantastic, providing that word is more than a generic word. If you had a car and the word was *Unbreakable*, then immediately that opens doors that are very exciting. But that word has to strike at the heart of the brand, not some word that a planner has whipped out of a hat like *Empowerment*..." Droga's concern is always the calibre of people who write briefs. "You're still at the mercy of them."

"Most great ideas come from the brief," asserts French. "The Campaign Palace used that principle on their briefing forms. In a place that was marked Headline, the suit had to write the promise, the basic premise of the ad. Where it said Copy, he used to write all the guff. Where it said Logo, he put what actually had to go on at the end of the ad. So what you actually had was an ad. Now with any luck, it wasn't very good. If it *was* very good, then the creative people would panic, which is a good thing occasionally. It's even more irritating when the brief is better than the ad. Every now and again that happens, but not via a planner, I have to say..."

"The brief is an ad to influence the creative team." Steel tries to boil the whole brief down to one paragraph, "which is for the benefit of Rich Silverstein, who has a very short attention span," he quips. Steel maintains that if it's not relevant to the consumer, it's not relevant to the brief. Creatives should work *from* a brief, not to it. His briefing format uses a series of questions: "What's the business situation the advertising has to affect?" ... "Why are we advertising at all?" ... "What do we know about the target audience?" ... "What is the main idea the advertising needs to communicate?" ... "What is the best way of planting that idea?" ... "How do we know we're right?"

"The best briefs take you away from very obvious areas." Saatchi & Saatchi's Kes Gray has written some of Britain's funniest, most memorable television commercials, Carling Black Label *Dambusters* for one. "I don't mind whether the brief has a big budget or a small budget. Half the fun of advertising is cutting your cloth accordingly."

Butterworth describes the briefing system at BMP DDB. "You get a brief from the client, and you might need to do some research to refine things. I'll then translate the strategy I've ended up with into a creative brief. It will be a page, with boxes on it, and the main box will be the proposition, a single-minded statement. The particular creative teams assigned to it will get the paper first, and a day later the account team gives them a verbal brief as well. The verbal briefing serves to highlight the main points that need attention, and the planner is there..." Butterworth aims for a single-minded statement, but does he ever condense it down to a single word? "It's nice to have one-word briefs, but sometimes what's different or most attractive about a brand is actually a combination of two things. At the end of the day, the brief's main job is to inspire the creatives."

Butterworth revisits his Volkswagen Polo brief that led to the award-winning *Surprisingly ordinary prices* campaign. "The original brief was based on a very simple product truth, that Volkswagen had in previous years brought down their prices. Most of the time, most people aren't in the market for a car and don't really care, so not surprisingly, perceptions hadn't caught up with reality. So the role of advertising was simply to challenge them and say, hang on a minute, these cars do cost less than you think. Specifically, we were targetting people who probably in their heart of hearts already wanted a Volkswagen, but were thinking, I won't even look into it further because they're beyond my price range, and it'd just be embarrassing walking into a dealership and then realising I can't afford it." The issue of tonality complicated the problem; people just weren't getting the price message. "We needed to do price stuff that was tonally very different. Despite all the cues to the contrary, in previous price-related tactical ads people had taken out reliability rather than well-equipped car or good value for money car. So, the biggest planning contribution in terms of this campaign was working out *what constituted a Volkswagen tone of voice* at that time, given what the competition was doing. On the one hand, you'd think that with a brand with Volkswagen's communications history, it would be quite simple to say, just do it 'Volkswageny'. The spirit of Bernbach for the 90s or whatever. But actually that's not very helpful. We found we needed to define what we meant by 'Volkswageny', given the time

A woman with hiccups is reading the paper at her kitchen table.

She turns a page and notices an ad that reads: *Polo, from only £7990.*

Her hiccups stop.

She continues reading and we fade to black.

Volkswagen logo and title: *Surprisingly ordinary prices.*

A surprisingly simple idea, economically presented by BMP DDB London. In both the 1999 and 2000 Gunn Reports, Volkswagen was the world's most awarded advertiser.

A grenadier guard stands rigidly on duty at his sentry box.

A flock of tourists, kids trying to make him laugh, even a dog sniffing his shoes can't distract him.

He doesn't move a muscle — until he sees a bus drive past with an ad that says: *Polo L, only £8145.*

Fade to black.

Volkswagen logo and title: *Surprisingly ordinary prices.*

Planner Richard Butterworth at BMP DDB London prescribed a realistic, down-to-earth tonality for the Volkswagen Polo campaign.

and given the prevailing environment. It was based on looking at loads of car ads, seeing how glossy and glitzy and hyperbolic they were, and saying, look, there's an opportunity here to do stuff that tonally is much more realistic, much more down-to-earth."

"I like to be as smart as I can before I put pen to paper." Ron Lawner is managing partner and chief creative officer of Arnold Communications, the Boston agency that won the Volkswagen pitch for North America in 1995. Lawner wants to know what business niche a company or product occupies, what the issues are in that industry, and most importantly, what consumers are thinking. The agency's research department is called the Consumer Insight Group. *"Demographics don't buy things, people do.* And when you have a clear idea what their mindset is, and you put that in some kind of meaningful cultural context, what's happening in the world around them, where do those products fit into their lives, you're working from a strong, very strategically sound platform."

"Good briefs keep the *client's* expectations realistic about what an ad can or can't do," stresses Tracy Wong. "It's only thirty seconds! When briefs are written poorly, they set false expectations and set the creatives up for a fall. Essentially, they become doomed architectural plans for a building that can't possibly stand." Wong favours briefs with ideas. "I call it creative kindling. With the short timetables we have, it really helps the creatives get off to a good start. This assumes, of course, a fairly egoless environment."

Chris O'Shea of London's Banks Hoggins O'Shea FCB believes there's no such thing as a perfect briefing system. "You hear things about it should be short, the proposition should be one word, which is true, all that helps, but the brief is just some thoughts put on a piece of paper. The real brief is when the account person or the planner comes and talks to me, because things are said that you can never, ever write down on paper. You've got to hear someone talk, then you fully understand what the problem is." O'Shea uses the brief as a useful reminder to keep himself on track.

What can creative people do when they receive a brief that doesn't have a genuinely clear direction, or genuine insights, let alone a genuine idea in it?

"If you feel *under*planned, or if you really believe a brief is *under*informed and not quite focused enough," Best advises, "you should open up your mind to the world outside the brief. What do you know about the realities of the market and the people out there? Try to get out there yourself if no one else is going to do it for you. If your agency doesn't have the benefit of planning, talk to the client; he is probably the best source. Planners are magpies, and so often are creative people. Ideas, inspirations, metaphors, analogies, can come from anywhere. The difficulty is marshalling them, knowing what's important, unless you've got a process and discipline to do so." The problem is, Best acknowledges, that you might just grab at the wrong shiny bauble and it will be fool's gold, not a nugget.

CONCEPT TESTING: YES OR NO?

In the words of Bill Bernbach: "One of the disadvantages of doing everything mathematically, by research and by mandate, is that after a while everybody does it the same way … We are spending so much darn' money for efficiency to measure things that we're achieving boredom like we've never achieved before. We're right about everything, but nobody looks." Besides, he asks: *"How do you storyboard a smile…?"*

Delaney discusses a television tracking study of all the major financial institutions in the UK, conducted by Barclays Bank. "After five years, and two and a half billion pounds spent on advertising, it showed that every financial institution had exactly the same profile on the four leading dimensions. It was a diamond, and they all overlapped. They were all identical, because they'd all done the *same* research, they'd all done the *same* kind of advertising, and they all ended up in the *same* little quadrant. And they'd spent two and a half billion pounds doing so! You could build a hospital with that money…"

In Japanese Noh theatre, they say that you must unify one thousand eyes. But can research prove that everyone is seeing the same thing?

As far as Arthur Bijur is concerned, testing concepts in focus groups totally eliminates the production. "It eliminates the tone of the finished commercial, it eliminates all the good stuff." For example, it's impossible to test all the nuances of comedy unless you have the finished commercial. "However, that's not to say that some concept testing may not be useful diagnostically. I think it's useful for testing whether a particular concept is relevant to someone or not. But I don't think it should ever be used to determine whether something is good or not, and the problem is, *it is*." If they have time, some of his clients test finished commercials before they go to air. Usually the work is validated, not destroyed. "There have been times when something in the commercial becomes a problem; a voice-over treatment that isn't communicating clearly enough, so we might fine-tune it. But we've had experiences with research that just show that the research was flawed." Bijur recalls how the famous Wendy's campaign was almost aborted. "They told us not to put *Where's the beef?* on air. It was tested as a produced commercial. Once you get people talking, they'll create problems that aren't really there, just so they can express something about themselves. The research people told us, do *not* put this commercial on air, and of course we all know what happened…"

Bijur believes the best research happens out in the marketplace. "A lot of clients have a long timeline from commercial-on-air to results. In the retail area, you put a commercial on and you get results within a week. In the packaged goods area, you put a commercial on and you might need five, six, seven months before you get reorders so you don't really know how effective it is. One of our biggest clients does a tremendous amount of research not on concepts but on *strategies*. Then there's research done on finished commercials, but they *don't* test commercials before they're produced. It doesn't work for their timeline and they know you can't always accurately predict from a pre-test what is going to happen."

"Researching scripts is the death of the business as we know it." Cozens thinks research is great up front, finding out about the consumer, the types of things they like. "There are some clients now who want three different ideas, and they need four or five different executions within each idea just to prove it's campaignable. It always comes down to the lowest common denominator, it really does." He recounts the episode of his Puma commercial with Steve McQueen. "It was the most successful car launch that Ford ever had, but it didn't research particularly well. But the marketing director down there said, well, I can understand why; there are things on paper that people can't imagine until it becomes a film. The punters out there don't have the imagination, nor should they have, they're not part of the business. And you've got to take that into consideration."

"Inspiration can't be defined or explained or justified." Stacy Wall observes that the majority of times our work is praised is because an ad really nailed a brief, or an ad said exactly what it needed to say, or that you can tell exactly what you're supposed to get from an ad. "But you can't stand in front of a work of art and tell me exactly what it's supposed to mean because it's open-ended. The meaning is what is between the individual and the work. The enigmatic qualities of our work are what's intriguing about it. The stuff that's left *unsaid*. People will either love or hate great work. *We're at our worst when we've been beaten down by the process and create stuff that's not going to be loved* or *hated*."

"While I might like to quarrel about the usefulness of focus groups and other methods employed to 'predetermine' the consumers' response to an ad, it would be a waste of time and breath," admits Riney. "Anyway, the fact of the matter is that while such research has never helped us very much, it hasn't really hurt us much, either." Research, he says, is a fact of advertising life, and will be as long as there are clients who need reassurance and researchers around to overpromise their wares.

Of course, not every client embraces predictive research. "A few clever people made loads of money by playing on client insecurities," charges Simonds-Gooding. "It strikes me as being something that the client psyche badly needs. My experience tells me that it's often of no value. Perhaps others have been more lucky than me…" When Simonds-Gooding used focus groups, he was fishing for insights or trying "to expose gross negatives, which strangely can sometimes be overlooked." They never played a mandatory role. "Rather, they were used or not used as my experience and judgement indicated. Logic tells one that the truly great new idea is *unlikely* to flourish in a focus group. Certainly, the first Heineken advertisements didn't."

"I think if your goal is to kill a good idea, focus groups are the right way to do it." Lawner says they're murder on any fresh approach or anything out of the norm. Clients who use research so they can become all things to all people will end up being nothing to anybody. "You don't get the truth. There's a dynamic that happens in a focus group. You're putting people in a place unlike where they normally consume advertising. You're asking them to be judges and that's a whole different headset. If testing worked they wouldn't have changed the taste of Coca-Cola." Lawner says you can check communications one-on-one to see whether consumers *understand* them. "But you can't check creativity in focus groups. A good client will know that. He will use them as a tool, not to protect his behind. If between you and your client, you don't have enough confidence and experience in what you're doing, you shouldn't be in this business," says Lawner. "You should be in a focus group."

"Predictive research is one of the greatest cons of the twentieth century." John Hegarty says everybody really knows it doesn't work, but corporations *want* it to. "But it doesn't work in the new world that they're now living in. It might have been fine when you were dealing with products that had an absolute performance advantage over their competitors. But now, what separates you from other brands is your attitude, the way you talk to people, so increasingly *your advertising is your competitive edge.* So in that sense, trying to measure the emotional values that a piece of film can deliver is almost impossible."

Hegarty describes how his agency's Levi's commercials were pre-tested before they went to air, so the client could secure affiliate contributions. "So many times there was a so-what reaction to a piece of advertising. *Flat Eric* is a fantastic example. It went down very well in the UK, quite well in Germany, not at all well in France. It was very strange, very odd, and people didn't know quite what to make of it. Now, in most companies, that piece of advertising would have been killed. But it's been a huge success for Levi's throughout Europe. The *Flat Eric* phenomenon is amazing. It also won a Gold at Cannes." The same thing happened when arguably one of the greatest Levi's classics was pre-tested. As Hegarty recounts, "Even when we tested *Launderette* before it went out, it was just kind of alright. And yet, when it actually ran, it was like wild fire. It's peculiar. The danger with this predictive research is that you show it to maybe twenty or thirty people. Just get the wrong percentage of people, and the whole thing's out the window. And the smaller the group, the more incredibly they're influenced by the people around them. You've only got to have one person who's a bit negative, and they can easily drive everybody else, and it becomes harder for somebody else to say, no, I think it's really good. It becomes harder for somebody to stick their neck out, and that's what you're asking people to do." Research exists, says Hegarty, because corporations want it to. "Because it makes their life easier, it justifies their decisions. If you're in a corporation, you've got to find some rational way of justifying what you're doing; you can't work from the heart…"

Delbridge dismisses focus group methodology as largely charlatan. "The research business in Australia has a respect which it hasn't earned. It's just psychobabble. I don't think the recruiting is accurate enough. And the people who want to sit in a room for two hours and get twenty bucks for it have to be a little bit suspect; they have to be of a certain type. The moderators vary hugely. Too often they're relatively inexperienced kids." Delbridge would only use focus groups to tell him about the market, as Hugh Mackay does, but not for concept testing. "When advertising is different, it doesn't work well in research. Now 'different' doesn't necessarily mean good, but it's not a bad start point…"

"Research is one of the great corporate frauds of the twentieth century. If chief executives knew the total amount of money spent on research to justify mediocre ideas *to them*, they would be shocked." Delaney believes you should use television to change things, rather than discussing them. "Most clients around the world test television commercials. They are led to believe that this is the right thing to do by their agencies, and certainly by research companies. The research companies, who are in many cases charlatans, lead clients to believe that they can get results which are empirical and that they have devices for judging whether things will work. It's not that I'm impatient, but I just don't believe that advertising is being used correctly. The large FMCG companies spend years developing advertising, by which time the brand has gone sour, or something else is happening in the market. One of the great things about television is that you can be on air in three days if you want to be. You can change things overnight. But these companies have a culture that's a really neurotic, fear-ridden process where people won't make decisions and will defer to any form of research whatsoever, even if it costs a fortune to do it. They test to exhaustion an idea that's mediocre in the first place, and will become even more mediocre once everybody's finished with it. They spend the kind of money that would build a village in Africa to find out whether people like an idea, when they can judge it themselves, otherwise it wouldn't have got into research. I don't mind research; I'm interested, but I don't want people telling me what an ad is. That's not what we're here for. In the end, whether anyone likes it or not, if you're good at this job it's because of an instinctive, intuitive talent."

"I'm not a big fan of focus groups," Garfinkel confesses. "If I'm not sure about something, I don't mind running an idea past focus groups, not so much in terms of execution but in terms of core idea. I don't mind occasionally running ideas by people to see if we can get a gauge if it's going to influence them in terms of buying a product, but even then I'm not 100% sure. I remember a focus group for Subaru, and one of the commercials was based on this big, heavy-set, redheaded guy who talked about his Subaru. And in the focus group was this big, heavy-set, redheaded guy, who said after viewing the rough cut, I don't believe that commercial, nobody looks like that guy." Garfinkel questions whether the industry has let itself down. "We're getting paid to be the experts. Some of us have had incredible success with a number of clients, not only in coming up with good advertising for them, but improving so many of our clients' businesses. And then, all of a sudden, a client will say, we don't totally trust you; we want to put the idea up in front of ten people who don't know anything about advertising and get their opinion. And the industry has *allowed* that to happen. I don't know if anybody's come up with a real, foolproof way of testing an idea on people. My biggest successes have *never* been focus-grouped…"

Reinhard seeks relevance, originality and impact in advertising. "I believe the purpose of research is to fuel the creative process with knowledge and insights, and to check creative hunches. It is essential in this role, but *dangerously inept when it attempts to predict the future.*"

Dan Wieden is adamantly against research, as Michael Prieve

explains. "For the most part we don't do any. One client does post-testing. We don't ever pre-test. You can read research any way you want. It's crazy. *Seinfeld* failed miserably in research. He got the lowest test scores in the history of NBC. We don't have a process beyond telling clients that they're going to have some really talented people who care about their business who are going to come up with some really great ideas. But a lot of clients don't want that, they want the process so they can drag out their jobs," Prieve concedes. "Sometimes it's a difficult place for clients to go. It's not all that reassuring."

Colleague Stacy Wall adds: "In general, we've got to create interest and get attention from people who are *not* in a room, being *told* to listen. That's why the whole process is flawed. Our agency mantra is the Orson Welles quote, *Don't give them what they want, give them what they never believed was possible.*"

"If there's any area of research that makes me weep tears of blood, it's television pre-testing." Hugh Mackay condemns pre-testing in general as a very, very dubious art. To pretend it's a science, he says, is rubbish. "No one knows how to do it because it's a very odd thing to try and do. The way people go about it is bizarre. Think about how people watch television; they watch it in their own homes, often in groups of two or three, increasingly in isolation. So we'd better pre-test in people's homes, with individuals or groups of two or three who normally watch television together, and we'd better embed it in a programme. *But that's not what we do.* What we do as an industry, typically, is assemble a collection of total strangers, shove them into a room somewhere and play them a television commercial or show them some storyboards, or worst of all, and now increasingly standard practice, show them some storyboards and play an audio track, which is not the track of the commercial, but is an *explanatory* audio track. So you get this nonsense where you show people pictures from the commercial while an announcer's voice says, 'In this commercial we are going to see Mr. and Mrs. Jones, who are a happily married couple, in their modern kitchen...' In other words, explain the whole thing, crack the code, reveal the formula, and then expect people to respond to it as though they're responding to television, let alone responding to a television commercial. *It's the most arrant nonsense* … and the big danger, which I've been watching for thirty-five years, is that creative people will write to win the test, instead of writing for the consumer."

Mackay advocates the elimination of pre-testing, except in the very occasional case where major disagreement exists between the creator, the client, and the researcher who did the preliminary work on understanding the consumer. If together those three people can't agree whether the commercial is right, then Mackay suggests doing some laboratory work, as naturalistically as possible, just to see whether people comprehend it. "But that should be the exception. It should be one little element to be *added* to the judgement of the experts. Trust the experts. That's why they're there; that's why they're paid." One of those experts should be the client. However, expertise on the client side is seriously threatened. "So many clients, in the interests of downsizing and cost-cutting, have stripped out very mature people from the middle management ranks and trimmed down their marketing departments. What's lost is a lot of corporate wisdom. So what you're often dealing with are only very senior people, who don't have time to get involved in the creative process, and relatively junior people who have no corporate memory and not much experience at all, being asked to make million-dollar creative campaign decisions. Of course they feel insecure, so they fly to the arms of research for reasons to do with their own insecurity, rather than because the research has a track record of saying we can tell you which ad is going to work and which one isn't."

There are many campaigns, Mackay argues, which in terms of the standard measures of advertising, such as the recall of the advertising, have done brilliantly. But they were never effective. Other campaigns, which have not produced high levels of recall, have done a brilliant job for the brand. "The thing that advertisers are slow to understand, and slowest of all in relation to television, is that we shouldn't care whether people remember the ad. Nor should we care how people feel about the ad. *All we should care about is do they remember the brand, and how do they feel about the brand.* The ad makes an input to that, but it's quite a mysterious input. It's subtle. It's not direct; it's not, here's the ad, here's the brand, now we'll graft that ad onto that brand, and that's how people will feel about the brand. But, because so much money is spent on television advertising, advertisers feel even more insecure about their television advertising budget than any other media budget. They see it as a high risk spend, therefore they want research to give them reassurance. In television, more than any other medium, the hunt has been on for ways to quantify the effectiveness of a television commercial before it's shown. So what you find is *professionally disgraceful work* generating statistical analyses of audience reactions to television, *based on tiny numbers of unscientifically selected people*, where there is no professional basis for measurement at all; the laws of statistics don't apply, so we're talking about *meaningless numbers.* Yet the statistics are spat out and clients seize on them, because at last they've got a number. They can say, this is a 78% effective commercial, that one is only 63%, so let's go with the 78%."

Mackay believes the pre-testing process is a house of cards that will collapse one day for a very obvious reason. "Smart clients will look more broadly at what's happening in advertising. They will realise that some of the best work they've seen on television was never pre-tested, and some of the dullest work they've seen on television was pre-tested almost to death, but passed the test. *There are many examples of really good advertising based on research, but not based on pre-testing.* In fact, as a general rule, if a client has decided as policy that every commercial will be pre-tested, and that they will use the pre-test scores as a *substitute* for their own judgement, then you can guarantee that over time, that client will find their advertising effectiveness will diminish."

"The only criterion we can use to judge advertising is its effectiveness," asserts Professor John Philip Jones. "This effectiveness must be measured in *behavioural* and not just in cognitive terms. *I would never recommend using focus groups to predict campaign effectiveness.* They are not just bad, they are counterproductive. Focus groups have some value in helping creative people generate creative ideas. This is because of the interaction within the group. Soft research of this sort simply does not predict what will happen in the marketplace, despite the protestations of the British advertising establishment. The sole method that predicts reliably the marketplace performance of an advertisement is quantitative persuasion testing; quantitative recall testing does not work. Quantitative persuasion testing is used by virtually all important advertisers in the United States. It is not used in Britain, mainly because British agencies, and account planners in particular, have an emotional aversion to it. It is the British clients who are the losers. It is not surprising that the top 30% of campaigns in the United States are far more effective than the top 30% of campaigns in Britain."

Breaking The Right Rules

Ironically, some of the world's most admired cutting edge agencies happily test concepts in focus groups.

BMP DDB, London. Ranked by *The Gunn Report* as the world's most creatively awarded agency in 1999, BMP DDB has enshrined concept testing in its culture. In fact, over the last thirty years, the agency has recruited more advertising focus groups than any other organisation in London, even more than the major market research companies.

As Butterworth explains, the agency believes that no matter how brilliant an idea is, there are always ways of making it better. "We always go in with the attitude that it's a glass half full and it could get fuller. We treat focus groups more as a tool to inspire one's own thinking than as a kind of black box that provides Yea or Nay judgement on either a strategy or a piece of work. At best, they're a bunch of people you chat to. You might get ideas from them, you might not; and that's it. When you're researching creative work, you might suddenly discover stuff that hadn't occurred to you. At that point, everyone on the account team and the client will have lived with it for a long time. Inevitably, because of that, it's very difficult to look at a piece of work and, forgetting the strategy, react to it afresh. So it's amazing how many times we've gone and done creative development research on something thinking, this will be fine, it's totally easy to understand, there's no possible way of misunderstanding this idea, and then you show it to consumers. Basically they're the first people seeing it who haven't been through three strategic presentations and six drafts of a creative brief, and quite often they'll react to it in a different way. They might take out a message you hadn't anticipated that people would take out. Perfectly good ideas can founder at this point, but everyone, and the creatives here as well, are mature enough to recognise that if the consumers are struggling with it for a very, very sensible reason, then the research has been useful."

When John Webster wanted to use popular cartoon character Andy Capp for John Smith's Bitter, the concept bombed in research. Capp was perceived as lazy, a miserable loner. However Best believed the underlying idea was right; it was a question of modifying certain executional elements. Capp was given a dog, a wife and a social network, and the rest is history. In other hands, though, the concept might have been doomed.

Webster himself believes most good ideas, "if they're good enough", will get through research. *"The worst enemy is silence.* If they watch something and there's silence after it, you've failed. I've often had things that go on and they're either very animated after it, or they're attacking it, but at least I've got a reaction. The death of any commercial is boredom. You have to get a reaction. I'm quite excited when I get a reaction, even if it's an *anti* reaction — there must have been something in there that touched a nerve. I'm always looking for that liveliness and polarising people. If you can do that in research, you'll do so much better when the film's made properly. To be honest, if I put my hand on my heart, very, very few things have been turned down in research that I can actually say were great in retrospect. They were probably right to turn them down, although it hurt at the time."

Not only does the agency operate its own network of recruiters, says Butterworth, the planners are trained to do their own focus groups as often as possible. The standard focus group size is eight. On a typical project of six focus groups, some are conducted in the north or in the Midlands, and two in London. Maybe two out of those six will be in a viewing facility with one-way mirror, a camera, and the client watching. "But usually you end up doing them in someone's front room in Manchester or Sheffield…" The role of planner as moderator is crucial. "By definition, good advertising has to be different and consumers, quite often, *in the context of research*, don't react well to things that are different. They're much more comfortable with what's familiar to them. A lot depends on how imaginative the planner is. We'd never claim to be as good a moderator as a full-time qualitative research practitioner, but because we're advertising specialists, and because we're familiar with the account, we can bring more to particular creative research than any independent qualitative researcher ever could. Some clients don't want agencies to do creative development research. They say it's like asking a child to mark his own homework. He won't be objective. Which sometimes is fair enough, sometimes not."

Butterworth believes the nature of the television idea should dictate the choice of stimulus material used in the test. "Ideas that are story-based are best researched on animatics, or a storyboard with a narrative tape." Depending on time and money, an animatic could be shot using a film storyboard, quite often enhanced with computer graphics to introduce movement. "John Webster is the classic exponent of quite simple black-and-white line drawings. Sometimes it will be just a narrative tape with a few pictures of key frames. Sometimes it's as simple as reading scripts. And, in a way, it's quite nice doing that; you're almost anecdotally chatting people through an idea. Maybe you've got the end line written down, so you could show them that; maybe you've got some tapes of music. Quite often that degree of informality and flexibility makes it much easier." Butterworth's clients rarely post-test commercials. One exception was the black-and-white Polo *Protection* commercial. Between doing initial creative development research and making the film, the end line had to be changed. The agency tested the finished commercial to make sure that the new line made sense.

Goodby, Silverstein & Partners. As Jeff Goodby explains: "We put scripts through focus groups all the time. The number of odd spots that have been sold to clients this way far outstrips the number that have been killed. However, one has to be wary of letting consumers make decisions in cases where commercials are *very hard to imagine*. We always reserve the right to overrule consumers and decide they'll love it when they see it. Groups are also helpful for adjusting spots, finding out that this or that part doesn't work, and finding a way to fix things."

Intelligent use of focus groups by planner Jon Steel paved the way for art director Tracy Wong and writer Steve Simpson to shoot their radical Fresh TV/Fresh Mex *campaign. Goodby, Silverstein & Partners for Chevys Mexican Restaurants.*

Which was precisely what happened when art director Tracy Wong and writer Steve Simpson developed their famous Chevys Mexican Restaurants campaign. The idea was for the advertising to reflect the freshness of the food by running "fresh" TV commercials on the same day they were shot.

"Actually, the original idea to make the commercials as fresh as the food was Steve's," reports Wong. "Chevys really did have a point of difference. They made everything from scratch that day and threw everything out that night. No canned tomatoes. No processed cheeses. No packaged tortillas. They had been living with the tagline *Fresh Mex* for years. It had just never been correctly articulated or brought to life in advertising. We wrestled around with the idea of making the spots as fresh as the food like some wild alligator, trying to get it to work in a 30-second format that was fun and engaging. The concept was great. The first few executions, however, were very flat-footed…"

The first focus groups panned the concept. The rough home video-style execution did not communicate freshness. It sent the opposite signal; that Chevys didn't care much for the quality of its food. Jon Steel probed for a solution. As he suspected, the concept was the right one; the voice-over just needed refinement so that the proposition was absolutely clear: *"We made this commercial a few hours ago. We call this fresh TV … At Chevys, we made our salsa just minutes ago. We call this Fresh Mex…"*

"The idea of *Fresh TV/Fresh Mex* as well as the squiggly graphic treatment really helped us turn the corner executionally," says Wong. "At first, no one believed we could do it. That included the client, the account people, the TV stations — and, to a certain extent, us. We ended up doing nineteen *Fresh Mex* spots over the course of three months. Waking at 3.30am, chasing unsuspecting people with camera and mike minutes before sunrise at 5.30am, finishing the shoot by 7am, reviewing the cut with Rich Silverstein and the client at 10am and reporting to the office by 11am for a full day's work. Not once did we fail to deliver."

Steel was the first *real* planner that Wong had worked with. "Technically, I'd worked with some research people in New York who had just had their titles changed to 'planners'. They were no different after the change. Jon, to me, was the ultimate. He was really part of the creative team — as a player, as a coach, as a fan, all those things."

What Steel rejects about focus groups is the unnatural atmosphere in which most are conducted. He believes we should replicate the environment and mood the respondents might be in when they have contact with the brand or the advertising. When GS&P pitched for Sega, all the research was done in kids' bedrooms. Family restaurants, hip bars and cruise liners have been other research environments. Steel is also convinced that *the planner should conduct the group*; no one else is as close to the brand or the creative work. Good planners are good qualitative research moderators.

Howell Henry Chaldecott Lury & Partners. Mary Stow, head of planning, describes how the agency's dedicated teams do the research together, set the strategy together, then develop the creative together.

Stow says the agency starts with research, but not with the consumer. "We tend to do a lot of research into the client organisation which is either behind the brand or is itself the brand. That's where the point of difference will be," Stow maintains, "in the cultural values of the organisation, or in the beliefs of the people working there. We do not start by doing focus groups so that we can understand consumer attitudes to the product. Focus groups can so easily hold you back. People can only tell you what is *now*, not what might be possible."

However, the agency — which describes itself as "professional radicals" — uses research for creative development, and always tests more than one idea. "By researching creative work which takes a brand in a different direction, we can discover what *is* possible," says Stow. The most controversial aspect of the agency's approach is the way it treats *likeability*. "In a lot of focus groups that are being watched from behind the mirror, everybody's looking for the 'that's nice' reaction, 'that's lovely', because the client behind the mirror will feel good. We actually have an allergic reaction to that response. People can say 'that's nice', then file it away and ignore it. We're looking for the ideas that *worry* people a bit." After the groups, Stow confesses, "we try to eavesdrop on people as they leave. We try to find out which idea they're still talking about. It's an indication that it stayed in their mind, registered enough, did enough. That kind of reaction means the shock value is not just shock value; it's got something intrinsic to it that's both shocking and interesting to people, but not irrelevantly so."

What shocks many creatives is the fact that the agency produces Britain's most radical work using a disciplined, almost clinical, research-based process.

"You have to build a structure that allows you to offer what reassurances there are." Steve Henry's logic bridges the realities of creativity and business. "Creativity in advertising, as much as there is creativity in advertising, and there are days when it feels like there isn't, is an area where you don't know if something is going to work or not. It's like in Hollywood, *the one truth is that nobody knows anything.* So when you do something genuinely creative, you just don't know. I don't want to copy. I don't want us to be dragged into areas where we are being asked to repeat the success that somebody else has achieved in the marketplace. *I want to go where nobody's been before.* But the forces in the industry, not just the advertising industry, but the entire creative industry, the entire entertainment industry, don't generally like that. These industries are full of people who want results. They want security. And they want to know if it's going to work. And absolutely correct, too, because there are large sums of money involved. So in order to really make a difference in the marketplace with an ad, a book, a CD, a movie, anything, you've got to go somewhere new — *and you have to provide a process that offers reassurance and security along that path.* That's what we did. Our culture here is about breaking the rules, but breaking the right rules. It's about being innovative, but being innovative in a way that is relevant. And that's about doing the right kind of research, because the *worst* kind of research will kill anything."

Henry is adamant about research. "From my point of view, if we're going to go somewhere that nobody's been before, *I want to know that the consumers are going to go there with me.*" Time is always built into creative development for research that has been specifically designed by the agency for each project. "Everybody uses research. But research, the way it's used currently in the industry, doesn't work. It has to be done in the right way. If you talk to most people, they would just reflect the *status quo* back at you. So research has to be conducted among the opinion formers, the early adopters, the bright people in the target market. And then you have to have very sensitive research. It isn't about eight people saying, I like this because it fits into my view of what's acceptable in the marketplace. You have to find the work that people are talking about when they *leave* the room. You have to find the piece of work that they're talking about the most. *They might not like it, but somehow it's got past their defences.*"

Sadly, such sensitive and strategic use of focus groups is the exception, not the rule. Mostly, clients and agencies abdicate their responsibilities, encouraging groups to become amateur copywriters and art directors. The groups play God. Shoddy questions and flawed interpretations abound. The process of feeding ideas into focus groups is akin to sending troops over the top in World War I.

PROCTER & GAMBLE: PALACE REVOLUTION?

Satirist H. L. Mencken might well have been referring to Procter & Gamble when he observed: "No one ever lost money by under-estimating the intelligence of the great masses of the people."

For years, P&G commercials embodied all that was bad about television advertising: unremitting hard sell, endless side-by-side demonstrations, mind-numbing repetition, and tonality pitched to the lowest common denominator.

But all that is history. Peter Carter, P&G's director of advertising development for global haircare, explains: "We're trying to change the type of advertising that we use. In the past it was very formulaic. It was dull. We've discovered that consumers can still get an informative message, but they *like it better* when it's a little entertaining. They like it better, and *maybe they'll even buy more of the product*, when they can associate with the brand on a personal level, when the brand character is something that they aspire to. So we're investigating other ways of coming at the consumer than just, hey, we've got the best product and here's a side-by-side to show you that, or here's the standard presenter who's going to tell you

Adding personality to function. A housewife digs up and shifts a tree in her garden, extending her washing line because Procter & Gamble's Ace now contains 10% more detergent in every pack. Leo Burnett Peru.

everything you ever wanted to know about haircare. We're now looking to expand our repertoire…"

Carter, a 20-year P&G veteran, discusses a recent analysis of the company's advertising around the world. "It was a big revelation for us. We believe that advertising must persuade people. That's why we've been so functional, so rational, in our approach. We've been very good at identifying the consumer need, and identifying how to tell the consumer that this product performs a certain way. We've not been very good at adding personality and attitude to the way that we tell the consumer about ourselves. We are not using personality to our advantage as much as we should."

P&G makes 1,200 to 1,500 commercials a year around the world and spends four billion dollars on advertising; Carter calls it a big part of the company's culture. P&G does not believe in or use focus groups for concept testing; it has developed its own proprietary research method. The company also believes that recall of brand is important, not the recall of advertising. "For the last 160 years, Procter & Gamble has sold products to consumers that are very different from the kind of image products that we like to talk about when we talk about advertising, the sodas, the cars, the clothing, the badge products. Our products are very functional. Out of sixty to seventy international brands, we have only one brand in the company that is a pure emotional sale, and that's for a fine fragrance. All our other brands are functional, like shampoos that clean your hair, or condition your hair, or do something to your hair, or paper products that have some advantage in absorbency, or breathability, so we've actually done very well at selling functionality. The *way* we sell functionality is what's going to change. Typically, we've done it in a very left-brain sort of approach. We still want our advertising to sell the consumer; we believe thoroughly that advertising can make a difference between product sales in one area versus another. We've seen it a million times and we believe in it wholeheartedly. So our idea is, let's get our people to take *bigger risks…*"

How does P&G define a risk? "Being open to alternate ways of having the advertising work with the consumer, to try something really revolutionary. Typically the P&G manager would say they're taking a risk if they did a Folgers commercial and it only had two coffee shots instead of three, as opposed to, let's do a Folgers ad with no coffee shot at all!" In the new corporate culture, managers and advertising agencies will no longer be rewarded for maintaining the *status quo*. Slight growth was acceptable in the past; now the company wants to set big goals and achieve big changes. "If we set big goals, we will make big changes, and we will take big risks instead of small ones when it comes to our advertising."

Accompanying the call for a new voice is a new agency briefing system. "We're walking away from long, involved briefs on paper. Our new thinking is that briefs are not something that the account people and the brand people spend months to craft so that *they* feel comfortable. The current briefing system was not inspiring the creatives." P&G is experimenting with something called A Creative Briefing Experience. "The creatives get a one- or two-line strategy and communication objective. The experience fills in the gaps…" Carter took several creatives from Leo Burnett Hong Kong to a Vidal Sassoon fashion show in Beijing. "We gave them the brand strategy, and sat them down in a swanky restaurant. Vidal was there, the media was there. They attended a master class where hairdressers are trained how to style hair; they got the sights and sounds and smells of it and a couple of weeks later they wrote some great advertising as a result of this total immersion."

Andrew Bell of Leo Burnett Thailand talks about the duality of the comfort barrier. "The biggest challenge of working on P&G was to actually step outside their comfort barrier and get them to step outside as well. But agencies were also afraid to step outside the boundaries that they've found quite comfortable to work within. Now, when P&G is ready to step forward, the agencies must not hold them back."

Avon Talking

Another century-old Fortune 500 corporation, Avon Products, Inc., has redefined its approach to advertising creativity. The company is also seeding a new campaign line, *Let's talk*.

"We are building share of soul and long-term relationships with new generations of women around the world," says Robert Gibralter, group vice president, advertising and creative agency. "*Let's talk* is a more modern and interactive interpretation of that wonderful woman-to-woman relationship that is us and nobody else."

Gibralter believes in planning and an intuitively-led campaign development process. "Great planning provides insights, the right resources, the best possible timing, and a plan — ideas, budgets, resources and timetables — to tackle the most complex of marketing challenges." Gibralter heads one of the major in-house agencies in the beauty business; he is also responsible for building Avon's brand worldwide through advertising. "Add flexibility to planning," he recommends. "Bring your team to peak interpersonal sensitivity and keep them open-minded, intuitive, even impulsive, capable of seizing opportunities during the creative development and production process."

Gibralter never discounts the role of luck in the equation. "It's what lets the team make great, unanticipated leaps. Faith and acceptance of the luck factor spice up the process with creativity. We should never close our minds to fresh insights and opportunities." Gibralter practises what he preaches. "We were doing a sunrise shoot in Majorca for our new international television campaign. It was a landscape; no talent was planned. Then the director, Simon Peters of Alias Films London, saw a beautiful woman open a window to welcome the morning sun and totally reset the team to capture the moment. No casting, no storyboards, but the group responded in time to catch it. And wouldn't you know, it turned out to be the shot that carries the film."

TOWARDS THE CUTTING EDGE

"What held the big agencies back in the past," observes Warren Berger, "was fear of controversy and risk. But in the age of Oddvertising, it's pretty hard to offend or cause controversy. So being rebellious and full of attitude is becoming acceptable to larger companies."

It takes more than being outrageous to reach the cutting edge. It takes more than being out there to actually get there. As Berger says, "They still have a problem with complete originality. They like to do things that someone else has tried already." Berger has chronicled American advertising over two decades for *Communication Arts*, *Graphis*, *Advertising Age* and *One*. "The top shops have one thing in common. They are run by very smart, charismatic, confident people; not just ad geeks, but witty, well-read people who understand art, pop culture, human behaviour. This is true of Delaney, Goodby, Wieden, Clow. You can't sit down twenty minutes with these people without liking them and being really impressed by them. And this enables them to do two things: inspire the creative troops and persuade clients to try new things. People will follow these guys anywhere."

By definition, therefore, the cutting edge is reached not so much by having brave clients, as it is by being a brave agency. As Steel says, speaking of his own agency, Goodby, Silverstein & Partners: "All we're interested in is working with clients whom we like and respect, who demand great advertising. If we can consistently produce great advertising, we believe, the future might take care of itself."

"A lot of life is to do with taste, a lot of judgement in advertising is to do with taste, and you don't — as some people think — leave that taste to consumers," argues Delaney. "If you want to use the medium at its most powerful, then *you've got to be prepared to lead* and help people to see things that are new and fresh. Something they haven't seen before will engage them at a different level. By going as far as you can with the medium, by being relevant to them and to the product, by expressing something in an interesting way, not being gratuitous or extraneous, you are being *responsible*. People only need to see it once or twice. The irony is, the irresponsibility is with the people who use the medium just through weight of spend. *Mediocre advertising costs more*; it costs more to whack people over the head to pay attention to it, six or eight or ten times, when it's so ordinary and they've seen it all before." That fact is slowly dawning on clients, Delaney asserts, and they have a right to get something better when they sit down to approve a commercial. Creative people in many agencies are capable of delivering it, says Delaney; agency managements are the ones that resist change. "Unfortunately, advertising is possibly the most conservative business on earth. It changes very, very slowly because the people who run advertising agencies are generally account men, and account people's imaginations are well known, and their terms of reference relate entirely to the status quo. Ultimately the creative people lose. In this agency, they tend to win because I run the agency."

If brand building methodologies change faster than advertising, will the big, monolithic agencies become irrelevant?

"Not necessarily, but the value of 'bigness' to clients can be sometimes less important than it is to the financial interests of a big agency." Berlin says, "To understand this, follow the money." Berlin calls advertising an *intellectual capital business*. "Its greatest value is the tangible value of ideas. We create ideas that contribute to the experience of brands. We can make a car more interesting by creating a context in which we can appreciate its styling and performance better. We can make a computer more valuable by getting people to understand the character and emotional issues that its makers infused into it. And absolutely, we can make a beer taste better. *Our work and the product merge in the consumer's mind.* Advertising, the best advertising, really is doing these things right now in our culture. That's intellectual capital. It's all about how good the ad is, and that means how good the agency is — which is the quality of the people in it, and not some rubbish about agency 'culture' or 'process' — at a given moment."

Where it went weird, says Berlin, is that we don't structure or value ourselves as an intellectual capital industry. "Not fundamentally, not anymore. *The bulk of advertising today — and by far the bulk of the wealth it creates for its practitioners — is driven by 'selling' advertising's moderate operating earnings on public markets at high price earning multiples.* How high?" he speculates. "As of this moment, Grey Advertising is trading at *seventy times* its yearly after-tax earnings. That's an extreme example, but the point is that the money to be made this new way can't help but change the focus of a business. You *have* to be big to do this, or you won't get 'taken public'. You have to be worldwide and diversified to appeal to most large clients and to spread your income risk. And in the process of doing these things, your basic nature subtly shifts from an intellectual capital-based business to a distribution-based business. You buy and merge agencies. *You become a business abstraction focused on making money as a means, instead of as an end.*" It doesn't happen overnight, explains Berlin. "And most people in a big agency have no reason to be aware of it, unless the agency is missing its profit goals. And because life is rarely simple, there are big agencies that still operate in a sincere belief system that they are foremost about the work. But the foundations have changed. By far and away most of the advertising in the world is done by the distribution-based models. There's billions of dollars at stake, and there's no real going back — unless you choose to stay small and therefore about seventy times less well off than you might otherwise be."

Which begs the question, is there anybody still left in advertising?

"Dan Wieden gave the creatives here the ability to fail, to make what I like to call Glorious Mistakes." If you are not willing to make a glorious mistake, says Jim Riswold, then you are not willing to do anything completely outstanding. "We all admire the trapeze artists that don't have a net. If they fall, they'll kill themselves. That's a far greater risk than advertising. What's the worst thing that's going to happen if you try for greatness in advertising and fail?"

3

HOW TO GET IDEAS

A s early as 1890, the German philosopher Christian von Ehrenfels coined the term *gestalt* to describe experiences that needed *more* than our basic sensory capacities to comprehend. Soon, German psychologists had taken the idea further; human perception, they said, can organise sensory stimuli in any number of ways so that the whole is *greater* than the sum of its parts.

All well and good, but how do we get ideas? Where do they come from? Do we really grab them from the ether?

Paul Arden once said, "They're not your ideas, they're God's ideas."

"Well, He doesn't give them up without a fight, you know." Siimon Reynolds, founder of Love e-branding in Sydney and the driving force behind seminal agencies Andromeda and OMON, says you have to be committed to getting them. "Ideas appear in the world at the same time, and the issue is whether we have strong enough antennae. You see it all the time. The same movies, the same ad ideas, all come out at once. Anybody *not* highly creative will say that's rubbish. But anybody who has to conceive ideas for a living well knows that sometimes ideas arrive on the page, fully formed, in a nanosecond, and they've come from somewhere else."

Nigel Dawson, creative director of Grey Advertising Melbourne, defines an idea as something that makes you look at a product or service "from an angle that it's never been looked at before."

Similarly, Japanese actor Yoshi Oida once described how Kabuki performers "look at the moon" by pointing skywards with their index fingers. One actor performed the gesture so beautifully, audiences gasped. Another actor made the same gesture. Audiences didn't notice his craft. They simply saw the moon.

IDEAS: DO WE STILL NEED THEM?

"There is an increasing danger," cautions Anthony Simonds-Gooding, "that extraordinary production effects and visuals are replacing advertising ideas…"

"It's like a meal that's too rich." Noel Delbridge believes there isn't anything surprising anymore. Anything you can imagine, you can do. "When that's the case, *you've really got to swim against that stream*, because you're not going to awe anyone into saying, what a fantastic effect. Particularly on the small screen. You've got cinema working against you. The small screen is not the greatest medium for technique." A television commercial, he says, has got to have demonstrably a big idea, usually an immensely simple idea, which has legs. Weak commercials, on the other hand, "have *too many ideas* — they demonstrate an inability to simplify, to be ferociously direct, and to have a central single idea."

"A lot of the stuff we see coming out of England currently seems to me to be executionally driven," observes Lionel Hunt. "And it is interesting because the execution is so fantastic, but it's very shallow, not much depth to it. The best stuff that comes out of England, or America, or anywhere for that matter, always has a powerful idea at its core." Advertising is incestuous, and executions are rapidly duplicated. Hunt acknowledges this, but nevertheless finds stimulus material useful. "I like looking at *Shots*. It's great to see the best work from all over the world. It's stimulating. It makes you aim higher. Sometimes, of course, you inadvertently copy things, forgetting that you've seen it before. That seems to happen more with some people than others…"

Marcello Serpa believes in ideas one hundred percent. "The production values in Brazil are not so high, so to make a point, you have to be bold, you have to make something different, and it has to have something unexpected."

"For me, it's about ideas." Naresh Ramchandani chalked up the Maxell and First Direct campaigns at Howell Henry Chaldecott Lury, Boots No. 7 and IKEA at St. Luke's. "When ideas are really big and really good, they somehow can't be contained. I always try to imagine that *the real medium is people's conversations*, and that the media we buy in terms of advertising is — to use an American football term — just a hand-off."

Execution is the icing, says Ron Mather. "You still need the cake. The real bit you get paid for is the thinking. You should always look for an idea. If an ad's got an idea, a good idea, it's bulletproof. Don't get seduced by techniques, by all the trimmings." Mather suggests training young creatives to work on pads the size of matchboxes, "so the thoughts they write have to be just so simple."

"It is a fundamental article of faith of every Lowe agency that there should be an idea at the centre of what we do." Adrian Holmes worked in a photographic darkroom with a radio playing all day; hearing one dreadful commercial after another, he tried his hand at writing some and discovered the existence of advertising agencies. He worked his way up from junior copywriter and admits his photographic and film training made him a "right nuisance" to art directors. He talks about the need for briefs to focus on one thing so the advertising idea can also be singular. "If you throw somebody one tennis ball, they'll catch it. If you throw them five, their arms will flay around in the air but they'll end up catching nothing. You can't have a great solution until you have a great problem to begin with."

A lot of clients are threatened by ideas, warns Roy Grace. "There's nothing more threatening than something different to them, and if it fails, they fail. It's like getting into a nice warm tub if you can approve something that has nice music, nice film, and nothing challenging. You're not going to get into trouble for that and that's why there aren't a lot of clients saying, Give Me The Big Idea." Cinematographically, says Grace, there are so many skilled and talented people that it's too easy to fall prey to big expensive productions with everything except an idea.

"A 30-second commercial without an idea does not have the same power as a 30-second commercial with an idea. In human terms, it's a neuter." Jack Vaughan of Sydney's Principals has held the posts of executive creative director and chairman of agencies like Young & Rubicam, George Patterson Bates and The Campaign Palace in London and Australia. Vaughan defines the idea as the driver that helps people understand the purpose of the brand. Some creatives are too lazy to put ideas into commercials, he says, some may not know what ideas are. "Sometimes, committees take them out, piece by piece, and that can happen without people realising it. When a commercial goes through a lot of checks and balances, committees and ducks, you've got to know when it's gone beyond the point of no return. To some extent, a robust idea can take a bit of battering and still survive. In other cases, imperceptibly, the idea has gone and that's the time to tear it up. You have to be objective enough to know when it's clinically dead." If the committee accuses you of throwing a temper tantrum, Vaughan's advice is to tactfully thank them for their new inputs and suggest that they now deserve a fresh, cohesive idea. "It's best to start again." At the other end of the scale, total freedom is as bad as people trying to do it by the numbers. "It bypasses the concept stage. What you get are executions looking for an idea." Vaughan is also very conscious of originality and not doing derivative work. "I don't care if it's been done by the Icelandic Art Directors Club in 1935; if you know that a similar idea exists anywhere it is an ethical issue that you must not do something that is the same or similar. You have to be original at all costs."

"Clients can come to any agency and say, well, the most successful marketing in my area obeys these rules, so can you give us an ad like that." But Steve Henry believes *advertising should be competitive.* "I want to give them something different. I hate advertising that just disappears into the void. Advertising by its nature is ephemeral and transient, but my ambition is to always shake it up and make a difference. That's what I love about advertising. I want to go to the client with a media idea they've never heard of before … the strategy will be something completely out of the blue … and the creative work will be an execution they'll have to get their heads around. Breaking rules, breaking rules, breaking rules. There are so many rules and so many people in this business

Ventilated Hush Puppies.

Fallon Minneapolis gained early fame by turning great print ideas into great television commercials. Agency art director Bob Barrie used the Hush Puppies dog as the icon. In the television version of Ventilated Hush Puppies, *the dog sits on the grating of an underground railroad. When a train goes through below, the rush of air causes his ears to lift. It was the first commercial ever directed by stills photographer Rick Dublin and it won a Gold Lion at Cannes.*

In the Gunn Report 2000, *Fallon was ranked the world's third most awarded agency.*

are just lazy." Henry cites the jeans market as an example. "Levi's dominated the jeans market. Their formula a few years ago was Americana, sex, rock'n'roll; so for a period of time, everybody was doing ads in the jeans market that had Americana, sex, rock'n'roll. Probably with all three, but certainly two out of the three. Then Diesel came along and completely broke all those rules and shook up the marketplace. And so Levi's had to get where Diesel was."

IDEAS, of course, serve another function.

The idea — *not* the size of the client's logo — should brand the commercial, says David Lubars, president and creative director of Fallon Minneapolis, originally Fallon McElligott. Lubars was formerly chief executive officer and creative director of BBDO Los Angeles. "The commercial should give you *an idea about the brand.* Something real that you can use. So you know who that company is, so you personally understand them. But while the idea should be big enough to be a big branding idea, it must also contain *how you can touch the brand today.* You can't just do branding; you have to tell people what you need them to do. Especially with dot.com, there's so much access."

Fallon was probably the first regional American agency to gain international creative acclaim. The Minneapolis-based shop earned its early fame with great ideas taken to television from print ads. Soon, they became a house style, as group creative director Bruce Bildsten recalls. "Originally we didn't have clients who did big budget television. So by necessity we kept it very simple; usually a locked-down camera, a simple little joke or smile to them, and a lot of them hold up very well today."

Today, the opposite is the case, says Lubars. "Each client gets its own flavour, as opposed to a Fallon's template. We should be everywhere, all over the map, based on what's right for the client." He likes to see big ideas that suggest big pictures of a brand. One example: "There's a guy who lives at home with his parents. He's a big schmuck loser and he wants them to keep providing him with things, and they say, what does this look like, a Holiday Inn?"

Bildsten references Joe Pytka. "Pytka once said either be elegant or outrageous, and that's what we're doing now. Either things that are really beautiful and thoughtful, or else they're a good laugh." Bildsten still reveres the simplicity of a great idea. "The best things usually have very simple ideas behind them, although they may not be simple to shoot. They are fully realised, every detail is worked out, and you wouldn't have done anything differently. The pacing is right, the film looks the way it should, the lines are delivered the way they should be, and it's something I don't think I've seen before." However, it is possible to have a small idea with a huge execution such as the Guinness *Surfers* commercial.

"A visual can come and go," observes veteran Australian writer John Kingsmill. "If someone said to you, ten years ago, something strikingly true, you'd remember that person because he said that strikingly true thing, and yet you might forget his face. Ideas must be simply presented and have a tremendous, almost unarguable truth in them," Kingsmill says. "An idea is likely to stay in the mind because it is an abstraction, and that appeals more to the mind than a pure visual. It passes belief that anyone would present visuals and leave it to the public to add in what else was required."

Nothing can replace an idea, says Matt McGrath, executive creative director at George Patterson Bates Sydney. "If you just do a big execution with no foundation, it's something that just goes over the top of you. It's just fluff, it doesn't impact in any way."

"You live or die by an idea." Jim Riswold disputes the old saying that God is in the details. "No, He's not. He just throws an idea into the air and says, make out of it as you will. Strong execution can make a great idea better. Poor execution will not harm a great idea. People will never get sick of great ideas. People are enamoured by execution for a while, but then they just figure you're trying to pull the wool over their eyes a different way. But a great idea that resounds in somebody's soul is timeless."

"An overproduced little idea will never be as good as an underproduced big idea." David Perry heads broadcast at Saatchi & Saatchi New York, and co-selects finalists for the agency's famed New Directors Showcase. "You can use execution in place of an *ownable* idea, but it will never be as good. The amount of money you need to execute a commercial is inversely proportionate to the size of the idea. A big idea doesn't need a lot of money, while there's not enough money in the National Treasury to make a little idea into a good ad. Everybody's got money. *Money's easier to come by than ideas*."

"If you've got a good idea, you don't have to try too hard to make it a great commercial." Graham Fink, now a director at the Paul Weiland Film Company, was president of Britain's Design & Art Direction in 1996. "The idea is the most important thing. If you haven't really got much to start with, then you need to get in funny lenses, and put weird bits of glass in front of it, and use your swing and tilt, and start shaking the camera, and do weird colours in telecine, and do tons of post. You're forever trying to add all this sort of stuff to try and jazz up what wasn't there in the first place."

"Ideas don't need to be overworked," agrees Andy Bridge, publisher of *Campaign Screen*. "We're identifying great ideas, as well as great execution and craft, but we wouldn't necessarily display huge budget ads simply because they were huge budget." Bridge believes his editors share similar instinctive responses to consumers. "Simple ideas, simply and freshly done, are ultimately the things that people remember."

"Television is always about a very simple idea." Nick Cohen believes his agency's print orientation helps it create very simple commercials. "Our approach is the same as it is for print. You're connecting with someone. It's all about not taking yourself too seriously, not being boring." Cohen's budgets are lower. "There's not a theatre of fear that surrounds the production. You retain control of the idea. But when you're spending hundreds of thousands of dollars making TV commercials you're making decisions which you then can't unmake."

Execution alone cannot build brands. Scott Whybin maintains you need an idea first. "Executional obsession is getting in the way of what is really our business, which is ideas. Execution alone is vacuous."

"An idea has to be big enough to spit out fifteen executions, and they're all different but they all hang together." Bill Oberlander stresses that big ideas should have many different ways to express themselves. "The *got milk?* work brought us a more cinematographic complexity that's more alluring, more engaging, more stimulating. But undeniably it could never have happened without a simple idea based on a human truth." How do you choose the best big idea? "I don't know if it's a science or a gut thing. You might think, this idea is interesting and cute and fun and clever, but it's kind of ... *fleeting*. And you try to not fall in love with it, even though you can almost see the commercial in your head, you can see who should shoot it, and which track will really bring it to life. *Try to imagine who the brand would be if it were a person*, and try to imagine if this idea is appropriate for them. If we were making a suit for them, would this fit? If we were building a house for them, would they feel comfortable in it?"

HAVE all the great ideas been done? Many creatives believe there is no such thing as an "original" idea.

"Don't believe them," urges Kes Gray. "To say that everything is in some way derivative is just a pseudo excuse for being lazy-minded. I believe my job is to *have* ideas, not find them." Every script should be anchored with a strong, original idea. "If you didn't have a client, you wouldn't have a script. Products should be heroes. I have never believed that branding is a dirty word."

When Bill Bernbach said, *"Execution becomes content in a work of genius"*, he unwittingly became the surrogate father of style-over-content advertising. His successor at DDB, Keith Reinhard, clarifies the need for ideas. "There must be an idea. There must be an idea that is relevant to the viewer. And that idea, to be worth anything, has to be delivered in an original way, and it must strike with impact. But that idea doesn't have to come from the intrinsic product itself. The only disagreement I have with Bernbach is in the area of what advertising actually adds to a product. He said on several occasions that we are not the product, we only convey the values of the product. And indeed that might have been true when products had intrinsic values that could be sustained." Reinhard recalls how curious Bernbach was about the agency's work for McDonald's. "We didn't go to the product as he understood product; we went to the experience, or we added value. Today there are people lining up on Lexington Avenue to pay $100 for a pair of Diesel jeans and it's nothing to do with their intrinsic value. What you're paying for as a consumer, and what you value, is what the product stands for."

"Forget about techniques completely," Indra Sinha suggests. "You have to look for something other than surface gloss. The first thing to do is *rediscover the human heart* in television commercials. I think it's what people are crying out for in a way. The society we inhabit right now is overwhelmed by commercial messages of all sorts. You cannot even dial up for the time without being told it's according to so-and-so. Everything we do has got some badge on it. The food we eat we buy from supermarkets without thinking. Decisions have already been made that you will be eating genetically modified starch; you might not mind, or you might mind, but you don't have the choice. Increasingly we see how little of our lives we

How execution separates brands: Diesel zigged while others zagged, defying category conventions through Paradiset DDB Stockholm. "There must be an idea," says DDB's Keith Reinhard, but it doesn't have to come from the intrinsic product itself. "What you're paying for as a consumer, and what you value, is what the product stands for."

own. But when you get into the realms of the human heart, by which I mean just the quirks of human life, what makes us human, when you can look at that with a really discerning fresh eye, then *you touch something that's beyond all commercialism.* You've touched deep truths about people. It doesn't have to be solemn or profound; the Hamlet commercials are perfect examples. They were very, very funny. They ignite that sense of the ridiculous in us."

Sinha is adamant that you have to have an idea. "Try and do something different in the world. When you look at the world as it is, and you look at the world as portrayed by advertising, *there is no relation between the two.* And yet advertisers are sitting on one of the hugest pots of money there is, which is destined for the purpose of communication. The power of that communication rests in the hands of the people who create the ideas. Whether you do a concept for a press ad by drawing a little rectangle or a concept for a TV ad by drawing a frame for a storyboard, you pin it on your curtain and look at it and maybe it does win awards. Now unpin the diagram, screw it up and throw it away. Pull back the curtain and you'll see there's a window there. And that window opens onto the real world. Now let that light shine in on you and your problem. And my advice then is to open the window. Don't just look through it. Climb out. And if you can do that, then you've done something."

"It's dangerous if you start getting inspired by other advertising because maybe you're just looking at the *surface* of things." Swedish art director Paul Malmström at Fallon Minneapolis believes there must always be a creative idea that conveys something of the company. The idea must be different and powerful somehow. "Powerful emotionally, or so that it makes you laugh." Malmström was formerly with famous Paradiset DDB Stockholm. "I started at Paradiset in 1990. I was their first employee. My writer Linus Karlsson and I were working late one night when Bill Westbrook, the former creative director at Fallon's, called us for our reel. He said, 'Your work is sick and twisted and I love it'. So we decided to go. We didn't know that much about Fallon's, but when we looked at the walls here we said, hey, that's the work we've been referring to all these years. We didn't even know where Minneapolis was until we came here. We looked in our thick atlas and it was right in the crease; we had to press down the pages." Malmström says it is very important not to get stuck in a certain style. "You can never avoid your work reflecting some of your personality and what you think of advertising in general. Over the years, Linus and I have a certain point of view on what's good and bad advertising. We've worked from potato chips, where you can be a little more 'out there', to insurance companies. You've got to be interested in the strategy. You've got to be a good team with your account people; you can't see them as an enemy. You've got to dig in to the client and their business so you know that what you are doing is solving something for them."

Neil French passionately demands ideas in print creativity, but sees television from a different perspective. "It's probably the one place where it's less important to have an idea. It's wonderful if you *can* have an idea, but if you haven't got one, at least your execution can look different from everyone else's. But I don't think it's something you should aim for. Because I'm a copywriter, I *have* to have an idea first. A lot of art directors will tell you otherwise." *French's priority in television is watchability.* "The reward part of a television commercial should be greater than the reward part of a press ad. I'm constantly aware of the fact that we invade people's living rooms very rudely and say, I'm going to sell you something you don't care about in the middle of the motor racing. It is the one point where I get absolutely lunatic. I hate it. If you're rude enough to interrupt what people *want* to see, you'd better give them a good reason to watch you. If you don't, you're going to antagonise them as opposed to selling them."

IS IT TIME TO REDEFINE THE IDEA?

"What once identified an idea as an idea is not necessarily that anymore." Andy Berlin explains that ideas have become less linear, less rational. "And executions bleed over; Bartle Bogle Hegarty is a good example of that. What is an execution? Think about it in terms of Olympic judging. Is it artistic merit? Often you can't tell the difference between the two. And it's not always wrong that you can't tell the difference between the two. Sometimes not being able to tell the difference doesn't mean that it's bereft of an idea — it means the idea has taken some different form." Berlin talks about the movie *Titanic.* "I think it was a bad motion picture. Why? Because the extent to which it had a filmic idea, it was like a Danielle Steel novel. The real attraction of the movie was that it did something that was *more* than our imaginations could do. We become peep show watchers in that way. Is that an idea? I don't know…"

Almost all of Wieden's work, Berlin says, is not ideational in a linear sense. "*It is about much more interesting things.* The ESPN SportsCenter work, for example, disappeared the distance between people on one side of the TV and people on the other. That's its merit. It makes the people you see on SportsCenter like somebody that you'd meet in a bar, or a friend of yours. It makes them people like you. It makes them affable and approachable. But is there an idea there? It's charming, it's entertainment, it serves a purpose. The best of the Nike work — are there ideas there? There are some where there are ideas, some where there are none."

Warren Berger also scans the American scene. "The film technique being used in commercials right now is dazzling, and it has to be to catch people's attention. Directors like Tarsem, Kinka Usher and Joe Pytka are doing amazing things, better than movies, which is why they're being hired for movies now. You hear some classic ad people complain that these star director commercials may be all-execution-no-concept, but as Chiat's Bob Kuperman says, sometimes the execution *is* the concept." Berger himself believes ideas are important, but they can take *all kinds of forms*. "The shaky-cam wasn't just a technique," he asserts. "It was a brilliant idea that conveyed authenticity, until it was imitated and played out. An idea doesn't have to be a punchline, and it doesn't have to be a unique selling proposition. It just has to be interesting, and somehow relevant."

"*The idea is what you own*," proposes Australia's Ted Horton, quoting one example: Volvo owns safety. "Because you own that property, it's a very easy thing to go and execute. You don't have to have fancy ideas in the commercial, just one simple image born out of the truth. *All* great advertising is born out of an indisputable truth, and that truth is either real or perceived. Especially with international campaigns, that truth is often born out of the national characteristics of a country. For instance, with all due respects to my German colleagues, one would find it hard to say, *Fly the fun-filled skies with Lufthansa*. It's not because Germans aren't fun people, but there's a perception, a truth, that they are more methodical and disciplined. So you could have the *'Arrive-on-time'* type campaign which Lufthansa did many years ago, and which you'd believe because it's born out of the truth of a national characteristic. It's true of all the great campaigns. Look at the *Singapore Girl*. It's a 25-year-old campaign based on the Western perception of Asian women. I don't mean that to be offensive, but that is the Western perception. At that time, there was no perceived truth that Singaporeans were brilliant engineers, so if you were going to build an airline you couldn't build it on engineering. And if you've ever smoked Marlboro, the indisputable truth is it's a pretty tough cigarette. It's also American. So the American symbol of *macho* is a cowboy."

However, as Horton demonstrates, the truth is that the "truth"

A car is driving through a harsh Australian desert.

It is a desolate, unforgiving place of skeletal trees and parched earth.

MVO: *There's no tougher place on tyres than Australia. And there are no tougher tyres in Australia than Olympic tyres. In fact, Olympic tyres are made in Australia for Australian conditions. Which means they'll probably last a lot longer in Australia than a lot of cars ever will...*

The car is slowing down, but not its Olympic tyres. As the car finally grinds to a halt, the tyres drive on regardless in perfect formation. The driver is left staring out the window of his immobile car, while the tyres run unstoppably up the road.

MVO and end super: *Olympic tyres. Aussie tough.*

Australia's Olympic tyres own toughness. Writer Ted Horton and art director Ron Mather present a simple idea that your tyres could last longer than your car. Saatchi & Saatchi Melbourne.

may not yet be acceptable in many agencies. "Just imagine walking into the office of a creative director and saying, I've got the two best campaigns that you're ever going to get out of this agency. In fact, they're probably going to be the best airline and best cigarette campaign in the history of advertising. And what are they? For Singapore Airlines, we just go to a fantastic city, we shoot lots of beautiful shots, and about the 55-second mark, we just cut to the flight attendant who turns and smiles at camera. And for the Marlboro one, we're just going to show a cowboy smoking a cigarette, and that's it. Now, what interests me is that many advertising people would say there's no idea in either. But to me there are very powerful ideas in both, because you very quickly establish what it is you own ... Marlboro owns American *machismo*; Singapore Airlines owns service symbolised by a demure Asian woman." As Horton argues, there is even an indisputable truth behind British Airways wanting to own the world. The symbol of the globe resonates for him. "People like myself who grew up in Australia, which is a British Commonwealth country, saw pink on every map in the atlas. We believe they *can* own the world, born out of the truth of the Empire..."

Can Execution Separate Brands?

When unique selling propositions ceased to differentiate brands, emotional selling propositions took over. As John Hegarty says, "We shouldn't be ashamed of that. How one *feels* about something is incredibly important."

With emotion came more elaborate execution. Once, relying entirely on filmic devices would have been a completely *illogical* way of making a commercial. Today, advertising is rarely logical. However, in cutting edge agencies, there is logic aplenty *behind* the anarchy.

"There's an old school way of thinking that defined an idea as a logical process," warns Henry. "A viewer is taken from position A where the ad has started to position B where the ad has finished. By position B, the viewer has been logically persuaded that the product is better than its competitors. I don't think it is relevant anymore. It was the unique selling proposition — u.s.p. — way of thinking. When we launched, we challenged all that. Logical propositions for ads seemed to us to be outdated. The logical u.s.p. was no longer universally relevant; in fact, it seemed almost universally irrelevant. If you come up with a product today, if it's any good it's going to get copied within six hours. So our thinking was, what we really needed to develop for our clients, for our brands, was a *tone of voice*. That then became the challenge, developing the tone of voice." Henry references the GAP ads. "They're done in-house by people who really understand the tone of voice of that brand." HHCL launched the magazine *Marie Claire* in Britain. "I really learned about tone of voice working with that client. They had this book, developed in Paris. It was full of images of fashion, sex, humour, gardening, furniture. On one side it said, *Oui*; on the other side, *Non*. This is *Marie Claire*; this isn't. Looking at it you ask, why is that in, and that not in? When you read through it, you got a real sense of the tone of voice of that brand, what was *Marie Claire* and what wasn't." In the context of communicating a tone of voice, says Henry, *execution is massively important*.

Henry explores the difference between an idea and a tone of voice, a personality. "One of my favourite ads of all time is Jon Glazer's Guinness *Surfers* commercial with the white horses coming out of the sea. The proposition that was sold to the client was *Good things come to those who wait*. To me, that's the kind of quasi-logical proposition that the client can buy into, but it's a terrible end line. I know quite a lot about that marketplace. Kids don't want to wait for anything. They want everything now. The problem young people have with Guinness is they think it's heavy, slow, ponderous stuff. They might respect it, but they don't actually want to drink it. They want stuff they can throw down their necks that will get them dancing, moving, flirting, and all the rest of it. *Good things come to those who wait* plays to the wrong mental image, but what's interesting about the *Surfers* film is that it jettisons that idea and reinvigorates the brand. It takes the image of Guinness, which is this dark liquid that is heavy, and in the film you get this dark liquid which is the sea, and it's suddenly invigorated by all these white horses. It says Guinness isn't heavy, it's *powerful and energising*. In fact, the waiting element in the *Surfers* ad is irrelevant. What's important is that the ad takes the brand, and the reality of people's emotional relationship with the brand, and it changes that visually, and emotionally, and makes it energetic."

If Henry is right, emotional bridges between brands and consumers are wrought by creatives who understand how to engage with their audience. He quotes John Webster. "There are responders inside the human brain. There's a response of laughter, there's a response of smiles, there's a response of compassion, or sadness, or exhilaration. The response, 'that's an interesting new video technique' is about number seventeen." The conjunction Henry looks for in an ad is where the newness grabs people's attention, but isn't just new and funky and out there. "It's not where you only appreciate it intellectually. It *has* to be underpinned by a strong understanding of the emotional bridge you are building from the brand to the consumer. And that is *not* logical anymore."

"If it's genuinely fresh, you can create a tone of voice and a personality that will make a brand an individual in a crowd." Vaughan argues that there are ideas all the way through the chain. "The strategy itself should be a powerful idea, then that leads to a central creative idea, and that in turn leads to executional ideas, the particular way to shooting or casting or lighting or audio that adds to the central idea. Bad commercials come about when an execution is done before the idea or to replace one."

Dawson believes that a commercial should match the culture of a company. "Rather than choose production techniques for the sake of it, which could be spurious, let the culture of the advertiser guide you. The product image should come from the right source so it reflects that culture to the viewer, rather than one that is out of kilter with reality. Really get to know the people who make the product; what they're about, what their work ethic is and the way they do things — which is the best definition of culture. When you know all that, you can start to impose that on the television commercials you're making for them. Assuming all companies are different, which they are, by extracting that culture your commercial will be different because it is reflecting a company that is different."

The watchword for Tim Delaney is *appropriateness*. "Why I think Nike has been so useful to television is their whole irreverence. If it's not in your face or rude or cheeky, they won't do it. It's pushed the boundaries, not just of sports advertising, but of television. And that comes from the positioning of Nike, which has found its way into very appropriate advertising. I've often said to people at Adidas, while of course you see Nike as your competitor, you should also see Nike as your saviour. Not only have they grown the business *so big* they've left room for a number two and a number three, but they've conditioned people to expect advertising. So when Adidas started advertising to a young audience on television, they became part of Nike's gang. Then Adidas split off and has become slightly different. Now the two brands sit side by side in a way, because they're pretty much on the same side, but they have different personalities; one is pushy and irreverent and still a bit out there, while Adidas has a more neo-classical feel and an appeal that's slightly different."

Lubars strikes a similar balance: *appropriate* execution for brilliant ideas. "Execution can separate you, but it can never separate you like an idea can. Execution is the price of entry, especially in this market where people are so sophisticated. When we first saw Apple's *1984*, it was executed like a movie, it was mind-boggling. A lot of commercials before that weren't. Now movies copy commercials. There was a trend in the last few years, *anti-*execution; low budgets, grainy, bad lighting, just to go against the grain, but that's executional too."

"In almost every category, you'll find almost every commercial is very similar." Which is why Hunt advocates looking at the category first, and then trying to do something *completely the opposite* to what everyone else is doing. "As long as it's the opposite, and *right*. In the early days of my career, I would just put type on a screen and play music." Hunt's Climacel commercial, a typographic message set to music, remains a creative landmark to this day. "When the Palace started, we had mainly print clients, that was all we knew how to do. So when we went to television, we started doing print ads on TV. Funnily enough, they worked really well because they were unlike all the other ads that were pretty pictures and technique." He adopts a similar tactic with radio commercials. "On radio, I tend not to use music at all because everyone else does. Just talking."

"Only in advertising do we look for ideas," reflects Ted Horton, whereas the execution "might be *all* that's required." He reconstructs a familiar agency scenario. "A creative team is sitting down in their office. One of the team is going through a *Shots* reel. The other one has a bit of music playing in the background, and he's sitting down reading a book, maybe a photographic book, all it has is lovely images, nothing more than that. Then an ad comes on and his partner asks, well, what do you think of that one? And he says, no idea, where's the idea? Now I find it interesting that the man could be listening to music because he likes it, but there's probably no idea in it, looking at a book that has got fundamentally no idea in it, it's just a nice lot of photographs. When it comes to his own entertainment, his own pleasure, he applies one set of rules; but when an ad comes on, he applies another." Horton argues that execution is what separates a little Dior black dress from a little £5 black one. "In fashion advertising, the *garment* is the idea. What do you think would happen if you reduced the size of the photo by half so you could fit in a clever headline?"

When Should You Start Thinking About Execution?

"Sometimes I start thinking about execution before I actually get the idea," confides Lee Garfinkel, "but I try not to. I want to stay focused on what the strategy is. If I start to think of execution, I can see I'm going to get into a trap. The worst thing for me is a blank piece of paper because I can go in too many directions. So I like having that core idea, it anchors me. When teams come in to me and start showing me work, and they start showing me individual commercials and not telling me what the big idea for the campaign is, I stop them right away because I *know* I'm not going to hear a big idea. The team has gone off and done a bunch of little spots, or Big Spots in their mind, but don't have a big idea, and they're going to do a lot of spots to make up for the fact that they don't have a big idea." Garfinkel pinpoints the acid test for himself, or for anybody who comes in to present to him. "You should be able to say, here's what the big idea is, here's what every spot is going to be about, and now we'll go into the specific spots."

John Webster considers the best commercials are conceived as a whole, visuals and words, as one. "I used to direct commercials, so I approach it from a filmic point of view. You have to."

"I think of execution the minute I hear the problem," says Hal Riney. "Once I was invited to a meeting, the last of a sequence of unsuccessful meetings where the agency had failed to answer the client's problem, at least to the client's satisfaction. The client had a product so unique and appealing that the product and its properties were simply *unbelievable.* I thought it would be interesting, since people were unlikely to believe us anyway, to employ as a series of spokespeople the world's most famous *liars.* I suggested this to the clients, and they loved it. That was an answer, and at the same time, an execution. Naturally, any idea involves a *series* of decisions and refinements, continuing into production." Riney's work resonates with humanity and a very distinctive visual feel, although he is quick to resist such typecasting. "I prefer to think in terms of middle America. I myself grew up in a small town in the Northwest. In my experience, creative people from small towns or the Midwest have a better feel for people than do their counterparts in our two largest cities. I have little respect for the typical New Yorker, who by no means represents the nature or the attitudes of the majority of people of this country. I could probably say the same about Southern Californians. Mind you, this is my point of view. It is not an agency policy, and it couldn't be even if I wanted it to be. No creative people think entirely alike." Riney talks about his personal creative style. "Any particular visual style reflected in the things I've been proud of may well stem from the fact that while I am necessarily a writer, I am first and foremost an art director. That was my talent, my training, and my early background in the business."

"If I've got an idea for a commercial, I've kind of shot it already." Holmes says he will shoot it, cut it and project it in the private viewing theatre in his mind. "In the UK you find young teams rushing half-formed ideas to a director and it will be further refined. It becomes almost a 3-person creative team." The risk is that the wrong director might muddy a simple idea with film technique. "You have to act as the idea police. You have to go to the pre-production meeting and on set and to the editing. Your main task is to make sure that no one loses sight of what the film is about."

Delaney sees the execution as he writes the concept. "You start thinking about how it will look quite early on. You start to think about the influence of music. Then you're very surprised by a director who'll come in with a *different* angle."

It's much the same when Mike Cozens writes a script. The idea is often the way that he sees the execution. "I'll then sit down with a couple of directors. They may see it in a *very* different way. We originally saw the Pirelli Carl Lewis commercial as him running around the world. It started at the Sydney Harbour Bridge, and then he'd run past the Taj Mahal. Then Gerard de Thame, the director, saw it. He said it would be better if it was slightly more *contained*. It was supposed to be a test rather than a marathon, and people might be confused into thinking it was about longevity."

"Eighty percent of a commercial is in the making. Technique can seriously improve and empower an idea." In fact, says Hegarty, having an idea is the closest a man will ever come to giving birth. "An idea is an entity, it has a being, it almost has a soul. And you've got to listen to that. You've got to understand what you can do with that idea, and where it can go, and where it can be taken; what's right for it and what's wrong for it. *I think great ideas force their views back on to you.* If you say, I'd like to do this in colour, the idea might say, no, this has *got* to be made in black-and-white, or no, it *mustn't* be made with a shaky, hand-held camera, *the idea does not want that.* And when you've got a powerful idea, it does those things to you. You feel it. You know it. You just think that's wrong, it's not right, the idea wouldn't do this."

His agency's famous Levi's television campaign is one example where technique influenced the ideas. "We probably wrote forty odd scripts per commercial we made. Out of those forty scripts, five of them would be very interesting. Then you'd look at those five commercials and you'd ask, *which* of these allows us to be *very* different and distinctive? You'd look at them, and you'd think about directors, and you'd think about what would work and what wouldn't. When we made the *Clay Man* commercial, we'd had that script on the table for some time. We knew we wanted to make an animated commercial for Levi's, we just thought it would be funny. But what form of animation? Animation can be very childlike. How do you give it edge? How do you make it appeal to an audience that is very much on the edge of style? It wasn't until we saw some work by these two animators in Cardiff, who do clay animation, that we suddenly saw the way to do it. So although the script was there, we knew we couldn't do anything with it until we found the people who could make it happen."

Hegarty talks about Tarsem's contribution to the Levi's *Swimmer* commercial. "The script was based on the film *The Swimmer* with Burt Lancaster, and it would have been very easy to make that in a very boring way, with all the filters. It could have been very Beverly Hills in the way it was shot, and that would have been wrong. Then Tarsem came in and he said, this is how it should be shot. It should be *Life* magazine, 1963. It's right at the height of the American dream; swimming pools are a symbol of American wealth, of Americana. The music is *Mad About The Boy*, which was quite different, and he played it to us. And he *conceptualised* that script; he took that script from being a very interesting script to being a very outstanding piece of film."

"Everything comes from the idea," Arthur Bijur believes. "You see a lot of commercials where there's a tremendous cinematic feeling, but there's something missing in the idea. It's a good cover-up sometimes. I think our work actually tends to be fairly simple compared to a lot of agencies' work. Some of our Fanta work is more cinematic. Outpost.com has some very cinematic elements, at least the band spot with the raving mad wolves, but that all just comes from the idea. You start off with a simple, good, clear idea, and the way it's shot has to follow that. *The way it's shot is always intended to heighten the idea, and not to lead it.*"

"It's important that a brand has a look, its own identity, but the look should come through the concept," says Harvey Marco, a group creative director at Fallon Minneapolis; he was an illustration major from the Art Center College of Design, Pasadena and a classmate of Tarsem. "The director's technique shouldn't take away from the idea. Some directors take your idea and push it so far out that you can't bring it back in. I look for someone who can tell a story and has good taste. Usually we look for a director we can collaborate with, who appreciates the concept and has ideas of his or her own to bring to it. You're buying a brain, not just an eye."

"The way in which you shoot it should have something to do with the idea," acknowledges Fink. Sometimes, techniques have to be grafted onto ideas. "What's quite nice is if you can get a technique that comes out of the idea."

"I'm not big on art directors' TV commercials," says Hunt, "but I'm big on doing great TV commercials with art directors."

Focus on the idea, says Malmström, and the technique will follow. "For our Jukka Brothers campaign for MTV, we really went into the Jukka brain, and the Jukka world, and asked how will it best be done. It's dangerous to get your inspiration from other commercials. If you do, you start at the wrong starting point. For inspiration, we go to real life, real stories, what real people think, not what ad people think."

NOT everyone sees technique and technology as creative liberators.

"The world of computers has made the impossible possible. They have *subtracted* some colours from my palette…" Grace talks about his famous American Tourister commercial with the gorilla and the suitcase. "Truthfully, I don't know if I would do that today. Today it would be much, much easier to do, you could manipulate the gorilla with computers, and a lot of the drama of it would be gone. I used to like doing things that were impossible to do. How do you get a gorilla to act for you with a suitcase? The answer is, you have to be very, very lucky. Today, it would not have the impact that it did twenty-five, thirty years ago." Grace says there is an area he just doesn't work in anymore, an area he privately calls, "It's-impossible-that-this-is-happening". These days, he believes, there is nothing that startles people anymore. "That kind of work has lost its effectiveness and will continue to do so. Now you can do anything. It's just a question of who's going to sign the cheque."

Inevitably, budgets come into the equation.

As a rule of thumb, Whybin's advice holds good: "*If you have a $200,000 budget, write a $100,000 idea. In your head, always write with half the budget so you've got enough room to play.*" The simpler the script the better, Whybin says. The logic is, you can then afford the best director to work on your idea.

Gray also offers two timely reminders. "Don't overwrite. And don't write over budget. Bigger budgets don't make for better television." Gray's *Hair in the Gate* commercial for Vidal Sassoon was a low budget spot that came within a hair's breadth of winning a D&AD Pencil. His Volkswagen *Bus Sandwich* was shot on a shoestring and won Gold at Cannes. "Big budgets are harder to do justice to. They can create unreasonable expectations. Small budgets have the benefit of simplifying your thinking; I might even go as far as to say that I prefer small budgets."

But when everything is said and done, Professor John Philip Jones reminds us: "Rich production values cannot compensate for a feeble message."

SHOULD A GREAT TV IDEA BE ABLE TO WORK IN OTHER MEDIA?

"Today, more than ever, it's not about creating *just* an interesting piece of visual communication," asserts Hegarty. "You've got to make that visual communication work through a multitude of other media, to tie the whole thing together, so people get *a cohesive view of the brand.*"

Hegarty advocates a strong thought or mnemonic device. It is not simply a case of using the same visual representation across all media. "I start work now by saying, how is this advertising going to stand out? And what can I take from it that's going to work *through the line*, on a leaflet, on point-of-sale? It's very important that you give the advertising you're creating some kind of visual recognition." He cites his agency's famous campaign for Boddingtons. "The print campaign was very distinctive, very black, with a creamy beer product in the middle. But we didn't try to just put the ads on television. We took *The cream of Manchester* as a thought, and that became the strong mnemonic that went through all the advertising." Hegarty refers to what he calls dot.com madness. "Huge numbers of brands are now trying to establish themselves. So increasingly it's very, very important that your advertising really has to work in a much more cohesive way than it did maybe ten, fifteen, twenty years ago."

"It's dying and going to heaven when that happens…" Grace's

American Tourister television commercial adapted to other media. "It worked in print. It worked in point-of-sale, with little gorilla tags to demonstrate strength on the product. The gorilla became the company's logo. To this day, thirty years later, although they don't do the advertising, their semi-trailers have a gorilla on the side with a suitcase, driving up and down American highways." But developing television ideas that would interlink with other media wasn't a conscious effort. "It may have been part of our arrogance, our creativity; we said, well, that's print, this is television. I think it makes sense to have them all connected. If you take an agency like Leo Burnett, their mnemonic devices like the Marlboro Man transcend all media. If a client came to our agency today and said I have an assignment for you, but the rules are that television, print and point-of-sale all have to be exactly the same, I would take it. I wouldn't find that restriction so crippling that I wouldn't take it. It's an interesting way of approaching a problem and ultimately, in truth, it may be the best way of approaching a problem…" However, Grace would never scrap a great television idea if it couldn't work in other media. "Not in a million years. There are other ways to create linkages. The main thing is to get people to the same place and they don't necessarily have to go in through the same doors."

"The sort of ideas that are great television ideas tend to be the sort of ideas that would work in print or radio." Hunt talks about Lowe Howard-Spink's Gold Lion-winning television commercial for *The Independent*. "It's a litany of don'ts. If you take that as the kind of idea I adore, it clearly could be a lovely print campaign using exactly the same words, and a lovely radio commercial." According to Hunt, the same could not be said for big visual extravaganzas without much of an idea.

"The future of advertising is going to be called communication." Cozens believes that advertising agencies will become complete communication agencies. Ideas will have to work across all media as well as the Internet. His famous Pirelli campaign, for example, started in print with Carl Lewis dressed in red high heels before it went to television. "I'm not suggesting that the executions be the same, but the ideas will have to work everywhere."

An *umbrella effect* is what Mather aims for. "When you build a personality for a product, and you know the tone of voice, how that personality would talk, it makes it so much easier. Then you can do TV and posters and radio, all with a similar tone, a similar sentiment, a similar umbrella feeling. You see a lot of products where they've got totally the wrong personality, and the commercials are saying things that the product would never say." Mather would never junk a great television concept if it didn't work in other media. "It's the old-fashioned idea that ads have to look exactly the same. It's clunky."

French says the same thought, the same personality and the same attitude should be behind everything. Every ad should leave you with the same *impression* of the brand. "But to expect the same idea to work in everything is unfair." Would French discard a great television idea because it wouldn't work in other media? "Certainly not. I'd be so grateful to get one in the first place."

"Sometimes there are ideas that will *only* work really powerfully on television," says McGrath. "If it can work as powerfully in other media, it's almost like there's a flaw, it's not quite as unique as a television idea should be." An exception he quotes is Volkswagen. "They had a position, and that position worked in all different media."

Horton believes great campaigns that own properties can be executed in any medium. It's very easy, he says, for British Airways to own the world in television or print, radio or posters. "I'm not interested so much in the commercial, as I am in what ownership you've established. I believe most briefs are wrong. It should be *mandatory* that whenever an ad is done, it should enhance — and prove — the brand's ownership of a property, and that mandatory should apply to *every* medium. For example, if I were writing briefs, I would say the purpose of this commercial is to enhance our ownership of service through the introduction of a new business class seat. Or, the purpose of this commercial is to enhance our ownership of the world with the introduction of this new route from London to Venice. What I find is that most agencies would say, oh, just sell the new seat, or just sell the new route. They're myopic."

"The line should move from one medium to another, but the execution shouldn't be compromised." Dawson advocates being more open-minded, more flexible. "If it won't work in other media, maybe it should be a TV and cinema campaign only. Talk to the media department."

David Blackley argues that the campaign thought should be capable of expression in all media. He cites his agency's *Legendary stuff* milk campaign. "I don't think it has to literally translate. You don't have to say we're using the character Roger Daly, *Retired Milkman*, on television, therefore his head must appear in the print. But you should keep the basic thought, *Milk, Legendary stuff*. The underlying evidence behind that thought can be covered off in other areas, like milk has more protein than fruit juice."

The commonality should be the proposition, the sentiment, and the tone of voice, agrees Whybin. "In a metaphoric sense, it's the same person speaking. Taking the essence of the strategy and making that work in each medium is much cleverer than trying to just take a frame from a TV commercial. If you get good print writers in terms of distillation of strategy, more often than not they're good television writers. It's fantastic if you've got a simplicity of message in a television commercial. *Any simple message is transferable to any medium.*"

Sean Cummins is convinced that if a TV thought is good enough, it should have possibilities in other media. But taking a still from a TV commercial is like taking a still from a movie and expecting people to enjoy it. It's also relegating other media to support media, when in fact they can play very different roles. "Radio suffers the most. People just take the whole soundtrack and run it on radio." It can work sometimes, but it denies radio the chance to contribute its own unique character to the campaign.

"Usually, tone and some simple style things will hold a campaign together without being literally the same." Bildsten warns against selling each different medium short. "The big packaged goods agencies start with television. The print has to come out of the television, so print is an afterthought. It's just a reminder of what the television was. One of the things that allowed us to become successful was because we treated the print just as importantly as the television. These days the expectation is that it will work on the website, direct mail and other things as well." Because print and television serve very different purposes, Bildsten would never junk a great television idea if it couldn't work in other media. "Sometimes we don't have a direct linear print component of our TV campaigns."

"An idea, a territory, should be big enough to work in different media, but in different ways." Vaughan believes the television expression might be completely different to the print execution, *but they converge on the same brand idea.* "A lot of people aren't comfortable with the fact you can have disparate ways of expressing the same concept."

GETTING IDEAS

Jeff Goodby never presumes what the finished product will be; a story, or even a certain kind of visual. "This would automatically obviate many other kinds of solutions — demonstrations, testimonials, animation, etcetera — that might be just the thing. Instead, *we try to keep our minds open as long as possible,* to find the very best, most economical, relevant and emotionally true way to convey our agreed-upon strategy."

Webster says there is no formula. "The first thing I try and do now is get the tone. *What sort of thing are we looking for here?* Are we looking for a farce? Are we looking for a joke? Are we looking for a serious thing? I'm trying to place it in my mind. Very often when I'm thinking about the very beginning of a problem, I'll put on different pieces of music. Music, more than anything else, sets the tone, so I know what area we're looking into. You can have some serious music, you can have a brass band, you can have some rock. It immediately sets the mood. Then I try to think of a piece of film or a previous commercial, or something that is in that area. And then you start playing around. But it varies a lot. Sometimes a picture will come to mind, like the one I did with Jack Dee and the penguins for John Smith's. Jack Dee is a real cynic. What would be funny, I thought, would be to put something ridiculous in front of him. And I drew a penguin. I started with that image, and the penguin was singing a jingle…" Webster always soaks himself in the competition first. "You're trying to build a brand. It's got to have its *own* personality before it can stand out from the crowd."

French agrees. "The first thing I do is get the reel of the competition to find out what *not* to do. And frankly, that's the most

Roy Grace, generating ideas. Grace & Rothschild New York.

important part of it. As soon as I know what not to do, then my options are frequently pointing to the *only possible direction I can go in*, because everybody else has done everything else." The second thing is to find out what image he can put on the screen that will stop people. "And I think the *image* on TV is far more important than anything else. I try to think of one image that will make people go, I don't mind sitting through this." The image should set the brand apart from its competitors, but it doesn't necessarily have to be relevant. "Relevant to what? The image doesn't have to be relevant, as long as it *turns* relevant by the end." French dismisses the old notion of the vampire video, consigning it to the Thou-Shalt-Not school of advertising. "I also don't believe in taglines. I don't think I've ever written a tagline in my life."

"*The worst way is to start verbally,* because you'll be in a trap; what you wind up doing is illustrating the words." Grace will start with a proposition, sometimes vague, sometimes very precise. "What you have to do is come up with a visual *gestalt*, a visual idea. Sometimes you may not need words at all. Sometimes you need four words, sometimes more. Any writer I've ever worked with, although they may be sitting with me and thinking verbally, ultimately we come to something that has a *fundamental visual foundation.* Volkswagen *Funeral* was a visual idea."

"*Forget about what is fashionable.*" Famous British art director Neil Godfrey warns against following a prevailing genre. Start from the common denominator of a piece of communication, he says, which is one person talking to another person. "Put an idea around the product you're trying to sell which by its very nature is different. It doesn't have to be a huge leap in some lateral direction. It doesn't have to be a great clash of cymbals. It could be something everybody recognises, something that could happen to them. It could be what makes great film, a piece of fantastic observation." Godfrey discusses a viewers' poll that voted a scene from *Only Fools and Horses* as the funniest comedy sequence on British television. "There's a little flap in the counter in a British pub that lifts up so the barman can get through to collect the empty glasses. In this scene, there's a spiv in a camelhair coat and a trilby hat, trying to look very suave, sipping his drink and making eyes at a girl in the bar. And he's standing next to the flap while it's actually down. Then the guy from behind the bar lifts it up and walks out. The spiv doesn't notice and he goes to lean on the counter and he just goes straight over. Now that was voted the best sequence from any comedy show *and it sounds like nothing.*"

Tim Delaney discusses his methodology. "When it comes to television, the most important thing to do is be *discursive.* The print medium demands that you focus very tightly on one expression, so you tend to write lines. With television, you are much more discursive. You are writing sketches, you are writing scenes from a film. You are thinking about music, you are thinking about atmosphere. You are thinking about the kind of mood that you want to create. You engage in a different way with the medium, because the medium is so powerful." Great films, Delaney contends, don't simply tell you things you already know. They change the way you think. The techniques of film, he argues, allow you to reorder people's ideas about what they should or not believe. "That's not to say we manipulate with television, but television is the most powerful of all the media that exist. You can do things in television that you can't do in any other medium. You can use all the techniques that Hollywood has used, and you can invent some of your own. People can admire the idea and admire the technique. While I would never subscribe to the idea of form-over-content, I can understand people getting engaged by it." Doesn't that make the writing job harder, more awesome? "All kinds of things are open to you, and in some respects, yes, you could say that gives you *too much* to play with. But a disciplined thinker with a good strategy says, okay, how do we want to order our thoughts; how do we want to narrow it down and down. There is a reductive process in creating an ad, and that applies to television as well." Delaney's advice: *don't write scripts, write ideas.* "The idea might be two or three lines. It's the absolute starting point for the whole film. That, in itself, is a kind of heresy because most agencies build for two years towards this bit of paper, which has gone through the copy department and then been tested. My view is that the script is simply the A to get you to Z; *it's not the Z by any means*. I don't believe that what is on paper is going to end up on film. I hope it won't…"

Don't be afraid to write anything down, Mather advises. "A lot of people get a bit frightened of a brief. But it's like exercising. You warm up first until you're ready to go. Get all the rubbish out first. The first ideas, the clichés. It doesn't matter. Write it all down. When you look at a blank sheet of paper, don't see a blank sheet of paper. See an opportunity." Mather likes to work on more than one job at the same time. He can skip from one to the other. Images come to him first. "We work extremely quickly, which is great," he says. Long deadlines don't necessarily equate with greatness.

Chris O'Shea also puts down anything that comes into his mind.

"My layout pads are full of little scribbles and jottings. A half sentence, a thought, and as I'm thinking I'm continually reviewing them. I always start with words. That doesn't necessarily mean it will be a dialogue commercial. Words are my strength, whereas with a lot of young kids music is their first dimension. I don't think of moods or atmosphere; it's too early to go down that path. I think as wide and as free as I possibly can. I'm a great believer that the subconscious will solve problems, so I like to get the brief and then forget about it for a couple of days. It's a bit like a coffee percolator; something will filter down…" When O'Shea and his art director partner Ken Hoggins have resolved an idea, they will each write it in script form *independently*. "Then I'll read his, and he'll read mine, and we'll marry the two together; the first sentence of his with the second sentence of mine. You get a better, more rounded commercial."

Holmes doodles around with words, too. "It's like a ball of wool, or a big knot, and you pull at it in an abstract way. You're not quite sure what you're doing, but you're looking for a loose thread to come out that might pull the whole thing out. It's difficult to begin with; sometimes there are long periods of silence where you're both thinking about something, and it's advisable that those don't go on too long, otherwise you and your partner will drift away. In fact, there's an old joke: why don't creative teams stare out of the window in the morning? Answer: so they've got something to do in the afternoon." Somehow, Holmes says, he will have pen to paper. "I'll just get words down; they may suggest pictures. That physical act is not just thoughts going down through the pen, it's the paper hitting the pen, which hits your hand, which goes back up to your brain." Holmes believes the brain behaves differently when you've got a pen in your hand.

Garfinkel starts with *the core truth in the brand*. "If the strategy is big enough, and right, it's amazing how quickly the ideas will come. It's when it doesn't work, or it sounds good on paper but you realise there's something missing in terms of the truth behind it, that's when the problems start. That's when I start looking for tricks, or I start all over again in terms of what the brief should be. When it's a couple of days of struggling, then I would guess that as good as it might have sounded, there is something wrong with the basic idea." One trick

Garfinkel uses a lot to get him there? "I just like to play music in the background a lot of times. If it's a car commercial, sometimes I'll put on some kind of music that I would like to have as a background, to give me some kind of guide of·where I want to go. *But I know if I start to get too wrapped up in something like that, I don't have the big idea.*"

Garfinkel identifies a problem facing creatives today. "Everything now has to be turned around in hours, days, weeks at the most. Even ten years ago, if you had to do a major campaign for a client, you had weeks or months to come up with something." Garfinkel remembers working in 1988 with Sal DeVito on a small account called Beneficial Finance. "We didn't have planners back in those days. It probably took Sal and me about a month to come up with a core idea that we believed in, and then another month to figure out the best way to execute it." Beneficial Finance gave loans to people who couldn't get loans from banks. As Garfinkel explains, the problem was they charged 20% to 25% interest, so he and DeVito couldn't talk about that. Nor did they want to follow other finance companies that made fun of banks by showing how miserable the borrowing experience was. Finally, after a month, they came up with the notion that banks will happily loan billions and billions of dollars to *foreign countries*, but they make it tough on the small guy. Because Beneficial made it easy for the small guy, the advertising could create a human connection based on a truth. "So we used the foreign countries as the fall guys. The hard part then was, how do we execute it, because you don't really want to dump on other countries. Eventually we came up with the notion, let's not make fun of the countries, let's make fun of the leaders, *the leaders that people hate.* So we got stock footage of Noriega, Marcos, Gaddafi and Brezhnev. The whole notion was, *Instead of loaning money to people like that, we believe in loaning money to people like you.* The last line was, *At Beneficial, we're not a bank so we don't have to act like one.*" The campaign won at all the award shows, including Best of Show at the ANDYs. "Those spots must have cost under $50,000 at the most. It was a nice simple idea, simply executed, and it was based on a truth; people could say, that's right, why should Gaddafi get all the money and not me? And when you looked at it, it would have seemed like the most simplistic idea and why would it have taken two months to come up with?"

Riney believes that a visual idea will intrigue viewers and get them involved long enough to consider the facts. "As both a writer and an art director, I begin thinking *entirely in visual terms.* What would be beautiful, or emotional, or funny, or dramatic? Then I work backwards, to see how it will fit, or to make it fit. Sadly, not enough writers work this way. Most writers write something they think is smart or funny, and then get someone else to show them what it might look like."

Serpa searches for what he calls the G-point. "Every single commercial has a G-point. *This is the point where everything turns,* where the idea becomes relevant, where the product becomes relevant. It could be in the beginning; it could be in the end. It could be something in the beginning that leads to something in the end. You have to find out where the G-point is, where the people are laughing, where the people say, *ah-hah,* you've got me." Brazilians, according to Serpa, are very happy people. "We don't get very emotional, with sad stories, or depressing stories. We like to laugh. Humour is a very good part of Brazilian advertising; humour, and simplicity, and intelligence. So in a commercial with a lot of humour, you have to find out where is the G-point for people to laugh. Maybe have two; there's one and people laugh, then you make a twist, then people laugh once again. Defining that G-point, you can build a commercial. If you don't define it, you start looking for photography, for soundtrack, for editing; the commercial loses its structure, and you have something very beautiful, but what is the point of this commercial? If there is no G-point, there is no point at all."

For Riswold, it's as simple as putting yourself in the place of the consumer. "You put your feet in the shoes of a basketball player for Nike. Who am I speaking to? But *not* 'who am I speaking to' based upon eight hundred reams of research and demographics! Why do they like this sport as much as they do? And where does this idea fit in the voice of this brand?" If you've done your job right, Riswold says, people will know what the brand's voice is. He is opposed to being different just for the sake of being different. "Bernbach had a great quote about a man standing on his head. You don't show a man standing on his head just to show a man standing on his head. You show him standing on his head if the idea is that he's wearing pants where the change will never fall out of his pockets."

When David Blackley faces a blank sheet of paper, he tries to get the thinking right first and worry about the brilliance later. "The biggest influence on me as a writer was a fellow called Noel Delbridge. Early in my career, Noel was a tough taskmaster. He is the best strategic writer I have ever met. At Masius Melbourne, in the late 60s, he had Lionel Hunt and me there, and on it goes. He taught all of us that the strategy behind the ad was the most important thing. So I always go back to Noel, to working out what the ad should say. What is the way in? What is going to trigger the response? I *don't* look at award annuals. It's the old Ogilvy thing, *first get it right, then get it brilliant.*"

Ken Schuldman, executive creative director of DDB New York, looks first for *the voice of the brand.* "I once heard Helmut Krone say, you should look at a page and see the brand. If you look at his work, you'll understand that. If you look at a Polaroid page, you see simplicity. If you look at an Audi page, you see technology, the brains, the gears, beautifully packaged. Those pages had voices." The same principle works on television, says Schuldman. "Just turn on TV and you see a hundred dot.com commercials, all trying to be more wacky than the other. There should be a recognisable voice talking to you, so you know who that person is." Schuldman was a musician who entered advertising late at age thirty-three. He has only ever worked at DDB. Ironically, he was hired the same year he got married. "My wife and I eloped at the UN Chapel on 49th Street. When we went to sign our papers, we were given a bouquet of flowers from a funeral that had just ended. Bill Bernbach's funeral." Schuldman's first boss was Roy Grace. One of Bernbach's great legacies is the formation of writer and art director teams, says Schuldman. "Sitting in a room, closing the door and working. And yes, it's better if one's Italian and one's Jewish."

Michael Newman, executive creative director at Saatchi & Saatchi Sydney, looks for *a campaignable idea.* "Even if the brief is for a one-off, I know if I've got a campaignable idea that there will be more than one script in it. It's a good discipline. And with the number of twists and turns that an ad must negotiate these days to survive, it's comforting to know there is room for other executions if the first script collides with a wall on the way to work. It also helps me avoid the young writer's trap of falling in love with one particular script or one particular gag and then being unable or too reluctant about abandoning it."

Newman says the pictures often come to him first. "In which case I work back to try and explain exactly what those pictures are conveying. This is the time for *intellectual honesty*, two unusual words in commerce. I often find younger creatives want their images and words to say something that they're frequently not quite achieving. You've got to be straight with yourself about what your idea is *really* saying. Another thing I try to remember is the philosophical tool called Occam's Razor: when there are two correct answers which solve the problem equally well, the more correct answer is the simplest one."

Steve Henry looks for *an emotion.* "We build emotional bridges between brands and consumers. But if you want to innovate, it's a balancing act. The people who really innovate and play radical games with structure and form are always on that borderline of, *Do you lose the emotional engagement with people?* I could write something that would emotionally engage you with a product, and that is *half* of what we need to do. But if I don't do it in a new way, my belief is that that piece of commercial communication will get lost in the clutter. Making it new, making it bizarre, sometimes can shake up the process so much that the consumers get a different relationship with the communication. You have to make it new and surprising every time, *but it still has to have an emotional connection.*"

The whole point about breaking rules, Henry stresses, is making sure consumers go with you. "You can just go barking mad, and do stuff that's crazy, and people will go, oh, that's different, but they won't emotionally engage with you. I want something that's different, that people are going to emotionally engage with." The first thing is to identify the emotion you need. Henry revisits Orange Tango. "You have to look at what everyone else is doing in the market. You have to analyse the assumptions that other marketers have made. With

Tango, we knew you didn't need to make those assumptions. Tango didn't have to be American, it didn't have to be sunny days, it didn't have to be boy-meets-girl, it didn't have to be a fire hydrant going off, the refreshment cue." The agency broke the rules. Tango became British, real, urban and gritty, a bit of a "lad" on the street. Henry points to an interesting advertising dynamic. "A lot of the time, clients want their image to be whiter-than-white and perfect, but what people emotionally engage with is *humanity*. The underdog, like VW, it's ugly but it works. Or a fat orange guy in a nappy."

Kirk Souder looks for *a big creative platform*, "a huge advertising idea that exists independent of a TV spot, print ad, radio spot, *something that matters to people*." Souder cites *Just do it* and *United Colours of Benetton*. "Without that, your spot may be clever, or funny, or cool, and wow that group of hungover judges in Barbados, but it won't be important to people, and if it's not that, then you've wasted the miraculous opportunity of being one person who gets to send a message to millions."

"You have to get down to the ground with an idea, *then* build it up." Scott Vincent, a group creative director at Fallon, is a trained hydrologist. "We studied streams and groundwater and I was always wet…" By chance he discovered advertising. A writer, Vincent prefers a collaborative creative relationship. "All my best ideas have happened with someone else in the room. If I'm too internal, something gets stuck. The process of explaining an idea helps me see it better." He started writing television commercials at TBWA Chiat/Day and won Gold Pencils at the One Show for his famous California Sunkist Pistachios campaign. "I always try to see things from angles. If you were working on X you'd ask, what would happen if there was no X, or what would happen if there was too much X?" Some creatives, he says, do TV with a print accent; others do print with a TV accent. Advertising was a far cry from geology, he admits. "It takes a while before you '*get it*'. You grab at things, you're not sure why. You think, maybe it was funny; that's why people liked it. You start to understand."

Kingsmill got ideas in a flash. "Let what happens happen. React to the challenge of the brief, to what you've been told. Whatever came to me first, I just put it down. A word flash, a picture flash. And I would reject nothing. I didn't try to impose order on it until later." If a dominant train of thought emerged, Kingsmill would follow that until words and pictures started to come into his mind together. "But I wouldn't force them to come together." Sometimes the brief would lead Kingsmill beyond the brief. "The copywriter's task is to sift away all the unimportant aspects and come to *the* important aspect." Sometimes that was not what he was told in the brief.

At Fallon's, Bildsten and his team start working with a key idea that is a joint effort between account people, planners and creatives. A key idea, for example, might be *BMW feels like no other car on the road*. Assuming Bildsten agrees that the key idea is valid, he starts thinking about the way the commercial should look. "I definitely would not start with a theme line or a tagline. I don't think about a story, because I don't think that every ad needs to have a story with a

Fallon Minneapolis romancing the car. Bruce Bildsten says his team starts working with a key idea such as BMW feels like no other car on the road. *Bildsten looks for appropriateness, not a theme line or a story. "I need to have a sense of what it should feel like in the end. The words are definitely last for me. They might even be written after the storyboard is drawn."*

punch line to it. Unless it's all dialogue, the words are definitely last for me; they might even be written after the storyboard is drawn." Bildsten looks for *appropriateness*. "I like to set some parameters on myself. Not that I want to limit myself, but it helps me to focus if I have a sense of what is right as far as the feeling is concerned; what is right for the budget; and what is right in terms of what the competition is doing. I need to have a sense of what it should feel like in the end. The reference for that might be a film, or another commercial that was done twenty years ago for something else. It might be a book. I especially like travel magazines about experiences that people have. I'll break down everything that comes into my brain. I need to start in a place, even though I might move from that place."

"I don't work on a word logic," says McGrath. He first establishes tonality. What will the commercial "feel" like? Is it going to be flamboyant? Is it going to be simple? "Then I get a visual idea, and then it's rooted in a thought. Sometimes one thought becomes the campaign. I've even done posters that become TV."

Ron Lawner is another writer who doesn't start with words. "I start with asking, *how* do I want you to feel? And it isn't much more complicated than that. What evokes that feeling? What kind of language? What kind of visuals? What kind of attitude or voice makes you feel like that?" Once he knows, Lawner says he is then working in a smaller, more defined box. "But I have all the freedom, because I'm not considering every possible response, just *one*."

Paul Fishlock likes to have an idea of what the commercial will feel like, well ahead of any sense of content. "Then as you actually come up with the content, whether it's visual ideas or a presenter or music or whatever, you judge them against that initial sense of what you think the finished piece is going to feel like."

Warren Brown always tries to start with something he thinks the consumer would like and find endearing or entertaining. "It's like I have this little Avid suite in my head. I can virtually see the whole thing in my mind and I just write down what I see."

Horton starts by asking: "*What do we want to own? And if it isn't a key category motivator, can we make it one?*" Horton cites bleach; efficacy and pleasant fragrance are key motivators worth owning, but having the best packaging probably isn't. "Then I try to create the *symbol* of what it is that I want to own that's born out of some truth. If I say Marlboro, you think of the cowboy. If I say Singapore Airlines, you think of the Girl. If I say Chanel, you think of the bottle or of her. If I say Levi's, you think of youth and rebellion and James Dean. Didn't David Ogilvy say that truth lies in the eye of the beholder?"

Despite the fact that writer Chuck McBride's work is hallmarked by some of the strongest end lines in contemporary advertising, he lets the picture determine the line. "I now prefer to write out of the picture as opposed to just writing the line. I'd rather write a line *based on what I've seen* as opposed to writing a line and then building a picture to that." McBride debates a writer's options. "You can do an ad that ends with a line that summarises the story, that basically tells you what you just saw, like *got milk?* We've been telling you a story about not having milk, *got milk?*, did you get it? Or you can create a line that doesn't just answer the ad, but lets you go a little bit further. It actually gives the ad a perspective, or takes you further away from where the ad is; it's like, what are you going to do with this now? Where should you go with this now?" McBride wrote hundreds of end lines for his Isuzu *Toyshop* commercial. "I played with lots of 'clever' ways to talk about the car or the ad. *Batteries not included* could have been the line! But I knew I'd finally hit it when I talked about the person who'd be using it. *Grow up, not old*, helped people understand the context of the ad but actually said, 'Don't be an old man — live'."

Dion Hughes talks about what he calls the supreme mystery of creativity. His Fosters *Salad* idea came to him out of the blue, fully and perfectly formed, when he was cleaning up his office, getting ready to go home, and wondering if there was still anyone around to go have a beer with. "I know Maradona talked about The Hand of God, and I myself am not a church-going chap, but I swear that's what it feels like; as though someone picked up the idea, rolled it into a tiny ball, and pea-shot it into my ear. Really, we can pretend that it was a bunch of steps that got us to a place, and that most people, given enough time and the right input and stimulus, would get there. But it isn't true. So much of the time it's just plain magical."

Throughout this commercial, things made by Dunlop that we take for granted disappear out of our lives.

We open on a woman playing tennis.

MVO: *You'd be surprised how much you'd miss Dunlop. Dunlop tennis balls...*

The ball suddenly vanishes.

MVO: *Dunlop inflatable boats...*

A yachtsman is climbing down into his dinghy. It disappears and he ends up in the water.

Similar situations unfold for Dunlop travel bags, road surfaces, carpet tiles, Wellington boots, fire-fighting equipment, wheels and tyres, moving pavements, playing surfaces, Dunlopillo beds, golf equipment...

A pen signs a cheque made payable to Great Britain. Suddenly the film runs in reverse until the cheque is blank.

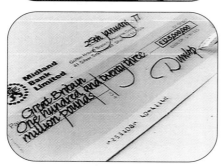

MVO: *Dunlop make 152 products for over 160 countries and last year, Dunlop exports earned over £120 million for Britain. You'd be surprised how much you'd miss Dunlop.*

What happens without the product? Art director Ron Mather and writer Andrew Rutherford prove that corporate commercials don't have to be dull — even when the client wants so many products in the one ad. Saatchi & Saatchi London.

Hughes definitely doesn't start with a line. "That's usually the last element. But pretty much anything else will do. Most often lately it's been stories, exaggerations, vignettes, visuals, an emotion. I have a preference for spots that tell a story. I agree with the theory that human beings have an inbuilt need for set-up, complication and resolution."

"Impose the product on yourself, not yourself on the product." Gray's advice: don't develop just one style of writing. "Be flexible. Be versatile. Have lots of hats and wear them accordingly. If humour is appropriate, be as funny as you can be. If there's licence to be wacky, go wacky wacky. But don't confuse lateral thinking with wackiness," he warns. "Lateral thinking simply takes you two steps sideways from the obvious. Always avoid the obvious." While everyone loves a funny ad, Gray says he has never wanted to be pigeonholed as a comedy writer. "If I had four briefs on a desk, I'd like one of them to be a serious brief, one to be a funny brief, one to be a tabletop brief, and one to be one of those weird, crazy, massive budget jobs that you can't pin down." Gray stresses that television advertising is a very difficult discipline to learn. "You have to understand what people expect within a genre. Unless you understand that, you cannot surprise people. The truth is, a lot of people can't write television. Having an idea for television and writing television are two completely different things."

How To Generate Ideas

All advertising ideas fall into one of these three categories. They will either show:

1. What happens *with* the product,
2. What happens *without* the product,
   or
3. What happens *with* and *without* the product — in the *same* ad.

Getting those ideas doesn't always have to be a mystical process, as some of the world's most respected creative leaders can prove. And while the creative process itself can be deconstructed into four stages — preparation, incubation, illumination and verification — the way we interrelate, overlap and repeat the various stages will stamp our ideas with our own creative DNA.

1. Start with the end first

"If you don't know where you're going, all roads will take you there. So I always start at the end and work my way back," explains Horton. "Say I want to draw a straight line between here and point X. If I start here I could end up anywhere. It's better if I go to point X and just work back. My endings will invariably be the truth: the line, with the symbol born out of that truth. It opens the way for the most fantastic creativity. All you have to do is finish at X; so you can excite us with where you start, how you start. A lot of creative people in my experience have had an idea, but couldn't quite finish it. But if they had known *where* they were finishing, then they could have started anywhere…"

Dawson also starts with the end line, or at least a rough line, first. "I would always try to start by summing up something different about the product or service, and then work back. If you can't get the line, you probably start attacking it from the wrong end, which means having an idea from something that can be related to the product. The problem is, you are likely to end up with something that isn't absolutely relevant." If it's just a funny, or a different, or a curious idea, he warns, it will usually require manipulation to marry it with the key thought. Dawson needs information; without it, trying to conjure ideas out of nothing means that the blank sheet of paper will stay blank a lot longer. He goes swimming at lunchtime to find ideas; he counts the tiles in the pool and things slip into place. He works alone. "I don't believe Picasso came up with an idea for a picture with somebody else, or that Mozart came up with an idea for a symphony with somebody else. Ideas can only come into one person's brain at a time."

Delbridge starts with a line. "And I'll hone and hone that line until I've got something really sharp, and then I'll spring off that into a myriad of possible visual interpretations. I rarely have a visual idea first. The line encapsulates the positioning I want; it forces me intellectually to see it so singly, so clearly, but the line itself may not even appear in the final commercial."

Newman says great lines are now more important than ever. "The 'slogan' was actually a Highland war cry. A great slogan can do more than neatly distil the essence of an organisation: *We try harder*. It can do more than get a product into the vernacular: *A diamond is forever*. If it's potent enough, a great slogan can actually drive the culture of an entire company: *Just do it*. Our client, Toyota Australia, has the value of their slogan — *Oh what a feeling* — listed on their balance sheet for many millions. Interestingly, Toyota is probably Australia's most creatively awarded campaign of the last ten years." Newman points to his campaign theme for the NRMA, a road service and insurance organisation. "Claiming the high ground generic of 'help' was strategically important, but it didn't come alive for me until I turned it into the simple branding mnemonic of the letters *H-E-L-P* always being spelt out after the name *N-R-M-A*." Getting into the vernacular, becoming part of popular culture, is what every campaign should aim for, says Newman. "I think 'Make it famous' should be a mandatory on every creative brief." Newman's discipline is that the idea should be reducible to a poster. "A sentence and a visual idea. Of course, the commercial might develop that visual idea into a multi-layered story, but if the thought can be reduced to a handful of nut hard words and a single unmoving visual, then at least you know you've got a real idea and not just an execution or not just a joke."

Cummins has three personal creative route maps. "One way is that I'll try to write it like a poster, a moving poster, and the headline next to the image in real terms is the voice-over. Another approach that I use, particularly if it's a complicated message, is to write out all the mandatories in a very straight and unadorned way. I'll then actually sit down and time what it is I have to say in its barest minimum form, and try to weave a story around it. Other times, I'll just start writing end lines and punchlines, and then work my way back to the beginning. My belief is, you may have a weak start but at least you'll always have a great finish."

"If I get stuck, I've always resorted to doing the TV as a print execution." Tracy Wong says this will force you to crystallise the concept in its *purest* form. "It's getting a concept to turn on a dime, as if it had to exist as one image and one headline, or one without the other. Yes, it might mean writing a bunch of headlines. It might mean thinking of a key visual."

Fallon writer Mike Gibbs adopted a similar strategy for BMW. "We started working on print ideas. We wrote down a print idea that was very simple, and added the ideas of things that you can do in film. We added sound, music, a way to deal with the supers, and it became a much stronger TV spot than it was a print ad." Gibbs admits that he tends to start from the back of the spot and write forward to the opening scene. "For me it's always knowing that I've got to have the logo at the end, and that's going to take a certain amount of time, and it seems like it's always stealing that little extra second that I want somewhere else in the commercial. So I start off being aware of that, and build from the back and say, okay, no matter what happens, I know right now this is a 27-second commercial. And sometimes clients like BMW not only want a logo at the end but also a dealer message and a price, so now you're down to 22 seconds."

"I'm trying to nail what the thing is about," says Blackley. "I try to get the central thought down on paper. It may be the theme line eventually, or it may lead to the final theme line. Because I've thought of what the theme line should be, I'll work my way through from the beginning to the end."

Writer, creative director and independent film director Antony Redman starts work on TV scripts in much the same way he does on print concepts. "You should always start with an idea, whether it's a proposition or an end line. You can then work from there. You've got something to base your ideas around." Redman also finds it useful to

The principle of the toolbox — with wheels attached. Toyota Hiace seen in a fresh, single-minded way by writer Michael Newman and art director Jonathan Teo at Saatchi & Saatchi Sydney. The Wagnerian-style music was welded with tool noises to build the necessary sense of size and strength, says Newman.

explore the feeling he wants to get across. Once a feeling is established, ideas can be steered into that area. "Often I'll start drawing little three- or four-frame storyboards, including the little logo-pack-shot-sign-off at the end; the fewer the frames, the better. If it's just one frame, fantastic. You're trying to find a succinct visual idea that sometimes doesn't need any copy. Just like the best posters."

"I'd like to say I always sit there and go, gee, what's the visual essence of this concept, because it's television, but to be honest I don't." Vaughan, a writer, admits that he tries to capture ideas in words. "In a funny sort of way you can argue that all ideas are words, even if they're visual. So I'd begin with a phrase that captures what the brand idea is, and from that what the commercial idea would be. I'd also try to think in terms of a campaign. I know there are instances in which you do get a one-off thing, but I don't think any client wants to spend money on a one-off approach that has to change next time around. People have finally understood that there is a synergistic effect when a family of communications cleaves to a strategy, an idea and a style that's central to them all. I like to create a pool of ideas. I will always rule out a clever idea that I can't follow up, no matter how wonderful it is. *You* might be the bunny who has to follow it up in a year's time so you'll have made a rod for your own back." Vaughan says you can to some extent measure the merit of an idea by the way it "pools" itself quickly. "Writers talk about how ads write themselves when they're right. There's an elegance about it. When it does happen, you know you've got the right answer. When it doesn't happen, when it's like pulling teeth, then I'm concerned that something's missing." Sometimes, Vaughan says, a gem from the client has been filtered out during the briefing process. Or, the strategy turns out to be a nice sentiment, nothing more. When it comes to writing an ad, the brief turns out not to contain the essence of the proposition but the out-take you want people to have once they've seen the commercial. "You know the sentiment is right, it's very sound, but there's no dimension in it and it takes you a while to wake up to what's wrong. It is very hard to think single-mindedly when you don't have to write ads for a living." The trouble is, says Vaughan, planners and account service people who write briefs are

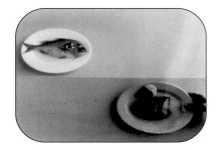

Open on a screen horizontally divided into two pastel halves. In the top left corner is a steamed snapper on a plate.

VO: *This steamed snapper...*

A plate of steak is placed in the bottom right corner.

VO: *Or this grilled lean rump steak will give you half your daily iron needs. So let's see them side by side.*

Suddenly a woman steps into frame and picks up the plate of snapper. As she lifts it, we realise that the fish and steak aren't on a split screen. The fish is actually a metre long and was on the floor while the steak was on the tabletop. When they are side by side, the snapper totally dwarfs the steak.

Super under the steak: *122 grams*

Super under the fish: *7.9 kilograms*

VO with end super: *Lean Beef. Your best source of essential daily iron.*

Writer Paul Fishlock and art director Warren Brown were handed an amazing fact on a plate. A special homemade camera lens used for nature photography made the side-by-side demonstration totally compelling. The Campaign Palace Sydney for the Australian Meat & Livestock Corporation.

never in a position where they are *judged* by the singularity of what they do.

Australian Meat & Livestock Corporation. At the Campaign Palace Sydney, writer Paul Fishlock and art director Warren Brown were briefed on a campaign to reverse the decline of red meat consumption in Australia. The proposition: a skimpy 122 grams of lean beef was all it took to deliver half of one's daily needs of iron, compared to a whale-size chunk of fish weighing 7.9 *kilo*grams. "We started from the end frame," recalls Fishlock. "We had this huge fish and this sensible plate of lean meat. It was a case of having this amazing side-by-side fact, but *how* could we make it fly?"

They explored lots of scenarios. Then one night Fishlock caught a TV show about an Aussie nature photographer called Jim Frazier. "He'd developed this peculiar snorkel lens so that he could get into spiders' holes and maintain the focus. He'd cobbled it together with old toilet rolls and chewing gum."

"The lens made it possible for us to make the visuals an extraordinary event," explains Brown, "a real trick of the eye." The split-screen-that-isn't had been done before. But making it a *depth-of-field* split-screen was totally new. At first, viewers think they are seeing the snapper and the steak side-by-side on the same surface; it is only when a woman steps into frame and lifts the fish that people realise that the steak is on the tabletop while the fish had been on the floor beyond. "People were gobsmacked at the amount of fish they had to eat as opposed to the amount of beef. Having it all in one shot, and 'live', without any evidence of technical trickery made it even more compelling," says Brown. At first, Frazier's lens was so rickety it couldn't be attached to a normal film camera. "The lens would shake so much everything would go out of focus. We had to get a military-style camera that had absolutely no vibration whatsoever." Brown says the effect could not have been achieved in post-production. "It would have been very difficult, as soon as you put the human element into it."

Brown art directed the commercial and the accompanying print campaign using pastel colours. "Most people would have viewed them as being exceedingly unfashionable and probably not very complimentary towards food. Sometimes, if you try to do the 'wrong'

A Japanese woman is in the final stages of labour. Her husband watches anxiously. The doctor and nurses call encouragement.

When the baby is born, the medical team proudly presents the bundle of joy to its happy parents.

There are lots of *ooohs* and *ahhhs*, until suddenly the baby produces a camera from beneath its shawl and photographs its astonished parents.

Cut to product shot. Super end line.

MVO: *Fuji Film. As used by the world's top photographers.*

Lionel Hunt started with the end line first when he wrote Born Photographer *for Fuji Film at The Campaign Palace Sydney. Ron Mather art directed.*

thing and not what's expected, you can come up with something that's purely original and fresh. But because the ads were aimed at women, I also wanted something that looked distinctive, yet was soft enough to be easy on the eye; a soft-graphic look. The backgrounds had to be recessive enough so they wouldn't compete with the food. No one else at the time was using pastels, especially for food, so I knew the ads would stand out."

"Personally I love demonstration commercials because you go through on the screen what the shopper does in their head." Fishlock says the commercial can follow the consumer's thought pattern precisely. "They're faced with two or three options; shall I buy this, or shall I buy that? They have to make that decision and your commercial has armed them with the necessary information to say, don't buy that one, buy this one."

Fuji Film. Hunt, faced with a blank sheet of paper, almost always draws the shape of a 24-sheet poster and writes the end line of the commercial into the box first. "I try and do a poster, as well as I can. Which means, in the ideal poster, very few words. If you can do that, you've got the whole campaign cracked. Then you spin a creative idea off that, be it a television commercial, a print ad, or a radio commercial. But I always start by drawing that oblong. And I always start with the *words* first."

His *Born Photographer* commercial, from Australia's Campaign Palace, was conceptualised that way with art director Ron Mather. "We started with the line *Fuji Film, as used by the world's top photographers* — meaning the Japanese — and then thought of the baby. So we actually had the 24-sheet poster or the showcard first, and that was expanded into the commercial." The story of the Japanese baby being born and then photographing his parents became, in effect, the lead up to the end line. It is the same process as comedy writing; the punch line is written first and the script then builds towards it. "I *have* to end with a thought, with a statement, a precis of what you've just seen." Hunt almost always works with an art director. "We see the commercial in collaboration; but that's not to say that I think of the line and he thinks of the picture, it's often the other way round."

Hunt notices that a lot of people don't have end lines on

commercials these days. "My view is that they can't think of them. They just end up with the name of the product, or the pack, and nothing. I'm very suspicious of ads, be they print or television, that don't have end lines. You can probably show me hundreds of good ads that don't have end lines, and I'll still be suspicious of them."

Mercedes-Benz E-Class. "When we first saw the car, it was a big departure." Writer Kash Sree, now at Wieden & Kennedy Portland, revisits his commercial that launched the Mercedes-Benz E-Class in Asia through Batey Ads Singapore. "It looked more flowing, rounded, a beautiful object which could have sold itself. But you couldn't forget it was a Mercedes-Benz. It wasn't a Honda, it wasn't a BMW, it was a Mercedes; it had all that background of engineering. So we wanted to give the impression that it was more than just a pretty face. We also wanted a deeper idea that could be continued beyond the launch phase. Eventually, we got onto a thought that came from a truth: that as beautiful as that car was on the outside, it was even more beautiful inside." Sree's end line was, *The real beauty comes from within.*

Asian values inspired the execution. Sree and his art director Andy Fackrell initially searched for symbols that epitomised the thought of not outwardly showing wealth, about being less ostentatious. "We had certain symbols that didn't make it into the commercial. In parts of India and the Middle East, you've got bangles that are plain and make a little shaking noise as you walk along with them. Now people 'in the know' know that those bangles are hollow and are full of diamonds, but that would have been too hard to translate into a television idea. We looked at snuff bottles in Asia, which are meticulously painted on the inside, so their real beauty comes from within. And a pregnant woman is outwardly beautiful, but what's going on inside her is even more beautiful." Sree and Fackrell also had a whole shopping list of marque values which had to be touched on in the commercial and in the accompanying print campaign: safety, engineering, precision, performance, craftsman-ship. "So the pregnant woman symbolised safety, because the womb is the safest place for the child. And a strong but intricate nautilus shell symbolised precision."

In the final execution, the connections between the symbols and

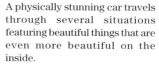

A physically stunning car travels through several situations featuring beautiful things that are even more beautiful on the inside.

Everyone it passes has their eyes closed as though in meditation, discovering their own inner beauty.

We begin with a pregnant woman in a forest, holding her stomach. Then a child with a zoetrope, followed by another playing with marbles whose perfect spheres contain marvellous crystal worlds.

The car continues its journey. A nautilus shell is held up to it, as though a party to its secret.

A man's watch reveals the inner beauty of its elaborate workings.

End super: *Mercedes-Benz E-Class. The real beauty comes from within.*

Once writer Kash Sree had established the end line, he and art director Andy Fackrell searched for symbols whose inner beauty exceeded their external attraction. Director Jeff Darling's execution was twice recognised by D&AD. Batey Ads Singapore.

the car are subtle and organic. As Sree stresses, "You shouldn't see the way it works. You shouldn't see the strategy. You should see the ad and buy into it with your guard down. These days you can see the strategy in a lot of ads and therefore your defences go up. If you can get anyone to lower his or her defences, you're on a winner."

2.   Find a moment

"I've never tried to solve a problem the same way twice," explains McBride. "Sometimes, by accident, the structure or the logic could be similar to other campaigns I've worked on, but the truth is always about boiling things down, trying to make them simple, and *finding yourself inside of a moment*."

McBride's work has explored many diverse moments, from the young man's dilemma in *Aaron Burr* to the pilot in *Airplane* going into a dive so the drinks cart rolls down the aisle with the milk. McBride crafts his moments to reflect what could have realistically happened in thirty seconds in real life. "Finding yourself inside a moment, and seeing it out, is finding the simplest way of telling a very powerful truth." McBride revisits the "moment" of the *Airplane* commercial. An airline pilot chomps a cookie on the flight deck and suddenly needs milk. He turns to see a pitcher of milk on the beverage cart at the rear of the plane. "He first puts the plane into a small dive. The cart starts rolling forward towards him, but its wheels get lodged against a peanut. So now he's desperate. He puts the plane into a steeper dive, the cart crushes the peanut and rushes forward down the aisle towards the pilot. And right then someone comes out of the restroom and — *POW!* He takes the cart right in the stomach, leaving the pilot inches away from what would have been a sure thing."

Writer Michael Patti at BBDO New York recalls his Pepsi *Diner* commercial. "Sometimes things that start off very big get better when they become smaller. We started off with the concept of that old 60s music about getting together, peace and love, and we said, what if all the Coke drinkers in the world and all the Pepsi drinkers in the world got together to celebrate the end of the cola wars. It would be this big statement. And then we thought, wouldn't it be much better if it got very small? If it was the same theme, but representing Pepsi was one of their hardworking guys on Christmas Eve, and representing Coke was the same counterpart, and they have a *small moment*, maybe in a diner. When the idea got smaller like that, it became a bigger idea, a better idea, and more human. Two guys *could* end up on Christmas Eve, sharing a burger, and showing pictures of their families, it wasn't too far-fetched, and that way it set up the premise for the funny surprise ending. We love to do Pepsi ads that poke a little fun at Coke, but we try never to be heavy-handed. We think it's important that we *never* say, Pepsi is great and Coke isn't. You'll notice in the *Diner* spot the Pepsi driver tries the Coke and says, 'Not bad; here, try mine'." The commercial was directed by Joe Pytka and art-directed by Don Schneider. "Without a great client you're never going to get the great advertising done," adds Patti.

3. Is there an idea in the strategy?

"Distil the strategy and treat it like a poster" is Whybin's advice. "In many ways, it's no different to the print medium. You've got to put down, in a square, the most succinct distillation of the proposition. And the greatest way you can do it is without any words, just a picture. The picture should distil the strategy and the proposition. I start that way, doing a poster first." *Once you distil the strategy, Whybin says the ad will just drop into place.* "Pull your ideas from *within* the brand. Don't try to create ideas and *attach* them to brands." It helps, Whybin says, if you can visualise the product in your mind and see the idea coming out of it. That way, you can sense whether the idea belongs inherently to the brand, or is just an unrelated or generic graft. "A lot of people try to grab at creative ideas, they're battling all the time, but actually I think there's quite a logical order to it. In many ways, it's not creative at all, it's quite rational. You keep working until the left side of the brain and the right side of the brain click together, and *then* you start to build emotion into that." Once he gets the idea, Whybin can see the whole commercial straightaway. He then works on the compression of the argument.

"Ideas come from within the brief." Saatchi & Saatchi Sydney senior art director Jonathan Teo says you would only run out of ideas if every brief you received was the same. "But every brief is

Jonathan Teo, David Rollins and Michael Linke took the classic glass beer posters found in Sydney hotels (above) and brought them to life for Nibble Nobby's Nuts *commercials (below) at The Campaign Palace Sydney. "All ideas come from within the brief," says Teo.*

different. Every clue is inside the brief. Yes, the idea might be new and creative, but it comes from the brief." Teo art directed the Australian *Nibble Nobby's Nuts* campaign at The Campaign Palace. The brief talked about nibbling the product with friends over drinks, which led to the idea of animating the classic glass beer posters found in many Australian hotels. Teo starts by analysing typical work in the category so he knows what *not* to do. "Then tell me what the client wants. Tell me all the boxes you want ticked — ten boxes, twenty boxes. My challenge is to come with a good, fresh, new idea and still tick all the boxes." Teo believes his job is not to create something out of nothing. "I create from the brief, I am a translator of words into pictures, but my pictures have to say more than they got from the words."

David Droga works back from the key insight in the brief. "You take the key insight, *Refreshment*, or *Unbreakable*, and you say what does that mean to me? What kind of emotion does *Refreshing* mean? *Refreshing* can sometimes be *Surprising*, and *Surprising* can sometimes be..." Droga says he has to convey emotions and that is where scenarios come from. "Essentially I like to tell a story."

Award-winning copywriter and director Rowan Dean of Rowan Dean Films Sydney, has evolved a seamless creative formula. "Strategic thinking is a creative process; for me, *the strategy, the idea and the execution are the same thing.* I don't see them as three separate elements. That's why it was easy for me to go from writing into film direction. They were also the same. When I was writing, I would write by drawing a little storyboard long before I put any words on paper. If it worked as a storyboard, it was funny. If it didn't, forget it." Dean is highly suspicious of the planning and briefing process. "Strategy? There are only two or three strategies. You're either selling more of the same stuff, or you're selling the same stuff with bells and whistles attached, or you're selling it to different people than the ones who have been buying it, or you're getting the same people to buy more of it. That's *every* strategy. So this thing about you've got to have a great strategy or a great brief, forget it. The best stuff I ever wrote didn't have a brief. Fosters didn't have a brief, except get the Poms to buy Aussie beer without offending the Poms or the Aussies. Hamlet didn't have a brief that we ever saw. We used to just sit around every morning saying, what's another negative emotion — humiliation, embarrassment, awkwardness?"

Clarks Shoes. Neil Godfrey describes a simple, strategic commercial for Clarks Shoes that he co-directed at Collett Dickenson Pearce. It showed a shoe being drawn onto a real child's foot to communicate the specific problem areas that the shoes were designed to safeguard.

"It was almost a still life. A big masculine hand picks up a delicate child's foot. The voice-over would say something like, if you get a shoe that is too tight across here, and the hand would draw a line across the toes, it will cause corns and bunions. The hand kept drawing lines to show you where all the potential problems would be — down the sides and around the heel — until it ends up having drawn a Clarks shoe on the foot. And then the foot match dissolved into the real Clarks shoe. It was the ideal commercial."

Little Caesars Pizza. Bijur's personal style is story driven. "I like having a progression, a beginning and an end. That's a style I really like, but it's not the only style we'll do here. It comes so much out of the strategy. It all depends on the proposition. *Is there a relatable truth in there?*" Good creative is always a bit of a leap from the strategy to the execution, Bijur says, and sometimes connections are made in conversation. "I always start with conversation. We talk among ourselves. It can lead in any direction."

He cites the Little Caesars Pizza commercial in which a young man finds everything getting better and better. "We always start with a very simple premise that's relevant to people. That commercial was just an offer. We really didn't have too much to talk about. There were two offers; one good, one was even better." For $7.98, consumers could purchase two pizzas with free bread. For an additional $2, they could upgrade to deluxe pizzas with more cheese and toppings. "Somehow in the conversation about what we were going to do to communicate this, the notion came out that here's something good, but what could be even better? Things just keep getting better. And that led to the idea where this guy has everything go absolutely right for him on that day. Things couldn't possibly be getting any better, but yet they do. He finds his wallet. Then his girlfriend decides she's not going to leave him, she will marry him. Then he finds his dog that was lost. Then he finds he has a brother." At that point, the offer is introduced: *Just when you thought things couldn't get any better...* "It turned out to be a great one. The clue to the Caesars campaign was that it always seemed to go like that. Simple things to say, fun ways to say them."

NRMA Insurance. Sue Carey, senior writer at Saatchi & Saatchi Sydney, was struggling with the type of brief so typical of the insurance category: "professional but caring, big but small, red yet blue, etcetera!" The problem was compounded by the company's profile. "In the state of New South Wales, the NRMA had been around for seventy years," Carey explains. "Their heritage as a road service organisation created an enormous amount of goodwill. Everyone has a story about the nice NRMA bloke who came out in the rain and got their car going, and it was no great leap to go to them, as they grew, for car or home insurance, or even investments. Our task was to introduce some facts about the company to new markets in other states, Queensland and Victoria, where the road service credentials meant nothing. The fact that they'd entered those markets offering cheap premiums left some people unsure if it was okay to trust them." As Carey sums it up: "So all we had to do was show they were big and strong and helped lots of people all the time. Maybe it's just me, but I found the brief extremely hard. It was very broad and I really had to circle around it for a long time before finding a way in…"

Carey made a connection using the "big and yet small" cliché. "It got me thinking about a raging storm in what turns out to be a tiny, safe back garden." To a ladybird, the garden is huge and threatening in a storm. The child that rescues it helped NRMA introduce themselves with a degree of modesty as the voice-over delivered a few impressive facts. "The ad was only going to work if it all looked absolutely real. The storm had to be scary. We had to care about the plight of the ladybird, and have the wilderness turn into a peaceful sanctuary at the end."

"The people who turned it into something really special came into the picture next," Carey recounts. "Phil Meatchem, the director at Film Graphics, believed 3D animation was the way to achieve the realism we were after. He worked with Zelko Dejanovic at Sydney's Animal Logic to create the entire cast in 3D. As they worked, we gradually saw the ladybird and grasshopper and ants and beetles grow from spinning wire frames into completely believable creatures." To ensure the insects all walked with the correct gait, live insects were kept on hand for reference. "Some of the feistier ones, like the honey ants, had to do a bit of time in the fridge to slow them down. It didn't seem to harm them, although they'd get pretty

In the style of the film *Microcosmos*, we see the effects of a storm on the tiny inhabitants of a small field.

Blades of grass sway in the wind like huge tree trunks.

Leaves crash to the ground like heavy sheets of metal.

Ants flee into a hole. Little insects shelter under rocks, away from the tidal wave of an overfull puddle. The sounds of the storm are magnified and quite surreal.

We follow the plight of a ladybird. As it tries to run across a branch, it is pelted by gigantic raindrops.

One heavy drop knocks it onto its back.

Super: *Need help?*

Cut to the *NRMA* logo. The letters dissolve into the word *HELP*.

A child's hand delicately picks up the ladybird and puts it back on its feet.

MVO: *Every day, we help more Australians with the big things in life, their cars, their homes, than any other company. N-R-M-A for H-E-L-P.*

Richly deserving a D&AD Silver Pencil for the most outstanding special effects, NRMA's Ladybird was written by Sue Carey, art directed by Stuart Robinson, and directed by Phil Meatchem at Film Graphics Sydney.

stroppy once they warmed up again."

Carey says it's sometimes hard to convince people that there are any special effects or animation involved at all. "The team at Animal Logic pulled out all the stops to create something that looked real. It seems they didn't get the chance to do this as often as they'd like. The creatures they usually build in 3D are 'characters' and they seized this chance to really show what they could do."

"My preference is usually for production-proof scripts," observes her creative director Newman, "especially with the relatively small budgets we work with in Australia." He also explains his reservations about "heartwarming" commercials. "Good commercials are usually of the *ha-ha* variety or the *ah-ha* variety. It's much harder to do the heartwarming *aah* variety. Miss the mark and you're covered in saccharine syrup, the *uurgh* variety. The *Ladybird* commercial managed to pull off a sweet ending *by charging the rest of the commercial with high drama.*"

To see it pull off a Silver Pencil at D&AD for the most outstanding Special Effects, says Newman, was very satisfying.

Outpost.com. Bijur references his agency's work for Outpost.com. "There's no way to ever completely understand where an idea comes from. When you really look at Outpost, *it's very strategically driven.* What the client wanted was to just get his name out there. So Eric Silver and Roger Camp started with a very simple premise. Let's do things that are outrageous to get the name out there. And that was it." One commercial opened with the statement *We want you to remember our name,* upon which gerbils were fired from a cannon through the 'O' in Outpost. "It wasn't really intended to build the brand *per se.* It was intended to make a lot of noise very quickly and to get a lot of awareness very quickly."

Partnership for a Drug-Free America. Sometimes, Bijur says, the idea comes out of a very new kind of proposition. "The *Lenny* commercial for the Partnership for a Drug-Free America, which was done by a very talented art director who was here named David Angelo, came about because there had been so many commercials done which lectured people, proselytised, and his idea was very simple. Just go out and show people how really horrible it is. Shoot the real person. That was a real heroin addict of course, anybody

We are alone in a room with Lenny, a heroin addict.

LENNY: *I'm, you know, I consider myself pretty intelligent.*

I could do whatever I want to do, man.

Whatever I want to do, I could do.

And I had, uh, gangrene on my foot that they — almost took my foot off, you know.

(Pointing to vein on his hand) *See if I can get this here. Yeah.*

But I got these tracks all over my body. That pus was just coming out of the little hole here. I threw up, man, my guts. And as I'm throwing up, I'm like, damn, boy this is (BLEEP) *what I want.*

By the time '97 rolls around...'96 at this time, right, 1996, August 17th, 18th, whatever it is, you can come here with your cameras and I'll be a totally different person. I'll be successful. And I'll bet my life on it.

End super: *Heroin. Want some? Partnership for a Drug-Free America.*

Art director David Angelo's concept was to shoot a real addict. Tony Kaye directed. Cliff Freeman & Partners New York, for Partnership for a Drug-Free America.

could see that. Not a word was scripted. Tony Kaye shot that stuff. He just spent a tremendous amount of time with him, alone in a room, running thousands and thousands and thousands of feet of film in conversation." Little bits and pieces from that extended conversation became the final, harrowing commercial. "There was a follow-up idea to that, which never came off, that was very sad. In the commercial he said, "Come back and see me in a year's time. Well, a date was set up a year later, and there was some conversation with his sister to try to get him to meet with us, and the meet was set, but he never showed up. He was still a heroin addict at that time…"

Rolo. Currently executive creative director of BBDO Düsseldorf, Jan van Meel recalls the development of the famous Rolo *Elephant* commercial at Lintas Amsterdam. "It sounds very logical when you look back, but it wasn't that simple then. There were lots of other scripts."

According to van Meel, the brief had existed for many years. "We distilled it down to one word: sharing. Every pack of Rolo has a last Rolo. Sharing that one is difficult. This thought was expressed in the line, *Think twice what you do with your last Rolo.*" Lateral thinking then took over. "Assuming you are egoistic about your last Rolo, someone else might be offended and remember that for a long time. And who has an especially good memory? An elephant."

The commercial opens in sepia. A young boy is taunting a baby elephant with a Rolo. The boy pops the Rolo into his own mouth going "Nah-nah-nah-nah-nah". The time frame changes. We are now in colour, the young boy has become a dad, but he still eats Rolos. He is standing in the street as a circus parade goes past. Suddenly an elephant's trunk swings into frame and taps him on the shoulder. *Whaaack!* The elephant, now also fully grown, exacts its revenge with a deeply meaningful "Nah-nah-nah-nah-nah…" The commercial broke its category conventions and carried off major international awards including the Grand Prix at Cannes in 1996.

Singapore Airlines. "The brief was very simple: ask people to stop over in Singapore for twenty-four hours on their way from the UK to Australia." Dean wrote the commercial that French later

An idea that flowed seamlessly from the strategy: Granny has so much fun on her Singapore stopover that she forgets about her family waiting to meet her in Australia. Written by Rowan Dean, directed by Neil French for Batey Ads Singapore.

directed for Batey Ads Singapore. "I have a very simple method of arriving an idea. You don't want the person watching the commercial to know what the brief is. It's all a huge sleight of hand. You've got to get them to accept the message without them realising it. It's like the conjurer at a kids' party; if you can see how he does it, he's boring. So the last thing you can do is say, 'you can stop over in Singapore for twenty-four hours'. So you keep mentally twisting the brief around until you find an angle that gives you an opportunity for a gag. Stop over for twenty-four hours … what happens if someone like a grandmother doesn't stop over for twenty-four hours? What happens if she has such a good time that she stops over for three weeks? What are the consequences of her staying longer? And you've got a gag. There's a family waiting at the airport for hours and hours, while gran is still having the time of her life in Singapore."

Singapore Tourism Board. French says he always writes to communicate propositions. "What's the *one* thing I want the person to take away? What's the *one* thing I want them to think about my product or service? And I *only* want them to think one thing. In terms of Martell it was, if I watch this I will know more about brandy than any of my friends. With Union Bank of Switzerland it was, these are people I would like to deal with. With *Billion Dollar Smile* it

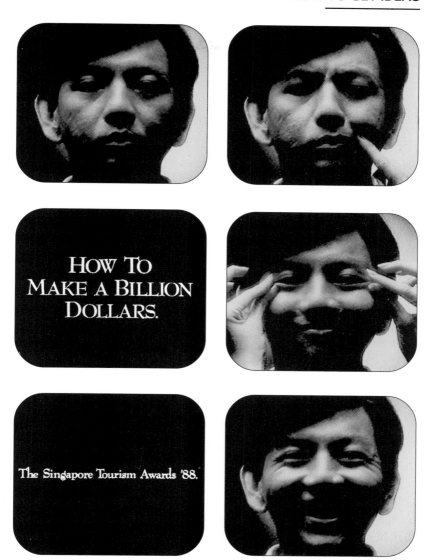

Nothing moves in this commercial except the idea. By locking-down the camera, Neil French focused attention on the importance of a smile to earn Singapore more tourist revenue. The woman's hands rearranging the man's lips and eyes, and the subsequent change in facial expression, were precisely timed to the voice-over. As a result, a Gold Lion at Cannes moved in French's direction. Agency: Euro RSCG Partnership (The Ball Partnership) for the Singapore Tourism Board.

wasn't 'be nice to foreigners because it's nice to be nice', but 'be nice to foreigners because you will make money out of it'."

In the same way a photographer frames a shot, French framed his idea and the logic of his argument. The commercial was addressed to everyone working in Singapore's billion-dollar tourism industry and related sectors like retailing. The Tourism Board's message was single-minded: a grumpy island isn't good for business. French's masterpiece of simplicity demonstrates what he calls "Zen direction". A locked-off camera remains focused on "yer average Singaporean". The man's face appears set in a rather bleak, bored scowl. As the voice-over explained why everyone had to greet tourists with a smile to boost the country's tourism earnings, a woman's hand entered frame and began to reshape the man's expression: the lips were pushed into a chirpy grin, his eyes were pulled back into a nice crinkly smile.

French underscores his focus on simplicity with a story of an old Indian wood carver. "He was famous all over India for carving elephants. He had never had any training, yet he carved perfect elephants. Somebody asked him, how can you carve such perfect elephants? And he replied, I take my little knife, and I take a block of wood, and I cut away everything that does not look like an elephant."

Billion Dollar Smile, written and directed by French when he was creative director at Euro RSCG Partnership (The Ball Partnership), Singapore, won a Gold at Cannes. It was rumoured to have been in the running for the Grand Prix, but sidestepped at the last minute because it had been shot on "the lesser medium" of videotape, not film. French and his cinematographer Han Chew had skilfully filtered back the sharpness of the video picture and pushed up the contrast to achieve a film texture. "We couldn't afford film; it had to be shot in one take and the human face is a difficult thing to control. It took a lot of practice and an enormous number of takes for the talent to control his facial muscles perfectly. It's all for real."

4. Be a sponge

"Be a sponge," says Fink. "Go and soak up as much information as you can. Read books, read magazines, go to the theatre, go to the cinema, go swimming, go walking, read a book about bringing up a dog, find out about glassblowing. There's a magazine in Britain called *Loot*, where people put in all their secondhand stuff they want to get rid of; there's everything in there from wardrobes to cars to exhaust pipes to cutlery. Just flicking through it, there are so many different kinds of things out there. The Internet is like the greatest encyclopaedia in the world. *There are too many advertising people who just sit in an office and say we've got to do an ad.* And they just stare at each other for three weeks. The worst thing they can do is look in the award books. All that stuff's been done." The best creative people are engaged in a constant process of observing, storing and connecting. Even a simple walk to work can yield interesting dividends. "I was watching the way everyone else was walking and everyone seemed to be waddling a bit more than usual. I think it was because I was just really concentrating hard on what happens to people's heads when they walk. They *do* go up and down. There's a Truffaut movie called *Shoot the Pianist.* In it, the main character falls in love with this girl and every time he walks with her, they walk absolutely perfectly together so their heads bounce up and down in sync. And I began to notice it throughout the movie, whenever you see the two walking together, their heads would move up and down together. And then there's a point where they argue, and suddenly their heads are no longer together."

Webster's cutting edge regimen includes going to art exhibitions and the theatre, and listening to the latest music. "Any creative person has a duty to keep himself fuelled with all the latest creativity and techniques, so he's got a full tank at his disposal. I collect things. Anything I hear that is unusual, or touching in music, I compile it. If I see any photographs in the paper, things like that, I'm always ripping them out. I've got a whole library of stuff that's caught my attention. You never know, in two years' time something might click, and I could use it or follow it up. Any good creative guy will always have his finger on the pulse of what's going on."

Screening new reels has become a regular lunchtime event at Fallon's. The creative staff can take time out together to update their knowledge without disrupting their schedules. "We work very hard at staying current." Bildsten believes all creatives should watch as many films as they can from different places. "Don't let Hollywood supply your only dose of film. People who are best at television really have something to draw from. You'll have a richer background. There'll be more in your memory banks. Take film classes. See more films. Rent more films. Not just the serious ones."

"Make your mind an attic." Buster Keaton's advice resonates for French. "Whatever happens to you, gather little bits of information, little experiences, little somethings, and stow them away in the attic because one day they *will* come in handy. And that's something I've really discovered. Everything that happens to you is an opportunity. Just put them away and one day you'll think to yourself, that was funny, I can use that now. Cutting the films of Buster Keaton together you can see an extraordinary range of ideas the man had, a thousand different ideas, much funnier than Chaplin because he kept using the stuff he'd seen." French can't see how anyone can be an advertising person straight from college or university. "You'd have a mind like a library, not an attic. There's a world out there. Become a street sweeper, a bouncer, a bull fighter, and you'll have more information than you'll ever need."

"Forget about looking for your idea in old issues of *CA*. It's not in there…" Berlin loathes the imitative style of doing advertising. "Don't look in the annuals. The idea may be in a conversation, maybe in playing pool with your partner. Probably, if it's going to be a great idea, it's going to be in some combination of images that have been loaded into your head by your culture and experiences."

"Write from the heart and draw upon your own personal experiences." They are your greatest creative weapons, insists Ramchandani. "Don't worry about searching for techniques; they come afterwards. Have some emotional truth that you really feel about something. Put in little characters, little situations that you've spotted and you've felt that might chime with other people. And be very happy to do things that don't feel like advertisements because if it feels right to you, and you're a human being, it'll be right for other human beings, too."

"Use life as your primary reference source." Keep a little book of observed experiences, Fishlock says. "When you can bring one of those into focus, then you'll galvanise millions of people at a time to go yes, that's what it's like, I've been there, I've done that."

Be aware of life around you, agrees Hal Curtis. "Live a life. It's important to not be too consumed by this business and to be a part of what's around you, because that's where ideas come from. If you're too insular, you're derivative. It's very healthy to look to anything *but* other advertising for inspiration."

As American writer Steven James said, creativity is not seeing something that no one else can see; it is seeing what anyone else could see *if only they were looking*.

Audi. Hegarty still recalls a real-life observation: "I saw two people walking along in the rain. They only had one umbrella. So one got immediately behind the other, and walked along completely in unison, as though they were glued together, so they wouldn't get wet. I thought at the time, what a wonderful image that is." It stuck in Hegarty's mind and resurfaced much later in the Audi commercial where two designers follow each other around.

Cozens takes up the story. "The original Audi brief was simply 'technology'. Also, Audi was not actually known for its German-ness. At that time, if you'd thought of German cars, you'd have thought of BMW and Mercedes-Benz, but you would never have thought of Audi. People just didn't have an idea where Audi came from. So we wanted to get a bit of German-ness into it, but we also wanted to make it a bit lighter; we could've gone very Teutonic on it, but we wanted the ads to be more whimsical. Which is why we came up with a two-part line: *Vorsprung durch technick, as they say in Germany.* Funnily enough, it'd been on a sign outside the Audi factory for forty years, *Vorsprung durch technick, Forward through technology.* You go past it on your way to Munich. So John Hegarty and I added the English bit and the rest is history. Years later, we were driving down there to do a bit of skiing in the Alps and my son was in the back. We passed the Audi factory and he said, Dad, they're even using your line over here."

Cozens believes the thinking process should never become too mechanical. "Once it does, then you come up with too similar ideas. I think if you start looking for a line, it's almost like an American way of doing things. They say, hey, let's have twenty-eight people working on the line; they come up with a line and everyone works to that. Do you need a line? If you'd had twenty-eight people working on a line, would anyone have come up with anything as fresh as *Vorsprung durch technick*? It would have never, ever got off the ground." He much prefers sitting in a room with a writer and art director. "You just mull over things, talk about the weather, talk about what you did last night. You're kind of stalling for time really. When you've got a deadline, fear is one of the great motivators. Can you do it? Can you *not* do it?"

Coca-Cola. One of Coca-Cola's most endearing commercials had its genesis in some big metal files at Fallon Minneapolis, in which art director Dean Hanson assiduously stores away dozens of ideas, typefaces, cuttings and videos. "When I hit a wall, I go and dig in there. I'm constantly refreshing my memory about what's in the files."

Three years before the Coca-Cola brief landed on his desk, Hanson had seen a Jacques Cousteau special on the Discovery Channel. The image of an elephant swimming off the Andaman Islands stayed in his mind. And the tape stayed in his files. He believes that we, the creators, are the audience as much as anybody else is. If something strikes our imagination, chances are it will appeal to the rest of the audience as well.

"If you want to do good work, *you have to look at the world around you*, at the stuff that stimulates you, and you have to write down ideas all the time, then file them. Everyone should have those gems stored away…"

Mobil 1. Grace remembers suffering over the final scene of his legendary DDB commercial in which a can of Mobil 1 oil is passed around the world. "The client wanted to communicate that this was an international brand and that you could go 25,000 miles without an oil change. And it came to me that we could violate reality, where people who exist in Hong Kong could pass the can of Mobil 1 out of the frame into another reality, let's say Rome, and someone in Rome could pass the can to someone in yet another reality in Paris. It was the first time something like this had been done. It was charming, it worked very well, but I knew it needed an ending. It came to me in a gush and I never thought the client would buy it…"

At that time, reports Grace, New York City was full of homeless people with their little cups and cans, all looking for a handout.

We are beneath the surface of an idyllic blue ocean. We can't quite believe our eyes, however...an elephant is swimming along above us!

An old 20s-style song is heard playing. The lyrics ask: *Is it love... is it love...is it love that brings me back into your arms...?*

The elephant spies a beautiful woman relaxing on a distant platform with her iced bottles of Coca-Cola.

He swims towards her, trunk uplifted so he looks for all the world like the Loch Ness monster.

The woman is unaware of his presence. His trunk discreetly drops some peanuts beside the ice bucket, picks up the Coke and he swims off.

An elephant swims out to exchange his precious peanuts for some Coca-Cola. A brilliant creative connection made by art director Dean Hanson who had seen a Jacques Cousteau special about the Andaman Islands. Fallon Minneapolis.

CHAPTER 3

Grace's ending called for the can to be passed into frame where the presenter is delivering the final pitch on a New York street. "The thought was that the spokesperson for this major industrial corporation would be standing there with a can of Mobil 1, and a little old woman passing by, seeing this poor, well-dressed but homeless man, would throw in a few coins to help him get along. The client loved it. They read into the ending that the product saved money. Which was never my intention, but I took it."

Grace calls it a perfect, lucky accident. Others might call it being alert to the ideas that are all around us.

NACAIDS. Two dozen Grim Reapers in a tenpin bowling alley with people for targets launched Australia's first AIDS awareness campaign in 1987 as well as the career of writer Siimon Reynolds. Reynolds, then aged twenty-two and based at Grey Advertising, Sydney, became overnight the icon for young Australian creatives and a media celebrity for the press. "I wanted to do a commercial that would stun people. And I knew I had to kill a lot of people in the ad. I knew that was a sound basis for doing an interesting ad. Every Christmas as a kid I used to watch the animated version of Scrooge on TV. I was always fascinated when the Grim Reaper came and visited Scrooge. I thought the Grim Reaper was a great visual symbol."

The only question was, how could Reynolds use the Grim Reaper to kill people in an interesting and relevant way? "I first thought he could machine gun them, but it was too fast for a 60-second ad. At the time I was doing a lot of tenpin bowling at the local bowling alley and the idea popped into my head that the Reaper could bowl the people over. I went to see a few directors but no one thought they could do it. One had the thought that the people could be made of ceramic so that they smashed on impact. Ian Macdonald was the only director who said he could do it for the money and that it would work. And it was absolutely extraordinary. They literally bowled a 9-foot high bowl down the lane towards real people and as it 'hit' them, they had to fall back into the gutter and get out of its way. There was one scene where a kid cried as the bowl came towards him. Everything was done through the camera lens. The last scene showed twenty lanes where other Grim Reapers were all bowling away, and it wasn't duplicated film; it was all through the camera."

Macdonald saw his task as making the vision big enough to support the words. "The facts about AIDS, issued by the World Health Organisation, which were almost unbelievable at the time, stayed in my head throughout the entire project. There couldn't be just one Grim Reaper, I thought, but a hundred, a thousand of them, systematically killing people from all walks of life. The biggest challenge was the Reaper himself; his form, skull, cloak, scythe, without him appearing comedic or phony. Then the performances of the actors; they had to be totally believable to pull this off. The set, which we presented in model form, had a deliberate industrial, decayed look to the finish, yet it had to be able to work as a fully functioning bowling alley. Kim Buddee solved the set, and Andy Pollard was responsible for creating the mechanics that allowed us to lower and release the real people as if they were actually bowling pins. The velocity of the giant ball striking the 'nine pin' people was a great safety concern because we were working with children and older people." If the Grim Reaper script were to appear on his desk now, Macdonald would not necessarily rely on post-effects. "As a photographer, I am a total believer in organic film making. I would take advantage of the ability to perhaps increase the number of alleyways, Grim Reapers and people, but I would fight very hard to retain the organic look of the film. There are tools out there that every director should be aware of, and I have thoroughly enjoyed the learning process and have worked with the best operators." Macdonald, formerly based in Los Angeles and now working from Marbella in Spain, believes post-effects should be a seamless part of the film.

The metaphor of the bowling alley and its AIDS victims being bowled over brought home a harrowing message. The sight of a child perishing at the hands of the Grim Reaper was an indelible image. Outrage erupted. "I actually did two scripts," admits Reynolds. "One super hard-core and one modified. We got the modified script approved all the way through, but I shot both. Then I had a one-on-one meeting with the Health Minister. In the hard-core version, people were bowled over and died. The modified version was like ten government officials had worked on it. Fortunately, he bought the hard-core version."

Nike. Wieden & Kennedy's Nike "Training" campaign won a Silver Pencil at D&AD. The *Footwork* commercial was written by Kash Sree and art directed by Linda Knight. "I started off memorising award books, so I could learn 'the language'," Sree confesses. "Then you learn how many different voices there are, you learn to do ads in different styles, and sometimes they win awards, but it's still aping, it's still derivative. Jim Riswold and Dan Wieden hate people reading award books because then you're going to do something similar. It's like anything else, once you learn the ropes you start discovering *your own voice*. So you start digging deeper, *you start digging into things that mean something to you*."

Which was precisely what happened when the Nike brief landed on his desk. "A great part of the sports market was being left unclaimed — training," explains Sree. "Nike was connected with performance, with on-the-field activity, whereas most people aren't great sports stars. At grassroots level, people train. We were trying to find a way of making training 'cool', showing the obsession that people have with sport, because when you are involved with sport you do it all the time. Luckily that comes from truths, from things that people have actually experienced. I used to be a martial artist. I was obsessed with it. So I'd be turning on light switches, flushing the toilet, doing everything with my feet so I could kick better. Chuck McBride said, yeah, that's a great idea, but we don't sell karate gear — do something for *soccer*." In *Footwork*, a teenage boy uses his foot to turn off his alarm and open his bedroom door. He deftly flushes the toilet and lowers the seat, again with his foot. In the kitchen, he channel surfs the TV with his foot and we hear the sound of a soccer game. A box of cereal tumbles from a cupboard; he chests down and juggles it with his feet before kicking it perfectly onto the table. "Chuck was a really good guide. He said, don't make heroes of these people. People are bored with heroes. Make them fallible. That's why the kid at the end is trying to feed himself with a spoon held between his toes. You can see he's got something 'wrong' with him, you can see what his obsession is."

Sree and Knight wanted the commercial to look "raw" like a

public service ad. "We didn't want to go to commercials directors. At every point we had to fight it looking like a commercial. So we went to a film director who'd only made one commercial. We tried to keep it as real as possible. We did not want to get into things that would make it look like an ad. The more disturbing it got, the better it was. We even tried to hint that it was a public service film, so it had this observational, detached, distant look to it. There were no closeups of feet coming towards you, no fancy shots, no music, always just distance and observation, which made it feel like a charity ad."

Other examples of preparation become even more extreme. A wheelchair-bound champion skier embarks on a training run through the corridors of her hospital. A man goes for an innocent training run only to be pursued and challenged by a pack of famous athletes. A boy squeezes raw steak juices onto his soccer ball so the neighbourhood dogs will become his opponents. A man is choking on his meal; Gabby Reese spikes him in the back and the piece of meat flies across the restaurant to everyone's amazement.

McBride elaborates. "There is a behavioural 'tick' that athletes have, where everything they do becomes an act of sport. The idea was training. We had to say training, and I thought that was a really inhuman way to talk to somebody. I said, why don't we engage with a language that doesn't use the word 'training'? At the time, training was a really bankrupt thought. We said training is about preparation, preparation is about being ready so the line was, *What are you getting ready for?* A lot of people looked at it and said, no, too many words. Hal Curtis and I said, no, it sums it up. We had it nice and big across the frame so I said, if you're worried about it being too many words, how about this ... how about we put it in parentheses and put it really small down in the corner? And that's what we did."

Singapore Traffic Police. The commercial that won a rare Gold at Britain's Design & Art Direction Awards and a Gold at Cannes in 1993 was the product of an art director's despair at a Singapore beer stall. Saatchi & Saatchi's Francis Wee, a self-confessed observer of life, vividly recalls what happened.

"The brief was to say, *Don't drink and drive.* But so many great commercials had been done on this subject. That was the pressure. We'd presented one direction to the client and they loved it. It used a

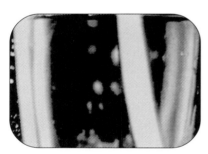

We are in a moving car, looking ahead from the driver's point-of-view.

A hand places an empty beer glass in front of us. Our view of the road and traffic ahead is no longer clear.

Another glass is placed in front of the first. Then another, and another, until our view is totally distorted.

SFX: *Skidding.*

MVO: *The problem with drinking is you don't know when to stop.*

Super end line.

MVO: *Don't drink and drive.*

Art director Francis Wee literally saw his concept through empty beer glasses. A D&AD Gold for Saatchi & Saatchi and the Singapore Traffic Police.

child, showing the accident scene, the usual stuff. They'd asked for the production cost and we were supposed to have a second meeting to go through the schedule. But we thought, maybe that commercial wasn't good enough, it was nothing refreshing, it was still going on a scare tactic, maybe there was a better, simpler idea somewhere. We'd been struggling for two weeks. It was the day before the next presentation. I'd had an early lunch, but I still couldn't get the idea, so I went downstairs to the food court. I went to the drinks stall and ordered a fruit juice. I was leaning my forehead against the table, waiting and thinking. Then I lifted my eyes, and there were these empty beer glasses in front of me, they hadn't been cleared away yet, they were still dirty, and I just saw blurred images through them. And I said, that's it, man. And I just knew, the more glasses I put in front of me, the more blurred the images would be."

Wee recalls having goose bumps. "I knew you couldn't use the same idea for something else — *it could only be used for drunk driving.* So I knew it was relevant *and* original. But I didn't know it would go as far as it did." He drew up a thumbnail storyboard and discussed it with his writer Dean Turney and creative director Linda Locke. "*I've always believed in being observant of life.* I love sitting around watching people, looking at the things they do, talking to all sorts of people regardless of their levels. You never know what you can learn from them…"

The client appreciated the agency's efforts; the new idea was not only better, but also cheaper to produce. Ace director Larry Shiu from Hong Kong's Shooting Gallery agreed to tackle the job; a jeep-mounted camera shot the traffic scenes, while the beer-smeared glasses were filmed against black in the studio. Video Headquarters Singapore provided post-production. Traffic authorities in fifteen countries have since screened the commercial.

It took Wee two weeks to recover from the news of his D&AD Gold Pencil. Ironically, it was the year when Wieden & Kennedy's Black Star Beer campaign, at the opposite end of the production spectrum, also won Gold.

5.   Work outside your tendency

Gary Goldsmith of Lowe Lintas & Partners US developed a theory

Famous movie titles begin fading in and out:

Perfect Strangers

Fatal Attraction

The Apartment

Dangerous Liaisons

Dirty Harry

Exposed

The Naked Gun

Chitty Chitty Bang Bang

The Black Hole

Breathless

Tremors

The Verdict

Dying Young

The Fool

Sleeping With The Enemy

The End

End graphic: *Wearing a condom can protect you from AIDS and other STDs.*

Two art directors working outside their tendency communicate AIDS with words in Dirty Harry. *Eddie Wong and Wilton Boey for Action for AIDS, Singapore.*

that people should do the opposite to what they would normally do creatively.

Action for AIDS, Singapore. Two young art directors, Eddie Wong and Wilton Boey, did precisely that. They set out to prove that they could communicate a message using words rather than visuals. "Everyone had seen thousands of AIDS commercials," recalls Wong. "At that stage, visuals were the trend. We started off thinking of visuals, too, but instead of going the obvious route as art directors, we thought words would be new for us."

The result was *Dirty Harry*, in which a series of famous movie titles faded in and out. "Only words appeared on the screen. We had in mind that whatever movies we picked out, right from the start to the end, the names had to tell a story. So we started short-listing potential names. It was a lot of discipline on our side, to throw out some really funny movie titles." The commercial ran in cinema and on house videos in clubs and discos.

More critical decisions followed. The original plan had been to use a different typographic treatment for each movie title, and bring them on with different executional techniques — fading on, popping off. "After a long time, we decided simplicity was the route to go. We kept with just one typeface, Franklin Gothic, and one typesize; back to basics, get the message across. Another big decision was just to fade the titles on and off. Minimise the art direction. The words became the visual to communicate the idea. We were originally thinking of using sound effects to go with the visual treatment, but when we settled on fading in and out, we knew there shouldn't be much in the way of sound effects." Wong and Boey opted for sound design, something rhythmic that would underscore the sequence of titles without intruding. "We had to be very disciplined with the music as well. Never let the music kill your concept..."

The decision to keep it simple paid off. The client, Dr Roy Chan, had never before seen a commercial communicating the AIDS subject in words alone. And neither had the judges at Britain's Design and Art Direction awards.

6.   Free-associate

It has been said that creativity occurs when ideas intersect; when two thoughts that first appeared to have nothing in common are connected to make something that did not exist before.

American Tourister. The gorilla hurling a suitcase around in his cage is still rated one of the world's five greatest landmark commercials. Roy Grace created it by free-associating.

"The client said we have this really strong suitcase nobody knows about, what can we do? And for years they'd always wanted to say they had a beautiful suitcase. My biggest battle with them always was, you can't *say* that you're beautiful. Either you're beautiful or you're not. People will think you're beautiful if you *are* beautiful." How could the agency demonstrate that American Tourister had a strong, beautiful suitcase that kept clothes neat and tidy and protected the contents from breakage? How could beauty coexist with brawn? "I was in the shower one morning and I thought to myself, we'll throw it into the cage of a gorilla. Well, easier said than done!"

Grace soon discovered that gorillas didn't grow on trees. "Even back then, they were protected. We wound up going to Mexico City. It wasn't a gorilla, it was something called a king chimpanzee. It was very large and totally unco-operative. It didn't look at the storyboard. It didn't know that my life was depending on it."

American Tourister was a pet account of Mac Dane, the second D in DDB. He had told Grace, if you don't come back with a commercial, don't come back. "We threw the suitcase into the cage and the gorilla couldn't care less. Whatever we did, we put food in it, we rubbed it with the scent of a female chimpanzee, he just wasn't interested. My voice was getting to a higher and higher pitch. And then someone mentioned that the chimpanzee was an ex-circus monkey and loved crowds and his name was Oofie. So we started chanting his name, Oo-fie, Oo-fie. Show business! He came to life for truly eighty-five minutes and we got five minutes of film." What Grace called a "magical piece of editing" created one of America's best-loved 30-second commercials, a patchwork of tiny intercuts and shots strategically printed in reverse.

While the gorilla hurls the suitcase around the cage, pounding it, jumping on it, smashing it against the bars, the voice-over irreverently addresses the message not to the consumer, but to those who will handle the consumer's luggage:

"Dear clumsy bellboys, brutal cab drivers, careless doormen, ruthless porters, and all butterfingered luggage handlers all over the world, have we got a suitcase for you..."

American Tourister made history not only for its creativity, but also for its media buy. "It was one of the first 30-second-only buys for an advertiser on television and the first 30-second commercial I ever did," Grace recalls. "Nobody at Doyle Dane Bernbach ever wanted to work on 30s. What we did at that time were 60-second commercials; the 30s were 'lifts' from the 60s. All you cared about was your 60." American Tourister helped define the potential of the new, shorter commercial. "What was happening then, the 60s were the great dialogue commercials, the little stories, the mini films, and I had an understanding that you *couldn't* do the same thing in a 30. They just didn't work as well. You couldn't milk an expression, nor have as many lines, they all had to be edited. So the 30 had to be a more graphic concept. It was more like a poster. It was stripping away the dialogue, doing more of a demonstration type commercial, and it worked."

Volkswagen. "Whatever product or area you're working, the ideas are always better when they're relevant ideas." Roy Grace describes the genesis of *Funeral*, ranked one of the three best commercials of all time. "We owed the client two commercials and the reason we were way behind showing them anything, we didn't have any ideas, or any ideas that were deemed worthy. And that's always a problem. I was away for the weekend. We had a little place up at Woodstock, New York. I came back early because I wanted to work on this thing. I often would try and work on the drive back, just sort of free-associate with things, and as I drove down this parkway, a funeral cortege was coming the other way. And my wife said to me, if that is not the worst idea I have ever seen for a car commercial, I don't know what is. And I said to her, then it must be a really *good* idea and some way or another I'm going to work something out with a funeral and a Volkswagen in it. *It just seemed like the wrong thing to do!*"

Grace had started work, in this instance, without a proposition. "Sometimes I believe you have to approach an idea from a different

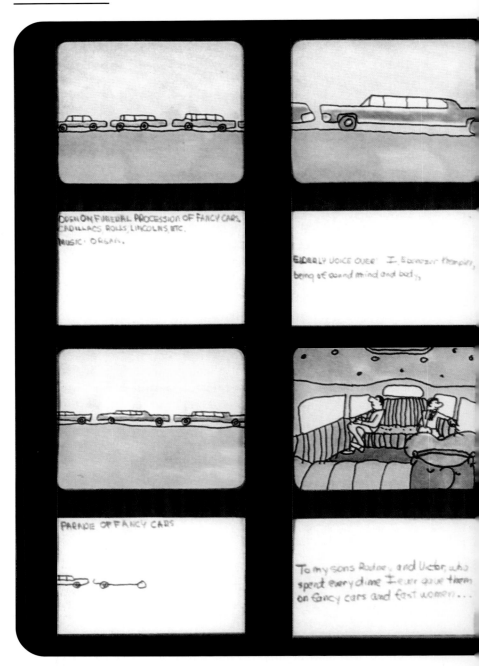

Doyle Dane Bernbach, 1969. Job No. VWSB 95321. Roy Grace's original storyboard for Volkswagen Funeral, *ranked as one of the three best commercials of all time.*

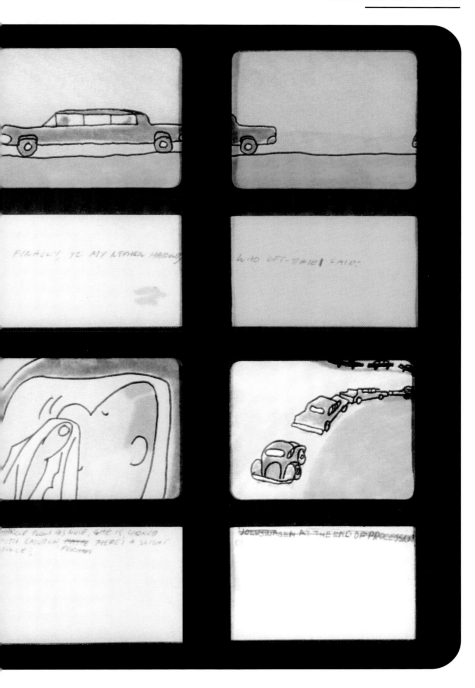

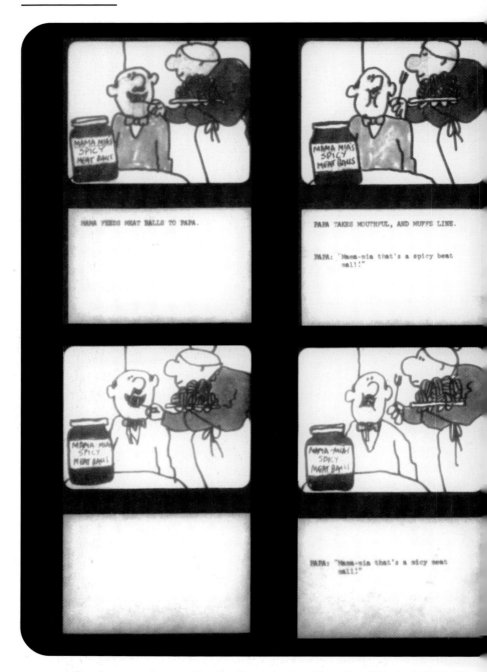

Opening scenes from another Roy Grace classic at Doyle Dane Bernbach, 1970. The original storyboard for Alka-Seltzer Spicy Meatball.

angle. Sometimes when you're approaching something from a purely logical angle, and you're not getting anywhere, it's because you're being *too literal* about getting to your final destination and there are *too many barriers.* So you have to come at it differently. You have to abandon the logic, and just sort of free-associate — and that's what I also mean by relevancy — *by finding parallel worlds and introducing the logic to them.* For me, the funeral was a parallel world. How do I introduce logic to it? How do I introduce the traditional Volkswagen story of economy? It became apparent to me, when I saw this funeral cortege with that line-up of Cadillac limousines, one after another, that someone in a Volkswagen would really be out of place in that. But then I thought, the reason he's driving in a Volkswagen is because he is the person who is loyal and faithful to this concept of economy. *Or, is he...?* Was he really just being manipulative to impress his uncle because he was a multi-billionaire? So I started trying to weave a story from the back end rather than from the front end, and the pieces started to fit, and the reason they did was because it was a parallel world; it was cars, and you could fit a car in to a funeral. But it wouldn't have worked for a candy bar, because candy bars have nothing to do with funerals..."

In the commercial, Grace opens on a cortege of big limousines, cutting to glimpses of their occupants as a rich man's will is read aloud:

"I, Max E. Mably, being of sound mind and body, do hereby bequeath the following: To my wife, Rose, who spent money like there was no tomorrow, I leave one hundred dollars and a calendar. To my sons, Rodney and Victor, who spent every dime I ever gave them on fancy cars and fast women, I leave fifty dollars ... in dimes. To my business partner, Jules, whose only motto was 'Spend! Spend! Spend!', I leave Nothing! Nothing! Nothing!"

At the tail end of the cortege we discover a sober, respectful young man driving a lone Volkswagen.

"Finally, to my nephew, Harold, who oft-times said, 'A penny saved is a penny earned', and who also oft-times said, 'Gee, Uncle Max, it sure pays to own a Volkswagen', I leave my entire fortune of one hundred billion dollars."

Grace is a firm believer that any ingredient of *irreverence* in communication really makes people pay attention, wins their favour and amuses them. "Everyone likes to see you take a poke at the establishment. So I worked this all out in my head, and I worked out virtually all the copy, and I got home and scribbled it down. I was so excited about the idea, I did not have the guts to present it to the client because I thought it was too controversial. You don't fool around with funerals. Nor did I know that the client's brother had just died and he had gone to the funeral that previous week. But the client bought it. And that's the difference in the world today. You didn't have to sell those things; they bought them."

It seems the only thing that changed along the way was the billionaire's name. In Grace's drawn storyboard he was Ebenezer Krempler. In subsequent references he became Maxwell E. Snavely and then Max E. Mably.

7.   Create fiction and film it

"Joe Pytka once said that a lot of our work is of the style of creating a fictional event, or pretending something is real, and filming it." Stacy Wall excludes the fad for making mockumentaries. "It's all about *appropriation*. But you don't just appropriate one thing, you appropriate about four things, then mesh them together to create something that potentially masquerades to be something original."

Wall has always been fascinated by the notion of telling a fictional story as truth. *Zelig* and *Spinal Tap* are two of his favourite movies. "I grew up watching tons of TV. I can remember characters from shows like *The Andy Griffith Show*. I'm still a huge fan of those things. I just hope that no one else is paying as much close attention as I am, then I bring it all back here and cobble it together."

As Wall frankly admits: "Everything that I've done that's been successful has definitely been inspired and influenced by something very concrete. I've never been afraid to say it because I don't think that what we create here is on the level of an artist or a filmmaker who is really putting themselves on the line and creating a work of art. Our work has an agenda, though there are elements of artistry in it."

Black Star Beer. "From the time we got briefed to the time we finished was an entire year. I didn't work on anything else for a year.

When I look back on it I think, why was I willing to do that? That was a lot of work. Why did I do that to myself?" Wall's year was well-spent. An elusive Gold Pencil at D&AD brought some compensation for him, art director Larry Frey and Australian film director Alex Proyas.

"From day one, the client wanted something really interesting and different so that gives you confidence. We went in with a presentation that initially wasn't about scripts at all. It was about a very marketing driven premise that I knew would be attractive to him. He was trying to create a premium beer. He wasn't going to be like a little micro beer. He wanted to go up against Budweiser, Coors and Miller. At the meeting I asked him, what did they have that we don't? He said, a lot of things. And I said, well, one of the main things they have is a *heritage*. We showed him their bottles. 'Brewed since 1898…' That's something that they have which we won't have because we were born in 1993. So I said, *let's create a heritage*. That will, in turn, not only mock the idea that you need to have one, but also play around with people's perceptions. They'll go, *was* Black Star around a long time ago?"

Wall then took the client through a series of *what if* scenarios. "*What if* the commercials were literally mini-documentaries on the history of the company?" Each new scenario ensured the brand would have a life beyond television. "In Portland, I used to walk to work. I'd pass by all these old warehouse buildings, and they had the remnants of painted billboards on their facades. You could barely read them, they were all degraded, but you could see they used to be ads for a tyre manufacturer or something. So we said *what if* we buy some old walls in Seattle, which was going to be our test market, paint them with Black Star ads, and then sandblast them so they look like they're aged. And — I'm embarrassed about this because it's 'advertising as litter' — *what if* we put bottle caps through an acid bath so they rusted. Then during the night we could scatter them in the corners of parking lots so people would find them and think, oh, it's an old Black Star Beer cap. That's how we got him into it, so by the fifth or sixth meeting we said, you're into this, you think it's fun, so let's show you exactly what we think a script would be like…"

ESPN. "We needed to sell WNBA games on ESPN, so we created a band and pretended it was real. All their songs were about the WNBA. They were obsessed with the WNBA. They were called 'The WNBAs'. We did a campaign the first year that was them just in their rehearsal rooms singing songs. It was so popular the next year we did a concert."

Wall has always been fascinated with documentaries and archival films. "We did this thing for ESPN in 1998 where we imagined that these old films of Ty Cobb, the baseball player from the 20s, were found in a barn somewhere. Somehow we stumbled upon these films where he was being interviewed about what he thought was going to happen to the game of baseball at the end of the century."

8.   Ask what if...

Horace Walpole wrote about *serendipity*: "the facility of making happy chance discoveries". Advertising rarely permits creativity to happen by chance; the discoveries are mostly driven by sharply honed creative methodologies.

Any time a creative team presents ideas to Stacy Wall and Michael Prieve and their opening phrase is "Open on a shot of..." they're dead, says Wall.

"You see a lot of stuff like that. 'Open on a tight shot of a clock, we pan over to reveal a man...' That commercial is not going to be good. It is not a big enough idea if the only way you can talk about it is to talk about it in a storyboard. It doesn't have any resonance and life beyond itself."

Nike. Wall demonstrates the *"What if..."* approach. "*What if* there was a sitcom on TV about college basketball... The idea can be summed up in about two sentences and opens up a world of things."

Another famous example: "*What if* there was a barbershop where all the Nike basketball players hung out and talked and joked, and as a fan our consumer would love to be a fly on the wall in that room and hear what it's like to be a professional basketball player. And Nike said, what are the scripts? And we said, we don't know, because we're going to put professional basketball players in a room and let them go. And then we got down to how we wanted it to feel, how we wanted to film it, what the music would be like; we wanted it influenced by James Brown and early soul and R&B because that was the vibe we wanted. All those choices were made along the way."

Wall and Prieve talk about the power of evolution.

"We encourage our people to work with really great, interesting people," Prieve says. "You've got to see where ideas go. The worst thing is when you hire a director and you already know what you're going to get before you even shoot."

"And that's what's so hard," observes Wall. "Because this is a business where you're supposed to justify every decision. Everybody needs to know exactly what you're going to do because you're going to spend a lot of money doing it."

9. Is the medium the message?

Sometimes, the best way to hijack the commercial break is to hijack the medium itself. Howell Henry Chaldecott Lury screened two opposing views of its client First Direct, *Optimistic* and *Pessimistic*, on two different channels simultaneously. The characters in a British Airways cinema commercial had an "argument" with an actress planted in the audience.

Toyota Landcruiser. It was Australia's first 3-minute 'roadblock' television commercial. It ran once, on every commercial network in Australia, at exactly the same time — Sunday night movie time. "Viewers simply assumed it *was* the movie, until the twist at the end and the Toyota logo appeared," recalls Newman.

"It was the launch of the first all-new Landcruiser model in ten years, a generational change, and Toyota wanted everything about the new vehicle in the commercial; even the Australia-wide 200-plus dealer network had to be mentioned. He wanted it to be bigger than *Ben Hur* — so we gave him *Lawrence of Arabia!*" The territory they wanted to own, says Newman, was the feeling of security you get in a Landcruiser because you know you'll come back alive from wherever you're crazy enough to go.

The idea was to painstakingly shoot a frame-by-frame remake of the famous rescue scene from David Lean's classic film, the only difference being that the Lawrence character returns with his friend in a Landcruiser rather than on camelback. The brochure-like list of features that the client had made mandatory were disguised as movie credits. Newman wrote the commercial. Bob Isherwood, now

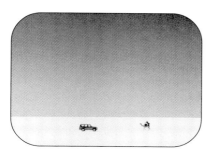

It seems we are watching the movie *Lawrence of Arabia*...

The familiar theme music is playing as we watch the famous rescue scene in the vast expanse of the Arabian desert...

Only *this* time the hero is crossing the desert in a new Toyota Landcruiser.

The dramatic 3-minute remake reaches its climax, the music swells up to the heroic crescendo and the product features roll like movie credits.

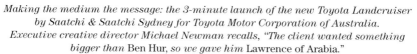

Making the medium the message: the 3-minute launch of the new Toyota Landcruiser by Saatchi & Saatchi Sydney for Toyota Motor Corporation of Australia. Executive creative director Michael Newman recalls, "The client wanted something bigger than Ben Hur, *so we gave him* Lawrence of Arabia."

A film leader starts counting down…

10, 9, 8, 7…

An eclipse begins to happen…

6, 5, 4…

Eventually all that is left of the film leader is the shape of a crescent moon.

End graphic: *Epson Moonlight Cinema. Starts soon.*

Using the conventions of the medium to communicate the message. A typical film leader sustains attention as it is progressively turned into a moon. A very simple and effective idea from Whybin TBWA & Partners Melbourne.

Saatchi & Saatchi's worldwide creative director, art directed it. "Director David Denneen, with Jeff Darling as DOP, captured the full filmic glory in 180 seconds of epic adventure."

Happily, says Newman, the client immediately sold out six-months' supply of Landcruisers. "A couple of years later, the ad ran again for the introduction of the faster turbo diesel model, only this time we sped up the three minutes of film into a 60-seconder, then added a voice-over which pointed out that the new Landcruiser is now *faster*."

Vidal Sassoon Hair Salon. Everyone has seen a hair caught in the gate of a cinema projector. Kes Gray turned one into an ad. "I don't know if there's ever been a simpler commercial." Gray believes structuring a commercial is "a bit like telling a joke. You wind your way in, and then you go wallop! You have to work every single moment of your film to the end, and you don't let up on the pack shot either."

Gray wrote his famous Vidal Sassoon commercial in his first two years in advertising. He was at the London agency, Masius, nicknamed the grocers of St. James, "the butt of a lot of jokes. It wasn't considered one of the elite agencies, the creative output wasn't startling, but to be honest it was a different style of agency. I grew up and spent four very happy years making mistakes at Masius. We had a brilliant creative director who put people like myself on accounts we couldn't damage too much."

Gray believes you have to try and find opportunities wherever you can. His was a cinema spot for the small, boutiquey Vidal Sassoon Salon. "I had a very simple idea for a cinema commercial. It was just a white screen and all it had was a hair flickering away. Imagine you're sitting in a cinema, the screen suddenly goes white, there's a hair that flicks and flicks and flicks, and at the end a super comes on and says *Hair*, with a little arrow, and then *Vidal Sassoon*."

A few months later, Gray and his wife were invited to go to D&AD one night. "I sat down at the table and didn't have a clue. I'd never been to D&AD before. I picked up this little booklet and Vidal Sassoon *Hair in the Gate* was in it. And I put it back down and I thought, why is my commercial in the booklet? And I looked at it again, and put it back down; I still didn't understand. Then they started to do the nominations for the categories and I suddenly realised we were up for a Pencil in the cinema category. And I couldn't speak. It was the first time in Masius history. We got pipped for the Pencil, but I didn't care. I had a Silver Nomination, I was twenty-seven, and it was the most exciting moment in my career."

10. Try word associations

Graham Fink reveals his technique to unblock creative thinking and stimulate unconventional solutions. "Say you're working on a product like lager. And you've been down all the lager routes and chatted about lager all week. Now get your partner to give you a number between one and a thousand, and say he calls out 257. Go to your dictionary and open at page 257. Go down until you find the first *noun*. Being an art director I never knew what a noun was, so I had to get a writer to help me. Say the first noun is 'frog'. So then you've got to try and fit frog and lager together. And there has to be a point where they do cross. It's just like chucking two pebbles into a river; the ripples get wider and wider until eventually the two ripples will cross. It will shake your thinking and even if it isn't right, *at least it's moved your thinking into another area...*"

11. Fill fifty boxes

It would be impossible to come up with one hundred potentially great ideas in a week, right? At Australia's OMON, and later at his own agency Andromeda, Siimon Reynolds pioneered his famous "Fifty Boxes" formula for generating creative ideas. Layout pages are ruled up into twenty squares. For each print ad or television concept they do, a creative team must fill each of their fifty boxes with a different idea. "The mission is *not* to do a great ad. The mission is to fill the page. Why is that? It's the difference between being potentially great or mediocre. If your mission is to do a great ad, you stop when you've done *one*. But if your mission is to fill the page, you might have to do another fifteen or twenty or thirty ads, and somewhere in those fifteen or twenty or thirty ads is one that's *twice* as good."

The system started, Reynolds admits, because he feared not coming up with anything. "The concept was to do so many ads that at least *one* would be good. With TV ideas, we used to write one line, like 'purple moose walks into a bar and starts eating potato crisps'. That's *all* we'd do on the ad. It's better to cover more ground in the time you've got, rather than waste time detailing out scripts. But a lot of people would waste half an hour fine-tuning a script before concluding it's not good enough. When you're only writing a few lines on the general idea, no detail, when you're not pausing to script them out, *it's not at all hard to do one hundred TV ideas*. After you've done one hundred, you then go through them over a couple of hours and choose the ones which are worth actually writing up as scripts. You could easily end up with fifteen promising commercials, whereas the old way you would have stopped at two or three."

After a few years of working to this system, asserts Reynolds, your brain will be getting very used to coming up with literally twenty ideas for an ad in sixty minutes. "So if you work three hours a day, and I don't know many copywriters or art directors who work more than four, within a week you should easily have one hundred commercials to play with. It always amazed me that our whole life was coming up with ideas, but no one had ever tried to finesse the technique of coming up with them." Reynolds estimates that he has taught this technique to over five hundred people. "There are people using it around the world; a lot of Australians have travelled and taken it with them."

Reynolds challenges the concept of the traditional creative team. "At any of the agencies where I've been involved, the writers have worked by themselves. There's a lot to be said for having teams, but there is also a lot of politics in them. Ideas are let through that aren't the best because you think it's about time the 'other person' got a shot at it. Talking things through produces pressure so that one of you will crack it, but *the real canvas of creation is silence* so your higher self can find something out there in the ether. You think you need two people so you can mix and match ideas, whereas you can mix and match with yourself."

12. Use the Adrian Holmes Swiss Army Knife

Holmes describes them as "mechanisms": five different idea types which creative teams can apply to any problem. "It's a bit like having

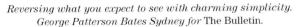

A newspaper delivery boy cycles down a leafy suburban street. But instead of throwing newspapers, he's catching them.

Boy: *Thanks...thanks...thank you...thanks...thank you...*

We see one of the boy's customers tossing back his paper, and then settling down to read his copy of the weekly newsmagazine, *The Bulletin.*

MVO: The Bulletin. *It's all you need to read.*

Reversing what you expect to see with charming simplicity. George Patterson Bates Sydney for The Bulletin.

a Swiss Army knife," says Holmes. "They are formulae for thinking, but not for thinking of formulaic ideas."

Reversal. "You would simply ask: what would the reverse of this proposition be?" For example, a perfect family would be an imperfect family. "Alan Waldie wrote a commercial in the Heineken *Refreshes the Parts* campaign called *Water in Majorca*. It featured an upper class English girl trying to learn to speak Cockney, which is a complete reverse of the *My Fair Lady* scenario where Eliza Doolittle, the Cockney girl, was trying to learn how to speak posh." Holmes says that if you get reversibility as a habit in your head it can be very useful. "You can just turn things upside down and see what happens."

Collision. "What's the most unlikely thing that we can put this up against to see what would happen? The Fiat Strada commercial takes automated car manufacture and makes it collide with Italian opera." Further collision occurs in the end line. How can something be *handmade* by a *robot*?

Snowball. "You take some small fact from the brief and you say how can we dramatise that? How can we make that bigger and bigger and *bigger*? How big will that little fact go?" Holmes uses the British Airways *Manhattan* commercial as an example, in which the island of Manhattan is seen flying above Britain. "I'm guessing, but for the sake of argument, let's say that it said in the brief that as an illustration of the number of passengers British Airways carries on that route, we actually bring over from America to Europe more people than live in Manhattan. It's just a supposition, but one could have said, well, that's an interesting fact, so British Airways is like bringing over the population of Manhattan, and then some little magic jump occurred and — let's bring over Manhattan. That's the snowball mechanism at work. That's why creative people have those kinds of brains that are looking for patterns and connections, that sort of playfulness and irreverence." That permission to go mad is essential to nurture the creative mindset, insists Holmes.

Ambush. "Set something up; lead the viewer to think something, and then at the end catch them out. There's John Webster's commercial for *The Guardian*, where a man is apparently being attacked by a skinhead, and not until the end do you see that the

A teenage boy looks over the hedge in an upscale street.

We follow his rather nervous progress up the drive towards a magnificent house.

This is where his friend Bradley lives. He sounds the doorbell.

A very attractive woman opens the door and greets him.

Bradley's mum: *Oh, hi. You've just missed Bradley. He's out playing football.*

The boy: *But I... didn't exactly come to see Bradley.*

Female VO: *Mill Creek's Age Defiant Skin Preservation System. Could you do with looking younger?*

Shades of The Graduate. *Mad Dogs & Englishmen New York busts the category with a new way of selling younger looking skin for client Mill Creek. The older woman-younger man relationship is a totally unexpected ambush.*

skinhead is actually trying to push the man out of the way of some falling material. There's a Volkswagen spot, where there's just a single shot of a man standing next to a very old VW Polo and the voice-over says, *After many, many years and many, many miles, time finally takes its toll.* And the man disappears, leaving the car. You would have expected the car to go because it was an old VW." Another ambush spot showed a handsome young man going to confession. The priest sniffs and asks if he is wearing Tuscany; when the young man says he is, the priest says, well, I'm not surprised you've sinned.

Lateral Leap. "That's where some other form of description or set of circumstances is used to describe what you want to describe." He quotes a commercial for French Railways. The brief was that French trains always run on time. "It was a charming commercial of a little guy who opens the level crossing gates in the countryside. As he closes the gates and a train goes past, he shouts to his wife, 'That's the 10.23', and you see his wife put some boiled eggs on the stove. Then another train goes the other way and he calls, 'That's the 10.30, you can take the eggs out now'. They've used the boiling of eggs to demonstrate the punctuality of trains." Another example Holmes gives is the Chevys *Fresh Mex* concept where the commercials were made as fresh as the food. The technique, he says, was in the service of the idea.

13. Have a hectic halfhour

When Mather was creative director at Saatchi & Saatchi Sydney, he instituted the Hectic Halfhour every Tuesday morning. "Actually it went for about an hour. We got all the briefs that no one wanted to do, all those jobs that just hang around in an agency. Then all the people in the creative department would come in and everyone had one minute on each ad. It was fun, and it turned it into a game. It achieved a lot; all the ads would get done, and 70% to 80% of them were quite good. And it took away any of that preciousness of people trying to hold onto ideas. I could say to someone, no, that's a bit ordinary. The worst thing is you get a bad idea and if no one kills it at birth it starts to grow, and before you know it, the client has seen it and you've got this monster."

How To Evaluate Creative Work

"We don't necessarily evaluate it against the brief," says Jon Steel. "The advertising may well be — and should be — better and more expansive than the brief." Steel evaluates by instinct, "and against some knowledge of the target and the client, against the objectives, and against our own standards of creativity."

"If you can't phone it over, as someone once said, then it probably isn't a good idea." Hegarty believes simplicity is key to a good television idea. "*Weak ideas, complicated ideas, don't give the director space to direct.* We've made mistakes in our spots. When we made the Levi's commercial based on *Cinderella*, it was good, it was nice, and Tarsem shot it. But in a sense — because he had such a complicated story to tell, and although he told it very well — it really didn't give him a chance to breathe and let the idea spread. It didn't allow him the ability to be the director he could be. He just literally had to tell the story. Whereas if I say, a man jumps in and out of swimming pools and at the end of it, it says *The more you wash them the better they get*, that's the idea. You should be able to write the idea down, in one paragraph, *if not in one sentence*."

According to Holmes: "The best test of a commercial is to be able to say, it's the one where — " You should be able to describe in the next seven to ten words what happens, Holmes stresses. "Telephone-it-over, as we say. For some people, a commercial is all about mood and look. This company, Lowe's, believes that it is the concept at the heart of it that matters."

Droga does not accept ideas in script form. His department has to present synopses. "We all suffer from overwriting. I want to see just a paragraph to start with, and then I can be sure there's an idea in it. England is rich with directors and production companies; it's so easy to get lost in the technique that surrounds a commercial."

"It's much easier to judge someone else's work than your own." Sinha talks about the integrity of the message. "Most of the commercials you look at, you cannot respect because you see absolutely through them with this cynical, 3D, X-ray vision of the consumer. It's like shining a pitiless white light on this carefully arranged facade which the agency and the client erected."

Dawson takes a lot of notice of good account service people. "I think when they're judging creative work, a bright one can usually be better than anyone else in the agency because they come at it with more objectivity than anyone else. They can judge it for its correctness as well as its creativity. A creative person judging other people's creative work is often coloured by their own way of doing it."

"If you want to write a good TV script, get yourself a big pad." In Gray's experience, a lot of screwed up paper will need to hit the bin. "I worry my scripts to death. I work and rework the structure. I direct them in my head when I'm writing them. I play casting director and sound engineer. I listen to the rhythms of the dialogue. I work and rework the timing. I lose sleep over the pack shot, too. I try to give my scripts balance, but above all I try to keep things simple. Cut them to the bone."

"Brahms once said that writing music is easy; what is hard is knowing which notes to use and which to let fall to the ground." Newman shares Gray's bin theory. "You have to get all the more obvious answers out of your system quickly and get to the natural yet unexpected one. The river of truth, someone called it."

Godfrey also warns against being trapped in the narrow vision of one idea. "One of the problems with film is that once you think you've got a reasonable idea, you tend not to be able to pull yourself out of it and go on to something else. One of the strengths in creating an idea is being able to say, we've gone down this line and we've tried damned hard but we just haven't achieved it; we've just got to do a lateral jump and do it in another way. It sounds like an easy process to do, but it's actually an extremely difficult one." There are also the times when you think you've got a fantastic idea, but you can't make it work. "Very often there is a way of making it work and it may take a long time to do. I always found it was best to have an intense period where you throw ideas at each other, and then you say, let's work on this one and that one, and then walk away from it and allow yourself a bit of time to do that."

Prieve talks about the internal creative validation process at Wieden & Kennedy. The agency started in 1982. "Dan Wieden truly still believes that what matters is good work. So most people in the creative department are still trying to prove themselves through the work, and not through how much money they make. People are ultimately validated by the ads they make. There's still a sense of pride in the craftsmanship. There is not another agency that can lay down a reel or print work, ad for ad, like we can. Maybe there's another agency that can show you twenty good ads. But can they show you thirty? Can they show you fifty? Can they show you a *hundred*?"

Wall also questions the external validation process. "For all the awards that we've won, there's almost an assumption here that if you win an award you didn't go far enough. What we should *really* be doing is stuff that even people out there don't know what to do with; stuff that doesn't necessarily fall into the box, stuff that doesn't fit into the current standard of what is creative award-winning work. We're doing a commercial with Michael Jordan and in this day and age, when everything seems to be sarcastic, or ironic, or post-sarcastic, or post-ironic-sarcastic, we're trying to be incredibly sincere. And that in itself is going to be different. It seems like an odd world when sincerity in an ad is the new trick."

Can some ideas be in advance of themselves? Can they be so different, so far ahead, that people can't recognise and accept them at the time?

"Most of the advertising industry has not defined the difference between Good and New," agrees Reynolds, rationalising: "They applaud Good, but what is so much harder to do is New, and New is virtually never applauded until it has been around long enough to become just Good. Take the first few years of Howell Henry. People didn't recognise them. Award shows only recognise the Good because there's an evening-out process. Half the jury will vote ten out of ten for a brilliant, totally New piece of work, while the other half of the jury will give it zero. So the Good piece of work that everyone gave seven will win the Gong, and it will be like that forever. It's not a bad thing. Even if some great ads are never recognised, enough people will see them and get on the shoulders of those ads and do better work. Hegarty said a very interesting thing when he was asked if award shows were accurate. He said collectively they are, but individually they aren't. If at one award show your ad wins no award, it's no indication that it's not brilliant.

If over six or seven award shows it wins nothing, then that begins to be an indication. But, as we all know, there's fear. A lot of jurors, particularly new jurors, don't trust their own opinions. Someone might see a Levi's ad, done by another nation, and they'll presume it's Bartle Bogle Hegarty and they'll award it. Or a mediocre *Economist* ad wins an award on the back of jurors assuming Abbott Mead Vickers did it, but it actually came from somewhere else."

FEAR of failure can hold back creative ideas.

"Just keep being willing to make mistakes," insists Riswold. "If you wake up every morning and think, I've got to be different, you'll fail. It's just advertising. That's all it is." Riswold also talks about awards. "Years ago, awards allowed people to see integrity and merit in doing something good in this industry. You could achieve something artistic that sold something at the same time. Awards at that point defined something bigger and attracted people to the industry because you always heard that joke about the person who writes in to Dear Abby, 'My sister is a serial killer, my dad's a rapist, my mother's a bank robber, my brother is in advertising; I have a question — what should I do about my brother in advertising?' Today, there's just too much of it. And we should never broadcast them on television." The salaries paid in the business astound Riswold. "My wife is a nurse. She does something that is actually very important and we just sell trinkets."

Patti, too, addresses fear; especially working on an account with a heritage of great work. "Any time you get a brief, you sit down and put your head in your hands and say, we're never going to come up with an idea that will come anywhere close to anything that's been already done. People think it's the greatest assignment in the world. In many ways it's the most terrifying. My partner Don Schneider and I like to work weekends. During the week there are lots of things going on, there's a lot of noise. We figure if you're giving up your weekend time, you'd better walk out of the office on Saturday night with *something*. I don't believe anyone ever writes a great spot at home, or on a plane, or sitting by the pool at the Four Seasons. We have to be in the office, staring at each other, begging the other guy to come up with the idea. We have to tell each other we stink, that we're never going to come up with another idea, that we might as well throw all our awards out the window because next year we'll be working on ads for anal pads. We don't work alone. It's much better when you're working with somebody who is as scared as you are that you won't get it right, because you feed off each other." Is it fear of failure or hunger for success? Patti says it's both. "You're always successful the year before, but you start out every year a failure. You see yourself in a meeting with nothing." Patti references award annuals and reels of work that he admires. "You see how a team in Great Britain handled something and you think, it *can* be done."

BUT in the moment of creation, how do you know if you've come up with something great?

"Anyone knows when they've done something great," says Webster. "You just know. There are times, occasionally, when you hit it. There's a glow inside you. Instinct plays a huge part. You don't have to ask anyone. I find if I have to ask someone what do you think of this, then there might be something in it but it's not great. It's the hardest thing in the world to judge your own work; it's the easiest thing in the world to judge anyone else's." Webster recommends the overnight test. "Just go away, do something else, come back to it; then you'll see it like anyone else sees it the next day, because you're not involved."

Fink agrees. "You *do* know. You've just got to trust your inner self. Just sit, and think about it, and inwardly you'll know. Your unconscious *always* knows. You know when you've done something poor. You know when you've done something mediocre. And you know when you've done something really great. Of course, when you're a student and you've got a book full of ads, you think they're *all* really great. Then you go to a creative director like David Abbott, and he's flicking through the pages, and then he'll stop at an ad. And you'll know, all of a sudden, in your gut, that that is *not* a good ad, and if only he'd go on and turn the page, there's a brilliant poster. But he doesn't. He sits and talks about that ad, and *that's* the ad you've got to take out." Fink believes proper creativity and true originality only emerge when we trust our own inner selves. "And that's the most interesting bit, actually. You should always strive for greatness,

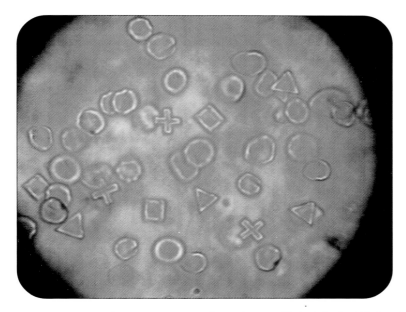

"You know when you've had a great idea," says Graham Fink of the Paul Weiland Film Company. Fink and Trevor Beattie put Sony PlayStation symbols into the blood of an obsessed user for TBWA London.

but I think the reality is, you eventually run out of time and you say, this is the best I've got, and you have to go with that and make it the best you can. There's always that compromise because of money and time. In the end, advertising is a business and you can push back all the boundaries as much as you like, and you can do the Tony Kaye thing and hijack time, but eventually you do have to commit something. There's that true greatness which you probably stumble upon from time to time, and for the rest of it, you have to be at least good."

Fink discusses a Sony PlayStation job he worked on with Trevor Beattie, TBWA London. "The idea that I had was, wouldn't it be great if you could take a blood sample from someone who was obsessed with their Sony PlayStation. And when you looked at their blood through a microscope you could see the little Sony symbols in it. And then you don't need to actually say *In the blood*, because it's obvious. When we did it, I actually went to the hospital and they took a sample of my blood. Then they prepared a little slide of it and I photographed it under a microscope. I put it in my Apple Mac and retouched it, put the Sony symbols in among the blood cells, and it's run as a TV commercial and on poster sites. Now I *knew* that was a great idea when I had it. I hadn't had an idea like that for a long time. You know when you get them because you go hot and cold…"

Fink's maxim, and his rally call for creative destruction, should be shouted from the rooftops of advertising: *Everything I know is wrong.*

Mather's maxim is equally potent: *I know nothing.* "Once you start thinking you're quite good, you're not very good. Every ad, you start again. I've been doing this since I was fifteen. I don't know where ideas come from, but you *do* get to the stage where you have an automatic filter system that goes through all the ideas in your head. That's a really good attribute to have, to know when you're doing rubbish rather than kid yourself it's pretty good."

BUT how objective can any of us be when it comes to judging our own work?

"A few years ago at Batey Ads, when Andrew Clarke was my boss, I asked him how do I get to the next level. And he said, just do stuff you don't know how to judge." Sree reviews his Nike *Footwork* commercial. "We didn't know how to judge that ad. It was interesting and quirky, and yet disturbing at the same time, which made it subversive."

Grace articulates a way to develop that skill.

"Watch a lot of television. Pick out the commercials you like and see if you can get hold of copies. Study them. Really try and analyse why you like them, why you think they work, why you think they're selling product. You should understand not only the visceral reaction to what you think is good, but intellectually dissect what you think is good. Analyse whether all these commercials had ideas of some sort, and ask is that what really provoked you? I would have a good guess that the majority of things you liked did have ideas that appealed to you emotionally, intellectually; that were provocative and made you think. I would begin to try to understand why, as humans, this is such great food for us, why this is such a joy for us as individuals. Start to look at your own endeavours and your work in the same way. Be as objective and ruthless as possible with your own work. Be your own worst enemy. The hardest thing in this business for beginners, middlers and enders is having that ruthless objectivity about what you do. That doesn't mean you're flawless. But it does mean you can look at something you've done and say, that stinks, or that's great. And when you come to the conclusion that something *is* great, it's having the courage to fight for it and also be able to articulate *why* you think it's great. *If you can't tell a client or a supervisor why it's great, maybe it's not.*"

Grace advocates total immersion in what you're doing, a real 360° understanding of *what* you're doing and *WHY* you're doing it. When Grace is asked to choose the best commercials of all time, Apple's *1984* tops his list; high praise from the man who contributed twenty-five spots to "The Hundred Best Commercials of All Time". "It was in a class by itself. The message was so important. It was a new age. The way it was directed and styled by Ridley Scott was fabulous. It was enormously effective and memorable. And when you realise it ran only *once*, the imprint it made on people was astonishing." Grace also liked a lot of the Federal Express commercials. "Truthfully, I don't like a lot of commercials that most people like. I often find the ones I like are sort of quirky and different and not necessarily in step with what everybody else likes. I saw one the other week, a low budget commercial for a movie; a couple of young kids so engrossed in talking about the movie that the girl gets late for her job as a life guard. By the time she shows up at the pool, you see two elderly people floating face down in the water. It was bizarre. It was the only movie commercial I've ever seen in this country that doesn't just merchandise film clips; it talked about the after-effects of seeing the movie and I thought that was a nice way of approaching it."

The commercial, promoting the movie *The Minus Man*, was produced by Cliff Freeman & Partners New York, creative director Cliff Freeman.

How Do You Know Which Rules To Break?

You have to understand the brand, understand the market, and understand the consumer, says Henry. "Think about a party. You're sitting next to someone at a party. Unless you like them, you can't talk to them. Why waste your best joke on someone you don't like? You have to like the people you're talking to, you have to like the brand, and then you have to have the energy to say we're *not* going to do it like it's been done before."

Henry articulates his process for communicating with a more media literate audience. "All you've got to do, in the time you've got, is engage with people in an interesting way, in a way they haven't seen before, so they end up *emotionally* in a different place from where they started. Previously, in the good old days, you would just build a logical argument in your ad. You'd start from position A, you feel like this about the brand, and logically you'd want to end the ad with people feeling differently about it. These days it's about doing that *emotionally*, not logically. *Logic is hugely overrated in advertising.* Most people in this industry cling to logic because there are large amounts of money involved." Henry sees direct parallels between advertising and the film industry. The fear syndrome cannot be discounted. "One of the best books for anyone trying to understand advertising is William Goldman's *Adventures in the Screen Trade*. You've got this whole nightmare structure in Hollywood of people who are not in their jobs for long. It matches exactly with client organisations. The average time a marketing director has in the job is eighteen months. The rule is, *nobody knows anything*. Research claims to tell you how to produce better advertising. If everyone knew how to produce better advertising, there wouldn't be an advertising industry. People would be doing it in-house all the time. So what is it that makes a difference? In great work, there is always a leap."

While Henry believes that our instincts can tell us whether something is going to work, he passionately advocates research. "I think we have to be measured by research because I know clients well enough to know they need that. The money in advertising is with the clients who have large marketing budgets. And that's where I want to work. I've never aspired to produce some five-quid charity ad that gets shown once in a corner cinema. I'm not interested in that. I'm interested in doing stuff that gets out there into the real marketplace and makes a difference. If you want to do that, you need

We spy a man drinking Tango at a bus stop.

Ralph: *Tony, a Tango taste sensation, perhaps?*

Tony: *Yes, Ralph, he's had a drink.*

The action freezes and we watch the replay. As soon as the young man lifts his Tango can, a strange Napoleon character sidles up and produces an enormous wet orange hand from under his coat.

Ralph: *Aye aye, Tony, just as I thought, there's some cheeky shenanaguns going on here.*

Tony: *Yes, it's a new look can.*

Napoleon's big orange hand wobbles all over the young man's face.

Ralph: *Wha-ho! Would you look at that...the tongue-tingling hit of Tango.*

Tony: *Yes, Ralph, little Napoleon's nipped in here and unleashed his big orange hand. Smashing...*

VO with end super: *You know when you've been Tango'd.*

"You have to do your homework to make sure you're breaking the right rules," says Steve Henry. "Engage with people in a way they haven't seen before so they end up in a different place emotionally from where they started." Howell Henry Chaldecott Lury's revolutionary campaign for Orange Tango.

to work with serious clients. And serious clients have serious boards, and they need research. *If I'm going to say to them, I'm going to advertise your product like it's never been advertised before, I need research, too.* We're working on research continually, trying to hone our research methods. It sounds really boring, but you have to get that bit right to have the fun, the enjoyment and the challenge to produce great new work. *You have to do your homework to make sure you're breaking the right rules.* Even then, there is always going to be a little corner where all the boxes *aren't* ticked, where you just *don't* know…"

4

HOW TO STRUCTURE COMMERCIALS

The legendary Hollywood screenwriter Ben Hecht considered that 90% of the success or failure of a movie lay in the writing of its script.

Nothing has changed.

"You're always trying to avoid *clichés*, you're always trying to avoid things which have been out there so long that they're devalued." Tim Delaney talks about the architecture of commercials. "Hollywood makes films, and they have titles on the front, and they show the stars quite early, and they unravel the narrative, and they come to a big end, there's an explosion of some sort, it could be emotional, and the titles come up. These are the conventions of a particular medium. I'm not worried about them. They're no different to writing a symphony with an *andante* and an *adagio*. Somehow or other, human beings have trained themselves to expect some conventions in expression. When it comes to art, people express themselves differently, and more freshly, than they do when it comes to commerce. *When you make a commercial, there is no art in it.* There is craft in it, and there is the art of persuasion in it about the position you're taking, but it's not art. Art is when somebody says I'm going to completely reframe the way you look at life via my talent, via my eyes, via my expression. We're not in that game. We don't do that. We don't reframe someone's life. We may reframe the way someone thinks about a certain brand, but that will only be within the context of other brands, and how much people will allow that brand to express itself. There is an elasticity in a brand that can snap if you take it too far away from its original core, both in personality and strategic terms…"

How does the art of persuasion come to terms with the conventions of the film medium?

"There is no formula for the curve of emotions a commercial should follow," attests Jeff Goodby. "We have made commercials for Sega in which things happen frantically throughout. We've made commercials for a restaurant here, the Velvet Turtle, in which nothing happens. It is important only that a commercial works within the time allotted for it. A 30-second TV spot that works in 35 seconds or 25 seconds, but not in 30, is a failure. This is the marvellous *haiku* that must be solved in making these things."

Nor is there a perfect formula for structuring a commercial. Matt McGrath says you cannot bolt an idea together. "That's how bad advertising is created, when every little box is ticked. You're constructing something to answer every question *except* the one in the consumer's mind: why are you showing me all this?" McGrath describes the structuring of a script with his art director as a flowing process. "It's generally done in a creative rush. It's not a really considered, slow, craftsman-like thing. It's a flash of inspiration. Suddenly it's just there."

Bill Oberlander doesn't have a formula. "I ask, does this fit for the client? Is this right for the category? Is this different to the competition? Will this really stand out on *Good Morning America*? Or will it be too standoutish? Every brand should have its own DNA code and we should subscribe to that."

"I don't have a general rule," agrees Jan van Meel. "It all depends on what makes the idea work best. The only general rule I have is that advertising should be three things: simple, original and relevant."

Michael Patti thinks in terms of total concepts. His ideas are presented in three key frames. "Once the client has bought into the concept, then we get someone like Joe Pytka involved. It's when we go to produce it that we add all the layers and textures, without consciously thinking that the first five seconds has to be this, or in the middle it has to be like this. It's more like, what do we want to end up with?" The payoff for the viewer is Patti's concern.

"Some kind of surprise should happen in a good commercial," John Webster says. "We're only talking about thirty seconds, but you need a surprise. *The end is almost the first thing you try and get right, because if you know where you're going, you can lead to it.* There is very much a rhythm to a commercial, with a beginning, a middle and an end. Of course you want to start by dragging people into it. They make a judgement very, very quickly, so you've got to hook them in somehow. I work out a storyboard in my mind; it's a bit like a symphony, I like to get the rhythm of the thing..."

Nigel Dawson agrees. "I know I've got it roughly right if I can play it as a movie in my mind." Some ideas don't play. "It may be the best idea you've ever had, but if it keeps breaking down it usually has to be abandoned. It's a pretty good test."

David Droga is increasingly suspicious of the *intrigue-intrigue-intrigue-big twist* formula. "The ultimate is to keep someone completely entertained and intrigued from *start to finish*. A lot of creative people try to display their cleverness with a twist at the end. You can't just rely on the twist, where you reveal it for two seconds and you're out. The idea should break convention from the start and *sustain* being viewed many times."

Neil French voices a similar concern about formulaic styles and structures. "Importantly, don't fall into the trap of making your ad look like an ad. The temptation is to go with the current style, or the current formula. Yes, *formula*; I didn't realise that even the best of us have one, until one day while judging the ANDYs, Spike Lee asked why all the winning ads were made to a formula. We all sat in amazement at his presumption. How dare he! And then he pointed out the formula: *situation set-up, joke, product*, and the *after-joke joke*. You could have cut the silence with a chainsaw. He was right, of course, the rascal." French muses that the two campaigns of which he is most proud did not look anything like ads. "They both worked brilliantly for the client; neither of them won any awards, which only proves that I'm right and award juries aren't."

Ken Schuldman says you can't trick people into watching. You have to do it with uniqueness and honesty, he contends. "People are just so wise, so savvy. You have all these shows on TV now about America's favourite commercials. People know about the media, about camera angles. You walk into focus groups these days and people are directing the spots. They're so savvy, I think you have to *un*savvy them. You have to get them with some refreshing honesty, but it's getting harder and harder. People are cynical. Oh, I've seen that, and I've seen that. I know it's a naughty word with some clients, but I think you have to *entertain*. People are not watching TV to see commercials." He describes great commercials as *inventions*. "Inventions are usually something that no one's done before. That's why they get patented and that's why they're original." He recalls the advent of the original Nike work. "Everybody was saying, what is this stuff? It's amazing; it's so fresh and so different. Then everybody latched on to it and everybody was doing the same. Now, Nike has gone back to simplicity, with portraits of athletes and their bruises, done to the music of the Joe Cocker song *You Are So Beautiful*. What is startling about it is its simplicity. Advertising becomes so me-too so fast."

"Sometimes, commercials are so simple people say, why didn't I think of that?" Noel Delbridge muses. As he points out, very often people walk away from the simple ideas because they seem too simple, too easy. They feel compelled to find something cleverer, which often means something *contrived*.

Commercials aren't islands, cautions Kirk Souder. "Don't conceive your commercial in the context of it existing as an island. Think about your spot as 30 seconds in the middle of a 180-second pod of other spots with the Johnson family on the other side of the screen, their itchy fingers on the remote, and Mr. Johnson dying to see a score on ESPN."

IS A 60 BETTER THAN A 30?

"There isn't an ideal length," maintains John Hegarty. "It should be as short as it can be. I think there is a great mistake in our business that length equals better, when in fact the whole driving force of advertising is about reduction. I get seriously, seriously worried if anything goes longer than sixty seconds. Rarely has anything been that good that it's been longer than sixty seconds. About the only one, I thought, was Fiat Strada, *Handmade by robots*. I thought that was outstanding. I can remember to this day watching it, and being intrigued by it, and thinking, what is this? But rarely is that the case..."

Steve Henry equates his agency's Blackcurrant Tango commercial with Fiat Strada. "Fiat Strada was a 2-minute ad. It dominated the break. If you were of that generation that saw Fiat Strada, you *had* to talk about it the next day. And I think we did something similar with Blackcurrant Tango. It broke so many rules. It was a 90-second ad that touched an emotional nerve. And it just didn't look like any ad you'd seen. It was one of the first ads that broke down the barrier between the brand and the consumer by opening the door and letting you meet, supposedly, the guy who's behind the brand. The fact that this guy was overweight, short-tempered, xenophobic was great. What you actually cherish with your friends, by and large, are their flaws, their failings and vices. And you emotionally engage with them." The British psyche engaged with the rotund "marketing manager" when he stood atop the White Cliffs of Dover, hurling abuse across the English Channel, with the Royal Air Force ready to have a go behind him. Somehow, the 90-second length was a media idea that underscored the substance, tone and humour of the creative idea. Beyond commercials, however, Henry points to a bigger issue. "Ultimately we've got to bust out of 30 seconds, we've got to start making thirty *minutes*. Programmes. Features. We even want to launch a channel for our clients."

"Almost the last frontier of television commercials is time length and weight," debates Delaney. "When you test ideas, there is no mechanism in the world — it hasn't been invented — which can tell you the impact of weight. You can't tell people in a focus group that this idea will have a million dollars spent on it, or that the same idea will have twenty million dollars spent on it. Yet the response to the one million-dollar campaign and to the twenty million-dollar

In one continuous shot, the "Tango marketing man" strips to defend Britain's honour and leads a crowd to the White Cliffs of Dover from where he hurls xenophobic abuse across the English Channel.

Ray: *Hi, I'm Ray Gardner, spokesperson for Tango. This letter is from Sebastien Loyes, a French exchange student. Sebastien says, 'I tried new Blackcurrant Tango, and didn't enjoy it as much as Tango's other flavours.' Well, Sebastien, all I can say is sorry. We've done all we can... You're an exchange student, aren't you, Sebastien? All hair gel and fancy loafers. What are your credentials, Sebastien? What drives you? When did you last get up at four in the morning for something you believed in, passionately? We don't need you, you hear. You're one dissenting voice in a billion, Johnny French... Look at us! Come on then, Sebastien! Come on! Right here, right now. You and me! Come on France! Europe! The world! I'll take you all on! I'm Ray Gardner, I drink Blackcurrant Tango! Come and get me!*

How long should a commercial be? Blackcurrant Tango ran ninety seconds — a media idea that underscored the substance, tone and humour of the creative idea. "It broke so many rules," says Steve Henry. It was also voted Best of Show at the London International Advertising Awards.

campaign will be totally different. The whole concept of testing is utterly specious for that reason alone."

Delaney reminds us that his acclaimed BBC commercial, *Perfect Day*, was a 4-minute film. "The conventions that say people sit there and watch and get hit over the head with 30-second commercials are basically outdated. Television is changing. The Internet is changing it. Thirty seconds ... *why* 30 seconds? Because the media guy says so? Because someone in 1950 said that's what the length of a film is? How stupid is that? It's like telling Shakespeare he's only allowed to write in sixty pages. It's mindless. Mindless because people don't challenge these things..." The impact of the Internet, says Delaney, has developed a new kind of audience. "Someone in America did a bit of research that said there is a sit-back audience and a sit-forward audience. We'll all become probably somewhere in between the two. We'll want to interact, so we won't slump. What it means is, people will stay longer, but they'll also browse and they'll scan. *Holding on to people will be key.*"

As the television medium becomes more fragmented, and as television viewing overlaps with the Internet, Delaney argues that the concept of 30 seconds being one where you save money and gain reach will be *less and less relevant.* "You'll still want that audience, but you'll realise that once you've got them, you've got to *keep* them. So you'll be more likely to do a 60-seconder than you are to do a 30 or a 10. In fact, you're more likely to do a 60 and a 10 than you are to do a 30. At least with a 60 you can make it stick and with the 10, you can say, hey, remember that 60? What you *won't* do is waste your time on a 30. You *won't* say, we're going to tell you something now, but we're going to truncate it all; we're going to try and pack a 60-second idea into a 30, and it won't work, and the ending won't work, so it'll be an idea that can't possibly express itself in that time. And you *won't* say it doesn't matter because the media guy says it works, because the media guy is someone who works for a media company, never been near an ad agency in his life because they're all split off, he doesn't understand advertising, he doesn't understand communication. The only thing he understands is what will tally in a computer. *That's not advertising...*"

"Painting a Picasso on a pinhead," Sean Cummins calls it. "Once, the 15-seconder was the saviour of the single-minded idea. Now we're being asked to cut down 30s to 15s, which is ridiculous."

French opts for brevity. The shorter the better, he says. "If you've got a really strong proposition, and you can punch it home in fifteen seconds, and then punch it home in fifteen seconds again later, that's better than thirty seconds or sixty seconds. If I could do the job in fifteen seconds, I'd be delighted to do so, and the client would be delighted if I could do so, too."

French discusses the parallel between writing for print and television. "If I can make my point in a press ad instantly, I will. Like Kaminomoto, for instance. Like XO Beer. But there are times when you actually have to keep someone's attention long enough to make quite difficult points. That's when you *have* to write long copy, and keep his attention from the moment you start to the moment you finish, and that is true art." Television is the same; more time is necessary … if it's necessary. " 'I'm a little teapot, short and stout' won't always work, actually."

No matter how long your commercial will be, Kes Gray talks about timing. "Writing overlength scripts is pointless and potentially disastrous. *There should be no more than sixty words in thirty seconds.* Alfredo Marcantonio once told me that 'only a fool breaks the two words per second rule'. He was right. The shoot is the wrong place to discover that a scene has to be cut or a line of dialogue lost."

How Should Your Commercial Start?

Former advertising executive and best-selling author of *The Christmas Box*, Richard Paul Evans says: "Advertising is an accidental encounter".

And perhaps television is where that encounter is more accidental, and arguably more avoidable, than anywhere else. According to conventional wisdom, we must grab the viewer's attention within the first few seconds or we are doomed.

Hegarty argues against the big-bang opening. "When I came into advertising, there was a kind of logic that that's what you did. I think it's very dangerous to do that. If you start judging things on that basis, and that becomes all-important, not the idea, you might reject something which could be incredibly powerful and which has the ability to be a very strong piece of advertising." Hegarty is always wary of formula. "You're there to create something as fresh as you possibly can, to make your brand stand out against the others. As soon as somebody says to me, you've got to start with a strong opening, well, you're just simply being like everyone else. Once formulae are established, they become very boring and people turn off from them. They're denying what it is that you're there to do."

Lionel Hunt agrees. "I think people often drift into commercials. They see one on, and they start to drift into it. Commercials have to build to the end, and not just start with a bang. Of course getting attention is important, but I'm not sure it's as important as people make out. People over the years have tried all sorts of techniques and most of them have been declared illegal. Like shooting a gun off in the first scene, a loud bang or something."

"It was a perception," affirms Francis Wee. "A lot of clients think a great impact at the opening will help get people to pay more attention to you. The *entire* commercial must be interesting, the opening scene, the middle, the end scene. Most importantly, it must be able to create some thoughts in the viewer's mind."

Marcello Serpa says the big-bang rule might have been true for a long time, but not any more. "Maybe you need a big bang if you have a boring commercial, but I don't trust that rule anymore." Serpa structures his commercials around a G-point, the pivotal moment when the surprise occurs, when all becomes clear.

"I'm not a big explosive-start sort of person," says Naresh Ramchandani. "I think starts should be intriguing. The greater requirement is to find some emotional chime somewhere along those thirty or sixty seconds where people are going to feel some sort of connection with it, some sort of complicity with it."

Arthur Bijur discusses the quiet, dignified opening scene in the Outpost.com commercials. "He's such a pleasant, grandfatherly character. He's actually fashioned a little bit after a character that appears on a television show called *Biography*. It always begins with someone sitting there, with his legs crossed, in a nice comfy chair, and he's very calm and he's talking about a person, and then you go into the biographical film about the person. When you see that in the commercial, you're expecting that kind of tonality throughout and then all the mayhem ensues." One Outpost.com commercial begins, *In an effort to get people to remember our name, we contacted the local high school marching band and asked them to help us out … and to help make this memorable, next we decided to release a pack of ravenous wolves…* "It just turned out to be a really funny kind of surprise. You don't know what's coming. It's unexpected. When that's contrasted with mayhem, the effect is that much more pronounced."

Henry argues for a "difference" more than a big bang. "I like the opening to be distinctive. I want it to look different, feel different. Is this an ad? What's going on? It could be very quiet, very still."

Cummins looks at a television commercial in terms of a window. "We are literally looking at a window when we watch television, not a window to the outside world, but a window to a television world. In the worst possible scenario, imagine there's been a noisy retail commercial in that window before your commercial, and there will be another one after yours. So let's stop. If there are lots of commercials using 60s tunes, for example, then I'll take the opposite approach, or I might use classical music, or dead silence. Format breaking is very important for me." Cummins says he conceptualises using that window mentality. "I like the theatre of TV, the stage, the window. A lot of my commercials happen left to right. Something minimal will happen in the left-hand side of the screen. Sometimes, I'll turn on the television. As soon as a commercial ends, I'll click my remote control and imagine *my* concept projected onto the screen next. That helps me to work in a real world." Cummins relishes simple, limbo, tabletop commercials. "I am never afraid of making an announcement. Strangely enough, we're seeing that a lot in research. People are so media savvy they're saying, why didn't you just tell me that, why did you have to take me on this highly brocaded experience?"

"In the age of the zapper, in the age where audiences are very disengaged from advertising or doing something on the Net, the early promise that this is going to be worth watching has to be delivered," rationalises Adrian Holmes. "But not to the extent that it distorts the way you go about doing commercials, otherwise everything turns into grab-them-by-the-throat. Likeability is an increasingly important component. Commercials are still seen often enough for people to say, oh, I like this one."

American director Bob Giraldi sees commercials in terms of movies. "Anybody who denies that is crazy. We have become a pop culture country. That's why our young people today are the best editors, not people who learned in classic film training, but who grew up on Nintendo and video games because that's the business of editing." Giraldi says viewer expectations are getting higher. "Ours is the only medium where our 'movies' are judged so quickly. The clicker has changed the pace by which our work is judged. If your work doesn't work in ten seconds, 'bye-bye'; in four seconds, 'bye-bye'. I remember when Procter & Gamble used to say, you have to say the name of the product in the first four seconds! I dare you to say 'Procter & Gamble' today on nighttime television in the first four seconds. 'Thank you, bye-bye. Next...' If you don't get me interested by something, by some man or some woman, by some story, by some colour, by *something*, you're gone!"

"I quite like intrigue, but there has to be a reason for it," explains Graham Fink from both a creator's and director's perspective. "I don't know if you have to start off with a bang, but it has to be sufficiently intriguing for them to watch the next three or four seconds. I think you could have a grey screen," he speculates, "and it looks grey for twenty seconds, and that isn't like a big bang but it *is* interesting. And you want to keep watching because you think, what's happening? And then maybe at the end of all that greyness you hear a foghorn and a ship comes through, and you realise you were in a mist."

Mike Cozens also likes intrigue up front, with the product revealed at the end. It's the best way to brand something, he says. "You try and be different with every commercial, but I think you become known for a certain style. The commercials I tend to do are fairly big blockbusters." The first time he worked with that structure was the Benson & Hedges *Swimming pool* commercial. More recently, Cozens put Carl Lewis into an odd suit and shot him running around New York. "It was a very intriguing start. He even runs across water. And you kind of pick up halfway through that the body suit he's wearing looks a bit like a tyre." It was a metaphor for a Pirelli tyre going through different situations: *Power is nothing without control.* "The reason we chose Carl Lewis was because if you think of Pirelli, you think of power, control and style, and Carl Lewis summed up all those three aspects."

Kash Sree believes people are very trigger-happy with their remotes. "It could mean doing nothing. It could mean holding still, so they think there's some kind of mistake. But you've got to get them in that first five seconds."

Antony Redman calls it seduction. "You have to convince people that this is going to be worth watching. You have to seduce them straightaway through the idea or through film technique. It may be an unusual shot, it could be casting a great character, it could be a great opening voice-over line. It's like the way the best jokes lead you one way and then hit you with the other hand." Bad advertising, on the other hand, presumes attention and tries to ram the message down the viewer's throat. "TV is very transient. Those first scenes are very important. Do whatever you can to make them stand out, but keep it relevant to the idea."

"The opening is vital." Ron Mather has worked as both an agency creative director and a film director. "We tell our clients that no one is interested in looking at their ad. Ads are unwelcome visitors. There you are on a Sunday night watching a movie and suddenly an ad comes on. You don't want to watch the ad, you want to watch the movie. Imagine going to the cinema and they stopped the film every fifteen minutes, and someone came out on the stage and started to sell you something. You wouldn't go to the cinema. But this happens every night on television. So if you're going to be a visitor in someone's house, in the middle of someone's entertainment, the opening scene is extremely important. You've got to get them in, but do it in a very clever way. I can't believe that you see so many ads that make you think, why, *why* would someone have thought that anyone would want to watch that? You can't pummel people into buying something. I don't think you sell anything anymore, *you make people want to buy.*" Think of that opening scene in terms of someone entering a room, Mather suggests. "If you like that person's personality, you are more liable to listen to what they have to say.

But if you don't like their personality, they could say anything and you won't listen to a word of it."

Mather pinpoints another issue: how commercials in the same category often open with virtually identical scenes. "Why would I want to herald that this is another ad for a particular product? I want quite the opposite. I want people to go, oh, this is interesting. *You shouldn't see communications coming.* Why not have six different ads for the same product?" Mather derides the wonderful world of advertising, where it's always sunny, everyone's handsome, all well-dressed, all live in lovely homes, nothing goes wrong. "It's like Pleasantville, it's a joke. You've got to get honest with people. You shouldn't con people, or annoy them."

French shares Mather's respect for the audience. "You don't have to whack somebody over the head. It's a bit like being a door-to-door salesman. If you arrive at the door, and throw a punch at the guy who opens the door, the likelihood is you're not going to sell him much. Basically, if you look halfway interesting for the first couple of seconds and you stick your little hand out, and you get his little hand in your hand, and you shake it, then you're cooking. Just intrigue him enough to make him *not* go away. I can't think of a great ad that started with an extraordinary thing. *Snow Plough* didn't. *Good and Evil* didn't."

Neil Godfrey argues it is very dangerous to think you have to do something dramatic to grab somebody. "Very often it's the other way round. It can start quietly. You want the viewer to be interested. If you were to relate a movie to a piece of advertising, and say had it been a piece of advertising it would have been one of the greatest, then it would have been *Twelve Angry Men*. It all takes place in one room. It is how to use film without apparently doing anything, but in fact there's a lot being done in it."

Paul Malmström considers the media environment. "I'm never worried about the first five seconds; I'm worried about the first thirty seconds, the first sixty seconds. You have a responsibility internally to be involved with what the media guys are doing. In the end, that's how your idea could get lost. You've got to be involved in every step. It's very dangerous when an idea becomes invisible."

Scott Whybin listens to what the strategy is telling him. "It's not that different to print. You're setting up the structure of the proposition. It's critical you get it right." Whybin revisits the first scene of his Dunlop Tyres *Aircraft Carrier* commercial. "When I read the research and the background strategy, it kept saying all the way through that people don't care what brand of tyres they put on their cars. It's the most boring grudge purchase in the world. So I followed that in whatever I did. In fact, that's how I got to the idea. It made me think, what would *not* make tyres boring? What would make them compelling? Well, if you were going to land a little Harrier jet on a few metres of tar in the ocean, then your tyres would stop being boring and become an absolute critical purchase. I knew the first line had to be, *You might think tyres are pretty boring...*" The result was a masterpiece of suspense as what we think is a Harrier jet descending to the deck of a rolling carrier turns out to be a family car.

Terry Bunton, Bunton Films Sydney, originally an award-winning creative director, directed the commercial for The Campaign Palace Melbourne. Bunton believes that the first scene in a television commercial is like the headline and first line in a print ad. "I still try to make the *first scene longer* than many people feel it should be, so that it gives the viewer more time to absorb what you're on about. I use it to really set up the rest of the commercial, as you would in a print ad. A lot of people, a lot of research, suggest you should get out of the first scene as quickly as you can and I disagree with that. It's a mistake a lot of people make." As Bunton sees it, television commercials don't have headlines and visuals to get people involved; therefore, the crucial first scene serves that purpose. He points to Hegarty's work for Levi's. "The first scene is usually the *only* scene; the story comes out of it. The first scene should be given the time to work effectively and make its impact on a viewer."

If Bunton is right, the viewer comes to it cold; it takes more than a nanosecond to register a new subject, a new story.

David Blackley talks about the art of storytelling and moving people emotionally in just thirty seconds. For him, the first few seconds are vital not for a big bang, but in terms of establishing the story. "It's setting up in the first four or five seconds what the situation is. It's good if you can base the situation on something that

We think a Harrier jet is about to land on an aircraft carrier.

But it's not a plane that touches down safely — it's a family car.

VO: *You might think tyres are pretty boring.*

But if you had to land a Harrier jet on an aircraft carrier 338 metres long you might think differently about the tyres you wear.

So keep your family safe. Stick with Dunlop.

End super: *Stick with Dunlop. The world's best roadholding tyres.*

How should you start a commercial? Scott Whybin listens to what the strategy is telling him. Because consumers thought tyres were a "boring" purchase, Whybin let his argument start there. Dunlop Tyres Aircraft Carrier, *directed by Terry Bunton for The Campaign Palace Melbourne.*

will get heads nodding at home. We did a very well-known commercial some years ago for Sorbent toilet tissue in which a kid's dad was locked in the toilet and the kid was busting to go. People could relate to it. You've got to set up the situation quickly, then have fun with it, and relate it back to the product."

Every frame is crucial, right from the start, argues Dion Hughes. "But the first few seconds of a spot are important for more than just grabbing attention. They also do a lot of work establishing the tone in which I'm going to talk to a viewer." Hughes believes structuring a script is different to the way we're taught to structure the body copy of a print ad. "The first line of boring copy is the last one the reader will bother with. The parallel doesn't work in TV. A boring few seconds just lets a viewer tune out, but you can get them back again just as quickly as you lost them. I suppose it's theoretically possible for the absent-minded, uncommitted TV viewer to watch any commercial in 1- or 2-second bites, with 1- or 2-second breaks in between, as they tune in and out at interesting or dull moments. The mind is the most effective remote control blocking device ever created."

Bruce Bildsten does not believe everything is won or lost in the first few seconds. "It should build, so they don't know what's coming." The composition of the opening frame, however, is very important to him.

"It's great when you can find that magic in the first scene." Harvey Marco does not believe that a commercial needs an explosive Jerry Bruckheimer beginning. "A lot of that happens *editorially*. You may do something with the music; you may do something with the dialogue or the sound." Marco looks at the standard story arc. "Something happens at the very beginning, then you go into your midsection, then into your backend. But is there a more compelling way to get people through the spot? When you make a movie, you can unfold a story slowly. When you've got only thirty or sixty seconds to unfold a story, it has to be very compelling up front to pull me into the middle. We never throw in too much layering, though I don't think that's a conscious decision."

Scott Vincent makes the idea his priority. "There should be something that holds your interest. There should be an idea to it,

Being the last lobster in the tank of a Chinese seafood restaurant is somewhat stressful.

As the commercial unfolds, the lobster darts behind a rock whenever a Chinese employee emerges from the kitchen. We hear only the Chinese restaurant ambience and underwater noises from the tank.

Just then a discreet super establishes the subject matter: *Living with stress?*

Cut to the product and end super with VO: *Executive B Stress Formula with Herbs from Blackmores. The best of health.*

"Every frame has got to earn its right to be there," says Paul Fishlock. Brown Melhuish Fishlock Sydney found a new way to demonstrate stress.

something that comes together and rewards you. *It doesn't always need to happen right in the first ten seconds.*"

"Every frame has got to earn its right to be there," insists Paul Fishlock. "In thirty seconds, you can't afford any wastage whatsoever. Every frame has to contribute, otherwise there is no place for it. It's a tough ask to tell a story well in thirty seconds without putting in something that's just some little wayward, indulgent diversion." There is only one mandatory for an opening scene, he says. "Does this look like it might be worth watching? If you start with a man in a car yard shouting, you've got a pretty good idea of what the next twenty-nine seconds are going to be."

STUDY STORY ARCS

Once, the conventional wisdom was that commercials had to tell very linear stories, to move from A to B to C in a logical manner, avoiding anything which might jar or confuse the viewer. Today, the best commercials more often than not are structured with layered stories and scenes. The texturing of stories can be quite dense — in some cases, *impenetrable*. Viewers are teased to decode scenes, rather than receive them in a crystal clear fashion. Interpretation is the viewer's responsibility.

Warren Berger recognises this more artful way of doing advertising. "We're moving away from linear, factual selling ads, which no one was paying any attention to anyway. One could lament that ads no longer provide useful consumer information, but did they ever?" Claims like "cleans brighter", Berger says, are now being replaced by unobtrusive sales messages woven seamlessly into entertaining stories. "There are people who think this is an insane way to do advertising, that it has lost touch with selling. Only a small percentage of commercials manage to pull this off, like Goodby's *got milk?* commercials. Many others have lost touch with the product. They could be commercials for anything."

"First be clear, then be clever." Too many commercials, says Holmes, have a beginning, a *muddle* and an end. "I'd welcome the return to structure and simplicity. The Volkswagen campaign is still the benchmark for clear, simple, spare storytelling. People may have their attention distracted by whizzy special effects, but in the end the classically-told story with relevance and impact will be remembered. But clarity of message has become unfashionable. I always get the impression that some people think that to be understood is somehow reprehensible. As though they were saying, how dare you understand my art…"

Holmes believes Goodby's *Aaron Burr* commercial observes the laws of good storytelling and film making as the young man who hadn't got milk struggled to say the word "Burr" after eating peanut butter. "However, a recurrent failure of creative teams is that they become over-intimate with their own concepts. They don't stand back from them; they don't go around into the auditorium and sit there in Row G and look at the idea from the perspective of somebody seeing it for the first time. The same phenomenon occurs when they're mixing the dub. You can't hear the words, but they can; because they've lived with them so long, they're crystal clear." A commercial that doesn't flow, says Holmes, is like a drawer that doesn't pull out smoothly. "If it keeps sticking, go and sandpaper it until it's absolutely effortless."

Giraldi discusses story arcs. "The first part and the ending are crucial. A 30-second arc is difficult because you always have to give about 4 seconds, 5 seconds, 6 seconds to the logo, so you're really only talking about 22- or 24-second stories. A 40-second commercial has a 30-second story arc." These days, Giraldi asserts, a 60-second commercial is much too much time to sell anything. "There aren't many products that need to be sold, or stories that need to be told, in 60 seconds. I think 30 seconds is short, but that's the kind of work I like. I like the fast beginning, the middle which just sort of lulls you, and then the instant ending that brings you back and lets you look at yourself when it's over and say, that was interesting, I can't wait to see that again."

Story compression drives Marco. "I have a tendency to over-storyboard. It's going back to ask, what are the most essential components for telling the story? Maybe you have to lose some of those great shots you've drawn, just to get into the story faster. That's always the most painful part. In the end, sometimes you do a 60-second spot, then you have to cut a 30 of it. And it works better as a 30, it arcs faster, it gets to the point faster."

"People are much more attuned to filling in a lot of the story for themselves, without you having to lay it all out for them." Warren Brown advocates making jumps in commercials to get to the story faster. "In the old days when they made a movie and they wanted to get someone from one side of the room to the other, they would film the person walking across the room. These days they cut from the person on one side of the room to the same person a millisecond later over on the other side of the room. The audience can fill in the walk in their heads."

Hegarty talks about narrative structure. "Because our Levi's work was crossing borders, we used visual narratives. What we found was that we could layer the narrative within the storytelling. It had texture to it, it had depth to it, so that when you came back to it, you realised it was telling you more than just a simple story." Deconstructing narratives is another technique borrowed from movies and books. "You've got to be a bit careful, so that in thirty or sixty seconds you're not making your communication so obtuse that in fact you're losing people. It's the old story, if you're leading somebody through the jungle, you've got to be ten yards in front of them; there's no point being a hundred yards in front of them. It's like everything in life, how far ahead am I? In deconstructing some of the dialogue and some of the narrative, you are in danger of losing the audience. But when people are into it, they are prepared to give it more time if it's interesting, and will therefore allow you to do something in a more stimulating way."

Delaney talks about shorthanding. "The skills that Hollywood utilises are now our skills. When you're compacting a story, when you're short-circuiting the messages, you don't follow the classical A to B to C, you can just cut and people go with you. You can see evidence of that in movies. The good storytellers, Tony Scott, Alan Parker, Ridley Scott, can compact a story and not leave the detail out. What we get from them is the idea that you can do a 60-second *epic*. You can do something big, you can make it awesome, and the music can turn it into a spine-tingling experience. And it's just 60 seconds. It's kind of loopy in a way…"

Cozens thinks the idea through in a direct line, A to B, then looks for ways to make it more intriguing, slightly more obscure. "It's kind of a series of clues. There's much more involvement, more reward, for the consumer. It's a much better way of branding things as well."

Narrative can be collapsed into tiny pieces of space. Andy Berlin admires the VLSI, or Very Large-Scale Integration of narrative used by John Milius and Oliver Stone in their screenplay for *Conan the Barbarian*. "When I worked for Hal Riney at Ogilvy, I saw him make narrative possible in 60 seconds. Real narrative. At Goodby's, we used the same fundamental ideas that Hal had used, but making a much more radical compression. If you are ambitious in the emotional content of advertising, then you have to compress narrative. The compression rate of advertising's narrative influenced the cinema. The first time I saw *Raiders of the Lost Ark*, I thought it was like a series of 60-second commercials." Berlin advocates purely visual techniques to replace any sort of verbal exposition. "If you can do an ad without any exposition, it will be a good ad. *Exposition kills stuff.*"

"Making commercials complicated to follow makes them interesting to see over and over and over again." Chuck McBride takes simple storylines, then layers and complicates them. He believes in building a more complicated puzzle, every element still directing people to the end, but meandering such that it keeps them wondering what the next frame might be. "After ESPN at Wieden & Kennedy, which was a very television-fluent agency, I'd seen what good television could be like. All I wanted to do was layer. ESPN was all about innuendo and metaphor." McBride quotes his friend Spike Jonze. "He tries to find a way to make sure the next frame isn't necessarily an extension of the frame right before it. It's actually trying to do something that's different to where you thought he might have been headed. It's a bunch of cues and miscues." McBride gives his characters a back story, communicated visually not verbally. Providing them with a past gives them more depth, more reality; they are not the usual one-dimensional stereotypes seen in the average commercial. The young man with the peanut butter sandwich in *Aaron Burr* demonstrates the principle of a character having a life of its own *before and beyond* the commercial. "Because the Aaron Burr storyline was simple, adding things was excellent. But nothing was verbal. Now, that language has become so adopted by so many

people that it's become the new Sedelmaier. The way to get people to laugh came to be having a really goofy guy and then compromise him in some sort of way."

Jack Vaughan talks about subverting predictable commercial structures: "You could do the classic problem-solution structure, where the lack of product is demonstrated in some ridiculous, hyperbolic way. A ridiculous version of the problem is much more entertaining than the solution. If solutions were interesting, newspapers would be full of good news." He draws a parallel between structuring a script and editing print copy. "Not all writers agree, but if you take out the first few paragraphs of print copy you get into the thing faster." The same process could apply equally well to scripts, he speculates. "However, in an attempt to break film storytelling patterns, people have taken it to a ridiculous point where it becomes obscure. You can get away with it in rock videos because it doesn't matter. When a verbal concept is right, it will suggest its own storyline." The idea should flow easily, says Vaughan. "It shouldn't be a strain."

Ted Horton advises us to write stories that can be reconstructed visually. He references an interview with David Lean, the great British director of *Lawrence of Arabia* and *Dr Zhivago*. "Lean was asked by a critic why he went to so much trouble with his visuals. And he said, well, you've seen lots of movies, you tell me all the lines of dialogue you can remember from them. And the truth is, if you ask anyone who's seen a movie — even in the last twenty-four hours — they'll be lucky if they can remember one or two lines, but they'll be able to reconstruct the film through imagery."

Neil French, however, maintains that one well-chosen phrase can recall the entire movie. " '*We'll always have Paris*', '*Go ahead, make my day*', '*Frankly, my dear, I don't give a damn*', '*It's been …
emotional*'. The problem today is that any buffoon can think of a picture, but most writers can't write dialogue."

The more things change, the more they remain the same. In a throwback to the days of silent movies when title cards carried the dialogue and filled in the gaps in the story, titles have again become a minor art form.

Public service commercials, particularly, alternate between live action and earnest lines of terse text, usually set in 6-point Squint and reversed out of serious black. Fortunately, commercials haven't quite resorted to the literary style of the titles in *The Birth of a Nation* which included such gems as: "Here I raise the ancient symbol of an unconquered race of men, the fiery cross of old Scotland's hills. I quench its flame in the sweetest blood that ever stained the sands of time."

"A lot of commercials I see now have pictures, and then give you the idea with a reverse super in the next frame," says Hunt. "I think it's cheating somewhat."

Fink pinpoints another form of cheating: the *dénouement*. If you lead people on, he says, you've got to give them some kind of reward at the end of it. Otherwise the next time they see it, they'll just switch off. "People write all this big stuff, open on aerial shot, a helicopter swoops down, they cràne through the window, and at the end it comes down to a tiny joke ... it's just *nothing*. I have to say I think 90% of the people in advertising aren't very good."

TRY THE SCENE CARD SHUFFLE

At film schools, screenwriters learn how to structure movie scripts with scene cards. A scene card is simply an index card — the typical 3" × 5" (7.6cm × 12.7cm) file card available from any stationery shop.

Every scene in the movie is summarised onto scene cards, one scene per card. The average movie might need from fifty to sixty cards. The cards are then laid out from beginning to end. It soon becomes obvious where the story doesn't flow smoothly from one card to the next; or where a scene is superfluous; or where a bridging scene is needed. If the structure feels too predictable, if the writer wants to subvert the conventional flow, the cards can be shuffled again and again. It is a process of elimination that makes a story bulletproof.

The same principle works for a commercial. Write out each shot on a card. Start with all the mandatories. One card for the final pack shot/end super. One card for the product demo shot. One card for each of the special feature shots. Next, the obligatory shots, one card for each of the basic shots without which you can't tell your story.

A cat is trying out a bowl of new Harpers Cat Chow.

Male VO: *The first thing any cat owner wants to know about a new cat food is, will my cat eat it?*

Suddenly a canary lands on the edge of the bowl. The cat ignores it and keeps eating Harpers Cat Chow. The canary pecks away at it, too.

Male VO: *New Harpers Cat Chow is a nutritionally complete cat food, which gives cats all the nourishment they require. As it's available in chicken, fish and liver flavours, it also gives cats all the variety they need. The unique star shape makes it easier for cats to eat and as you can see, cats would rather eat it than just about anything else.*

The cat and canary sit peacefully with the product.

Male VO and end super: *Harpers Cat Chow. If it could run, cats would chase it.*

Lionel Hunt says you can sustain viewer interest by "not doing terribly much". His famous Harpers Cat Chow commercial proves the point admirably. Can the Cat Chow really be better than the canary perched within paw's reach? You have to watch until the last frame to find out. "A nightmare to shoot," recalls art director Ron Mather. The Campaign Palace Melbourne.

Then add extra cards, one for each of the reaction shots, the cutaways and those crazy, wouldn't-it-be-great-if shots.

Lay out the cards, first in a logical, conventional sequence. Does the structure work? Does the commercial play? Does it need tightening? Does it need an unexpected twist or two? Now, experiment with structure. Take the opening series of shots and rearrange the cards. Start taking risks — *shuffle them*. Repeat the process for the middle of the commercial. Now, how far can you complicate it before it's convoluted? Take *all* the cards for the opening and middle sequences and shuffle them. What have you got? The shots that might have belonged in the middle may suddenly work better at the beginning. Who knows, the mandatory end shot may play better as the second or third last shot. Or maybe, the whole idea might work better in one single shot, with no cuts.

How To Sustain Interest

"Generally speaking, I find it's good to sustain their interest *by not doing terribly much*," reflects Hunt. "Commercials I don't like are those without much of an idea, that have shot after shot, cut after cut, multi-scene commercials which seem to me to be a total waste of money. As the great British art director David Holmes said, what's wrong with a match striking for thirty seconds? It takes thirty seconds to strike and burn a match. In a French film, you'd think nothing of it. But if you showed the average creative director a match burning for thirty seconds, he'd say that's too long. But I don't think it is. I think sometimes using that slow pace can dramatically improve an idea. Things happen within a flame. That's exactly why people stare into the fire and call it country television…"

David Holmes elaborates: "A computer tells us that there are about 98 million different ways to strike a match. That's 98 million ideas. But what the computer doesn't tell us is that each time we create combustion in one of the 98 million ways, we could dramatise that individual event and make 98 million different ways of seeing it." The idea that a powerful image has to have a sack of money thrown at it is missing the point, says Holmes. "Simple new visual answers can be so strong. For example, who can forget the captivating little film called *The Red Balloon*? It had a cast of one." Albert Lamorisse's halfhour masterpiece captured the adventures of a little boy and the big red balloon he rescued from a lamppost in the backstreets of old Montparnasse. It won the 1957 Academy Award for best original screenplay. As Holmes reflects, "It's so sad that there are untold numbers of wonderful new ideas boxed up under our very noses. We've all at one time or another fallen into the trap of *trying far too hard*, ending up prettily dramatising events that have already occurred in the name of creativity. The challenge for me is still: have we seen it before?"

"When you give a speech, one of the most powerful things you can do is just stop," Henry reminds us. "You've got the audience thinking, what's he going to say? Maybe he's forgotten what he's going to say? Maybe he's lost it? It's the same with an ad. *You actually just stop.* Instead of saying, I've got thirty seconds, I've got to start, and off you go, buy this, buy this, which is what people expect from ads, you can have a confident, laid-back tone of voice." Pace, but not panic, says Henry.

"It's not a huge problem to keep people's attention," observes French. "I think most people are willing to be entertained. But you've got to start doing it within three seconds, or at least promise them that something good may happen. And that's the problem with being second in the break. You might have a P&G ad on first and by the time the good ad comes on, which is yours, they're out of there." French believes the trick of television creativity is to be either first in the break, or last. "Because they might have come back just in time for the programme and they'll catch your ad." French's own work is hallmarked by its simplicity. He hauls the viewer in slowly. "You've got to make them think, oh, this might be worth watching. A close-up of a human face is almost always worth watching."

Oberlander warns of *sensory overload*. "If it's just a short format like fifteen seconds, you do have to provoke. There's always the classic argument with the creative team saying, we want to do something that's really wild so the consumer says, what's that? So they pay 'more attention'." Actually, says Oberlander, the opposite happens. "The consumer turns off the channel because it's more confusing than it is provocative. We're always having that conversation: *is it provocative or is it confusing?* It's always a

We embark on the most boring Sunday afternoon drive of our lives. A repetitive music track kicks in:

Dah dah dah...

Dah dah dah...

Two extremely bored young men cruise through a mind-numbing industrial landscape in their Volkswagen Golf.

Inside the car, they indulge in such fascinating pastimes as playing games with the sun through their fingers and trying some pathetic martial art movements.

Coming to a mundane urbanscape, they discover an old chair abandoned by the roadside. They stop. When they set out again, the chair is in the back seat.

Becoming aware that it actually stinks, they unload it and drive on. And so it goes.

Female VO: *The German-engineered Volkswagen Golf. It fits your life — or your complete lack thereof.*

VW logo and end super: *Drivers wanted.*

Female VO: *On the road of life, there are passengers and there are drivers.*

How to make something boring interesting. Neat satire and storytelling that busts the category by Arnold Communications Boston.

negotiation. Viewers have so many options." Oberlander says human beings love stories. They love storytelling and they love storytellers. "Television directors must have the sensibility to capture human truths. The camera has to find a look or a scene or a series of narrative suggestions that really just grab the viewer and either make him laugh or cry or respond emotionally."

Horton acknowledges how quickly audiences can tire of commercials. He cuts a lot of his scenes a little bit shorter, "just a tad", so people want to catch them again to see what they *think* they've missed. Repeat viewings also need repeat rewards. "Having the odd, other 'little thing' going on in a commercial gives people a reason to come back to it."

Godfrey addresses that issue by referencing the work of Jacques Tati, the French actor-satirist-director. "He seems to have invented the idea of having something interesting going on in the foreground, but there are also little cameos going on in the *background*. Perhaps a guy tripping over a step and falling down and moving out of picture. His whole principle was if someone sees that, then that's terrific. If they don't see it, it really doesn't matter; it's not going to affect the film. But for the people who do recognise it, they will really love it." The principle would work well in commercials, argues Godfrey, because people would discover the background detail *eventually*.

Ramchandani believes that you can put a lot of layers into a commercial and it won't come over as something complex; it will still come over as something whole. "If you've seen everything there is in a commercial the first time you see it, and then the second time you see it you see *less*, then you're not being rewarded for watching it again. But if you see more, you're being rewarded. You've got to give people credit for taking stuff in. Each time someone watches it, they get something more out of it. Often there are quite a lot of little subtle things you see in the St Luke's work, maybe a connection between the second scene and the fifth scene and it might be something to do with a word. There's a Midland Bank commercial about someone setting up their own business and it's all done through a famous song with the lyrics stripped out and new words put in so you actually complete them in your own head, like mental karaoke. The visual imagery is all to do with light. The story is about turning an old cafe into a restaurant. Nobody would ever stand up and say that's 'light', but the fourth time you watch it you might start to sense something else is going on. I don't think people do enough with that." Layering should never stop, says Ramchandani. "Some ideas you can only put in the writing. Some ideas you can only put into the production. You just never stop. Even when you're post-producing it, you can't do enough of it. And you can put so much detail, so much interest and difference, into sound." Ramchandani remembers an IKEA commercial he worked on at St. Luke's with Dave Buonoguidi. "Halfway through there was a little gap in the sound and we thought, well, it's winter, it's a winter sale, what shall we do? So we just put a little sneeze in. I think those touches are really important because they make an ad sort of human and whole." He says it's also nice to work out people's characters, even though they're on screen for only ten seconds. "It's nice to work out their personality, their back stories, then you can wardrobe them right, and of course *you put glasses on them*." Ramchandani says you cannot believe that your first "hatch" of an idea is everything. "You not only have to give birth to ideas; you have to parent them."

The elements that matter most to Blackley are the honing and crafting of the script, immaculate casting and a director who can tell a story. *Great stories have an inherent ability to sustain interest*, he says. "We don't come from the big, George Lucas school of pyrotechnics, thousands of hours spent with Animal Logic to create effects. We are not that sort of agency. We write stories that people really relate to or have a laugh with."

Dawson relies on the idea itself to drive interest. Music, avoiding obvious jokes, developing interesting characters, even using a delightful piece of animation will help. "Keep asking yourself, what is the basic, essential idea of this commercial? Take out what you can until it starts falling apart, then you know you've taken out too much."

"The stuff that cuts through entertains," confirms David Lubars. "In the 70s, 6% of households in America had remote controls. Now everybody has them. In the 70s, we had an average of nine stations, including the local one, to choose from. Now there's three hundred!

So you *have* to entertain. It doesn't mean don't sell, don't explain why the product is good." Lubars talks about an advertising renaissance and a new generation of clients. "Clients know that creativity is not a dirty word, entertainment is not a dirty word. Marketing people want to make their mark also."

SHOULD THERE BE A MNEMONIC OR NOT?

According to conventional wisdom, a commercial should contain one key visual — one shot or one scene — that resonates in the viewer's memory.

"There are memorable scenes in many commercials," agrees Whybin, "but if it's a great ad, you probably won't remember a scene, you'll remember the sum of the parts. But if you've got an opportunity to have a *mnemonic* — like the use of the smoke in the Hamlet commercials — don't waste it."

If movies often have one or two key scenes that resonate long after we leave the cinema, shouldn't that be a valid objective for commercial makers?

"I think in a commercial it's not that important," considers French. "You've only got thirty or sixty seconds to worry about anyway. Thinking back to *Snow Plough*, there isn't really a moment you carry away; it's the entirety of it. In a commercial like *Perfect Day*, you may have a favourite bit; mine is Tom Jones', which is so hokey, and I like the Lou Reed bit. I can't remember a single one of the others, but I took away a great feeling from it as a whole."

"I think it's the total effect rather than one major visual." Hunt questions the whole hypothesis. "*Gone With the Wind* is actually remembered for the line, 'I don't give a damn'. Often commercials are remembered for the thought, or the words, more than anything else..."

Sometimes, Wee will remember key scenes from a movie. "But I don't think that should be the case for a commercial. It's the entire message you want people to remember, not just one key frame. One should link to the other. It may happen that people will pick up on one particular scene..."

One such scene in Nike's *Good and Evil* resonated for Redman. "It was the shot where Eric Cantona stops and lifts up his collar at the most crucial time in the ad. It was something someone had thought about and the reason it works is that Cantona always plays with his collar up. That's a good example of finding something memorable, but it's only memorable because people who love the game know him. It never hurts to start off thinking how you can make an ad more memorable, from the very first shot to the last, while still telling the story. The best thing you can do in an ad is to have some of those scenes, but they have to be relevant to the idea," Redman warns. "You can't go off at a tangent suddenly to show something just for the sake of people remembering it. You couldn't do more damage to an ad."

For Mike Gibbs, it's the combination of things that build up. "It's making something out of the small details, it's creating a mood and a setting. So it's not just one giant key image, it's the whole environment that it happens in."

Vaughan debates the popularity of the mnemonic. Does the industry still rely on such devices as a woman soaking her hands in dishwashing liquid, or a glass and a half of milk pouring into a Cadbury's chocolate bar? "We tend to try to avoid things that are spelling it out too obviously. Show-and-tell is the most banal thing you can do. There's come to be an understanding, which wasn't always with us, of the concept of *self-completion*; if you get the viewer to participate by not showing everything and not telling everything, there's a greater power to what they take out of the communication. Some clients worry that unless you tell people everything they won't 'get it', but if people put it together for themselves they feel rewarded for having figured it out. Maybe we weren't always conscious of that. We certainly didn't intellectualise it."

VO OR NO VO?

Does the end voice-over make a commercial feel more like an ad — a bit like the logo in the bottom right corner of a press ad?

Delaney doesn't worry about VOs too much. "Some things are fixtures, they're conventions of the medium, of the industry, and people accept them as such. They're not troubled by them. And you can move around them. Nike have shown how simple things can be, just by putting their swoosh on the end."

We are in a quiet neighbourhood park. We hear children playing in the background. Ambient sound continues throughout; there is no VO.

A man walks hand-in-hand with a little girl along a path around the park.

The man is talking to her as she skips along beside him. They walk into the distance.

Super: *A policeman would think he's her father.*

The man and girl walk around a corner.

A new super comes up: *A neighbour would know he's a stranger.*

Dissolve to black.

End super: *Neighbourhood Watch. Good neighbours look out for each other.*

VO or no VO? Two supers made the shock value far more intense. Copywriter Peter Moyse and art director Rashid Salleh relied on restraint and silence. Film director Sng Tong Beng made the familiar sinister. Agency: Saatchi & Saatchi Singapore.

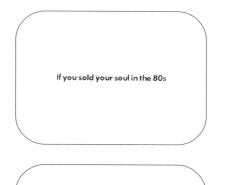

The familiar shape of a Volkswagen is approaching us through a haze. There is no VO.

First super: *If you sold your soul in the 80s...*

The Volkswagen materialises...

Second super: *Here's your chance to buy it back.*

...into the new Volkswagen.

End super: *Drivers wanted*

When you've got a great line, either super it or say it — but not both.
Arnold Communications Boston.

"There's nothing wrong with words in a commercial, there's nothing wrong with dialogue in a commercial, and there's nothing theoretically wrong with voice-overs." Hunt says the best commercials are a combination of words and pictures. He expresses concern when voice-overs and supers are used to explain what's going on, "because the commercial isn't really working. If they're used as a crutch like that, it's a mistake." Hunt experimented with voice-overs delivered by professional singers. "One of the techniques I used was not to use voice-over people to do voice-overs, but to use singers. *Their speaking voices weren't normally known, but they knew how to phrase things.*"

"If the idea comes across visually, and you've got your tagline in a super at the end, you don't *always* need to bash someone over the head with a voice-over just reiterating things." Redman believes it doesn't hurt to have a voice-over. "People obviously know they've been watching a commercial. It's a bit like the logo being in a print ad; does it really matter? I think you've got to remember that we're in the selling game. You have to put your businessman's hat on and ask, does the VO ruin the integrity of the idea? *Maybe*. Does it help sell? If it does, go with it. You start off seducing, but you've still got to let people know what you're offering."

"We did a lot of work for BMW with just titles," Bildsten explains. "The next batch of work we do will have a voice-over. It's simply because titles themselves have become a trend, whereas a voice-over may be a little more timeless." Bildsten believes there is a difference between how well people pay attention to a title versus a voice-over. "We advertising people like to believe that they're glued to the screen and they're going to read every word and take it all in, but they read it much slower than we or editors want to believe. It's amazing how much can go by them, how much they can miss." A voice-over does not have to make the ad overtly commercial or compromise its emotional impact. "It's a matter of how the words are delivered and what voice you're able to use."

Phil Webster of the Melbourne studio Flint Webster abolishes convention. Voice-over people lie on the floor when appropriate, or deliver their lines from deep armchairs.

Dialogue coaches insist that actors learn their lines by first writing them out by hand, removing all punctuation marks and capital letters. Once formal sentence structures are eliminated, the actor can concentrate on the meaning of the words and the truth of the scene. The same principle applies to voice-overs. Because people don't speak to each other in neatly broken lines with commas, voice-over copy should have all punctuation and spacing removed. Then it might sound more like a real voice saying something and less like a paid announcer.

French doesn't draw any rules. "It depends on the ad. There are times if you don't have a voice-over you won't have a film at all. The Martell *Legend* commercial needed a voice-over; in fact, you could argue that the pictures of the swallow were *an add-on to the voice*, as opposed to the voice being an add-on to the pictures. With the Union Bank of Switzerland, if you couldn't have seen the people it wouldn't have made a lot of difference; the poetry was the whole point. There are other times when you should leave the voice off altogether and assume that people are literate enough to read the words if you want them to read them." French nevertheless urges caution. "If you're not careful, though, voice-overs tend to be hokey."

"Everything should add to the communication," considers Wee. "Even the voice, the type in the supers, everything. But the voice shouldn't be saying exactly what the visual is doing. It's pointless. That means you have no confidence in visually communicating your message."

"I love it when you can do a commercial without any words, when you can have a clean strategic selling proposition without anything said." Whybin maintains there are no set rules. "But if the voice-over doesn't get in the way of the idea and actually adds to the selling proposition, do it."

5

How To Craft Campaigns

"For me, the idea is everything," declares Lee Garfinkel. "And especially a big *campaign* idea. I think anybody can come up with one good commercial, one good print ad, every now and then. But coming up with a big campaign idea, and *every* spot in that campaign living up to the standard of what the idea is — if you can deliver that, then you're on to something."

"What we're there to do is build a brand, not to do a one-off," stipulates Ron Lawner. "The challenge is to do commercial after commercial, ad after ad, year after year. You have to find the voice that can echo in a brand, yet keep it fresh at the same time. That's what great campaigns are, that's what great brands deserve, and that's what is so *rare* in our business today. In the States, you can count the great branding campaigns on one hand."

Adrian Holmes calls a campaign "an endless corridor of ideas". In his experience, the script-to-shooting ratio was fabulously high on such cutting edge campaigns as Heineken and Hamlet. "You might have *twenty-five scripts* written before one got made. That is how you get a campaign that great. The long-running campaign is the highest form of television commercial art."

Once, audiocassettes were a parity product until Howell Henry Chaldecott Lury's Maxell campaign. Writer Naresh Ramchandani made the connection between the brand and the potential embarrassment of mishearing song lyrics. The Cannes Grand Prix-winning commercials were shot in one take to Desmond Dekker's Israelites *(above) and* Into the Valley *by The Skids (below). Ramchandani called it the start of 'street' British advertising.*

Some mates have been working on home renovations. They are sharing a few beers. One of them is with his son. When he receives a tip-off by phone that the police "booze bus" is conducting random breath tests nearby, he decides it's time to call it a day. He whistles to his dog.

One of his mates gives him another beer: *Go on, one more's not going to kill you.*

The young father stops and takes it: *Hey, I'm still capable of driving...*

At last, he and his son drive off in their pick-up truck. He stops at the first intersection, but ignores the Stop sign at the next.

Son: *Dad!*

A huge tanker ploughs into the truck, crushing it into a mass of twisted metal.

Back at the work site, a mobile phone rings and one of his mates hears the news just as more beer arrives.

End super: *If you drink, then drive, you're a bloody idiot.*

If you drink, then drive, you're a bloody idiot.

TAC

The Transport Accident Commission campaign from Grey Advertising Melbourne.

We see speeding motorists through the eyes of young policemen. Their laser gun picks up one offender after another.

Everyone has an excuse...

Oh, 120's not fast on this road...

I had to drop my kid off at my mum's...

Well I find it hard to believe I was doing 119, I was just overtaking a car...

The two young policemen are suddenly called to a nearby accident. Details are still sketchy.

When they arrive they encounter a two-car head on collision which had occurred at around 120 kilometres an hour. It is a double fatality. Blood-streaked faces, a limb torn from a body, a traumatic experience far removed from the litany of excuses the young officers had been listening to before.

End super: *Don't fool yourself, speed kills.*

Dr Richard Gilhome.

10 kph less will save lives.

TAC

A man carrying a pizza steps onto the road, and into the path of a car. The impact is sickening. Witnesses scream in horror.

Cut to Dr Richard Gilhome who reconstructs the accident while the film runs again in slow motion, so we can see every detail.

Dr Gilhome: *I'm a trauma surgeon and I want to reconstruct what happens to the human body, in less than two-fifths of a second, when hit by a car braking from 70 kilometres per hour over a braking distance of 50 metres. Even in a car equipped with ABS, the first impact will occur at around 46 kilometres. The bumper hits the knee joints, tearing flesh and ligaments. The full weight of the skull smashes through the windscreen, the neck snaps, the skull shatters, and the pedestrian's brain is turned into pulp. In little more than a second, the pedestrian's body will hit the road with a 70% chance of being dead.*

We then see what happens when a car is driven at a slower speed…

Dr Gilhome: *But had you been braking from 60 kilometres, not 70, there's a good chance you could have stopped in time and the pedestrian would have suffered nothing worse than a severe fright. Think about it.*

End super: *10 kph less will save lives.*

The TAC demonstrates what happens when drivers reduce speed by ten kilometres per hour. Grey Advertising Melbourne.

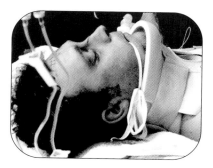

The *Twelve Days of Christmas* used an episodic format. A woman humming the famous song is an audio mnemonic.

On Monday, a father arrives home with a Christmas tree. His pregnant wife, son and daughter greet him.

Wednesday is the office party. Liquor flows. On the way home he grows impatient, loses control and a split second later has crashed into a tree.

On Thursday, the pregnant wife and her in-laws are convinced that her husband will regain consciousness at any time.

On Sunday, the doctors announce that his brain has stopped working and that he should be taken off life support. The curtains are drawn. *See you later, son*, says his distressed father.

The funeral takes place on Christmas Eve. Tempers are frayed. A child asks if Daddy will be at the church.

Christmas Day. The two children climb into bed with their mother.

We hear one ask: *Mummy, is Santa going to find Daddy?*

A budgerigar uses a touch phone with its beak.

Sound: *Beep, beep, beep, beep, beep, etc...*

Electronic VO: *DHL Customer Service. Please enter your account number.*

Sound: *Beep, beep, beep, beep, etc...*

Electronic VO: *Please enter the air express service you require.*

Sound: *Beep.*

Electronic VO: *Please enter your package's destination.*

Sound: *A very long and deliberate beep.* The budgie drops a card on a sleeping cat. It reads: *Darkest Africa.*

MVO: *DHL International Express Freight can take almost anything to just about anywhere.*

A DHL man enters and asks: *Package for Africa?* He sees the cat, scoops it up and goes. The budgie makes a triumphant twittering sound.

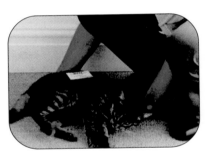

Michael Newman, Saatchi & Saatchi Sydney, calls a humorous TV commercial the original interactive ad. Budgie was written by Paul Fishlock, art directed by Jon Iles, and gave the DHL campaign a famous brand property.

A sprightly, elderly man is backing out of a front door, fondly kissing a lady about his own age goodbye. He strides down her garden path with a farewell wave.

What a vibrant, charismatic old boy, we're thinking to ourselves. Just as we're wondering what age he is, up comes a super: *Roger Daly. Age 67. Retired Milkman.*

Suddenly the old boy stops outside another suburban house. As he approaches the front door, another lady of about his age greets him with an enthusiastic embrace. He closes the door with a boyish smile. Up comes the next super: *Still doing the rounds.*

End on shot of Roger Daly drinking a glass of milk.

Final super: *Milk. Legendary stuff.*

Retired Milkman *won the Australian milk account, CAMA, for Clemenger BBDO Melbourne and became perhaps Australia's most highly awarded individual commercial. The campaign went from strength to strength, winning Golds at Cannes and a string of other accolades.*

One of Australia's longest running campaigns stars a stuffed chicken. "Ten years ago it first became the victim of Toyota Camry's surprisingly powerful performance," explains Michael Newman, Saatchi & Saatchi, Sydney. "The hapless chicken has been trying to cross the road only to have its feathers blown off by a passing Camry." Saatchi's ran a house ad in Australia headlined Don't waste money on advertising, invest in property. *"Brand properties such as the Michelin Man, Ronald McDonald, even the Nike swoosh, have a vivid reality off the page or screen. They are ideas bigger than ads, building the brand exponentially with each campaign execution." Toyota, says Newman, has sold a lot of Camry's and a lot of toy chickens.*

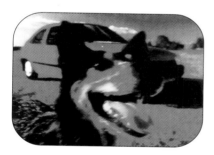

A Daewoo is undergoing an obedience trial with a dog.

The Daewoo and the dog respond to every command:

Back, back, back, stay!

Forward, forward, forward, forward and around, forward and around...

Back, back, back, and forward, forward — stay!

Now, right around, right around...

Aussie male VO: *The Daewoo. At $14,000, it handles better than a cattle dog. There's nothing you can't do in a Daewoo.*

End super: *3-Year 100,000km Factory Warranty.*

The dog and the Daewoo made their debut doing an obedience trial. Ron Mather calls it "the most successful car launch ever in Australia". The irreverent tonality has continued through many more executions from The Campaign Palace.

This is what it looks like to be buried in a $25,000 funeral.

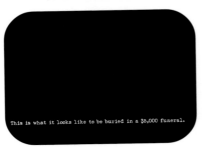

This is what it looks like to be buried in a $5,000 funeral.

No Frills
FUNERALS & CREMATIONS

When you're gone, you're gone.

Black screen and classical music throughout. No voice-over.

First super: *This is what it looks like to be buried in a $25,000 funeral.*

Next super: *This is what it looks like to be buried in a $5,000 funeral.*

Logo: *No Frills Funerals & Cremations. Call 9247 6895.*

Final super: *When you're gone, you're gone.*

"Every now and then you get an advertising brief that actually has something new to say," observes executive creative director Michael Newman, Saatchi & Saatchi Sydney. The brand name said it all and the execution took its cue accordingly. Newman believes the terminology "ad" sends a misleading subliminal message to clients. "The most effective procedure, when it comes to the number of elements in a communication, is actually to subtract."

Locked-off camera on a gravedigger, a rather bizarre figure standing in the midst of a cemetery. The same classical music heard throughout. No voice-over.

First super: *This is who buries you in a $25,000 funeral.*

Next super: *This is who buries you in a $5,000 funeral.*

Logo: *No Frills Funerals & Cremations. Call 9247 6895.*

Final super: *When you're gone, you're gone.*

The No Frills campaign had four no-frills executions: the same classical music, the same irony and the same use of supers to draw the comparisons. Written and directed by Jay Furby, art directed by Steve Carlin, at Saatchi & Saatchi Sydney.

The adventures of Buddy Lee, a big campaign idea that lets Fallon Minneapolis demonstrate how Lee Dungarees can't be busted.

Great campaigns are distinguished by what David Blackley calls "their creative handwriting and sets of values". They often originate in surprising places. The Australian city of Melbourne, for example, has produced two of the world's most highly and consistently awarded campaigns: the Australian Milk campaign from Clemenger BBDO and the Transport Accident Commission campaign from Grey Advertising.

Australian Broadcasting Corporation. When Australia's equivalent of the BBC first went to air in the 30s, its mission statement was "cultural enrichment, information, entertainment and gaiety". Over the decades, commercial broadcasting and television steadily stole Auntie's thunder. What was intended to be Australia's something-for-everyone public broadcaster became alienated from the audiences it served.

"The brand positioning was very much white, Anglo-Saxon Australian, elitist, Church of England; in other words, a dead stereotype," explains Steve Gray at Batey Kazoo, Sydney.

When Brian Johns became the ABC's new managing director, Batey Kazoo was invited to create a new on-air image for the national television network. "We had worked with Brian when he was at the Special Broadcasting Service, a multi-cultural channel. He knew that what the ABC represented and what the community thought of it were two different things. The number of Australians of non-English speaking backgrounds is 35% of the population. Australia has over 170 different ethnic communities. Did all these people feel *welcomed* by the ABC? Was the ABC *relevant* to them?"

The Australian Broadcasting Corporation is the Aussie equivalent of the BBC. Sadly, over the decades the ABC became alienated from the audience it served. Its logo — based on the shape of an analogue wave — symbolised an elitist broadcaster that didn't make people feel welcome.

Sydney agency Batey Kazoo was briefed to create a new on-air image. Overnight, the ABC logo was placed in the hands of the audience. People of different ages and cultures starred in a quirky series of grainy, slowmo trailers. As each video concluded, Muslim Australians, skateboarders, lawn bowlers and dancers would reach out to camera and trace the shape of the ABC logo across the screen, just like skywriting. The campaign won Australia's major television awards outright in 1996.

Creative director Russell Smyth had two elements he was hesitant to discard. "We had the ABC logo, actually an analogue wave, which was well entrenched. The other was the ABC signoff, *It's your ABC*, which had been used for years. It was based on the notion of the ABC's charter, and the fact that broadcast licence fees and taxpayers funded the ABC, not advertising revenue." Executionally, it was decided to show a diversity of different cultures and ages in station programme breaks. "Muslims, skateboarders, lawn bowlers, dancers, it *is* their ABC..." An intriguingly grainy, slowmo film technique was identified. Its quirkiness engaged the right tonal nerves.

Smyth then made the creative leap. "We knew the brand direction, the subject, the tonality. But how could we bring it to life? How could we attach value? How could we personalise the ABC?" Instead of using a graphic or digitised logo, Batey Kazoo literally placed the logo in the hands of the audience. As each video concluded, a dancer or a bowler or a skateboarder would reach out to the camera and, finger outstretched, trace the shape of the ABC logo across the scene, leaving a trail akin to skywriting.

Batey Kazoo won the ABC pitch against fifteen agencies; the campaign won Australia's major television awards outright. Batey Kazoo became Television Agency of the Year in 1996.

California Milk Processor Board (CMPB). Milk inspired two of the world's most acclaimed campaigns in the closing decade of the last century: Goodby, Silverstein & Partners' *got milk?* in America, and Clemenger BBDO's *Legendary Stuff* in Australia.

Jeff Manning, executive director of the California Milk Processor Board, wanted an advertising campaign that would *change consumer behaviour*. Milk had always been advertised to non-users solely for its nutritional value and as far as Manning was concerned, it hadn't worked. As its image improved, its sales volume went down. Manning believed there was a communications opportunity for a milk and food story; after all, most milk was consumed in the home, and rarely by itself. While focus groups confirmed Manning's theory, it was clear those consumers wanted the food first and the milk *second*. Milk was part of the equation, but incapable of creating any desire of its own ... unless, of course, they had the food but they had run out of milk. Goodby, Silverstein planning director Jon Steel probed further and discovered an intriguing truth: running out of milk was a traumatic experience for consumers. It led to his now famous deprivation strategy.

"I've lived a fairly charmed life in terms of advertising," says writer Chuck McBride who arrived at Goodby, Silverstein just in time for his *got milk?* assignment. "Jeff Goodby had the insight of *got milk?* The idea was, you only care about milk when it's not there. By the time they'd got to *got milk?*, I was on my way there to start work. I was faxed a sheet to work on while I was on the plane to the agency. It basically said, *got milk?*, write stories about people without milk. I came in with about twelve."

The 60-second *Aaron Burr* commercial launched the campaign. The storyline is simple enough. A strange young man, obsessed with the lives of Alexander Hamilton and Aaron Burr, is making himself a peanut butter sandwich while he listens to the radio. The deejay calls him to ask, who shot Alexander Hamilton? Because the young man has a mouthful of peanut butter and jelly sandwich, he desperately tries to utter "Burr, Burr…" but he is out of milk and can't talk. He loses the money. McBride worked with writer Scott Burns and art director Erich Joiner on *Aaron Burr*. "It was Scott's idea. He's a history buff and he said, what's the most obscure piece of history you know about? Wouldn't it be funny if we did something with this character?"

McBride shares their search for a new storytelling language. "Our scripts were very flat to begin with. We wrote very simple stories about people who needed milk but something got in their way or they were afflicted in some way by food in their mouth. So they were very formulaic on paper. It looked like you could screw them up really bad. Erich Joiner and I were teamed at the time and we were asking, how could we inject a *new visual language* inside of this stuff? For example, how do you get the back story that this guy is a nut about history? We had a lot of work to do to make this thing play out. It wasn't just as simple as setting down the camera and shooting this guy spreading peanut butter and then the phone call comes in and you know what's going on. How do we add the layers? Erich and I wanted to thicken the thing up. We wanted to stretch normalcy a little further by bringing in a far quirkier normalcy. If we're going to cast this character that lives in a castle of memorabilia, he's got to be pretty weird."

McBride and Joiner wanted a visual not verbal back story. "The one thing that kept on tripping us was, how do we *know* that this guy is completely obsessed with the lives of Alexander Hamilton and Aaron Burr? We had to give people an understanding of what he knew — visually — because that's like the third wheel, so the audience knows that he knows the answer well before he actually tries to deliver the line. So we massaged that and we came up with this world he was completely engulfed in. We created the cutaways. There was the memorabilia. There were the two portraits. The guns. The famous bullet." Even the angle on the knife spreading the peanut butter underscored impending disaster. "On the set, the client went nuts. You have guns, and you have bullets, and you have knives; what are you doing? This commercial is so violent! This is crazy, this is milk, this isn't anything but a simple, wholesome product! When I look back on it," admits McBride, "I wouldn't go as far now as I did then."

McBride and Joiner chose Michael Bay to direct. "Erich and I took a lot of pride in the fact that we had created a different dimension. We hired Michael Bay to direct our commercials. He'd done all the wacky Budweiser stuff. He added a lot. He said, let's put this guy in a loft, let's isolate him in a huge space in a small space. So we put him into a deserted warehouse, we put a few bookshelves in the centre of it, then spotlit it. Michael compresses a lot of good action into scenes, so you get quite a bit of eye direction, and he foreshortens lines. He calls it crowding the lens. Michael and I have done some of our best work together. We've formed a pretty good relationship; it's kind of tumultuous…"

McBride authored the classic *Baby & Cat*, which was also used in the first round. "I had seen the movie *Delicatessen* and I was just so charmed at the way they'd used sound effects and people's body motions for that one scene where the bed is squeaking and everybody is going nuts. I really wanted to use that idea; if you didn't have milk, but your baby and the cat did, that suck-suck-lap-lap-suck-suck-lap-lap-suck-lap-suck-lap would drive you nuts!" Michael Bay directed again. "We used twin babies on the shoot. We even hairstyled the babies, the dad and the cat to look alike. Then their mother said they couldn't drink the milk because they'd been nursed two hours before. We said, sorry, you did *what?* Well, the mother said, I always do at that time, nobody told me not to. So there was panic; the babies were fed and wouldn't drink milk. We only had them for six hours. They just wouldn't take the bottle. So we shot indirect eye and we brought in a prosthetic baby; we could shoot over the top of its head and put the three characters together. Then at the last minute the babies grabbed their bottles and started drinking furiously. We had two cameras, shooting with different lenses. We picked up an amazing amount of film in a matter of seconds. I'll never forget the most brilliant moment when we had to have the baby react to the dad as he reached for the baby's bottle. The baby literally pulled his bottle out of his mouth and looked at the dad like, No Way!"

The campaign's original objective had been to halt the sales decline. In its first year, 1994, Californian retail milk sales actually increased by US$13 million. It was the first increase in milk sales recorded in the United States in a decade and did not go unnoticed by the national milk marketing association. By 1995, *got milk?* was running successfully across America and has now become a cultural icon.

In his book *got milk?*, Jeff Manning addresses an issue that many advertisers face. Although discussing comedy which he calls "a narrow path to tread", his remarks apply equally to any form of fresh creativity. Campaigns that are too unconventional, too radical, will upset people. On the other hand, campaigns that play it too safe, too "goody-goody", will bore them. "You won't get complaints," says Manning, "because no one will notice." Manning's preference? "Tick off only a few people and entertain the rest. If we don't get a few disgruntled calls from people, *I'm disappointed and a little worried.*"

Even *Aaron Burr* got complaints from people opposed to a young man speaking with his mouth full of food on television!

Confederation of Australian Milk Agencies (CAMA). Clemenger BBDO was the only Melbourne agency invited to pitch for Australia's national white milk campaign. The CAMA is a Sydney-based confederation representing milk industry interests. David Blackley recalls: "We'd already worked for the Dairy Corporation, so we knew a bit about milk. And we also knew a lot about the Goodby, Silverstein *got milk?* campaign. We knew it was the only campaign in America that had done anything for milk sales. I'd been to San Francisco and spent time at the agency with Jon Steel, the planner. I'd even interviewed him on digital video. So we knew *we had to do something in Australia that was completely out of the ordinary,* that gave milk a cachet and brought its front of mind awareness much higher."

The campaign, written by Sarah Barclay and Tony Greenwood, lives up to its name: *Legendary Stuff.* "The client brief was to sell milk to young males," explains Blackley. "The *Retired Milkman* commercial was a lateral thought. They got the psychology right, selling milk to young males by proving that milk was a virility potion that keeps you in good form for the rest of your life."

The irreverence resonated with the psyches of young Aussie males. The retired milkman has the seemingly innocuous name of Roger Daly. In Australian slang, to "roger" means to have sexual intercourse. Daly, aged sixty-seven, is seen slipping out the front door of a lover's house, with a big smile on his face. He goes down the front path, virtually skips down the street into the next house where another old flame lets him in. *Roger Daly, retired milkman, still doing the rounds ... Legendary stuff.* A Gold at Cannes was an appropriate trophy. Another commercial starred a younger milkman with the wry observation, *It was always the milkman.*

"Very rarely do you ever make the campaign that you use to win the business," says Blackley. The committee in charge of the advertising is very big and diverse, including traditionally conservative members like farmers. "It was the most unlikely campaign to get through that sort of committee. It was very thoroughly researched before it was made. The research results were overwhelmingly in favour. They couldn't really knock it back, although some of them were very nervous about it after it went to air because church groups wrote in and said it was disgraceful..."

The third commercial in the campaign addressed the issue of not having enough milk on hand. Called *Run-Out*, a mum dashes to the shop for milk, overpowers a masked holdup man in the process of robbing it, then heads home again — notching up another Gold at Cannes.

Retired Milkman is generally regarded as Australia's single most awarded commercial; Barclay and Greenwood were rated the tenth most creative team in the world in 1999.

First Direct. A bank without branches was a revolutionary product; the advertising that launched it remains some of Britain's most talked-about work. Howell Henry Chaldecott Lury disrupted the banking category creatively and in terms of the media buy.

The agency faced up to the potential negative: a brand new bank without branches would be basically an invisible bank. There would be no reassuring High Street presence, nor a long tradition of banking prudence to quell depositor nerves. So in a lateral leap, the agency launched the bank by televising its 21st anniversary celebration, which was being held at some point in the next century, a concept created by Steve Henry and Axel Chaldecott.

Then came the creative media breakthrough. Two commercials were screened simultaneously on two different channels. One portrayed the *Optimistic* view of the new bank; the other provided the *Pessimistic* opinion. A very serious female presenter introduced the commercials, inviting viewers to stay tuned for one aspect of the product, or suggesting they switch to the second channel for the other side of the coin. "It was shocking then and is shocking now, the fact that we even pulled it off," considers Naresh Ramchandani. "It was a logistical nightmare." It was also a very expensive media buy, but the phones lit up whenever it was aired.

In the *Optimistic* view, a bespectacled man in a pink suit prances and dances to a cheesy jingle extolling the convenience of the new service. In the *Pessimistic* version, a truculent Luddite demolishes the idea of a bank without branches. At one point, the man from the *Optimistic* commercial visits the *Pessimistic* commercial; he is glimpsed dancing past in the background. "It was very *Purple Rose of Cairo* to play those games, mixing fiction and fact, what's actually on the TV and what's actually out of real life."

First Direct was a very personal banking product, says Ramchandani. It was an individualistic bank that offered different people different options. "Jan Smith, the client, pushed us to be different. The strangeness in the commercials very much came from Adam Lury and the planner, Fiona Clancy. We gave people credit for being intelligent. If certain kinds of people weren't going to be right for this bank, the advertising would filter them out. But the second commercial, the negative one, is actually a bigger sell than the positive one."

Ramchandani adds a creative confession. "In the *Optimistic* commercial, the dorky man is wearing glasses. I've got this thing I do in most ads. I stick a pair of glasses on people. I really believe advertising has to be competitive and I think there are very few reasons to put glasses on people in commercials unless it's a glasses commercial. So I always stick a pair of glasses on them. Eight times out of ten I'll do it, just to make it look a bit different."

IKEA. London-based St. Luke's centred the IKEA campaign on an "amazingly shocking thought": that 90% of Britain's taste in furniture is rubbish. The furniture said very nasty things about British homemakers as social beings, the agency argued; women were constructing overly fussy and claustrophobic environments for their families. Dave Buonaguidi and Naresh Ramchandani created the campaign.

"If you've got a really outrageous thought, all you have to do is just soften it, then hand it over to people and let it explode within them. *Chuck out your chintz* was so friendly and catchy and supportive, and yet so incredibly subversive." Ramchandani traces the campaign's development. "I'd wanted to write a jingle for ages, like a sort of Mojo ad, a very subversive Mojo ad. We did this feminist, 60s kind of song, encouraging women to chuck out their chintz and did an ad with two hundred women chucking out their flowery furniture into this big blue skip. It was outrageous in focus groups. People were insulted. But we'd got their guards down enough to get the message through. So basically we just turned the 'volume' down a bit..." IKEA was a kind of cultural invader, showing people a new way. "Of course it didn't really feel like that," smiles Ramchandani. "It was very gentle and nice."

Gentle and nice it might have been, but the campaign provoked an emotional explosion. In line with Ramchandani's personal philosophy of advertising, the real media became "people's conversations". Everybody was talking. Feminists hated it. Others hailed its bravado. The media had a field day. "The end results were amazing. IKEA's sales were already pretty good. But they went up by about 30% year on year and for IKEA to achieve that is something quite astonishing. I'm very proud of that."

Maxell Cassettes. It was a watershed in British advertising. "Maxell, plus the next three or four campaigns that Howell Henry did, was the start of *'street'* British advertising," debates writer Naresh Ramchandani. "Before that, advertising had been Britain's film industry." There were really interesting things happening, he recalls, a lot of brilliant pop promos where people had abandoned thirty-five millimetre and lots of lighting and just gone and shot something on the street. "We just wanted to go and do something like that."

Ramchandani believes that the communication has to leap from one of three places: the product offering, or the strategy, or the creative execution. *And it should only leap once.* "If it leaps twice it gets really confusing. So if you had an amazingly strong product offering like 'British Airways fly anywhere for one day for one pound', then frankly you just leave it there. If you've got a parity product but a brilliant bit of planning like the Automobile Association, *The Fourth Emergency Service*, you just execute that strategy really simply. But what we had on Maxell was a parity product with a parity strategy, 'Cassettes that sound better'; so when you haven't leapt in the product and you haven't leapt in the strategy, then the creative execution *has* to leap." The planner, Chris McDonald, worked with Ramchandani night after night on the music and fine-tuning the end communication.

The creative breakthrough was born out of Ramchandani's belief that there are "power centres" advertising can tap into. "There are things just waiting to be touched, things that a lot of people think and feel but don't necessarily say to other people. Like this potentially embarrassing idea of mishearing lyrics. No one knows a single word of some songs; no one knows what they are really saying. It sounded like a common idea that hadn't been expressed yet."

Ramchandani chose two songs: Desmond Dekker's reggae classic *Israelites*, and a post-punk track *Into the Valley* by The Skids.

The commercials were shot in one take under a London flyover. "We wanted to shoot it really simply, one take, we didn't want to cut around like a bit of film." The directors, Steve Lowe and Martin Brierley, did standard casting as well as hauling people off the street. "The guy in *Israelites* was an actor, but the guy who did *Into the Valley* was a carpet layer. And he had a double-jointed neck. It was important for them to be like real people and have slightly odd faces and not be so polished in front of camera." Ramchandani recalls a young account handler previewing the commercials and saying: "I don't know what they are. I don't know if they're ads or bits of TV or trailers. They're really unexpected."

Overseas Telecommunications Commission, Australia. On a fateful day in the early 70s, deep within the staid bureaucracy of Australia's biggest agency, George Patterson Bates, writer John Kingsmill received a visit from "a creative director from the Upper Floor". Kingsmill was asked to please do a 10-second radio spot for OTC, the authority that provided Australia's international phone service at that time. The creative director, it seems, was a press man, unaccustomed to radio and television. Kingsmill dutifully obliged, and in the process wrote the line which millions of Australians would come to know by heart over the next ten years, a line addressed to the nation's immigrant population: *Go home on the telephone.* "And that took all of two minutes, because it was just one of those ideas that came to me straightaway. I had to be succinct about it, because in ten seconds, what can you say?"

Time passed. When OTC decided to do a television campaign, another creative director made the trip down to Kingsmill's office. Bruce Jarrett had the idea of using the Barbra Streisand song, *The Way We Were*, combined with Kingsmill's old radio line. Kingsmill was asked could he please do the campaign, which ultimately garnered twenty-nine awards from around the world.

"The lyrics were perfect," recalls Kingsmill. "The whole campaign was based on nostalgia for the past. The idea was to get Australia's immigrant population to remember what it was like in Greece or Holland or Britain or Germany, and to turn that particular screw to

Seven commercials ran for ten years, winning 29 awards from around the world.
John Kingsmill's campaign for Australia's Overseas Telecommunications
Commission. George Patterson Bates, Sydney.

make them pick up the phone and ring home." Some half dozen 60-second executions were produced and then rotated for ten years, usually running two at a time while the others "rested". "Like a repertory company," says Kingsmill. "You got the impression of a lot more commercials and you'd think, have I seen this, or have I not…"

Kingsmill began by interviewing over forty immigrants from various countries. "Someone would say, I know an old Greek man who might be interested in doing this, or I know a young German girl. They'd come into my office, we'd have a cup of tea, and I'd tape their memories. I didn't go out of my way to lull them into a feeling of nostalgia; that would have been insulting."

He devised his own interview structure to provide the raw material for the campaign. The migrants virtually storyboarded the commercials. "I might suddenly say to them, what did they remember about home. And if it had been a little Greek island, they would talk about the things they remembered; the vine leaves, the things they ate, the sounds in the little square, what it was like at night to go and sit in the square and listen to the bazooki. I was digging, digging, digging, for things that would then be put into the visuals. Out of those answers, we picked the images that would give us a *composite visual recollection*, a composite Greek recollection, a composite German recollection."

His second question, he regrets, was cruel. "But I had to do it, and it was a probe. I would say, try to remember your last day at home, and tell me how you felt that day. It deeply affected many people. I got some wonderful responses. Some of them burst into tears. We were pressing a button. We had pictures from my first question, and emotion from the second."

Each commercial opened with the Streisand song, and shots of a particular homeland based on the composite recollection. The visuals used people recruited on location. Then an actual immigrant voice would be heard, telling his or her story, exactly as it had been recorded in Kingsmill's office. "We picked out the actual voices of people that had the biggest emotional bang. We wanted the viewer to feel that this was a real person, not an actor. If you were a Greek, sitting in Melbourne, looking at the commercial, you'd think that's just like *me*, that's the way *I* feel." Kingsmill read the final tagline himself: *When you're thinking of home, go home on the telephone.*

The campaign produced immediate results. "We were told that within a minute of a commercial finishing on air, the OTC would light up as thousands of people picked up their phones to ring Greece." Kingsmill believes the same campaign would work today, just as it stands, because it would go against the tide of hard-edged, brutal, effects-driven work. "The fundamentals of advertising have not changed. The fundamental feelings that people have will never change. The only change is how you present the story, and *if you move too far away from the fundamentals you're likely to lose touch with the very button you want to press in the viewer.*"

Pepsi-Cola. At BBDO New York, writer Michael Patti has contributed some of the world's most famous, highly awarded commercials for Pepsi-Cola. He recalls the brief for *Stranded.* "My art director Don Schneider and I were faced with an assignment at the beginning of the *Nothing else is a Pepsi* campaign to do commercials that said there is really something about Pepsi that is worth waiting for. We look for what we call MacGuffins; Alfred

Hitchcock had them in all his movies. MacGuffins to us are truisms, *things that the average viewer can relate to and say, that's happened to me.* We came up with the idea that there are a lot of vending machines out there taking dollar bills. Everybody in the world has put a dollar bill into one of those things and had it spat out again; it's aggravating. You put it in; it's spat out again. So we thought, wouldn't it be great if you saw an entire commercial and you had no idea what was going on except there was this annoying noise that took place over the course of a day. And really it was because Pepsi was so terrific, that this guy will stay there from dawn to dusk just trying to feed that dollar into a vending machine. We said, everybody will like that because they can relate to it." Patti recalls what happened when the spot made its debut on the Super Bowl in 1996. "Every year, the newspaper *USA Today* has this poll that rates the commercials on Super Bowl. People have a meter and if they dislike the commercial they turn it down, and if they like the commercial they turn it up. Because the sound was so irritating for the first forty-five seconds, it was getting one of the lowest ratings of any commercial ever, until everyone saw the punchline and then it went off the wall. We'd sucked everyone in."

Given the power of the lateral idea, the execution could have been more linear, in traditional storytelling style. Instead layers of thought and detail abounded. "Joe Pytka gave it that grandeur. He pushed us to make it a longer piece, like dawn to dusk. It could have been just thirty seconds, and we could have just dollied in and it still would have been funny. But every shot is like an austere postcard that adds to the beauty of it while you're hearing the annoying noise. And the music, Ricky Nelson's *Lonesome Town*, which the editor put on the first day, raised it to yet another level."

A recent campaign, *The Joy of Cola*, was initiated by Pepsi-Cola to celebrate the taste of cola as a beverage vis-à-vis the infusion of New Age beverages and bottled waters. "We wanted to get people talking about colas, all colas," says Patti. The campaign gently and engagingly ascribed the joyous feelings of cola to Pepsi-Cola. "There are a lot of places you can go and order a Pepsi and they'll give you another brand without even telling you," Patti explains. So the commercial where a little girl demands a real Pepsi, overdubbed with Marlon Brando's *Godfather* voice, addressed that issue.

"We were on eggshells. We were all out in Los Angeles, and we thought Brando would go in and read it once or twice and say, that's it, give me my cheque. But he came in and the first thing he did, which I guess is very Marlon Brando, was to say, I don't like this script at all, who's the writer here? And I said, well, er, I am, and he said, The Godfather would never say these words quite this way, will you sit with me? And we sat for forty-five minutes while we went over the script line by line, and he would read it and interpret it, and as he did it you could see him getting into the role of Don Corleone. It was quite an amazing thing. By the time we had the script in great shape and sounding like Don Corleone, we thought he would just go into the booth and read it once or twice, and that would be it. But he went in there for about a halfhour and kept doing it over and over, asking our input, and getting the character exactly right. If he didn't like a take he told us. And after that, he stayed around and told us fabulous stories about Broadway and Hollywood for another hour." When the commercial was shot, the little girl mimed to Brando's lines on playback. New software allowed the computer to editorially compensate the track and improve her lip sync.

Singapore Airlines. It was all about defying conventional wisdom, recalls group chairman Ian Batey of Singapore's Batey Ads. The fledgling Asian airline sold itself on a platform of inflight service when no other airline did. It used television as the brand-building medium against all advice to the contrary. And it invested a higher-than-average proportion of its budget in producing a stable of world-class commercials.

"When we wanted to go on television, it was against very fierce arguments by local agencies. Going on television is totally wasteful, they said. You've got to be more focused against your target group." Batey remained adamant. "We went on TV to build a brand, and build it quickly, particularly in the case of London and West Coast USA, which were fairly new markets for the airline in the 70s. If you get your act right creatively, you can take a bit of wastage, because the impact will far transcend any wastage."

Batey envisioned a different kind of airline campaign. "We said, let's have a stable of up to six different commercials in any one year on a fairly thin budget and rotate them. That sort of menu gave them freshness. You never really saw one commercial for too long. You'd see another, then another, then another. That meant the client had to commit himself to a large production budget vis-à-vis his total spend. And he said, I'll buy off on that thinking."

We follow the Singapore Girl as she explores San Francisco.

She has a charming way about her and people always respond to her quiet dignity and grace. Not surprisingly, she is well recognised wherever she goes.

End line: *Singapore Airlines. A great way to fly.*

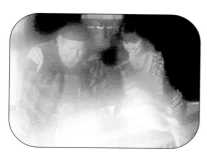

The campaign that launched an airline — and an agency. Batey Ads staked out the territory of service for Singapore Airlines while competitors advertised routes and fleet sizes. The Singapore Girl became the international branding icon for inflight service "that even other airlines talk about". Thirty years later, she still is. Creative director John Finn worked on the campaign since its inception. Pat Aulton's original theme song continues.

For the first ten years, the commercials focused on the Singapore Girl. And, from the first commercial ever shot right through to the present day, all the Singapore Girls have been actual flight stewardesses. No professional models have ever been used. "We were selling the icon," explains Batey. "The client's objective was to fill as many seats as possible for the best possible yield. So what we wanted the consumers to take out was a beautiful, rare travel experience — worth paying a little bit extra for." As Batey observes, "They were a brave and trusting client and they delivered on their promise to the consumer. But, in terms of a brand proposition, you just can't live by saying, aren't we nice people. You've got to give some rational arguments to support the emotional ones. After a while we had other product offerings. We promoted the world's most modern fleet, the best inflight entertainment." There's nothing wrong with that, says Batey, and you need to do that, but don't think for one minute that the way you can buy people is to spend money on product improvement all the time. "There's got to be an emotional connection and bonding, selling the soul of the brand; it can't be just 'here's a bigger seat, here's a fatter cocktail, here's a bigger screen', because money buys that and anyone with a thicker cheque book can go out and upstage you tomorrow. *What they can't buy is the soul that you're selling.*"

Most brands would not have run virtually the same campaign for almost thirty years. There must have been external and internal pressures to change. "It's conventional to change," argues Batey, "it's *unconventional* not to change. Everyone says we've got to change to survive. But if I know what my consumers are about and if I keep improving my product, then the way I talk to them won't change because I am what I am. When you're on a good thing, you don't change for the sake of changing. When you become a national institution like Singapore Airlines, you become like the national flag or the national anthem, and you don't change them every year. It's the same thing with the Singapore Girl. She should never really change; she is that same gentle personality forever and ever. What, however, does change around her is that she might offer you wider seats, she might offer you wider aisles, she might offer you more cocktails and better food, *but she herself never really changes.*

That's where you have to work out the relationship between the two. We can't stand still on technology, or services on the ground, and we have to keep on improving food and entertainment. But what shouldn't change are the Girl and the experience when you step on board."

On the other hand, the campaign doesn't stop evolving. "Yes, you have to make her relevant and contemporary," acknowledges Batey. "I maintain that a lot of that relates to the production values. You can contemporise the executional style, rather than the Girl herself. We always say we think it's a beautiful world out there, and we're part of that beautiful world and, whatever happens, we always believe in the romance of travel. Those two things, the beautiful world and the romance of travel, provide the canvas on which we paint."

Transport Accident Commission, Victoria. The TAC television campaign, from Grey Advertising in Melbourne, is probably the world's longest running campaign funded by a public authority through the same agency. It is certainly Australia's *most consistently awarded campaign*, and the only one that has ever won Best of Show at America's One Show. Creative director Nigel Dawson shares the philosophy behind the campaign: "Compared to other advocacy campaigns around the world, we make quite sure we don't have any *advertising* ideas in our commercials. We want them to show reality, to be believable and compelling; put an advertising idea in it, and it becomes an ad. It's a far more disciplined campaign than anything I've ever worked on. A kind of formula has evolved as a result of the tripartite relationship between Grey, TAC, and the researchers."

The campaign was launched on the eve of the Christmas party season in 1989. TAC is a state-owned enterprise set up by the Victorian State Government. "It's basically an insurance company," says Dawson. "When you register your vehicle, you also pay an insurance premium which goes direct to the TAC. If you have an accident anywhere in the State, whether you are at fault or not, you are covered by TAC for all your injuries. So it is in the TAC's interest to keep the incidence, and therefore the cost, of road accidents as low as possible."

The results are impressive. In 1989 the Victorian road toll was 776; in 1999 it was 383. Over ten years, the TAC campaign has contributed to *the saving of 3,514 lives and financial savings of US$1.8 billion in claims and costs to the community.* In tracking studies, it enjoys around 90% unaided recall and 98% community support. Victoria now boasts *one of the lowest road fatality rates in the world* (1.18 deaths per 10,000 vehicles registered). The annual media spend averages around US$6 million. Apart from creative recognition at D&AD, Gold at Cannes and the One Show, and dozens more accolades, the campaign has won many effectiveness awards around the world.

Back in 1989, the media played a key role in putting road safety on the public agenda. The community was angry about the road toll, and initial research gave the agency permission to "shock, outrage and appal", to be emotional, to establish a link between drink-driving, speeding and "real" accidents, and ensure that viewers would be left thinking "this could happen to me". Research warned against too much twisted metal, too many boring statistics, a lecturing tonality, people in uniforms, and telling the public they couldn't have a drink. The task was complicated by the huge variety of road safety ads, public relations campaigns, and good corporate citizen messages. The TAC had to establish a new, single voice on road safety.

After fifty executions that voice *hasn't* changed, Dawson reports. The campaign always applies the rules of documentary drama to advertising. "*The camera as observer*," he explains. "We always ask ourselves, when people see the ad will they say, that could so easily have been me. The camera therefore has to observe a person *that could be me*, having a drink or whatever, and then doing something stupid; not putting a seat belt on, or dropping off to sleep at the wheel. So I'm watching myself, rather than a piece of Hollywood, a piece of slick advertising. The audience has to be emotionally involved, firstly with the kind of behaviour that leads to a particular kind of crash, and then with the aftermath. Generally, it's behaviour, drive, crash, aftermath — death or serious injury, leading to the awful emotional trauma. We test things over and over again as a reality check. The minute it becomes unbelievable, the minute anybody can find a way out, they will; oh no, I wouldn't do that; oh no, people don't do that; no, I wouldn't drive that sort of car. It's got to be real accidents, real emotions, real people suffering real pain. The commercials are utterly credible; I've sat in double-head research groups and heard people say, but that's a real accident, isn't it, that's not actors." Dawson says the crashes can't be too big. "You cross the border from reality into entertainment. People start thinking, wow, that was a great crash, how did they do that? Thus they become less emotionally involved."

Dawson says TAC commercials rarely use voice-overs. *"We abide by the rule of letting people work things out for themselves.* They can fill in all the gaps." Sometimes, though, the commercials will deliberately give instructions. One famous example was the car hitting the man with a box of pizza. The man flips up into the air. "The message of that commercial was to cut your driving speed in urban areas by ten kilometres an hour. At seventy kilometres an hour, you'll kill him. At sixty, you'll just give him a severe shock. It's a more rational, more didactic commercial, but still very graphic. You don't feel for the guy as much because you don't get to know him. With our previous commercials people were saying, if I do something stupid, I might kill somebody. But with this commercial they could say, with this piece of information I can knock ten kilometres off my speed to *make sure* I don't kill somebody."

Grey has recently completed its fiftieth commercial for TAC, averaging four or five a year. The campaign was originated by Greg Harper and Stuart Byfield and continues with Nigel Dawson and Rob Dow.

6

HOW TO BE FUNNY

G eorge Bernard Shaw believed, "In order to educate or enlighten, you must first entertain."

Advertising, says Ron Lawner, is about getting people to like you. And humour is a very human approach. "Nobody likes being yelled at or scolded or lectured to. If you can get your point across to me, and you can do it with a sense of humanity and a sense of humour, and I get the sense that you don't take yourself too seriously, then I like you better."

Dion Hughes wishes he had done more funny commercials. "The truth is," he admits, "I have done plenty of serious work. It just hasn't received the attention the humorous stuff has." Hughes believes humour is one of the few irony-proof ways of communicating a message. "It consistently works with consumers."

While no one seriously believes the old adage, "People don't buy from comedians", humour in advertising is fraught with problems. Humour, like music, is subjective. It is one of the hardest genres to master. Ask any comedian how tough it is to be funny; except, of course, Tony Hancock. Being funny drove him to suicide.

Realistically, what reaction can we expect from a funny ad?

"Some people say, an outright laugh, and I'm not sure if that's asking too much or not," argues Chuck McBride. "My feeling is, if you can get them to lean forward in their chair a little bit, or if you can get someone in a bar to turn to someone else and say, hey, did you just see that? That usually means the next time they see it, they're going to be laughing their heads off."

WHAT KIND OF HUMOUR WORKS BEST?

The first issue to resolve is one of the hardest: who or what will be the butt of the joke? Obviously, if it's the consumer, it's not a good idea. What salesman would walk up to a prospect, laugh at their shortcomings and then try to sell them something?

"There is not a scientific theorem that proves what is or isn't funny," confirms director Frank Todaro, @radical.media New York. Todaro's forte is humour; within the genre, he has resisted any form of typecasting. "I was doing a lot of mockumentaries for ESPN SportsCenter; then I got lots of the same kind of ideas coming in. My favourite type of humour is very quiet, very dry humour, through to something more screwball, more slapstick. I tend to avoid very broad humour, not that I dismiss it out of hand, but it can be a little ham-fisted. Sometimes I'll get stuff where the script may not be hilarious, but with the right casting and performance twist it could be charming." Like other genres, Todaro warns, humour can become highly imitative. "When we were doing SportsCenter work five years ago, we occasionally had these guys walking by in the background in college mascot uniforms. There was an absurd quality to it. Now there's a spate of guys in silly outfits, dressed as huge corn flakes or chickens, and I'm sick to death of it. When you're in an agency you don't quite know what people are doing in other agencies. But here you see work coming in from everywhere and trying to change these cycles is like turning a huge yacht in a tiny harbour."

One of the safest ways to get laughs is self-deprecating humour. The joke is on you, the comedian. Few advertisers, though, are prepared to let their products be the butt of jokes. While Volkswagen happily endorsed the notion "it's ugly but it works", most would not.

The best humour, be it in movies, plays, books or commercials, is based on reality. It happens when a layer from real life is peeled back and reveals some facet that isn't quite what we expected. Looking at life through a cracked mirror means we can identify with the

Britain's Hamlet and (above) America's Little Caesars share top billing as the world's most consistent — and consistently funny — enduring campaigns. Little Caesars from Cliff Freeman & Partners New York.

humour, we can relate to the situation, but it doesn't make fun of us personally.

"People insights make for entertaining TV," considers Kes Gray. "They are rooted in life, and so is your audience. The highest praise you can receive will not come from an awards jury, but from your aunties, uncles and mates back home. For me, it doesn't get much better than that."

Comedy, says Ian Macdonald, is "not optically altered people, but good ideas, well-written, subtle and entertaining. I would travel a long way for a well-written script…"

Marcello Serpa believes the humour should come from the product benefit. And the humour should be iconoclastic. "Brazilians laugh a lot about themselves, and we make campaigns that let us laugh about ourselves." Serpa loves the humour of the Outpost.com campaign. "I think people are laughing about it because it's against all the political correctness. The humour is because everyone is so politically correct, society is so politically correct. You can't say anything that would offend women, or blacks, or Latinos, and then you have a guy shooting these small animals against a wall, and you make a point, you ask for complaints. It makes no concessions to anybody. That's what's fun about it. Finally, someone is breaking the rules. If you made this campaign in a country like Brazil, I don't think it would be as relevant as it is for the United States, because we don't care…"

BUT how do we know what kind of humour to use? How do we know what people will laugh at?

"When in doubt with comedy, *underplay it.*" Rowan Dean's advice is worth heeding. His famous *Photo Booth* commercial for Hamlet Cigars was voted Best Commercial of All Time at the Cannes International Advertising Festival in 1997. Less is more, he says. His formula for comedy: "The gag should be the selling message. If the gag is bolted on, I always find it's weaker." In his Singapore Airlines commercial, the joke about the grandmother who has forgotten all about her waiting family is also the message: stopover in Singapore. "The key emotions to avoid at all times are smugness, arrogance and cruelty. If something happens with a lack of innocence, if it happens deliberately to hurt someone, it's cruel and it's not funny."

Sadly, many supposedly funny commercials are anything but funny. There's a certain ploddiness about them; the humour is heavy-handed and obvious. Dean's view: "I always think commercials are like the drunks at a party. You're watching TV and there's this intrusion, basically by drunks. Some drunks are loud and obnoxious; most ads are loud and obnoxious. Some drunks are endlessly repetitive — let me make that point again — and you wish they'd go away; many commercials are endlessly repetitive. Some drunks are invisible, they're just comatose in the corner and you don't notice them; just like some ads. The ones you like, and remember, and talk about the next day — drunks or ads — are the ones who had a sense of humour, were probably self-effacing, didn't take themselves too seriously, and sold their positives through their negatives. You'd invite them next time round and you're quite happy to see them again. The best British and American commercials can do that with humour and humility." Dean stresses that the best ads are like telling

Politician Max Henderson is out canvassing door-to-door for votes.

Max: *Hello. Max Henderson. I'm standing for parliament in your electorate. Have you got a minute?*

The teenager offers him some Whittaker's Peanut Slab: *Huh...want one?*

Max: *Oh, thank you. Very kind.* (Chewing away...) *Well, anyway, our party stands for fiscal responsibility and more integrity in government.* (The good honest chocolate kicks in...) *But, obviously, we'll change our values depending on the poll results. As your MP, I'll be abusing the free airfares, as will my wife and my mistress...I'll go joyriding in the government limos. I'll spend a lot of time in bars, massage parlours, that sort of thing. And three months into my term, I'll change parties, refuse to resign, and basically try to hold the country to ransom.*

End VO and super: *Whittaker's Peanut Slab. Good Honest Chocolate since 1896.*

Good honest chocolate — so honest, in fact, it can make a politician tell the truth. More award-winning humour from Saatchi & Saatchi Wellington. Art director John Fisher and copywriter John Plimmer made the lateral leap.

A genial man steps in front of a police line-up chart.

Norman: *I'm Norman Price...*

He introduces an equally little woman.

Norman: *And this is my wife Shirley. I believe you're looking for us.*

MVO: *Looking for small prices? Hardwarehouse has hundreds.*

End super: *Hardwarehouse.*

Entertainment works for retailers. Hardwarehouse was written by Paul Fishlock and art directed by Ron Mather at The Campaign Palace Sydney.

a joke. "You don't tell a joke by explaining the punchline, you set up a series of premises and the connection happens in the audience's head, and they laugh because *they* made the connection. You've got to let the audience make the connection, whatever it is you're selling or whatever it is you're trying to say. The moment you *tell* them, they're going to switch off and walk away."

A lot depends on *how often* the commercial will run. You might think it's clever the first couple of times you see it, but not if you see it every day. Jokes wear thin if their creators don't allow for exposure. It helps, of course, says Dean, to build in additional rewards for the viewer. "Without ever overgilding the lily, I always like to put in little things that you mightn't notice until the tenth or fifteenth viewing, as long as they're in keeping with the whole thing," he adds.

Gray agrees, referencing the famous Carling Black Label Beer campaign from British agency WCRS. "The thing that killed a lot of Carling scripts was the question of repeat viewing. Would your script stand up to repeat viewing? Very often the answer to that was No, not once you've got the joke. It was never enough to have a one-joke Carling ad. It just wouldn't do. You had to keep working at it, get as many little twists and turns into it."

A lot also depends on *when* the commercial will run. Black humour doesn't play on American morning television, as Bill Oberlander discloses. "We did a commercial for Olympus cameras, shot by the Coen Brothers. The premise was that Olympus is used by more professional photographers to shoot their family photos. Professional photographers will use a Nikon or a Hasselblad or a Leica in their studio, but when they go home they shoot their kids on an Olympus pocket camera. So we turned that further and said, if an average person is seen with an Olympus camera they get mistaken for being a professional photographer. So we had this one commercial where these Eastern European thugs were interrogating this guy. They felt he was a spy or a journalist trying to get dirt because he had an Olympus camera. At the end of the commercial, they basically said to kill him. And the client said to us, we really want to push it, we really want to get people talking. And we said, are you sure? And they said, yes, really, we want to get our palms sweaty. And we said, are you *sure*…? So we just did it. Then I found out that the media buy was morning talk shows, Mom making the oatmeal, getting the kids ready for school, and suddenly on comes this commercial about killing American tourists in Eastern European countries." The extremely black, tongue-in-cheek humour did not click with the audience. "The client pulled the campaign because they got all these letters from upset consumers. It was just too much for them."

Can You Learn To Be Funny?

"Comedy is craft, and you learn what works and what doesn't. You kind of know instinctively what to avoid and what buttons to push." Cliff Freeman & Partners has a reputation for creating funny commercials that actually *are* funny. However, Arthur Bijur insists that not everything the agency does is funny, even when it's meant to be. "People are being kind. We just don't advertise the stuff that doesn't turn out funny," he quips. "Cliff has got a certain kind of a sensibility about comedy. I think I do, too. When you have really good people around you, you can figure out ways to make things work."

Having "people around you" can also prove counterproductive, as Todaro admits. "In your heart, you *know* how something will be funny. And of course, all the other people standing around you know how it will be funny, too. That's the thing you always come up against. Between your initial conceptualising it and the final edit, something can get lost. It happens all the time, more frequently than not. The director shoots and hands the film over to the agency. Once an agency left out one of the punchlines. Somebody had said, I think it's funnier without it." Todaro is philosophical. "When I was at an agency, I sat there, too, saying the director didn't understand the spot when we gave it to him…"

"You cannot go wrong with what Chaplin, Seinfeld, Mr. Bean and all the great comics have understood," says Dean. "It's the little bloke, whose head's spinning, who's got a mass of insecurities. You like him because everybody has insecurities. Everybody has foibles. Nobody is this 'picture-perfect presentation' that most commercials show. Most people are alienated when they see a good-looking, glamorous person with a great life. They're *ex*cluded. They're included when they see the bloke who's bald or whatever, or who's wearing a dodgy suit, or who makes mistakes. That's *in*clusive because we all do that, and we want him to win." How does Dean know when something is funny? "Pure instinct. You can feel very quickly when things aren't funny. There's a lot to be learned from great comedians like Woody Allen and Rowan Atkinson. *Anything contrived isn't funny*. Forget it. Often you have to discard a funny script because it is contrived. It has to have integrity, it has to be real, it has to be credible, and it has to be innocent."

"Comedians and scriptwriters know about timing and delivery." Gray believes writers must understand the metre of a script and the way to work all the elements into the structure to deliver a message. "Everything you write has to have rhythm and balance." Advertising isn't poetry, he says, but it is a writer's job to be aware of those things.

McBride reveals how to capture the humour of the moment and compress the time sequence of the joke. "We try to drop in on a conversation or a moment, and be with it for *that* moment. What television can do very easily is transport you through time relatively quickly, but it becomes rather a 'device' and I think you lose your contact with the *real circumstances that are at play*. In *Aaron Burr*, we created a visual interest by not staying on a shot for a long time — *but the time was in concert with the moment*. It was: a man is listening to music, the music stops, the radio comes on and says now it's time for our question — *all that could have happened in thirty seconds in life*. And I wanted most of the scripts I dealt with for *got milk?* to be that way." McBride's *Airplane* script was condensed to the thirty seconds prior to the climax of the story. "The sequence of time is pretty spot-on. We worked back from the 'milk moment'; the moment when someone realised they needed milk and couldn't get it. If the pilot wanted milk, this is what he'd do … he'd put the airplane into a dive … now, at what point doesn't he get it, and I'll back up the story from there. I'll keep it on time. So I don't write: early morning … everybody is getting onto a flight … we go up in the air … we find out what they're serving … she approaches with the cookies…" McBride's commercial was based on an observation of life. "I needed a situation. I was actually on a plane and I was sitting there, looking at the pilot. They were giving out cookies and I saw the pilot being given one and I looked back and there's the cart with milk on it, and I thought, wouldn't that be funny!"

SHOOTING FOR LAUGHS

Bruce Bildsten recalls his Timex *Torture Test* commercial shot by Joe Sedelmaier. An ugly lady's face shattered glass wherever she went. Her visit to a watch dealer was catastrophic. Only the Timex watches kept on ticking. "It was all about nuance. Certain comedy directors know how to tell a joke, know the little nuances, and know when to pull back and be restrained."

David Denneen of Sydney's Film Graphics discusses the art of comedy. "Most of the scripts I get to shoot are stories that have to be told in thirty seconds. I think with my animation background, I learnt the art of setting up shots in a clear and sequential way. Each tells its own little part of the story clearly and precisely and when strung together, the story unfolds in a seamless manner. Therefore I don't have to rely on tricks at post stage." A lot of comedy spots are shot in what Denneen describes as a raw, uninspiring way. "They just rely on the script and talent performance, and not on the standard of the visuals. This, to me, is not a good thing either."

Todaro elaborates on casting for comedy. "Sometimes somebody could be right, but they're nervous, or they're in a weird way; if you give them only two shots at it, that might be when they're just getting past whatever it is they have to get past. I'll work with somebody until I'm convinced they can't do it. Sometimes you get these guys who are not really funny people. They try to do it, but it's very bad, pandering joke-salesmanship. What I try to go for is somebody whose instincts are right; they're not acting it, they're *feeling* it. Everybody else can tell the difference, too, but they may not know why or how. It's a purely subjective thing." The risk of over-rehearsing is ever present. "Commercials are different from legit stuff. A lot always depends on the scripts. I'll sometimes say, here's the gist, just do it the way you feel like you'd *want* to do it, don't worry about hitting all these words, and a lot of times that will free them up a bit. Sometimes you'll get to a point where you do nothing."

A classic Fallon Minneapolis spoof of demonstration commercials. When three Penn Tennis Balls were dropped from the top of a 40-storey building, each bounced back to the same height every time. "Now we try the same test with our competitor..."

REPRODUCED WITH KIND PERMISSION OF PENN RACQUET SPORTS.

One of the greatest sins in comedy is *"indicating"*. As Todaro explains, "It's where they take you by the hand and point you right at the joke and say, see what we've done, 'Joke Here', with big arrows. It's shameful. Sometimes it's done with music or big reactions that make it very obvious. Why put in funny music? Put in serious music and cut against the joke; it's funnier, more absurd, to play it straight."

Rick Dublin of Dublin Productions Minneapolis, warns against *nuance-directing*. "Some directors direct every single move of the talent. It's a rare director who can nuance-direct and get away with it. Over time I've learned that the fewer words you use with an actor, the better. You need to let the actor do what you hired him for. The director's job is to explain the scenario. If you start nuance-directing you're in big trouble." Dublin believes the best results happen when agencies are open to new ideas. "When everybody stays in their own corner, it's not good. Fallon's not only know what they want, but they're always open to listening. It gives me a chance to have a lot of input. You get a chance to work with the creatives. Sometimes when you get very close to a project you get boxed in. You wrote it, you've lived with it for a long time." Dublin recalls one job when he asked

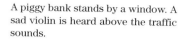

A piggy bank stands by a window. A sad violin is heard above the traffic sounds.

The pig looks down at the street. Is this the only way out?

Cut to super: *Jacoby & Meyers.*

Male VO: *Bankruptcy? A team of lawyers is waiting to help. Jacoby & Meyers. Problem solved.*

An irreverent 15-seconder on a low budget makes it possible for smaller clients to access television. Mad Dogs & Englishmen New York.

an agency if there was a different way to end their spots. "The agency said, well, we're wide open. But on the day of the shoot I still didn't have a new ending so I took the four actors into a room. Just me and the actors in this room, no one else. We went through a bunch of scenarios and I shot the new ending in two takes."

As Dean reminds us, everything has to work within the structure of the story. "I was doing a commercial where two people fall down.

How hot is Tabasco…? In this commercial from DDB Worldwide, Dallas, any mosquito that imbibes the blood of a Tabasco user will self-destruct.

The reaction from the third character who hadn't fallen down wasn't funny. The actor either wanted to do shock-horror or a smug, pleased look that he hadn't suffered the same fate. Smugness is death. We did fifteen takes with the actor and every expression just felt wrong. You've got all the pressures of a shoot, you just know the expression isn't right, you think come on, come on, get on with it. Then I thought back to how an innocent character would react, how a 7-year-old might react, and I could see a look of relief — 'glad that wasn't me' — and it was immediately perfect." Dean storyboards expressions. "When I do a storyboard, I draw these *Tintin*-like expressions, just a circle and a mouth, and you get a feeling of what the expression should be. If you can't convey the humour in those little pencil sketches, if you can't convey it in cartoon form, you *can't* convey it on film."

McBride discusses observed humour and how a camera angle can accentuate or *de*-accentuate the funny factor in a film. "What we've been playing around with over the last few years is going to a longer lens to compress backgrounds against the characters a little more, creating a soft background almost like a 70s style film. In the late

80s, early 90s, we were distorting people's faces to make them funny, whereas now we're flattening out the scene a little so that it plays a bit straighter." When the camera lens is not part of the joke, it functions as the observer, the human eye. When the camera gets involved, McBride says, suddenly you start to see the film making. "When the camera is not participating in the story, you're not doing a lot of lensing or dollying to create the idea that something funny is going on. *You let the action itself give you that sense*. It's a more sophisticated sense of humour. It lets the viewer participate more like they were there instead of going, oh, it was filmed that way, that's why it's funny. *It should be the absurdity of what's happening that makes you laugh.*" McBride questions a lot of filmic conventions. "Would modern horror films be all that scary if they didn't do all that camera trickery? I doubt it. Yet comedy was following that same rule of thumb for a long time. What we noticed was that if you had a really great standup comic, or if you had a great performance artist, you didn't need a camera to laugh. You just stood back and watched them. And if you were observing someone who was being very funny, you were a part of the comedy as opposed to just *being told* when to laugh, how to laugh, and, hey, isn't this guy weird looking." Television is so often used to drive fantasy, McBride says, that it's easy to dismiss some of the content. "If you set up your commercial as being real or observed, it's more unsettling for the viewer and they've *got* to find out where it's going to go…"

HOW do you get the right energy going on the shoot? "The place to do that is in your wide shots because the camera is the furthest removed from the action and therefore invading less space." The actors can enjoy a few mistakes, says McBride, and get used to the rhythm and the timings you want. McBride's methodology: "Try to get back on your wides for your opening sequences and do it in a place that feels natural, as opposed to coming down from the chandeliers which I used to love but now would not recommend. Just start straight, see the action, and have them go through the full commercial in the wide. Go front to back with mistakes. If there's a few in there, iron them out and have them do it again, front to back, all the way through. Then talk to your director, tell him what you saw." McBride says there will be extemporaneous things that happened in the wide shot that can be restaged and reshot from different angles, either looser or tighter. It is good to have a relationship with a director that allows for discussion and collaboration, he adds.

California Sunkist Pistachios. Scott Vincent recalls how he and his art director Jerry Gentile were getting nowhere on their Sunkist Pistachios job at TBWA Chiat/Day Venice. "A lot of time, planning helps. Unfortunately, planning had talked about pistachios being 'time for me'. We'd done a ton of campaigns, but in the end our creative director Steve Rabosky just came in and said, it's a nut, do something funny. So Jerry and I thought, well, it's a nut, and California was on the pack, and everyone thinks Californians are kind of nuts. We wrote the line, *Everybody knows the best nuts come from California*. We weren't going to present it. It was late at night and Jerry said, let's go down the street to Vidiots." Vidiots was a video store that stocked all kinds of bizarre tapes. "We decided to do a rip. We started out with people who were one-man bands, then we thought that's not really that funny. So we found this footage of an 'automatic painter' who stands and stares up at the ceiling while his hands paint perfectly, and we did the title card."

At the meeting, Gentile and Vincent presented three other concepts first. "The client's business people thought they were all too edgy. So we presented our last idea, the three rips for the *Nuts* campaign. We put it on. The business guys were horrified. But the owners, Linda and Stewart Resnik, were laughing." As so often happens, the people at the top appreciated the bizarre; the other layers were the Luddites.

Seven commercials were ultimately made. "They were all real people. There was even a couple who thought they had found a civilisation in the mountains of Santa Monica. They were deadly serious. We showed them all what we were doing; it wasn't like we hid it. We had a bunch of guys who dropped out because they didn't want to be made fun of."

The single commercial which won a Gold Pencil at the One Show featured August Priest, a sound toner. "He believed in what he did. He had rent due and car insurance. He said, I want more people to find out about me, even if you are making fun of me." Priest is seen cupping his hands and emitting a strange, howling sound into a man's lower back, while he explains what he is doing:

It opens your heart chakra, so you feel unconditional love just vibrating throughout all of you, comfortably and easily. You can feel your guardian angel surrounding you, creating balance and harmony.

Up comes some happy, bouncy music with the simple title card, *Everybody knows the best nuts come from California.*

The voice-over observes, *Sunkist California Pistachios ... now that's a nut.*

Another commercial in the Gold Pencil-winning campaign brings us face-to-face with an oddly garbed gentleman who announces:

My angel name is Sanfernandinaki. People call me Buddy.

After some heavy breathing and mysterious chanting, he delivers his final line:

We have spiritual parties at our house about once every other month. If you're at all interested, we'll invite you.

Vincent describes his music track as "work music". "I had all these cheesy songs, which we used to play at another agency when we had to do our timesheets."

The commercials were shot on video. "If we'd shot beautiful film, it would have looked 'produced', like 'you're making this happen'. It wouldn't have felt as real, even though the people were real. But we also didn't want to make it look crude or rough. So we didn't try to make it look anything. *We wanted the execution to go away and we wanted those guys to come forward.*" As Vincent reminds us, "When you get a good idea, it's almost like human nature to screw it up."

To their horror, Vincent and Gentile screened their work to unappreciative audiences. "No one at the agency thought they were funny except Steve. We were outcasts. The agency didn't enter them into awards, but Jeff Gorman, the director, did. They won at the Beldings and Cannes." Positive public reaction started coming in. "The agency did focus groups for other brands, and planners said that all people were talking about was the *Nuts* ads."

Vincent's advice to young creatives resonates for all creatives: "You can have a lot of fun in advertising, doing ads, going on shoots, but the hard part is when you really start to like something too much, and you care about it, like the *Nuts* thing. It makes the business kind of awful. It's when you do something, and you think about it when you go to sleep, and you know there's more than a likely chance it won't ever come to fruition. And people keep coming in and saying, you should change this, or do that, and you don't want to because you know in your head it's right." Advertising, says Vincent, makes you greedy. "You wake up, you put an idea together, and when you go to bed you can say, I built something. And then you want to build more and more stuff." Vincent talks about finding opportunities: "Nobody else really wanted the *Nuts* brief. It's not the assignments you're given that make you; it's what you do with the assignments when you get them. Stop looking at what everyone else is working on. When you get an assignment, it's like a present. For three years in one agency I just wrote coupons. If I did real good on the 'Save 50¢' ones, I'd get to do the 'Save $1' ones."

Carling Black Label Beer. The Carling campaign and its catchphrase, *I bet he drinks Carling Black Label*, became a British institution. "It was the reason I came into the business," confesses Gray who loved the Carling commercials while he was in college, years before his own *Dambusters* spot won Gold and Silver Pencils at D&AD. "I used to look out for them. I applauded how funny they were, right up to the pack shot. I liked the way they didn't just finish at the joke. Ironically, by the time I got to WCRS, nobody really wanted to work on Carling. It had kind of lost its way a little bit."

Gray wrote two Carling classics, *Dambusters* and *Squirrel*. Gray estimates that for every Carling script shot, probably forty or more were rejected. The creative directors made the final selection. "Alfredo Marcantonio presented *Dambusters*, Adrian Holmes presented *Squirrel*."

The idea for *Dambusters*, Gray says, didn't come from anywhere. "One of the things about this industry is that too many people think you 'find' or 'source' an idea. I believe my job is to *have* ideas, not to find them in annuals. Our job is to squirrel away things we see, things we hear, and apply them, twist them, expand on them or mix them up, and create something original with things that had once been original in their own time. Creative people watch and listen, it all goes in, and you have to have a very retentive memory. In the case of *Dambusters*, I'd seen the movie years before."

With Carling, Gray explains, thinking always began with the territory. "Where's a territory that no one else has been before? And that's hard. We hit upon the idea of the war thing. Carling had never been into the territory of black-and-white war films. You have to be careful with war because obviously it's a sensitive subject. We were just chatting away and then all of a sudden it just came. I'd grown up on *Dambusters* and *Reach for the Sky*; they were all the same genre. We were talking about the Dambusters raid, and bombs that bounced like balls, and we had the idea of the bloke who caught them like a football goalkeeper. We went from there to completely over-writing it. We had a football stadium completely redesigned like the Ruhr Valley and there were German football supporters down either side of this massive stadium."

Concepts play in Gray's mind like movies. "I can see the pictures in my head, I direct the scenes in my head, I cut them in my head. It's like a snowball effect." The *Dambusters* script took weeks and weeks of refining, and it also took a year to sell. "Once we had the idea of the 'goalkeeper' catching the bombs, things like the sausage sandwich joke happened on the shoot. When the German guard came out we wanted to give him something to do, so we gave him a sandwich, and then we pushed it a little bit more, and the sausage got longer and longer and funnier." Roger Woodburn directed the commercial. "It was very nicely paced."

The ending is a masterpiece of British comedy and a brilliant parody of black-and-white air force movies. Having observed the guard catching the bombs, one pilot removes his oxygen mask to deliver the Carling tagline in clear English: *I bet he drinks Carling Black Label*. The copilot removes his mask and still speaks in gibberish. According to Gray, "The client didn't think it would be funny. Perhaps I didn't write it properly on the script and we had to submit another ending before we were allowed to shoot it. The other ending was after he'd caught all the bombs, somebody lobbed in a toilet roll. He picked it up, tossed it over his shoulder, the whole dam shook and the wall was breached. We shot it as well." Were they ever tempted to run both endings, Version A rotating with Version B? "It was never a consideration. It'd be a bit self-indulgent. You've got to get it right the first time." Even the pack shot delivered another joke: a little bomb bouncing along five glasses of Carling in time to the jingle.

When they explored the black-and-white war movie genre, *Dambusters* was not the only idea they pursued. *The Wooden Horse* was another inspired concept. "It was about digging tunnels in POW camps. We had this guy who shook his trouser leg and a little bit of sand came out. Then he shook it again and a bit of earth came out. Then he shook it again and some rubble came out. Then he shook it again.... At the end there was this massive great pile of stuff he was shaking out of his trousers. A German guard watching him said, *I bet he drinks Carling Black Label*. It was never made."

Squirrel was a lateral leap. Cue the theme from *Mission Impossible*. Gray had a squirrel performing action movie "stunts" high above a suburban garden, darting up and down poles, skimming along a rope upside down, conquering all obstacles in its path. Two owls observe the action. One turns to the other and hoots, *I bet he drinks Carling Black Label*.

Fiat. At Collett Dickenson Pearce, Tony Brignull and Neil Godfrey made a commercial about an Italian man standing on his balcony one morning, torn between his wife and washing his Fiat.

"In England, people tend to wash their cars on a Sunday morning, but the Italians tend not to bother with that sort of thing," explains Godfrey. "We hear his wife, who's obviously had a good night with him, calling him back for a second helping. He has to make a decision. Does he clean the car or go back to her, and of course being Italian he'll always go back to his wife. There was just a backward glance to the car, *what can I do?* And then we showed the car and the voice-over talked about the fact that it didn't need to be cleaned that often because it had a good paint job on it. There was a nice line about it being made for a husband and wife and a family of two — and when she called him back to bed again the voice said, *Or maybe three*."

Fosters Lager. "I had no brief. I was given a weekend to write the thing." Dean revisits his Fosters campaign that starred Paul Hogan. The *Wine Cellar* commercial won a Gold Lion at Cannes. "I was at Cherry Hedger Seymour, London. I was little more than a despatch guy. They were English and having huge problems writing a Fosters commercial for the UK market that didn't offend the Australians. In those days, in the late 70s, as far as the Poms were concerned, they knew nothing about Australia. Every commercial they wrote was boomerangs, kangaroos and Rolf Harris. Fosters in Melbourne were going berserk saying, we will not present ourselves like this. So the agency said, you're an Aussie, you write them something they'll like."

Dean's own experiences in the UK triggered the creative breakthrough. "I'd been living over there for a couple of years and I'd met all sorts of resistance from English people; one person, after I'd been in despatch for six months, said to me, we're quite impressed, you really are intelligent for an Australian. And it was said without irony, without attempting to be clever, and with a genuine attempt to flatter me. And that was the attitude the English had then. So I thought, let's take that experience. Let's take an innocent Aussie who comes over to England to sell Fosters. As far as he is concerned, Fosters *is* beer; there is no other beer. So from his perspective, the Poms have never had beer; they don't know what they're missing out on. And from that, I just extrapolated everything he loved about Australia. When he looked around England and saw its counterpart, he misunderstood it. When he saw rain, he thought the drought was breaking. When he saw a foxhound, he thought it was a funny looking dingo. We called the campaign, *The Innocent Abroad.* Fosters just loved it and bought it within twelve hours of seeing the script."

Dean describes the campaign as basically the precursor to Paul Hogan's famous movie character *Crocodile Dundee.* "It was saying, here are our Australian values; we're going to take them with us. We're innocent when we go abroad, we love what's back there in Oz. What worked was that he wasn't boasting. I actually had a huge argument with Paul Hogan in the second year when we were doing the *Wine Cellar* and *Garden Party* commercials. Paul said, I don't want to wear this tee-shirt anymore, I've been accepted in England, I want to be funny, but I don't want them laughing at me. And we spent a day in a hotel in Park Lane thrashing this out. For me, that innocence, that vulnerability, was a critical component. It runs through the Hamlet campaign, it runs through all the great comedies. Paul said he was going to choose his own suit for the *Wine Cellar* commercial, and the director and I thought it would be much funnier if he was in a tee-shirt, jeans, some Australian gear. And in the *Garden Party* commercial, he wanted to wear a dinner jacket because he wanted to be the hero and lose his innocence. He wanted to be like the Great Gatsby. Anyhow, I lost that argument. Paul arrived at the shoot in this blue safari suit that he thought was terrific. The director and I just looked at each other and said, yes, perfect! All the extras were looking at the blue safari suit and covering their mouths. Paul had become the character, he had stepped into that innocence."

Where campaigns lose their way, says Dean, is when they say, we've gone past innocence, now let's be clever, let's be smarter. "The Hogan campaign ran off the rails after a couple of years. Year 3 was going to be Hogan returning to his little outback town in Australia. I had twisted the whole gag round. He would have been coming home as Mr. Know-It-All from England. He would then have been the wise one. I knew he'd have to lose his innocence eventually," adds Dean, "so I put the innocence on the town." The commercials were never made.

Hamlet Cigars. Dean joined Collett Dickenson Pearce London, in the early 80s. "It was a strange time for CDP. They were coming down from the heady late 70s. Frank Lowe had just left and set up Lowe Howard-Spink. There was a lot of emotion at the time over that, there was a lot of creative insecurity. One of the great accounts, Heineken, had just left the agency. I joined Garry Horner, who was already there working with Indra Sinha, and I'd worked with both of them at O&M a couple of years previously."

Campaigns like Hamlet, Dean recalls, were almost run by a Star Chamber or committee — the creative director, the agency chairman and some of the senior creatives would sit around and say, which script do we think is best? "Only *one* Hamlet commercial was made every year and obviously everyone wanted to do it."

Dean and Horner realised the odds were stacked against them. "We were both mid-level, so we set up our own little alternate

Hamlet commercial-making factory. We decided that virtually every single day we came into the office we would write a Hamlet commercial. That was our brief to ourselves, and we did that for the couple of years we were together at CDP." Horner is now creative director at DDB Sydney, not far from Rowan Dean Films. "So we can still recycle our old ideas today," jokes Dean.

The first script they presented internally was *Frankenstein*. "It was turned down flat. So we approached a new film director, a photographer called Stak, and said if you would like a Hamlet commercial on your reel, you can film this. So he financed it. We presented the finished commercial and everyone laughed, but it just so happened that someone involved in the business was gay and looked exactly like the actor we'd cast. It was felt that this particular individual would see the commercial as a personal affront, so it was shelved. But there was a Rumpole-esque character called John Ritchie who was a suit, and he looked after the Benson & Hedges account. He showed it to the client. Six months after we'd shot it, they decided to run it." Years later, Ritchie's son Guy married Madonna.

Hamlet *Frankenstein* won a Gold Lion at Cannes and many other awards and, according to Dean, ruffled a few feathers internally. "So we thought, we've done it once, let's do it again."

Their Hamlet factory had generated all sorts of different ideas, including a rather unlikely script about a man sitting in a photo booth. "One thing which every creative person wants to do at some stage is that classic locked-off camera commercial. My two all-time favourites from the fifty-eight commercials in the Hamlet campaign were the *Man in the Lift* and *Bunker*, which had been almost a

Based on Philip Differ's TV sketch, Rowan Dean and Garry Horner put the baldy man in a Photo Booth *for Hamlet Cigars. The commercial was voted Best Commercial of All Time at the Cannes Advertising Festival.*

locked-off shot. You didn't see the golfer at all. It wasn't a gag as such; it's just a scenario that's humiliating. The other one, which hardly anyone had seen, was a locked-off camera of a man in a lift. He had all his Xmas shopping and as more and more people got in, he got more and more bunched up and uncomfortable. Eventually, he lit a cigar. The Hamlet music was going throughout, like lift music; it wasn't just used to punctuate the point of humiliation. It was a 60-seconder, there was no particular gag, but it was just a great moment and we were looking to do something like that. Then we saw this sketch on a TV show. Philip Differ wrote it about a baldy man. So we had this script of a baldy guy just sitting in a photo booth with a locked-off camera, you don't know what he's doing, or why he's there. It was very unstructured. It wasn't a traditional gag as such. After *Frankenstein*, a couple of directors had said to us, look, if you happen to have another script, call us. But people didn't think it was funny. One director said, no, but if you do something as funny as *Frankenstein*, I'll film it for you. So we went to Graham Rose who'd done a lot of Hamlet work and he just leapt on it. So, in a tiny room, for no money, we shot *Photo Booth* with this Mr. Bean character from the 80s. We got him down from Scotland for the day. The only discussion we had was the colour of the curtain in the booth; what about green, what about orange? It was a one-hour shoot. It had to be all-in-one shot, no cuts. We did ten takes and we had a 60 and a 30."

Disaster struck. "When we showed it back at the agency, nobody liked it. In fact, a lot of senior, very talented creative guys told us we'd blown it. It wasn't funny. We'd been negligent in not getting a wide shot. How do you know he's in a photo booth? He could be anywhere. To make matters worse, my father had come over from Australia and thought it was a bloke in a dentist's chair. My mother-in-law thought it was someone being electrocuted! Nobody wanted to show it to the client. The director was devastated. So it languished. It just sat there. And then John Ritchie happened to wander in from his summer holiday, saw it, thought it was great, and took it to the client who loved it. I think there was another Hamlet commercial in the works at the time so it was agreed that *Photo Booth* wouldn't run on TV. They decided to run the 60-seconder in a huge cinema in Leicester Square and see how it went. Garry and I and our wives headed down for the first screening. We were so nervous. We sat there in the audience in a packed cinema and it came up second or third ad. There was silence, just people chomping on popcorn. Then the first flash went off and there were a couple of little chuckles. Then the second flash went off, followed by a ripple of chuckles. By 50 seconds through the commercial, the whole cinema was in stitches and I swear, at the end the audience stood up and applauded."

Photo Booth won a Gold Lion at Cannes and a D&AD Silver Pencil.

Little Caesar Enterprises, Inc. This campaign, more than any other, has showcased Cliff Freeman's flair for comedy and his strict adherence to the disciplines of the genre. Bijur says the right premise is critical. *"You always have to start with a funny idea, a funny premise.* Where a lot of agencies go wrong is they don't start with a good premise, and then they try to make something out of it and it doesn't resonate."

Training Camp was voted one of the top fifty commercials of the decade.

"It came about because Little Caesars was the last of the three pizza chains to deliver. Domino's had been delivering for years. Pizza Hut had been delivering for years. And then here comes Little Caesars, they had to make some sort of noise. We had to do the biggest, most ridiculous introduction of delivery possible, otherwise it would really have made no difference to anybody. When you have no news, sometimes you have to find pretty ridiculous ways of presenting it."

Bijur describes the lateral leap as a nice, simple notion. "These two kids, Matt Vescovo and Steve Dildarian, came up with the original idea. They said, to make the most out of this, we'd have to make it absurdly big. A training camp for delivery people. How ridiculous! It played off of a stored-up knowledge of Little Caesars. It was in a way a little bit of a parody of itself. It was just so perfect for Little Caesars *tone.*"

Miller Lite. Arguably one of America's funniest and most controversial campaigns, it was the product of a Swedish team that Fallon Minneapolis recruited from the celebrated Paradiset agency:

art director Paul Malmström and writer Linus Karlsson. Karlsson recalls: "The actual character of Dick came out of a need to invite the viewer to have some fun together with us. Dick invited people into *his* reality."

The device of an invitation was important for Karlsson. "Commercials are an intrusion into your privacy. They are an unwelcome break in a movie. They are unwelcome because a lot of times the commercials tell you what to think, what to do, how to act, how to look, how to be. No one would like to be interrupted like that every five minutes."

The first commercial had a voice-over explaining that a man called Dick was going to write these ads. A man walking through a field established the campaign. "We wanted to communicate that this company has a nice soul. It has a perspective on life and its beer. Yes, beer is a serious business, but it's also fun. Because you should enjoy beer, the ads communicated the fun."

Karlsson's personal advertising philosophy is refreshing. "Every day when I go to work, I have to remind myself advertising is not important. *Because it isn't.* To any hardworking normal person, they don't go round thinking advertising and taglines. The way advertising is looked upon is the advertising industry's own responsibility. The way you treat people is the way you are treated back. Creative people in advertising have a very big responsibility not to go into people's homes and *shame* them and *insult* them. We have 30-second opportunities to reach out to millions of people. We can *encourage* people. We can *inspire* people. We can actually make people enjoy our ads. I believe everybody is creative. I don't think there is an exceptional group of extra-talented people who can only do advertising." Karlsson calls for a new perspective on mass communications. "Everybody out there is different. Who is to tell what's right and what's wrong? It is important to be polite to people, not just tell them how to think." Karlsson's philosophy has a sound economic base. "This is a business about selling stuff. It's a business of numbers. You've got to be smarter, more sophisticated in mass communications."

MTV. What was the creative leap that led Fallon Minneapolis to make a campaign about the Jukka Brothers, four bizarre Finnish brothers who lived in the woods? "Both Linus and I think it is very important to sit down and talk about the business problem with the client before we start talking about ideas," explains Malmström who devised the concept with his writer, Karlsson. "We had this very simple idea about these remote guys. The only connection they have with the rest of the world is MTV, and the guys who watch it are cool, and the guy who doesn't watch it is *un*cool. Then, of course, it gets more tongue-in-cheek. Maybe the guy who doesn't watch it, he is the cool guy because he is an individual, whereas the other guys just follow. That's what you laugh about and that's why the whole spot within itself has integrity for MTV; they can poke fun at themselves."

In every commercial, the older brothers punish the younger brother who doesn't watch MTV. He is dragged outside by the ear to the fuse box where the paddle with an MTV stencil is kept. His trousers are pulled down. His backside is paddled. It was only logical, says Malmström. "We have four brothers, they live in the woods, what is the best way they could punish their little brother? The paddle was branding, a nice way to get the pack shot on his cheeks!"

Jukka, says Malmström, is a very common first name in Finland. Well and good, but how did they convince MTV to buy into such a bizarre concept for global use? "We made a little book about these four guys. We used the computer; we took a nose from here, a haircut from there. We showed where they lived, their psychological profile, the dynamics between them. It was a fun little book and it was our sales tool. We didn't have any animatics. We just told the client the story and he loved the whole idea. Allan Bruce was lovely to work with. We like to have that collaboration with the client and invite the client very early on into the creative process, so we can all have fun with it."

The commercials were shot in Sweden with a Swedish production company. "We wanted a different look from what you normally see on MTV because a good ad must stand out from its environment. It's easy to lose an idea through technique. If you have a good story, with something funny happening with some good actors, then the camera has to be just straight on — so you can really follow the story and appreciate it. You can't use a wide-angle lens and strange angles.

You've got to break the rules and stand out." Malmström and Karlsson have an uncompromising view on directors. "If you can talk on the same level and become friends, everything gets solved because it is fun to work together. It is not an effort to change things or have an open discussion. There are so many good people out there who *aren't* nice. We had a short turnaround time on MTV. We knew what we wanted, we knew the kind of vibe we wanted, it couldn't be shot in L.A. with typical actors, so we went to our old schoolfriends at Traktor." Malmström and Karlsson scoured the most obscure record stores in Minneapolis and developed the music track at Ash & Spencer.

As Malmström reflects: "Linus and I have worked such a long time together. Our roles are blurred. We just sit down and talk. We work fast. When you work with a new partner, there are a lot of things you have to go through. But if you work a long time together, you can skip all those first ideas and go directly into where you want to be."

How Do You Know When It's Funny?

Basically, when somebody laughs. That's why being funny takes courage.

"I've lost count of the number of times a team has marched into my office with the announcement that 'this is a comedy script', as if laughter is a given," Neil French reflects. "So many teams simply forget the First Rule of Comedy. The First Rule of Comedy is 'Be Funny'."

The only way to sell a humorous ad is to get up and tell it like a story, like a joke. Presenting a funny script in a client's boardroom is the acid test. It is easy to be intimidated into modifying the humour. Be warned: committees cannot write comedy. Corny, predictable humour is worse than hard sell. Nobody likes a bad comedian.

Study your own favourite comedians. Listen to their jokes, pick up their pacing, watch their expressions and above all, learn how hard they've worked to make their audiences laugh.

And if nobody laughs, maybe, just maybe, it wasn't funny anyhow.

We are in a cavernous hangar. A super reads: *Somewhere in the Gobi Desert.*

Teams of men are engaged in what must be a highly secret training programme.

Trainer: *Up the stairs! Down the stairs!*

Men with boxes of pizza are running up steps and learning how to knock on doors.

Trainer: *Bell, knocker, hand! Bell, knocker, hand!*

All becomes clear…

MVO: *Little Caesars introduces… Delivery!*

A simple notion: have an absurdly big introduction for home delivered pizza.
Cliff Freeman & Partners New York for Little Caesars.

Bored kids are manipulating sunlight through a magnifying glass. The Yellow Pages music throughout.

Super: *Entertain the kids*

Suddenly we realise the kids are training that sizzling beam of light onto some hapless ants.

Boy: *...you'll burn them!*

Boy: *...wow!*

Super: *or they'll entertain themselves.*

Cut to a glimpse of all the different Talking Guides displayed in the Yellow Pages. A woman's hand closes the book to leave the cover as the final product shot.

End super: *Look in the Talking Guides for ideas.*

The best humour is always based on little observations of life, observed truthfully by a director like Ray Lawrence of Window Productions. Agency: Clemenger BBDO Melbourne.

A young boy is picking his nose. The Yellow Pages music throughout.

Super: *Entertain the kids*

He is totally engrossed and examines his discoveries with interest.

Super: *or they'll entertain themselves.*

At this point, we're actually rather relieved to see a shot of the Talking Guides listing. A woman's hand closes the book to leave the cover as the final product shot.

End super: *Look in the Talking Guides for ideas.*

Aussie kids will always find disgusting ways to amuse themselves — and us. The Yellow Pages Talking Guides campaign from Clemenger BBDO Melbourne was written by Glen Ryan, and art directed by Peter Becker and Lynda Thompson.

Simple instructional diagrams accompany what sounds like an official MVO warning announcement:

Patrons, just a reminder that smoking in the cinema is prohibited.

Wearing tall hats in the cinema is also prohibited. As are extremely large wigs.

Unless you are in the very back row, in which case you can wear whatever you like.

Cooking is also prohibited in the cinema. However, if you are hungry there is a Nando's Restaurant nearby. And if you bring your movie ticket stub in, you'll receive two Nando's Burgers for the price of one.

And because Nando's is just around the corner, you can get there on foot. Or by bike. Or by horse. Or both.

A reminder, when exiting the cinema, please consider the people behind you. How are they feeling? What are their thoughts? Are they really happy?

And finally, patrons, no bootscooting. Ever.

Nando's Restaurants charmed cinema audiences with irreverent messages disguised as official announcements. Whybin TBWA & Partners Melbourne.

Typical instructional diagrams appear on the cinema screen. Pseudo official MVO throughout:

Patrons, in case of emergency, please observe the cinema exit signs here, here and here. Please do not attempt to exit here, or here.

If at any time rumblings occur here, do not be alarmed. There are Nando's Restaurants located here, here and here. Sorry, here.

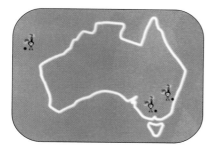

And for a free burger or quarter chicken with a drink and chips purchase, just bring in your movie ticket stub which can be found here or here. You can retrieve it with your hand, which can be found here.

And please be aware, if you order your Nando's with extra hot Peri Peri sauce, it may burn here...and then later, here.

So for a free burger or quarter chicken with a drink and chips purchase, just bring your ticket stub into here. And if someone tries to steal your ticket, just punch them here or knee them here.

Not just another boring retail ad for cinema audiences. Whybin TBWA & Partners Melbourne turns the medium into the message for Nando's Restaurants.

Saatchi & Saatchi London celebrates the British love of gravy for client Centura Foods, makers of Bisto. A family is dining out at a restaurant. The father asks for some gravy. When the waitress tells him that they don't serve gravy with their chops, he leaps up and strips to his underwear. Pointing to his scrawny body he asks: "Madam, do you find this acceptable?" She shakes her head in distaste. "Quite," he remonstrates. "Customers come with clothes, chops come with gravy."

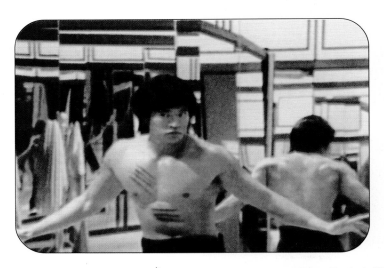

Proving that Procter & Gamble does have a sense of humour. A Bruce Lee lookalike searches for his enemy in a mirrored room, but can't resist the opportunity to check how Head & Shoulders has improved his hair. No sign of dandruff, his search continues... Agency Saatchi & Saatchi Singapore. Production by Axis Films Malaysia.

A man returns home with more than lunch on his mind.

He sheds his clothes as he hurries down the hall to the living room. A jaunty melody reinforces his mood.

Peering through the keyhole, he sees only his wife. He plucks a rose from a vase, places it between his teeth and flings the door wide open...

Only to discover his in-laws have decided to make a surprise visit.

While everyone looks suitably horrified, the final graphic comes up:

Warning: We're flying your in-laws at half price!

The classic Naked Lunch *commercial, from Leo Burnett Norway.*
The proposition was given a very lateral twist.

Our farming hero just can't get used to the extra power of his new Toyota Hilux. Everything he attempts with it goes wrong. After each catastrophe all he can say is "Bugger"...

He tries to straighten a sagging fence by nudging it with the bumper of his Toyota Hilux. The fence collapses.

Farmer: *Bugger...*

He tries to tow a tractor with his Hilux. Trouble is, the Hilux yanks the wheels off the tractor.

Farmer: *Bugger me...*

He pulls out a tree stump with his Hilux. It's so strong the stump is catapulted into the chicken coop, demolishing it.

Farmer: *Bugger...*

A cow is stuck in the mud. He starts towing it out with the Hilux. Suddenly he looks horrified and grimaces. We can only imagine what happened to the cow.

Farmer: *Bugger...*

The farmer's dog leaps for the Hilux but underestimates its speed. The dog plops down in the mud, splashing it onto the washing line and the farmer's wife...

Wife: *Bugger.*

The dog just stares balefully ahead, too buggered to get up.

Dog: *Bugger...*

A Gold Lion at Cannes and Commercial of the Year in Australia — Saatchi & Saatchi Wellington challenged politically correct language to the delight of New Zealanders. Written by Howard Greive and John Plimmer, art directed by John Fisher and directed by Tony Williams of Auckland Film Company.

A man is diligently washing his car — with his tongue!

His wife steps into frame holding a phone and addresses camera. We hear Frank's tongue slurping away throughout.

Wife: *My Frank! He likes to wash his car the old-fashioned way. He says the old way is the best. If he knew I was using Moviefone, he'd have a fit. Moviefone is the easy way to find out what movies are playing, where and when. It's so utterly modern. But don't tell Frank.*

End VO: *For movie showtimes, even tickets, call 777-FILM or say hello to moviefone.com.*

Cut back to Frank, still licking, but a bit grumpy. No wonder…

Frank: *Darn birds!*

More outrageous dot.com work, this time from Mad Dogs & Englishmen New York. That great mainstay of American television — the hard sell presenter commercial — is subverted for Moviefone, with an unusual crunch at the end.

A typical infomercial gets underway...

Barry: *Are you tired of being short of breath? Would you like a thinner, trimmer tummy? Well now you can with the revolutionary TreadMaster 2000!*

We cut to a close-up of what looks like a hamster exercise wheel.

Barry: *This has got to be the ultimate all-in-one workout machine. Now you might be thinking, "Barry, what is the secret to this patented machine?" Well the secret is this — it goes forwards and it also goes backwards! And to help me explain it — sports star D. Brown!*

D. Brown: *That's right, Barry, the multi-direction feature helps you go forwards and backwards; helps you target those hard to reach areas like your tummy and your legs.*

Barry: *Time-out D, are you trying to say that because this machine goes forwards and backwards, you're going to get a better workout?*

D. Brown: *You're going to get the ultimate workout! Just spend 40 minutes a day, you'll see results in just 4 months!*

Barry: *Wow, that is amazing. Is there anything this machine can't do?*

Super: *Animal Planet. Television with an animal twist.*

Saatchi & Saatchi Singapore subverts the infomercial for cable TV channel Animal Planet. Written by Troy Lim and Jagdish Ramakrishnan, art directed by Addy Khaotong. Silverscreen Productions Auckland.

7

How To Sell Great Work

According to one theory, clients hire the kind of agency that *they* would be if they were an agency. Very few clients know how to judge advertising, but they do know how to make judgements about human beings, and they do know how to make judgements about businesses of like kind.

It has also been said that clients prefer dancing with agencies that have the same size feet as they do. If you're a big client, you want control, and you can get *more* control of your brands around the world by hiring an agency that owns the people in its offices around the world; your wishes are carried out by two pyramidal structures working hand in hand.

Gloom and doom for cutting edge creativity? "Clients are not in business to be brave," says David Abbott, whose agency has created and sold some of Britain's most outstanding and enduring campaigns. "You must *educate them with evidence* by the way you work with them."

Great partnerships are born out of special relationships.

First Build A Relationship

Tim Delaney discusses what he calls the cap-touching mentality and the downward pressure on any kind of change or original thought. "A lot of companies attract anal people. Their desire for orthodoxy is built into their psyche. It's a cradle problem. You can't fix it. It happened too early for us to get to them. They won't open their mind to anything, therefore you can't work with them." Delaney prescribes a simple solution: agencies should choose their clients with their eyes wide open. "Clients think they're choosing us, but that's not true. We decide whom we want to work with. If they've got a hundred million pounds and they're disgusting, they wouldn't even be let past reception. I don't care. I've stopped meetings. Bang, I'll hit the table. That's enough. I tell them we're not right for each other. We don't deal with those kinds of people. We're not interested. *You have to have a sense of truth.* You have to have a sense of what the business is capable of being. It's such an interesting business. Brand consultancies only have the theoretical nature of what a brand can be. But advertising agencies have *expression*; we are creating things which fit into a strategic pattern, into a vision for the future of a brand."

David Blackley is a thirty-year veteran of Clemenger BBDO. He talks about mutual respect. "A lot of the clients have been here for fifteen, twenty, twenty-five years, so we have relationships that are different from other agencies where the people are new, the clients are new, and everybody's circling each other. Sometimes I'll call up a client and invite them in for a coffee. I won't have a script, but I'll talk the idea through with them, and they'll say, yes, we can see it, it's worth taking to the next stage." Blackley admits that he can't sell anything if he doesn't believe in it. "I worked that out twenty years ago. I presented the *Legendary stuff* milk campaign over and over again to various committees; I believed in it so strongly, I believed in the research that had been done, I had the background of the *got milk?* campaign. Just the power of conviction will carry it." The agency has no set formula for presentations; animatics are used occasionally, ripamatics rarely. "Sometimes we sell straight off a script."

Ted Horton believes you get a lot further if you are prepared to share and let lots of people have equity in your work. "There are only two sorts of commercials you can make as far as I'm concerned.

Let's say your client is a marketing manager and he's at home with his wife and two kids. The ad might come on and his wife will say, what's that, darling? And he'll say, oh, that's the ad the agency did for me. Or he might say, quick, sweetheart, come and look at my ad. The second response is far more successful. When ads are made, they have to go through a corporation and when it comes to advertising, everyone's an expert. People will cut it to shreds every opportunity they can get. And if you don't have someone in there, protecting it, championing it, then you're in trouble. A lot of advertising people forget that." Horton says the secret is client involvement. Clients should have a personal stake in the work because they believe in it. "The best way to do that is to actually sit down with your client right from the word go and work on the campaign together. Find out what's possible, what's not possible. It's just like entering a writer-art director relationship. And when you do give up ownership of your work to a client, no one ever questions your role in it. If you give up a little, you get a lot more back."

"Trust is the operative word." Mike Cozens also sits down with clients and explains his thinking. Trust is something you have to gain, he says.

"We spend time with clients helping them understand who they are and who they *could* be," says Bill Oberlander.

What happens when Wieden & Kennedy presents itself to a new business prospect? Stacy Wall explains: "Instead of paying lip service to creativity and saying we will create work that is impactful, we can ask if they have eight hours; we can invite them to sit in a room and show them everything we've done. Even the tiny Nike ad going into a gymnastics programme will be a great ad. It's because every individual team is challenged to try to live up to the standards and there are no second class citizens. Dan Wieden said, I don't care if we go down in flames, *we are going to always care about the work* and he just believes in that." Wall is proud of the fact that the agency and its clients never assume the audience is stupid. "Our clients never talk about themselves in their advertising. We find something the client loves and we talk about that instead. If you go to a party and want to be seen as an interesting person and you love sailing, you talk about sailing, not yourself. In Nike's case we're always talking about athletes or we're talking about sports, but we're never talking about Nike. I don't think we've ever done an ad that says, Nike, we're cool. Same thing with ESPN. We talk about how much we love sports, how much we love being a sports fan. You can even create something wacky, but at its soul it's *not* attractive if you're talking about yourself."

"Most clients do not understand the power of advertising." Nor do they believe in it, says Roy Grace. "Most clients do not understand how easy it would be to sell more of their products or services if they hired a good agency and listened to them. In my experience, all of the clients we work for, we have a good relationship with. A give-and-take relationship. They don't buy everything we do necessarily, but they do buy a lot of what we do."

Not all clients resist great work by any means. Some actively pursue it. According to Doyle Dane Bernbach history, the Mobil Oil Corporation called the agency in 1965 and invited it to pitch for a corporate project. DDB was assured that only two agencies would be competing for the business; the one that did the Volkswagen ads, and the one that did the Avis ads.

How Many Ideas Should You Present?

Anthony Simonds-Gooding is adamant. "Only one idea should reach the client." Handling this discipline, he maintains, whether you're an agency or a client, really does sort the men from the boys. "Very few can nail their colours to the mast." He believes the account service person entrusted with the brief should present the work, not the creators.

HHCL defies many conventions; presenting multiple ideas is one of them. "We have a process that gives us three or four ideas," Steve Henry explains. "Naresh Ramchandani had written three routes for Maxell tapes. Music and humour are relatively formulaic so the one that ran wasn't my favourite. The other two were just stunning. *We're Number One in America, but don't let that put you off ...* the idea was lots of vignettes of the worst things you hate about America. The other route was fantastically emotional. It was a guy speaking his thoughts about his father onto a tape. Everybody who heard it was on the edge of tears. The marketplace at that time for tape was all music and buzzy and young people, and I thought Naresh had just touched on a deeper truth. If we'd got the client to buy that approach maybe we wouldn't have won the Cannes Gold Prix, but we would have produced work that was completely unlike anything you'd ever seen."

SHOULD CREATIVES SELL THEIR OWN WORK?

"I've always thought that you need really great account directors to get ideas through, rather than try and do it yourself, which is the opposite to what most people think." Lionel Hunt acknowledges that some creative people can create and sell their own work. "I find it very difficult to be thinking of the idea and wondering how to sell it at the same time. I'd much rather concentrate on the idea, and have a really brilliant suit, who had gained the respect of the client, to get it through. Over my career, I've got half of them through myself, and been lucky enough to have people get the other half through for me." He acknowledges the prevailing school of thought, that the only way to get work through is if you sell it yourself. "I think what that does is let account service off the hook. You end up, in fact, taking the brief, writing the strategy, writing the ad, selling the ad *and* making it."

Despite having created Australia's most formidable agency brand and some of the nation's most admired campaigns over three decades, Hunt readily admits: "I don't like presenting my work to clients in case they don't like it. You live with an idea for a while, and you grow to love it, and you only present it if you are utterly enchanted by it, and then for someone to reject it, I find crushing. It's like being turned down at a dance — not that *that's* ever happened..."

Neil French is always there in person to present his work. He sold *Billion Dollar Smile* by performing it "live" in front of the client, with French pushing the talent's face about with his finger. "Make 'em laugh, make 'em laugh, make 'em laugh," was French's dictum. When he presented his animated Martell *Legend* concept, however, it was impossible to demonstrate the visuals. "I couldn't show them what I wanted to do because it had never been done. I blacked out the room and played a tape of myself reading the legend. By pre-recording it, I could make it sound booming, like Orson Welles. Then after that, I said we were going to tell the story but in pictures drawn by Vincent van Gogh. And they were sold without a moment's hesitation." When he presented his Union Bank of Switzerland campaign, he produced the commercials on video, with himself on camera reading the poems that Sir John Gielgud and other famous actors would eventually deliver. "The 'look' was almost identical to how they ended up. We pointed out how much better they would be if they had proper actors doing it, and they agreed — but there was a point when they actually wanted *me* to do the readings myself."

PRESENTATION TECHNIQUES

"An advertising agency should be the most exciting place a client will visit. You have to have theatre," believes Matt McGrath. "Take them through your thinking process so that it's happening in their heads at the same time. It should be a process of discovery for them, so that they come up with the idea at the same time. Never underestimate the value of playing music, showing visuals, bringing the whole drama of the television commercial into the room. Reading off a script or showing a storyboard in a cold environment isn't enough. Clients aren't constantly working with ideas and looking at scripts like we do every day. If you've taken a week to come up with an idea, you can't expect the client to latch on to it, and understand how great it is, in five minutes." You must also be willing to embarrass yourself, says McGrath, standing up and acting out the various parts in your script.

Ken Schuldman talks about respect and comfort. "You have to be incredibly honest with the client. You have to set the groundwork of what the idea will do, not just for them but for the category. You have to set up who the audience is. Sometimes we've used testing as a friend. We've said we've shown this to consumers, they've understood it, they got it, they loved it. We'll give them some verbatims. You have to make your case like a lawyer does with a jury. You've got to do it on a point-by-point basis, especially with something that's new."

"It could be seen as intellectual arrogance," begins John Kingsmill, "but it's not that at all. It's just that busy people haven't got time to sit down and sift through things. First of all, just like making a speech, you tell people what you're going to tell them about, then you tell them, and then at the end you tell them again what the speech was about. And, like a good chessplayer or footballer, be ready to handle any objections." Kingsmill advocates putting campaign themes on boards while you present the film treatments. "The client needs to be sold on that kernel inside the whole campaign, and if the statement can be put up on a board, all the better; nice, big, fat letters, so they are concentrating on that while you sell the treatment. But don't give them too much to think about. Give them two great ideas, either of which you'd be proud to stand by. Some people like to take along a straw man, one they want knocked over. But it's very dangerous. Sometimes the straw man gets up and wins."

SHOULD YOU SELL OFF A SCRIPT?

"Interestingly, I don't write scripts, and never have." Hunt prefers to tell a story. "Even though I've been looking at the old audio-one-side, video-the-other-side scripts for thirty years, I can never understand what they mean. So I just write a little story, *not* two sides of the page. And I tell the story point-by-point: one, a man walks into a shop; two, he takes off his hat; three, he falls over. However, in addition to that, we sometimes do a rough storyboard to help the client." Ideally, Hunt prefers to sell ideas just by talking about them, "like a radio story", without showing anything.

Naresh Ramchandani wants clients to find the idea and see it in their own heads without having it drawn for them. "I like to write a script in such a way that the client can see it themselves. It's not their job, but there are some clients who are very good at visualising things. Sometimes we do some very simple sketches, the looser the better. Sometimes we'll stick in a couple of videos and say, look, see that little effect, we're trying to create that; or, this is how dialogue like this could work; or this is how a frame like this could work. But I don't like doing that too much. It's fine having some early references, but you've got to jettison them pretty quickly to get to somewhere new and you have to encourage the client to think about that."

Chris O'Shea prefers to sell from a narrative script. "Keep it as loose as possible. Rather than left-hand side, right-hand side, I'd write something like, a door opens, a man comes in…" Occasionally he might show a scene from a movie as visual reference. "But try to avoid all that. Do all the more detailed stuff at the pre-production meeting with the director."

Given a choice, David Droga likes to read scripts. "It puts the theatre back into presentations. I like doing silly voices and noises and a bit of acting." Sometimes, he warns, storyboards and animatics can be misleading. "I don't want people picking apart executional things when I'm trying to convey an idea." In his first year as creative head of Saatchi & Saatchi London, Droga led the agency to win more new business than in its last eight years combined.

Sean Cummins likes to explain ideas in two sentences, selling punchlines and never getting into peripheral detail. "People can be very literal, so I keep it to bare bones. I concentrate on what you will see, what you feel, without going into detail like clothing colours. I never see commercials too literally in my head. I never attempt to write down the shots, cut here, close up there. I know what I want, but I keep it very open for someone to interpret it for me." When the idea is approved, then Cummins will present a director's storyboard in film language. "That allows me to sit back and worry about whether it's communicating. I can remove myself from the production process. By the time we get to the final pre-production, the client is seeing it all but shot."

"Reading off the script becomes too mechanical." Cozens uses visual stimuli. "Most people find it difficult to understand something from a script. I like to have as much reference material as possible. Anything that's relevant in some way. Even the style of cutting." Cozens has used thumbnail storyboards and animatics. "The best way is to present from a slide carousel with some music in the background. The slides should have very simple drawings. Nothing too executional. They're looking up at the screen and you can describe how you see each scene; then you can show a bit of stimulus material from a movie or a previous commercial."

The *got milk?* campaign was sold off scripts. Jeff Goodby, Jon Steel and the Milk Board's executive director Jeff Manning tabled six television scripts, including *Aaron Burr*, to the nine board members. Three million dollars of production was at stake. Goodby had offered to storyboard the commercials. Manning was tempted, but decided the ideas were strong enough to go unaided. Manning also decided to keep the numbers down; Goodby and Steel were the only agency representatives at the crucial meeting. According to Manning, they presented with "grace, humility, confidence and humour"; the board "listened, understood and laughed".

Warren Brown and Paul Fishlock sell from scripts; usually they are written in the conventional left-hand side, right-hand side format, although occasionally a treatment-style script might be presented. They would rarely if ever do animatics, even for a new business pitch. "The script is the first step of a journey and it should always be sold to the client as such," stresses Brown. The client should understand the *essence* of what you are trying to do. "They are buying into a concept, something that is quite fluid, open to a lot of influences throughout the process; they should always keep an open mind, all the way through to putting on the last title. Even at the eleventh hour, just before it has to go in, you can always improve it or take things out." The script will be acted out in front of the client.

"I've always found it easier to sell television than print." Antony Redman says the advantage is that he can get up and perform. "You can do little skits, you can get enthusiastic about certain scenes. It's like pitching in a film to a Hollywood studio." Redman presents his ideas from a script, never an animatic. "When you're pitching to a client, think of how a radio ad sells. Create images in their mind with your voice. I once sold a 2-minute commercial just reading them through the script. They were intrigued by it." A day or two before the presentation, Redman decides intuitively how he wants to sell the work. "I might show visual references, storyboards, atmosphere or feely boards. Sometimes they help, but they can also mislead. All of that can come well after the concept is sold. The presentation should be a logical progression: what is the brief ... what is the aim of the advertising ... here's a solution to the advertising ... and here's an ad that expresses that solution." Redman has never agreed with animatics; he says they create a state of confusion. "You're showing them, but you're saying this is *not* what it's going to look like, and this is *not* how it's going to be paced..." He finds them a waste of time and money. He prefers to work from a storyboard, which he calls an animatic that's just not on videotape. "Once the concept is sold, and the client agrees with where you're going, then you can workshop the commercial. The wardrobe, the photographic style, how pacy it's going to be or how slow, how noisy or how quiet…"

Kes Gray often writes *three different scripts*. "I take the idea, and I cut it right back for the creative director. I might then flesh it out a bit for my own sanity. Then I might go to town on the script for the client, because you have to remember that clients have different agendas. They want you to have a good idea as much as you do, but when they're listening to a script, very often they're listening for different things. They're listening for whether their product has a role in this script, and if it does have a role, what's the role going to be? They want to be reassured that you have the same love affair with their product that they have." For one thing, Gray says, don't just write: Cut to pack shot. "What does that mean to a client? You have to dress the product, describe how it will appear, make it look beautiful in the script." This script does not have to specify wardrobe, colours or locations in detail. "Those kinds of things come in later. There's a balance."

Before you can sell a script, says Gray, you have to sell yourself. "The best way to present a script is to allay their fears first, run through all of the concerns they might have, and make them feel comfortable about you and your understanding of their marketing problems and product. If you go straight into the creative idea, you can bet your life that while they're listening to your script, there'll be another voice going through their head that says, why hasn't he said anything about our marketing? What's the casting going to be? Is this person right for us?"

Jack Vaughan has reached a similar conclusion. "All the show business, all the tap dancing isn't going to make up for a situation in which the client is actually scared of you and the agency's risk-taking with their brand. Maybe the best tool of all is having a situation of trust between you and the client. I believe in bumbling sincerity; I'll act out the commercial, but I'm not a slick presenter." Vaughan believes the best way to sell an idea is to present a treatment-style script with the audio or dialogue woven in. "Storyboards and key frames get in the way. So do the old left-hand, right-hand scripts. I always used to read the right-hand side first, the audio, which is the least important." Doing a second-by-second shooting board is a good discipline so you know exactly how the story will be told filmically, but it is not a presentation tool. "What worries me is being congratulated when I sell a commercial. I can never relax until it's on air."

DO STORYBOARDS SELL?

"Storyboards are enormously dangerous. And animatics are even worse. Completely useless." John Hegarty suggests using stimulus material. "You can use photography as an example of the look or feel you want. You can use bits to film to say, see how that works, or look what happened there. But if you start writing storyboards, you are painting yourself into a corner and you're asking for trouble. It's all about trust. You've got to have built up trust with your client. You've got to make them understand what it is you're trying to do for them, and all your previous work adds to your ability to sell them what you're going to do with this."

Nigel Dawson says drawn storyboards lie. "They lie, they lie in every way. They lie to simple clients because they think they're going to get a cartoon. They lie because a director hasn't been involved, so the angles in the finished production will all be different. I find more and more times a written scenario is the best way to do it, and a good presenter to enact it, and you can usually get the client to understand what you're on about." Dawson advocates pre-selling an idea. By predisposing a client to the thinking, they start to know before the meeting a little of what to expect.

Hal Riney shares his distrust of storyboards. "A bad storyboard can go a long way towards killing a good idea. Our efforts are intangible, and often must be taken on faith. We need to be salesmen, and we need to present our thoughts with conviction and honesty. Most of my best stuff, humour at least, has been sold simply with a clear description, and something of a re-enactment before the client. We still use storyboards, but are using them less and less, perhaps because there are so few good storyboard artists around anymore." Riney believes that there is no one formula for selling ideas. "Some clients employing large committees require stacks of rationale, charts and research. Others, usually confident, strong client individuals who are empowered to make final decisions, require no more than a well-presented — entertaining, if appropriate — description of the commercial or campaign being recommended. Stealing film for animatics can be of great help, but that often tends to limit the creative solution to material that can be obtained from existing film. Also, these stealamatics can overpromise, dependent as they are on snippets of film from a bunch of multi-million dollar productions."

David Lubars shares Riney's reservations about ripamatics. "When you do a rip, you're using stuff that's been done before. A lot of times what we'll do is create a giant collage board, just in pictures, and we'll act out the spot, as opposed to a linear storyboard. We try to make it more conversational, less static. As opposed to us telling them, here's what we want you to think, it lets the client imagine." A lot depends on the client; there are no house rules, and Fallon's will do whatever it takes to sell the work. Sometimes, as Bruce Bildsten has observed, the process of producing a detailed storyboard or animatic pinpoints fundamental weaknesses in the concept. The commercial is actually made twice. "You get a chance to see, well, maybe it won't work as well as I thought."

"There should be no more than six frames in the storyboard for a 60-second commercial." Scott Whybin sells from rough boards. "You're not tying down a client's mind or a director's mind. You're opening up a much greater window of opportunity in terms of execution." The more finished and detailed your storyboard is, Whybin warns, *the more possibilities you take away.*

"We don't do detailed storyboards. We do three key frames," explains Michael Patti. "We don't want a client in a presentation looking at a storyboard, looking for their product. We want them to pay attention to what we're saying about what the idea is and we want them to buy into that concept."

Schuldman advocates one or two key frames, a script and perhaps some tonal references from a director. "The problem with ripamatics and animatics is that clients can fall in love with them."

One key frame is Mike Gibbs' preference. "One image is better than talking from a script. A lot of times, when you go through a storyboard or a flip board, the process of just flipping the pages tends to slow down what you're trying to build in their minds."

French would never present a good idea on a storyboard. "I've seen a client become obsessed with the tie the man is wearing in the storyboard because it's all he can understand. He'll spend the rest of the afternoon talking about the man's tie, which is perfectly reasonable cause for murdering somebody." Feely boards are another of French's *bêtes noires*. The idea of covering a board with a mosaic of shots that represent the "mood" and "visual contents" of a commercial is nonsense, he says. "It's very useful if you can't write, and haven't got an idea."

"I LOVE IT, BUT..."

"I used to tell people you have to be willing to die for your ideas," says Grace. "I felt that strongly. I would sell them like it was a life or death proposition. I wasn't always successful." One of his pet hates is people who say, *I love it, but let me make it better...*

Grace presented a Mobil 1 Oil commercial to his client. "They loved it, except they wanted to change it. After the client told me all the things he wanted done, I said, I understand where you're coming from, and I understand why you want to change these things, but I won't do it, because I think this is too good the way it is. So I told him I'd do another idea. And the client said, but I like this, and I said, no, you *don't* like it, and he said, okay, if you believe that strongly in it, do it."

It turned out to be one of the fifty best commercials in Doyle Dane Bernbach's history: *25,000 Miles*.

"It's just a map of the United States and nothing happens. Then the copy starts, *You can now drive from New York to Los Angeles without an oil change*, and a red glowing light crosses the map. *And back*. And another red light goes back to New York. *And back again*. And another light goes back to Los Angeles. *And back*. And it just keeps going. *And back again. And back*. And it was just so riveting. *25,000 miles without an oil change*. It was enormously successful. They actually saw the sales increase dramatically. Now I had been willing to die for it. I had been willing to kill my baby rather than see my baby mutilated."

Grace believes that creative people should make themselves bulletproof. "Like you'd rehearse for a play. Look at everything you're presenting, have all the answers ready, so when something comes up you can say, well, this is there because of that. You can't just do an ad and expect to walk in and people will say, I love it. I've seen it work for some people, but it's never worked for me."

THE HOLLYWOOD PITCH

"It's *Mrs. Doubtfire* meets *Gone With the Wind...*" Thus begins the typical Hollywood stand-up pitch to a studio executive. The pitch meeting will run around twenty to thirty minutes, including question time. Hollywood executives, not unlike clients, have no time to waste listening to rhetoric. Cut to the chase. As movie mogul Samuel Goldwyn once said about a script, "I read part of it all the way through..."

If a Hollywood feature can be pitched in fifteen minutes, it's more than enough time to outline a commercial. Advertising may not be show business, but it still calls for showmanship:

- Know your story inside out. Don't read it. *Tell it*, the same way you'd tell it to a friend. Rehearse it. Time it with your watch.
- Maintain eye contact. Let them see your enthusiasm and energy. Engage them. Let them see your passion. Let them see how important the idea is for you. Passion = commitment.
- Do you need a prop or two?
- Start with your best shot. Your opening line should contain the hook that captures their imagination. As the story unfolds, describe one or two scenes in detail so they can visualise them.
- Pitch your voice to underscore the story. Speak the action scenes quickly, slow the pacing when the mood slows.
- Let them see you enjoy telling your story.

NEW WAYS TO SELL WORK

The Campaign Palace. Australia's famous creative agency has introduced a new system called the 3 Ds. Ron Mather's rationale: "The old idea was the account service person going to get the brief from the client, then they gave it to the creative department, and two weeks later the client was supposed to come in and see what you've

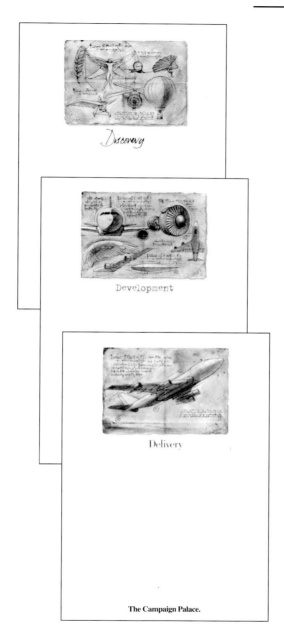

Even special stationery is distributed at 3 D meetings, The Campaign Palace's new way to involve clients in the creative process and spread creativity to all levels of the agency.

done and say yes or no. But clients now expect a lot more from an agency, not just a nice ad. They want to be part of the thinking." So the agency instituted a new critical path for all major projects. Three working sessions, over a 3- to 4-week period, bring the key agency and client players together for Discovery, Development and Delivery.

The initial Discovery meeting will be very well-structured. The client, account service people, planners, creative team and media would all sit down for three to four hours. *"Prior to this meeting, there is no brief.* This is where the brief originates. We talk about the market, what's happening, what the opportunities are." Ideas and directions begin to emerge. "We use special scribbling pads to write down ideas. They go up on the wall and everyone gets to stick a red tab on the ones they like. And the client is doing this as well." As a result of a Discovery session, the account director and client write the brief and set the deadline.

If the deadline was two weeks, then the Development meeting would be held one week later. "All the same people would be there, the client as well, and we'd be talking about directions. It's structured, but nothing is set in concrete. We'd show creative work. We don't say, do you like this idea or do you like that one? We say, given that brief you could go in this direction, or this one. Media things are talked about; do we just go on television, do we just use outdoor? It's a working session with the client there. It's a chance for the client to see all the ideas, all the thinking in progress, and it builds a good relationship. At the end of the Development meeting, we know *exactly* which way we're going."

Within another week, final storyboards or animatics are presented at the Delivery meeting. "Because the client understands the thinking and how you got there, you can sell better ads."

Mather says the process "had to happen". While clients want more involvement from their agencies, agencies also want creative thinking at all levels. "The days of the creative department being the only department that's creative are over. You want *everyone* to think creatively, to do things differently."

Fallon. Paul Malmström describes how the Miller Lite campaign was presented. "We did a video — not an animatic — but a video of *the world we were going to live in.* There was an interview with

Dick, and he explained certain things and how he would approach the Miller Lite advertising..." The client was able to get to know the character and appreciate the universe of the campaign before scripts were tabled. "Eventually, when you agree with your client on a strategy, it is so much easier to bend the rules on what you usually see on TV, because you can go back to the strategy and say, yes, this works within the strategy that we all agreed on. You agree on a strategy and everyone sticks to it."

Wieden & Kennedy. Michael Prieve reveals that scripts don't exist at initial presentations. The agency shows ideas and shares the influences behind them. "We presented the idea for a TV sitcom about college basketball. There weren't any storyboards. We presented it like most TV shows are presented in Hollywood." The presentation kit contained mocked-up photographs of the stars of the show, the lyrics of the show's theme song, how trade ads might look, and typical TV show merchandise like a jigsaw puzzle, lunchbox and an action figure. "Then we said, if you want us to go forward, we will script it in more detail. The client was very excited."

A CLIENT'S PERSPECTIVE

Anthony Simonds-Gooding sat through countless agency presentations. He was partial to intelligent advertising, humorous advertising, honest advertising, the implicit rather than the explicit, and an idea that would last. "I abhor the opposites."

He bought some of Britain's bravest work. Over the years he formulated a series of steps to evaluate each submission.

"I listened attentively and optimistically to the agency's presentation of work. *Optimistically, because I always wanted to buy.* I would then make them go through it again, in answer to some simple questions, such as:

1. Explain again how the submission is on strategy and on brief
2. Explain to me why the submission will stand out and be noticed
3. If it is on brief and distinctive, explain why it will be *persuasive* to the target group
4. Any good communication proposal carries with it some risks. *What does the agency see as the risks?*

5. Does the agency wish any of their proposals to be validated before going ahead? If yes, how? If not, why not?

Usually, having gone through these five questions, it became obvious not only to me *but also to the agency* whether we had something excellent on our hands, or a dog."

Occasionally though, despite this questioning, reiterative process, there was a failure to agree. "In those instances, I would do my very best to go with the agency, if they insisted, despite my misgivings. They knew this, and it is interesting to reflect on how often they went with my misgivings, *without my insistence*. The total trust that I put on agencies was a heavy load for them to carry. They hated letting me down."

Simonds-Gooding recommends that agencies and clients *use other people's ads* to learn about each other's tastes and preferences. "Every six months or so, spend an informal day discussing other people's advertisements. It's especially useful and fun when the advertising process lies in the hands of two large teams, both multi-layered and marking-at-both-ends. Often, where one has no emotional axe to grind, one can see clearly in seconds what is good and what is poor. You avoid win-lose situations, and it gives you an effective way of building a common viewpoint on those ever-recurring bones of contention like change versus continuity, selling off the negative versus the positive, good versus bad taste, information versus feelings, the use of humour..."

How To Survive Rejection

Advertising is a business of rejection. Ultimately, how you cope with rejection determines how long you stay in the business and how high you rise.

"Truthfully, I never got rejected that much," Roy Grace reflects. "I never got rejected by the people who were important to me. My only real boss in my mind, in my life, the only boss that I ever cared about, was Bill Bernbach. Ninety-five percent of the time we were on the same page. That meant a lot to me. It didn't mean that clients bought everything I ever did. No, but they did buy an extraordinarily high percentage. And that's what kept me interested."

Grace has little patience for compromise or rejection. It's not a question of being temperamental. Creative people have to preserve their dignity and self-belief in order to survive. "If I get into a situation where they don't buy what I do, I don't want that relationship. I didn't want it then and I don't want it now. Then, I would be as devious and manipulative as I could to get out of it, and now that I have my own agency, I can simply walk away from the client. If they don't want what I do, I don't want them. You have to maintain a certain amount of integrity and belief in yourself; you've got to be loyal to yourself. You can't just keep getting up to the plate every day, and doing what you think is great, and never having it come to fruition. I don't think *anybody* has that kind of perseverance."

"You're constantly doubting that you're any good at this job and that's what makes you strive harder and harder." Matt McGrath believes young people who aren't prepared to be passionate and get involved in the business should get out. "If you're committed enough, *you can turn any agency into a great agency*. Working under Neil Lawrence at Young & Rubicam Sydney proved to me that you can do *anything* in this industry." The agency had been on the brink of closing. Under Lawrence's creative directorship, it was transformed within eighteen months. It became Australia's Agency of the Year two years in a row. If we have doubts, McGrath points us to Gandhi. "He beat the British Empire. *One* man, basically. So if one person can't change an advertising agency, there's something seriously wrong. It's all a matter of what you're willing to lose or what you're willing to put on the line to succeed."

"You've got to work harder than anybody else," says Michael Patti. "You've got to be competitive with yourself, you've got to look at the awards reels and say, I'm going to do *better* than that. *The result of success is more success, if you can stay hungry.*"

"One of the reasons I came into advertising, having been to art school and then design school, was the excitement of doing things that were so public," John Hegarty recalls. "The fact that if I did a 48-sheet poster and it went up around the country, I was talking to the nation." He equates advertising creativity with movies. "I love the idea of movies that have incredible integrity and truth to them, and work at a number of levels, and yet are hugely popular. I'm not really interested in things that are very esoteric and talk to small numbers of people." Hegarty reviews options for young teams. "One of the great things about our business is that you have this opportunity to work on a huge number of things. Now as hard as that may be, if you can do it, do so. Every time you do something new, you learn something new. If you're not doing that, I think you're cutting yourself off from that kind of stimuli." Some people though, Hegarty admits, have made conscious decisions to specialise in one medium. "John Webster, in the UK, who is absolutely legendary, never used to do any print work. He was primarily a creator of TV commercials and was absolutely brilliant at it. I just think that John decided that was what he wanted to do, that was what he was good at doing. I can remember when John was a print art director…"

Webster himself advises young teams to look at what's good in the world, look at the great ads that are coming out, and keep those as their template. "You should write stuff that really gets you excited. Even if it's wrong, make it exciting rather than toe the line, trying to please the client. You've got to fight to get any good idea through. You've got to be prepared to fight and believe in yourself. *It's better to make a huge mistake than just toe the line and be ordinary.* Don't be ordinary." Webster says the best thing any young, bright teams can do is affiliate themselves to someone who is great and learn from them personally.

Chuck McBride agrees. "I've been fortunate enough to have worked with people who made things really exciting. The chance to work at Goodby and work at Wieden in the same lifetime is pretty extraordinary." McBride, quoting Hal Riney, says we are lucky because we have a new life every day in advertising. "The problems are all so different. I think I'm probably a frustrated mechanic in a weird sort of way, because I love that aspect of the business, finding out why something isn't running right." McBride remembers how he was expected to go into the family business. "I said, Dad, I love you, but I don't want to spend thirty years of my life doing something I don't want to do. I want to do something that I want to do every day, so that I never end up regretting a single moment of it."

"The key is getting into an agency in the first job or two or three where great television is done, by people who know how to do it," says Arthur Bijur. "It's pretty rare that beginners know enough to make television great themselves without any help. It does happen, but they need support. And they definitely need to be in an agency where there are clients who are going to be open to it. There are a lot of clients who are very nervous; they'll hug an idea to death and you'll end up with something that's not very good. You need strong leaders to help keep that from happening." While Cliff Freeman's uses beginners to do some of the grunt work, the agency gives them a chance at television jobs almost from day one. They also get immersed in radio, learning writing crafts and gaining the confidence to direct talent. "It's all based on opportunity."

FOR some creatives, opportunity knocks regularly. Others have never been given a shot. According to the *Hollywood Reporter*, screenwriters are nothing but "willing scribes". By definition, aren't advertising creatives the same?

"Advertising's like any industry," says Ron Mather. "It's a horrible industry if you're in a bad agency. If you're in an agency where the big thing is making as much money as you can at anyone's expense and forget the product, that's another business. But as far as I'm concerned, I want to be at the top end of an industry. I want to try to be the best in the business, I want to try to make my product better than anybody else's. I enjoy trying to push things forward a bit, to improve the business. There are a lot of people in the industry who *don't* enjoy it. They're just in it. Lots of people come and go, too. They do one little flash and they're gone. What keeps me going is that I love advertising. It's fun. I'm in a terrific environment, I love what I do, and I love working with good people."

"Advertising is not a cure for cancer." Scott Whybin advocates seeing the business for what it is. "It's not that serious. It's not going to change the world." Whybin was a young surfer when he entered Teece Promotions, a retail agency in the regional city of Newcastle, Australia. His radio commercial for a local used car dealer won Gold in Australia's top broadcasting awards. Whybin was lured to Sydney; a stint at Abbott Mead Vickers in London followed. Back in Australia, he won Commercial of the Year as a writer three years in a row. "You can have passion and ambition, and all those things, but at the end of the day you've got to have a deliberate detachment from it. The people who get it all wrong are the ones who get so worked up about it. If you're obsessed with awards, if you start thinking, oh, this one will be a short walk, you'll always be B-grade."

Paul Malmström shares a similar perspective. "How do you see yourself in this business? What is your role as a creative person? You're not an artist; you're a salesman. And that's a big and important difference. You are not here to fulfil your artistic dreams. You are here to sell the product for the client. Sometimes, face it — you're just *wrong* in an idea you presented, and the feedback you get is somehow good for you. It's for a reason. The times when it happens, when you didn't come up with something good enough, you come up with something better." He talks about working in Paradiset. "It was only twenty people. Then your role as an art director or copywriter automatically becomes broader. You have to be at the beginning of the food chain and the end of the food chain. You have to be more responsible towards your client. You can't hide in your room and have someone else sell your work. *You have to be involved in the client relationship yourself.*" You can't curse the client, he warns; it feeds bad energy somehow. Malmström advocates working in as many different styles as you can. *"You must be challenged at all levels, otherwise you die in your head."*

Malmström's partner, writer Linus Karlsson, offers equally pragmatic advice. "Work with really nice people. You might be super-talented, the world's best, I don't care, if you're not a nice person I don't want to spend my time with you. When you have a nice group of people coming together, that's when terrific things happen. That's when the remarkable work comes out. Out of that energy. You see it over and over and over again. It's reflected in the eyes of the consumer. I totally believe that the consumer can see a commercial and know when there were good people behind it, when there was a good intention behind it, and that's worth something." Karlsson believes in self-honesty. "Be open with yourself. Don't think you're right. Never be sure. *Be open, and see where it takes you.*"

David Blackley talks about young creatives and the burnout spiral. "They change agencies every eighteen months and get quite a bit of publicity for it, but they spin out of the business relatively early.

They're in it for some sort of ego reasons or they're so into advertising that they only mix with advertising people, they only go to advertising pubs, they only go to advertising club lunches, they only go to advertising parties on the weekends. They're so caught up in the peer group thing they lose reality for the things outside. I've always gone to the football, I drink in the public bar, I spend weekends in the bush, I get about as far away from advertising as I possibly can, as often as I can. I love good advertising with a passion, but I think you can only do it well if you have a wider perspective. *You've got to experience what real people experience.* You've got to love the real people. It's a bit like the old barrel; *if you've got the tap on, pouring the ideas out at the bottom, you've got to keep putting a wide variety of stuff in at the top."*

SOMETIMES, though, the internal approval process is more daunting than the external one. Creatives confronted with continual internal rejections can do one of three things: submit to the house rules — in other words, don't fight City Hall; or, leave and go to a more like-minded agency; or, open their own shop.

Marcello Serpa opened his own agency when he was twenty-nine. "If you have a proposition for the market, if you have something new to offer, if you really believe you can make a difference, and you have a chance to open an agency, you should do it. I was very lucky. I lived in Germany; I worked in a very creative agency at that time, GGK in Düsseldorf. I learned something that was very relevant about creative work. I didn't learn anything else. I just wanted to make good ads and good commercials. And I always found a way to work in agencies that had the same kind of philosophy that I had. I always worked in agencies that allowed me to do the work I believed in, and I always presented my work to the clients myself. I was very free in that sense." Serpa talks about the big monolithic agencies that profess a belief in creativity, but are not prepared to make the necessary sacrifices. "In those multinational companies, they have the wrong perspective about creativity. A lot of them come to festivals like Cannes and they see the lists of advertising agencies winning awards, and they say, I want to become one of those, I want to be creative like a BBDO or a DDB agency. I want to have the same kind of work that they have done, let's do it. But the problem is, those guys have no idea how to do it. *Nobody knows what it costs to produce good work. It may even cost the client. The moment it could cost the client, nobody pays the bill.*" Serpa believes there are no brave clients growing on trees. It is the agency that has to be brave. Every single agency, he says, deserves the clients it has. Why should the client be brave? Winning awards is not part of the brief. You have to prove to them that creativity will sell. You have to fight them. "I have said to clients, I want this campaign done, it is good for you. Sometimes I will pay for the campaign to be produced out of my own pocket, and I will even pay for it to be tested before it goes on air. If that's the only way I can get something through, I'll do it…"

Serpa offers advice to ambitious young creatives. "I still paint a lot. I like to stay at home, in my own country. I want to keep the agency the way it is. I don't want to have any kind of international duties. I can remember David Abbott winning a Gold at Cannes when he was about sixty. I admire that. He didn't want to be the CEO of the CEOs, or the Chairman of the Universe. He just stayed in his own agency and wrote great ads. I think that's a good ambition. The problem is, people always get 'there' because they're doing something, and the moment they get 'there', they are no longer doing it. I have had a lot of chances to be kicked upstairs, and I said, no, no, NO. This is what I do. I like to be in the kitchen. I am a chef, not a restaurant owner…"

THE thing that Hal Curtis has always admired about Wieden & Kennedy is the fact you are expected to do something different. "So much of the structure and apparatus of our business stifles communication. At the end of the day it's a conversation with another human being. It's not rocket science. It's very simple. And it's kind of weird, particularly in the media environment we live in, that advertisers don't understand the idea of risk, of taking a more entrepreneurial approach with their advertising. So much advertising looks the same, smells the same; it's derivative. A lot of the time the audience isn't the consumer, it's retailers and dealers; it's an internal thing and the job is to not ruffle feathers."

"It's not enough to have wacky ideas, you've got to have both sides of the brain." Stacy Wall has seen brilliant young creatives who last no more than two years in the business. "You've also got to have the thing that usually doesn't come along with being a creative person, and that's the patience to put up with the bureaucracy of the business and protect your ideas despite all the meetings and things that go counter to the way you think." However, he reminds us, pessimism and anger are not exclusive to advertising.

When Kash Sree joined Wieden & Kennedy, he had to make two transitions: from Asia to America, and from print to television. "Abject terror" is how Sree sums it up. "Thinking you weren't worthy to be among all those other people who had done great television ads. Wieden's gives you enough room to grow. It takes a while to learn. That's a nice luxury. So you talk to people, you see how they think. You try and throw out your old ways of working, which sets you back at first. It puts you in a very insecure place, but that gets your adrenaline going." Sree is wary of anything formulaic. "People get used to formulas on TV. As good as they are, people get used to the gag. People get used to the shock tactic, even to introspective, poetic work. Dan Wieden says, look for something in culture. That's where your answers will be. He's right." Sree studied graphic design, switched to advertising art direction and was hired at Batey Ads Singapore, as a writer. He has worked in India and Australia, too. "I started when I was thirty so I was always trying to catch up, which helped me and hindered me." Sree dismisses an enviable portfolio of work. "I haven't done anything yet. I haven't done anything that is so different or so great that I can sit back and think, I can't better that. The best advertising comes from really insecure people, people who are never satisfied." His advice: "Always be hungry, always work harder than the next guy, always question everything — especially yourself."

Warren Brown talks about insecurity and the need for recognition. "Most creative people that I've ever known, and I include myself among them, are usually a morass of insecurities and self-doubts, and need to constantly prove to themselves and those around them that they are capable of doing a good job. I haven't ever met any self-confident, self-assured creative people yet. I'm sure there are some, but they probably work in one of those huge American agencies on

Level Six." Brown is sustained by the impact his work has on the public. "There's nothing more enjoyable than hearing people adopting something you've created and making it part of their lives. It's gone way beyond being just an ad. You can have an impact in a very short space of time, and you get another opportunity to do it again in the very near future."

"You never lose the thrill of solving a problem creatively," agrees Paul Fishlock. "Taking a business situation or opportunity and doing something that has never been done before and making a difference; the thrill of that never goes away."

"I'VE been lucky, the last thirty years," considers Lionel Hunt, "because I've been running my own agency, or at least been at the top of the agency I was in, so I tended not to get too many knockbacks internally. If I was off strategy, I'd reject it myself once it was pointed out to me. Which isn't the same for most creative people, of course, who have to go through creative directors and review boards. It's very hard to do great work in an agency that isn't doing great work. Often they don't recognise it, often they reject it, and often they're not used to selling it. The absolute key is to be where great work is being done. I was very fortunate early in my career to go to Masius in Melbourne, which of all places had some really brilliant creative people. Noel Delbridge, a brilliant strategist and a great creative director; Gordon Trembath, Terry Durack, Peter Carey, it was a real creative hotbed. Just trying to emulate Peter Carey's ability had a tremendous effect on my ability." Hunt speaks with pride of The Campaign Palace, the agency he co-founded with Gordon Trembath. "The Palace almost immediately was recognised as the best creative agency in the country, and still is, twenty-six years later. Obviously that wasn't all to do with me, but I'm proud to at least have started an agency that was able to achieve that. David Ogilvy once said to me that he envied my talent, and Peter Carey, the author, once said to me that I had a way with words, and I'm rather pleased about both of those comments, too." What sustains Hunt? "An eternal quest, to do great work. When I think of the really phenomenal ads that have been done, I actually don't think I've ever done a really great television commercial, and I'm constantly hoping that I will, and that keeps me going, and I'm going to *keep* going till I do. I suppose what I'm really saying is you're only as good as your *next* ad."

Another writer who considers himself lucky is Naresh Ramchandani. "I spent nine months in the media department at BMP, then I spent a year trying to put a book together and I was one of the first people in at Howell Henry Chaldecott Lury when it was tiny." Ramchandani knew intuitively that people were more intelligent than advertisers gave them credit for. "I believe in pitching things more challengingly at consumers. Steve Henry and Axel Chaldecott believed in people trying things and that experimentation was a creative difference. Steve taught me how to be comfortable with writing stuff that was unusual and different. That was a big confidence to give to someone, not to feel you have to seek everyone's approval all the time and to understand that you *have* to have some people not liking it when you've done something different." Ramchandani says he also learned how a client rejection could lead to a better script. "It's a skill that Steve Henry taught me. He and Ax didn't fight the clients. If a client had fundamental problems with an idea, Steve would factor them in and rewrite it in such a way that he'd not only stepped around the problem, but made the work better." Ramchandani was teamed up with Tim Ashton. "My first two jobs, side by side, were the launch of First Direct and the TV campaign for Maxell cassettes." Ramchandani's first work was showered with awards. "Before I even knew what awards were, I had completely got all that out of my system. After that I didn't want to know what awards were, I just wanted to do things that were different; I haven't bothered at all with that whole awards system and that's been a real strength to me. For the last five years at St. Luke's we'd withdrawn from awards completely. I've been doing things a little bit texturally different, so they don't feel like advertising. It's stuff that cuts through and gets into the culture, but award juries don't respond well to it. I believe in competitive creativity that doesn't just say something differently but it *feels* really different as well."

FOR Noel Delbridge, it's the thrill of the chase. "Here's a problem, how are we going to solve it? And in all these years I've developed a capacity to soak up the brief, then read everything I possibly can about that market. Like a computer, just put it all in. Then I wake up in the middle of the night, and often it's all rolled out, lines, scenarios, and that makes the business very easy to be in. Because it doesn't worry me, *it doesn't threaten me.* I know I can always come up with an idea."

For David Perry, it's the thrill of creating something new and tangible every eight weeks. "A TV ad takes six to eight weeks to do, then you're on to something new, you're refreshing yourself as frequently as that. You're not on a movie that takes three years, you're not in a job that's repetitive. I've never wanted to go into features." Thirty years ago, he wanted to be a studio musician. His advice to young creatives: "Be a student of your craft. Know who your predecessors were. Have a global sense. Take something from everything you see. And do not assume that anyone older than you is old-fashioned, conservative or out of touch. Just because you're young doesn't mean you're good or smart; all you are is young." For young film makers: "Know more than the arena that you're working in. There isn't a good film maker that I've ever worked with who didn't have an encyclopaedic memory for feature films. Kinka Usher is a really good example. Kinka has seen every movie ever done, including some that no reasonable person could ever sit through. And if you're a young director, have a hero. Find someone whose work you really respect and learn from that person. Call that person up. Become his student."

For Steve Henry, it's never being satisfied. Creative people and agencies must keep evolving. "Coming up with ideas is not a difficult thing. The difficulty is making them happen. For a long time what we tried to do here was just break the rules, and that was great. But what's becoming increasingly apparent to me is break the rules, but make sure you make that emotional connection. It's not just enough to be new." The agencies that Henry most admires? "St Luke's, Mother, Goodby's, Fallon's; their best work has that emotional truth to it." Henry himself searches for new Holy Grails, for new rules to break, for what else might be possible. If he was not inspired to experiment and evolve, why stay in the business?

For Ken Schuldman, it's inventing things. "We've got to be true to ourselves. Try to give your brand a voice that no one else has. Then when you do, you'll see how much easier it becomes. Advertising has become a little soulless. We need to be aware of how people look at our work, how they see us. We shouldn't be car salesmen. We should respect their intelligence and their humanity."

Mike Cozens looks at creativity as having a deposit account and a current account. "You should live on your current account, which is coming up with new ideas all the time. But occasionally you've got to rely a little bit on experience. That's your deposit account. The awareness of all the great work. It's a stimulus. First you copy, then you write. I used to study David Abbott's copy, just for the simplicity of it, just to get the metre." Cozens still gets a huge amount of joy out of the business. His career tip for young creatives: "Concentrate on doing things other people don't want to do. Become a great radio writer because no one else is, then you can *blag* your way into doing TV commercials after that."

Why persist in thinking about advertising purely in craft terms, asks Andy Berlin. Getting involved in solving the strategy could well give you the breakthroughs to do great work that clients buy. "The way that you think about making an ad, you can use to think about solving a problem. Don't just think about the ad, think about a client who has a specific problem. The brief is going to articulate it in overly rational, inelegant terms, but basically it will be saying something like, General Motors wants to be loved. Creative people can use their non-linear processes. *Don't accept briefs at face value.* Don't believe that creative people don't have responsibilities and capabilities for dealing with strategic issues. Take responsibility for solving the problem. Use your non-linear thinking because the chairman of GM *can't.*" Clients can't be lateral, says Berlin; turn a brief that looks impossible and deadly boring into something that's wonderful if you're willing to do that. "And I don't think you need to be senior to do that. You can be quite junior and do it."

Sean Cummins is convinced that most people spend their lives doing what they are second best at. He read law until the day he walked into an advertising agency. "I met people who were exactly like me, kind of funny, kind of quirky. I was so relieved. I could enjoy the business side and the theatrical side of it." Cummins talks about the need to believe. "No one ever sees the sweat. Seventy percent of the time we're dealing with rejection. You've got to celebrate the 30% of the time you get approval. I like to believe in a cause, a standard, and that idealism has driven me through the business. I believe in this wonderful gift we have to create ideas. There is something spiritual about feeding in all the facts and then out comes this piece of theatre. It was there, inside me, all the time, and I found it."

Michael Prieve prescribes perseverance and personal integrity. "Most people don't have those two things. They're just as happy to cash in and take more money. Or they give up, they quit. You'd have a decent chance of succeeding if you got a job here at Wieden & Kennedy because we do a lot of TV and most of our budgets are pretty big. But I'm amazed how many people don't care. They're just not that interested."

"I will sacrifice everything to an idea." Jack Vaughan's career has taken him to high-profile creative directorships in Britain and Australia. "You don't come through unscathed if you throw everything into it. And you have to. *You can't be half in advertising.* You're either in it or you're out of it." What drives him on? "It's just plain old insecurity, Catholic upbringing, guilt, all that stuff helps. You're trying to prove something to yourself; you want to put things on paper. It's a frustration and it doesn't usually come from the most functional human beings." Vaughan believes young people shouldn't trifle with advertising unless they are fully committed. "You can't half do it. Or, you can do it half badly, but there are plenty of half-bad people in it already."

SIIMON REYNOLDS talks about the pressure that comes with early creative success. By twenty-two, he had become a media celebrity as well as the *enfant terrible* of Australian advertising. "It was very disturbing. I remember when I left Grey, it was on the tabloid banners outside newsagencies. To have that kind of notoriety was fun in a way, but I could never relax." Reynolds knew people were waiting for him to fail. But there was a positive side. "It's not such a big deal if you can do that at that age. The great thing about advertising is that you can get the gist of how to write ads in a year.

Unlike other businesses, it doesn't take ten years to learn; it may take years to master the craft, but to learn the core structures of great ads and how to build originality into them doesn't take long. You could teach the ten structures that lead to great ads in one day. The terrible part of our industry is that many people who have been in advertising for thirty years have never learned those structures themselves and they wonder why they don't do great work."

Reynolds argues the case for *creative quarantine*. "The average person's brain is 90% full of bad, ordinary ads because that's what you see all around you. But what we used to do was never read a newspaper and never watch TV. If we saw ads, they were only the world's best. We watched the world's best TV commercials on reels. If we saw print ads, they were only the world's best print ads in annuals. So after a few years all your brain had in it, as a point of reference, were great ads. Immediately when you sat down to do an ad, you worked to a different yardstick. Now if you create an environment where you only ever see great work, people will say, that's terrible, you don't know what's happening in your own country, but you *will* know what's happening in the top 1% of advertising and that's all you ever have to know." Advertising, says Reynolds, is a very difficult industry to be half-hearted in. What we expect and hope for deep down, he believes, we become. What we visualise we become, because we are our thoughts. "You must become a great creative in your mind before the reality can happen. You also need to distinguish between progress and drift. You can be a stick on a river and you appear to be getting ahead, but everything else on that river is travelling at the same speed so you aren't actually getting ahead of any other sticks. You're drifting."

Reynolds identifies three criteria for success: firstly, learn the structures of great work; secondly, learn to reject a lot of your own work; thirdly, you must really want success. "It can't be a casual ambition. All the great people have *desperately* wanted it." Reynolds tells the story of a young man who came up to Sophocles and asked him how to be wise. Sophocles took him to a trough, grabbed the boy by the hair and pushed him face down into the water. At first the boy didn't struggle; he thought it was some kind of trick. Then he realised that Sophocles wasn't going to let him up. He went berserk and still Sophocles wouldn't let him up. Just when he could endure no more, Sophocles hauled him up and said, when you want wisdom as much as you want air, you'll get it. And I think that's the case with doing great advertising."

David Droga worked for Reynolds at OMON. "I've been fortunate in my career. I've had a lot of opportunities. When you're just working as a team, not shouldering responsibility, you don't realise how much fun the business can be. You want to enjoy that and really experiment with it and not want to try and thrust yourself into too much responsibility too quickly. I can still remember the first day I took a job as a writer. I was so shocked that someone was paying me for my imagination." Use award annuals for motivation, says Droga, not emulation. "A lot of people look into award annuals and think, if I could just live up to the best of last year; that's why trends drag on longer than they should. As an industry we reflect more than we forecast. Whatever wins this year should be looked upon as what we should *not* do next year."

"Advertising isn't as tough as some of the other things I've done." Australia's legendary Ted Horton discovered his flair for advertising while cooking and waiting at tables in a restaurant at the age of thirty. "People from agencies would come in every day. Whenever I cleaned the kitchen after lunch, it would be 3.30 and all those people would still be in the restaurant. And then when I took out the rubbish I'd see all these fantastic cars lined up down the street and I thought, I don't know what these guys do but I wouldn't mind a bit of that myself. And when I found out they were in advertising, I started to knock on doors. If it had been The Campaign Palace having lunch, I probably would never have gone in because I wouldn't have thought I could do as good." Advertising never "scared" Horton; he always felt it was something he could do. Being a late starter in the industry gave him a broader perspective of life. It also gave him greater resilience to overcome rejection. "Draw from your own personal experience, as opposed to being this third-person observer and never putting anything of yourself into your work. Take the very ordinary, simple things that you find in life and make them special by making them personal." Horton is a firm advocate of doing work that reaches into the public consciousness. "I used to be very award-focused, because I was led to believe that this was very important. So I spent a lot of time in that part of the world. And then I came to the realisation that you can be working in the industry and doing stuff that means absolutely nothing to anyone other than the people in the industry. I'm very conscious of producing work that when I sit down at a dinner table and someone asks me what I do, and I tell them the commercials I've made, they *know* them. Don't be afraid to do work that's popular as opposed to stuff that's smart and award-winning. If we're popular and we do work that everyone likes, we're told that we've 'sold out'. I think that's pathetic really. Clients are trying to create mass market brands, and too often we try to create niche market advertising for them. We're creating for our own egos."

"EVERYBODY has had miserable failures, horrible public failures," David Lubars reminds us. "What keeps you going is that you did something else cool. And that something you thought of on a pad, or a piece of scrap paper, has now made a client successful." Lubars describes the route that young creatives have to take. "It's so easy now, to get a job with some decent money. But if you go for the money early, you're hurting yourself in the long term. The best places are either big — so they can afford not to give you so much money because everyone wants to go there — or they're small and they can't afford to give you that money. If you want to go into creative and have a long-term career, it's not about the money when you begin. In your twenties, don't think about money. The thing is, when you don't think about the money and you get the work, the money comes; much more money than you could have made working your way up in some middle-level company that's mediocre. The money comes from fame and success in the marketplace, so you have to be in a place where you can have that."

"You are not in a popularity contest." Francis Wee is pragmatic about criticism. "You can't ever please everybody. Everybody will have a different opinion. People are entitled to their opinions. You have to realise that what they are saying is because of some other hidden agenda. So I just gather all their comments. In the end, most creative people have their own instincts. You have to be comfortable with yourself. You have to listen to yourself. You have to be true to yourself." It also helps to treat your job as a hobby. "You shouldn't get too serious about the job itself. You should enjoy what you're doing, because you tend to contribute more to things you enjoy."

Veteran film director Bob Giraldi, himself a former agency art director, has very little patience for stupidity and fear. "Fear is scary. It makes people react badly. There is no reason for it. After all, at the end of the day, we're selling soap…"

"The real issue in this business," Tim Delaney stresses, "and it relates more to television than anything else because television takes more of the money, is that the people who lead advertising agencies are not visionaries. There are no Bernbachs. There are no people out there that want to stand up and speak out and say, look, we are an old-fashioned, dusty, crotchety, underpaid industry. There is no money in advertising anymore. And the reason for that is that we have shown no leadership. We have shown no way out of the jungle. When it comes to things like the Internet, you've got a lot of people talking, you can't shut them up. But there's no one talking about advertising. When it comes to things like how does advertising work, why does it work, why doesn't it work, we have simply given it to research people on one hand to tell everybody why, and we've given it to the media people to buy it. And then we say to the clients, oh, by the way, we can do a few ideas. And the clients say, for those few ideas we'll pay you nothing. And then we say, a *little* bit more than nothing? And they say, yeah, all right then, and we try and make a business out of it. And of course it's just a joke. There's no money in it." Delaney believes big clients have been allowed to hijack the industry. "They have made the advertising process anal and sophisticated to the point of stupidity. And everyone in advertising knows it, but no one argues about it. *It's a taboo subject.* Instead of saying why are we working with such ridiculous people, we say they're ridiculous but we're going to do it because the guys who run the agencies say I want the money, I've got another house I want to buy." It never used to be this way, maintains Delaney. "The conglomeration of agencies has prevented leaders from speaking out if it doesn't suit the other agencies in the group. No one has ever measured the effects of the conglomeration of agencies."

RISKS, REJECTION — AND RESILIENCE

If you want to be the best, you have to develop a working methodology that lets you hit your creative highs on demand. You can't rely on inspiration; it's too fickle. You can't rely on technique; that's shallow and ephemeral. There's about only one thing you can actually rely on in creativity — rejection. No matter who you are, you will fail and you will taste rejection.

The less formulaic your work becomes, the more your own creative style will develop. The more individual and original your work becomes, the more risks you take, the more you expose of yourself, the more you will be rejected, ridiculed and hurt. Fame always carries a price.

The most important thing about rejection is how you handle it.

Of course, the most you'll lose in advertising is a script, or a few headlines, or a layout or two. It's no big deal. What if you had a 600-page manuscript rejected, not just once, but again and again? What if producer after producer binned your screenplays? Would you have the resilience to keep trying? Would you still believe in yourself?

Next time you suffer rejection, smile. *The Good Earth* by Pearl S. Buck was rejected 14 times. Margaret Mitchell's *Gone With the Wind* was rejected 25 times. *Zen and the Art of Motorcycle Maintenance* was rejected 121 times.

Chicken Soup for the Soul was rejected by 33 New York publishers and some 111 others at the American Book Publishers Association convention. In 1998, 13 million *Chicken Soup* books were sold in the United States alone. By year 2020, total global sales of one billion copies are forecast.

Hans Christian Andersen was told his stories were unsuitable for children. Theodor Geisel, better known as Dr Seuss, was told the same thing, too — twenty-four times. Because he "did not know how to use the English language", the *San Francisco Chronicle* fired Rudyard Kipling.

Before selling their first manuscripts, Alex Haley and Louis L'Amour had each received 200 rejections; Jack London, 600 rejections; and British author John Creasey, 774 rejections. Creasey went on to write over 500 books under at least 10 different names. One poor soul suffered an entire lifetime of literary failure; he became a humble New York customs agent and forgot his dreams of writing. It was only after Herman Melville died that *Moby Dick* was hailed as a great American classic.

John Grisham's novels have sold over sixty million copies. He wrote his first book, *A Time To Kill*, by hand on legal pads while he worked as an attorney. It was rejected forty-five times. What if he had not mailed it out again for the forty-sixth time?

According to publishing legends, *Catch-22* was originally called *Catch-18*. But because Leon Uris was about to launch his book *Mila 18* at the same time, Joseph Heller was asked to change his book's title. He snapped back with *Catch-22* — because his publisher was the twenty-second house to which he had sent his manuscript.

Rejection is never personal. It's our work that's being shelled, not us. Ironically, a far greater threat to the creative spirit is success. Applause, too much applause, extinguishes the flame.

8

EXECUTING EXCELLENCE

Hollywood screenwriter Paul Schrader, whose credits include *Taxi Driver, Raging Bull* and *The Mosquito Coast*, said that movie scripts are not in themselves works of art. "They are invitations to others to *collaborate* on a work of art..."

A television commercial is no different.

"The script is the beginning of a journey," argues John Hegarty. "You say, that's a very interesting idea, now how can I make that idea really, *really* stand out?" Much more is demanded of things today, he believes. There is so much stuff being thrown at people. Commercials have to be more exacting, more pure, and they have to capture people's imaginations in a more single-minded way. "All my experience doing the commercials in the Levi's 501 series showed me that you can have four scripts on the table, and nobody could say which was going to be the best one. It was which one were you going to marry with which director, and with which technique, to make it really outstanding. Read William Goldman; he said, in Hollywood *nobody knows.*" You can be more certain in print, says Hegarty, whereas television is a journey into the unknown, irrespective of how much experience you have. "Each time I approach a script, I am always standing on a kind of precipice..."

In 1999, according to the American 4As, Hegarty's "journey" commanded a considerable price. An average 30-second commercial for a national advertiser cost $295,000 to make. Interestingly, the figure was down a little from the year before and included everything: about eighteen to nineteen hours of shooting on average, either on location or in a studio; talent costs; music; post-production; even agency travel.

KAIZAN: THE ART OF CONTINUOUS IMPROVEMENT

Kaizan, Michael Newman tells us, is the Japanese word for continuous improvement. "Advertising is a collaborative art, but there must be a conspiracy of good intentions among those involved in the process." Newman says an idea should ideally get better from concept to final script, from storyboard to director's treatment, and from first cut to final client presentation. "All this crafting should be considered part of the creative process, *not* part of the agency presentation process."

Newman is wary of what happens in the misguided interests of "relationship building". "Otherwise well meaning clients can unwittingly unravel a precisely balanced idea with the infamous picked-to-death-by-ducks syndrome, even after the concept has been approved. Once there's been a successful pre-production meeting, the client really should not see the commercial again until it is finished. That is the only way they have a hope of judging it *objectively*." However, Newman is adamant that time should *always* be left in every production schedule before the airdate to accommodate client modifications. "I have a map of the ocean floors of the globe, where what is normally hidden by water is detailed along with the dry land masses. When you can see the underwater chasms, peaks, channels and planes that are usually hidden beneath the surface all exposed, the reflux of the oceans and the patterns of the world's weather are far more easily comprehended. Unfortunately, there is no analogous map available which can indicate the subtle depths and undercurrents in communication. Creative people are the only navigators we have. They simply have an intuitive feeling for it, though it cannot always be articulated or readily made explicit. The truth is, fully half of all successful communication is subliminal, so perspicacious clients leave it to the experts to look after the 'body language' of their ads. This is where clients need to hold their breath, commit a little trust, and look to their agency's creative track record. Having approved the concept, the wise thing is to let the creative people and production house concentrate on producing, polishing and honing it. All good creative people deserve, and will respond to, an opportunity to do that."

Ken Schuldman sees the director as a collaborator, not an adversary. "These guys like Pytka and Tarsem and Andrew Douglas, who was a brilliant photographer and now is a brilliant director, are brilliant for a reason. When you send them a board and they're interested, I don't want to give them my idea of execution. I know what the tonality is, I know what I want people to feel, but I want to hear what *they* have to say. When a director 'gets it', or when they can describe your idea in a way you'd never thought of, they're hired."

Naresh Ramchandani sees the director's job as connecting ideas with consumers. "As you get close to the end of the chain, each new person is progressively more and more responsible for connecting the idea with the consumer. Some directors are incredibly good at taking messages that aren't necessarily connecting and giving them shape or form or palatability, even just through the casting and performances." Ramchandani gets his ideas "pretty finished" in his head. "I would never give a director something to make out of nothing. That's not my style. I need to be able to see it myself, then I want them to make it better. When you appoint a director, it should be someone who very much gets the *spirit* of the idea rather than having details worked out all the way through. Then what we try and do is build in a week or two where we just hang out together and go through it, shot by shot, and have ideas *within* the shots, or within each section of it."

"As a creative person you have to resist the temptation to interfere too much on set," counsels Adrian Holmes. "In a sense, every time I write a commercial I shoot it in my head anyway. I direct it in my imagination and I have a vision of what it should look like. And I have to say that so often the finished result is very different from that. Sometimes it's a disappointment; sometimes it's a lovely surprise because the director has added something that I didn't count on happening." Despite his film training, Holmes admits that feeling the urge to rush forward and take over is the closest he has ever come to wanting to be a director. "I'd rather be a control freak with the script, than with the film. If I own anything it would be at the script stage rather than interpreting someone else's work." If you've made your choice of director, he says, you should trust him or her to do it in the way that they want. A thorough pre-production is the stage when you should have ensured that everyone is shooting the same film and that the director's interpretation is not different to yours. "The thing you *should* be doing is policing the idea. You should be making sure that nobody has lost sight of it. You should be making sure that the way the shots are set up, the way the dialogue is delivered, shot by shot, is staying true to the idea. The director will thank you for not pestering him because he's got enough people on his back. On the rare occasions when you really feel strongly that you want to make a suggestion or disagree with what he's doing, he will then take even more notice of you than he would have done otherwise."

"One plus one equals four," muses Jack Vaughan. "There are occasions when outside opinions might actually stop you making a mistake. Another person keeps you honest."

Who's In Control Of Your Job?

"The storyboard is your best tool for making something happen, finding out all the problems you're going to face, and pre-thinking them." Roy Grace sold his Volkswagen *Funeral* from a detailed storyboard drawn in cartoon style. "When I do a storyboard, I'm pre-producing the commercial. One of the things I am always proud of, and it was a great frustration for the directors and cameramen I worked with, was they would find it hard to improve or change the way I laid out a storyboard. For me, the framing of camera angles, the staging, the propping is all part of the drama and pacing. It has to be well thought-out. I always take a lot of time doing it. I don't even have to go to the shoot, but you can take a commercial that I storyboarded and lay the frames against the finished commercial, and it will be the same. I think it behoves every art director to approach television that way."

While Grace acknowledges that some ideas can't be storyboarded, he is adamant that the majority can — and should — *be laid out and pre-edited*. Great directors like Alfred Hitchcock painstakingly storyboarded every scene of their movies. "I always used to admire other art directors who'd make a scribble and show up on the set and things would happen right there. I have never had that sort of confidence. I also have far too strong a desire to be in control of the end product. *I pre-think everything.*" Howard Zieff directed Volkswagen *Funeral*. "There was no better director of that kind of commercial at the time, and there hasn't been one since," states Grace. "Howard's real genius was his casting. There were a lot of directors I worked with, they might as well have not been there, but you could not say that about Howard. He made enormous contributions." But even Howard Zieff stuck to Roy Grace's original storyboard, "because it was right".

"Over hundreds of productions, I have learned what I can and cannot expect from a production company," Hal Riney attests. "In thousands of hours of looking over an editor's shoulder, I've learned editing better, I think, than most editors. I find today that young creative people expect too much from — and depend too much on — the production company and director. When I go into a production, I know every nuance and frame of the film I expect to end up with. Anything the director contributes in addition is a bonus. But I will *never* turn over the responsibility for my work to a director. He really has no responsibility, in fact, because when the shooting's over, he's outta there, and I'm left with the result." His advice resonates especially for young creatives. "The best advice I could give young teams is to get what they're unlikely to have — experience."

HAVING a single-minded idea is one thing; keeping a single-minded focus on the production is another. Who can you trust? Whose opinions should you take on board? The director's perhaps?

"It depends how I rate the director," admits Delaney. "If someone looks at the idea and nails the idea very quickly, I'd say fine. We've had directors in here and we've canned them a third of the way through a project because they've lost the plot. They try to take the idea somewhere it doesn't need to go. Equally, the directors that we use *do* bring a lot to the ideas, and we encourage them to. I actively say to them, look, go away and come back and tell us how you think it should be expressed. You choose a director because he understands the idea, and can give it a feel, and if required, a certain interpretation."

But if you're *not* a Grace or a Riney or a Delaney, if you're relatively junior in the scheme of things, how can you steer your idea towards the best finish?

The best analogy for advertising, says Stacy Wall, is Hemingway's *The Old Man and the Sea*. "Coming up with the idea is like the man catching the fish. It's no big deal. But he had to get the fish back to the shore with sharks eating away at it the whole time. That's what advertising is. You come up with an idea, and there are literally eighteen thousand hurdles and they're all explanations of the idea. And so this job is 98% about explaining yourself, over and over and over again. It varies according to client. Most of the time it's five or six meetings and conference calls and discussions just to get them to understand the idea. Then when you get to production you've got to explain that idea with the same enthusiasm and passion to a whole new raft of people from the production company. *You've got to keep focused on what you liked about the idea originally.* That's the hardest part of this job. Somehow you've got to balance the creative side of your brain with the methodical side."

"It's absolutely criminal if you write an idea on a page and then hand it over to a director without first wrestling that script to the floor and getting it exactly as you want it," asserts Kes Gray. "You can bet your life the director will have a slightly different agenda. Obviously a director will want to 'improve' on a script, but you have a duty as a writer to *own* it by getting that script as completely polished as you can, by getting the balance of it absolutely right, and by getting the structure absolutely right."

THE writer's craft should be bulletproof.

"You've got to see it yourself," argues Harvey Marco. "You've got to know what you're going to put together. Not a lot of people board now; they do just a key frame, or pull a visual out of a stock book, and write a script around it. Then they give it to the director and he turns it into something *he* sees." Marco boards all his work; the frames go up on his wall for review. Recently, he drew a 32-frame board so he could see every single shot that was possible. "I can't move forward without doing a very detailed storyboard, shot for shot. You can see what's not going to work. You can see that maybe there's a constant thing that could run through an entire spot. That's what you get from boarding. I hate to even talk to a director without a board." Young creatives, he says, often think they need million-dollar budgets to build a reputation. "Come up with a great idea, a simple idea that's a big idea. Block it out with your partner, how you want it to be. Then seek out your director. Until you've blocked it out, until you can see it in front of you, don't go forward with it."

"Great commercials are made in pre-production," attests Warren Brown, "not necessarily on the day of the shoot. You have to workshop everything. You have to go through every movement, every possibility of where you might be able to improve it or add something to it that will elevate it out of the pack of mediocrity." He also argues that scripts need to be meticulously and *honestly* timed. "It's a brutal process but you have to be prepared to hack out the stuff which you thought was actually going to make the commercial special." Brown has directed commercials himself. "It gave me a very strong appreciation of what a director has to achieve. On the day you're getting advice from everyone, the DOP, the camera operator, the producer; fortunately I didn't have an agency on my back or a client, but I could imagine trying to get clear space to just think about what I needed to achieve. What we're really trying to do is capture something that's only a few seconds long, but if you do get it right it is enormously rewarding."

"It's a retrograde step," Chris O'Shea observes, "but directors feel they *have* to alter the script, and if they don't alter it they're *not* doing their job. I believe the director should shoot it as it is scripted. Once I've got the shots I want and I can make the commercial as it was written, I can relax and the director can do whatever he likes. Very often the things he does are good ideas and we use them. But I don't like leaving a commercial entirely in the hands of a director because when you write a commercial you can see it on the back of your brain. When a director reads a commercial he can also see it on the back of his brain, but it might be a different image." O'Shea chooses directors who have come up by the agency route. "There's more chance of them understanding what you're trying to get at and how client approvals work. Paul Weiland was an agency man, so were Graham Fink and Frank Budgen."

"Be in control," says Nick Cohen. "In a print ad, you're in control completely and absolutely as a writer or an art director. But because in a TV commercial you get into subcontracting it to other people — directors, editors, music people — there's a danger for young people to enter into it in a kind of *submissive* way. They give up the authority and control over the idea to the people they're working with because they're not as secure in their own abilities. Don't ever do that because they won't see it the way you're seeing it and you'll end up with film in the can which may not be what you intended in the first place because you're too trusting." By all means, says Cohen, you've got to listen to directors, but you've got to take responsibility. At the end of the day when you're in the editing room, they're somewhere else on the next job. "If you can't cut that commercial in your mind while you're shooting it, you're abdicating your responsibility as the creative team."

IT helps to keep the numbers down and the chain of command short. In the more enlightened agencies, creative producers can help.

"Conventionally, a production department executes ideas that are already fully realised and are perfectly there on paper; but that's rarely the case." In Mark Sitley's experience, the vast majority of concepts in American agencies have no storyboards; they are more the manifestation of strategies. "Sometimes, the concepts are so thin; oh, we are celebrating 'individuality'. It just becomes generic Chevy heartbeat land — just pap, no core." Sitley describes his mission as a creative producer. "My role is to be the right arm of the executive creative director and make sure the production department becomes a kind of engine for the creative department." Inevitably Sitley deals with approving budgets and administration, but creative standards are also part of the job: seeing that concepts are stripped down and strong, and that client images are *imitation-proof*. Sometimes, Sitley has helped steer and shape skeletal ideas. He is well-qualified to do so; his mentors have included Roy Grace. He once spent a memorable afternoon at DDB New York, when Bill Bernbach sat him down in a screening room and personally told him the worth of advertising.

Unlike many agencies, Wieden & Kennedy is very open to extemporaneous execution. As Hal Curtis explains: "On ESPN, for instance, we didn't have a lot of money. Because we would show up at an ice rink with a stack of scripts but we didn't know which hockey players we were going to get, there were things that happened organically during the shoot. It was very different."

SHOULD THE CREATIVE TEAM BE AT THE SHOOT?

"You don't go to a dentist and tell him how to drill your molar." Scott Whybin himself does not attend every shoot. "I've got this theory about directors. The more I put trust in them, the harder they work for me. I don't believe in creative teams who sit behind a director and look through the lens. You don't need a cast of thousands at the shoot. It's a waste of time, except maybe in the case of dialogue spots where there's intonation the writer may need to hear." The critical part is hiring the right director, building up trust, and pre-producing so he's got a clear mind.

"I don't think the art director is of any use whatsoever unless he had the idea," reckons Neil French. "You only need one person who has the 'vision', in inverted commas, of what the commercial should look like. I think it is desperately important that he should go to the shoot. I also think it's desperately important that he should explain that vision to the nth degree before he gets there. To be fair, most directors have an exact feeling of what they want to shoot before they get there and a good director will have a shooting board, including all the cutaways. They're prepared for it. But what they're not prepared for is some spotty youth coming up to them, halfway through the shoot, and saying, oh, can we try it this way? Or somebody from the agency or the client saying, oh, have we covered it from this angle, just in case? And I'll say, no, you can't try it like that; I'm sorry, little spotty youth, but the angle we're going to use is this one. Why would I want to do thirty-five takes wrong, when I could do thirty takes of which one is right? Options should be decided in pre-production. Even producers I admire have said to me on the shoot, Neil, you'd better shoot a cutaway. And I know *why* they're saying it, because if something goes wrong you've got a safety net. But I can work without a safety net."

Budgets often preclude teams attending shoots. As Antony Redman recalls from his Singapore experience: "We might have wanted to send three people — the art director, the writer and a producer — but very often only the art director would go." Speaking from the perspective of other young creatives, he believes agencies have to invest in their future projects. "If you've got a department full of young people, it's crucial they go on shoots so they understand the technicalities of things; so they understand what it's like being on set with sixty people and how decisions have to be made quickly on the spot. There are some agencies where writers don't go on shoots, because it's 'out of their hands'. That's a mistake. Obviously there are lines of demarcation, but a writer can help by making a decision on the spot that will enhance the idea. A great art director will think that way as well, but often the art director has other concerns like the 'look', the camera angles, the movement of the camera, the lighting, the pacing, whereas the writer tends to just look at whether it's still supporting the idea." As a creative director, Redman was too busy to attend shoots but usually sought enhancements in post-production. "You make sure you can get in on the editing process and take a little bit of the glory there."

Brown warns against being sidelined by directors, especially "name" directors. It is very easy to be intimidated by the production process, he counsels. "If you see something that you genuinely think should be done another way, speak up. The first campaign I did when I went to Britain was for Irn Bru. The director wasn't getting it right. I wanted it done my way. By eleven o'clock at night, after a lot of *hrrmmphing* and stamping of feet, he changed it. Supposedly I was inexperienced, especially coming from Australia as well, but if I hadn't stood my ground I would have lost control. In the end it was the right thing to do. It ended up winning Commercial of the Year in Britain and two Silver Pencils at D&AD."

How Should You Use Technique?

"*Techniques,*" says Ron Mather, "*are all devices to elevate the idea.* They're all available to you. Use them to your advantage. But they have to help the idea. *The idea is still mandatory...*"

"Fads are basically for people without talent." Grace resists fads; in fact, he strikes out in the opposite direction. He maintains a sense of the culture he is in, without being obsessed by what other people are doing. "I believe that a commercial that is really great today should be great twenty-five years from now. It shouldn't be so ephemeral in its technique that it becomes that dated. We're still running commercials, in this agency, that we did twelve years ago. There's a classic way of approaching advertising that allows things to have a longer time line. One of the things that gives it that time line is the idea. *The idea should be the single predominant feature, not any technique.*" Grace flew in the face of cinematic fashion when he pioneered one-shot commercials for Volkswagen at DDB. "It was the age when everyone was discovering '*Cinematography*' ... when people were doing '*filme*' ... when everything was *Fellini-esque.* I liked to do things that were starkly boring." His most famous example was a VW approaching from one horizon and driving past towards another. "The camera just didn't move, or moved very little. I was trying to work against everything I was surrounded with. It was very effective." As Grace recalls, whenever his absolute locked camera commercial would come on, "it would be startling in its inactivity."

Neil Godfrey also praises the static camera. "It allows you to do things at what I would call *the pace of life.*" In *Closely Watched Trains*, he says, the static camera treated the screen like a painting. "For example, there's a scene on a railway station which is well-composed with a nice doorway and a window, which to a visual person is a pleasing thing to look at. It might be a painting of a door and window because the shapes are just in the right places. And then one character comes in from the left and another from the right; the camera remains static. They'll meet and have a conversation, then one will walk out of the screen and another person will come in and they'll do something different. It is what you call, in a sense, controlled filming, but it has to be done so beautifully and when it comes off, it really works a treat. It shows the skill of the cinematographer and the skill of the director being able to do that, against the principle of most American films now that use all the techniques, the quick cuts, all of that sort of thing in order to achieve pace and dynamism. It's like a comic book thing." Godfrey prefers to achieve pace quietly. Films like *The Third Man, Twelve Angry Men* and *High Noon*, he believes, are done at a pace where you feel you could actually *walk into the picture* and be one of the people involved in it."

"*The toughest commercials to make are the very minimalist ones*," affirms Sitley. "A single taker is harder to do than giving Ridley Scott millions of dollars. There are thousands of suppliers out there and I wouldn't even say there was a handful who were adept at doing minimalist work, or knew the *worth* of doing it." Sitley resists trends. He wants his clients to be imitation-proof. "First and foremost is the idea. What is the best execution of the idea? What's getting in the way of the idea? I truly do believe there has to be an idea, that what you're selling should be done in a low-key manner and it should be very intelligent. I can't stand any advertising that in any way patronises anybody or tells them what to do."

Sean Cummins is equally dismissive of fads like *cinema verité* or wobblycam. "I can look back on commercials I did fifteen years ago. Fashion never got in the way and they still hold up. Anything that is justifiable is fine; but anything that can pinpoint an era, isn't. I'm keen to keep it timeless."

Francis Wee reviews his Traffic Police commercial that won Gold at D&AD. It was patently a low budget commercial. Would it have been better with a bigger budget and a slicker, more expensive look? "It would not have contributed to the idea. In fact, it might even have devalued the idea." Wee does not rely on production values and a premium look.

Mike Gibbs reviews the techniques chosen for his "misdirect" commercials for Holiday Inn Express. "Misdirect," he explains, is building a beautiful stained glass window and then throwing a rock through it at the end. "We had one concept where a guy is pushing parachute students out of the aircraft. It could have been shot really big, up in the sky, amazing shots, but what we ended up doing was shooting handheld video. We found out that people who go to these parachuting schools for the first time usually have someone shoot them on video, so that technique felt more real and was a better misdirect." Another spot was about a surgeon who turns out to be someone else when his mask comes off. "We could have shot it like the surgery channel, but in the end we just felt it didn't belong. It would be better as a dramatic piece of film, with great angles and close-ups, and we could play on the characters in the operating room, as opposed to a locked-down, weird video shot that the science channels use. A lot of it comes down to gut feeling; how can you make the spot work better, or in the case of Holiday Inn Express, how can you make the misdirect feel much stronger? If it's an emotional sell, you can get away with a lot more freedom filmically. People will allow you to. If it's more cerebral, you have to be a lot more careful with techniques."

"I'd better be honest," French shrugs, "but there have been times when I've tried 'looks' and MTV cutting and I have to say I'm really sorry about that. I have commercials on my reel that look like pastiches of old MTV clips. In retrospect, however, my pastiches look no worse than the originals, but also no better. It's always proved to be a mistake and I've learned that *style just doesn't do the job*." French's advice: never try to be somebody else.

Tracy Wong is one of America's most-imitated art directors. For one thing, his Chevys *Fresh Mex* graphic style has been copied again and again. "Innovation, or discovering 'fresh' ideas, is born out of a deadline and a brief. You've got limited time and a limited range of what to say. Once you arrive at a concept, the execution conforms to it, not to the fact that you're trying to be 'edgy'." Wong insists he has done his share of ripping off, too. "Except I prefer to use the terms 'inspiration' and 'homage'..."

"Don't try and copy anyone else," urges O'Shea. "It's very easy to get into the current genre. Don't. If you actually analyse award-winning stuff, it's always different to the previous years."

Bad commercials are those when somebody jumps on a trend bandwagon, usually six months too late, observes Bruce Bildsten. "Or, in the case of packaged goods, five years too late." If you do something that is really technique driven, he warns, you have to assume others will copy it very quickly.

"It's dangerous to think in terms of trends. The reason they're trends is because they're popular." Redman is equally sceptical about category conventions. "In the car category, they always show a car whizzing down a winding coastal road, a leafy road or a desert road with vortices behind the car because there's a helicopter nearby. You've got to know what those conventions are so you can avoid them, subvert them or spoof them." It all goes back to the core idea, he says. "If black-and-white enhances the core idea and the point you're trying to make in the commercial, if it needs that particular feel, or if your category is full of colour ads, do it."

The use and abuse of black-and-white is hotly debated. For some, the moodier it is, the grainier it is, the better. It symbolises documentary truth and sincerity in the public service category; elsewhere, it lends an air of art cinema, class and quality. Interestingly, in certain Asian markets black-and-white is associated with old-fashioned films and days gone by; it is anything but contemporary and aspirational.

"There is nothing wrong with black-and-white," says Lionel Hunt, "but it is not in itself an idea." Hunt says it should be either one thing or the other. He loathes anything in between, either sepia tones on television, or duotones or spot colour in print. "Of course you must remember that when I started, all the commercials were black-and-white..."

NOT everyone is fussed by using the same technique as a competitive brand in the same category.

"If the execution was right for the idea, I'd still go with it," says Whybin. "Execution is a secondary issue. If it works, if it shines the idea brighter, I'd use it." The only enduring things you can have are strong ideas. Ideas, he believes, stop you subconsciously drifting.

Ted Horton agrees. "I'm not concerned whether I look like other ads in the same category, to be frank. I don't think anyone's ever rushed into Rupert Murdoch's office and said, hey, you can't put Princess Di on the cover this week, another magazine's done it. Everyone says, oh, you've got to be different, you've got to be different. I find this really interesting because the whole advertising industry is always telling you that you've got to be different, you've got to be different, you've got to be different, and then you go to an awards show and everyone's dressed the same. Or you go to their houses and they've got thirty CDs but it's all the same kind of music. Fundamentally, I think people find comfort in sameness. What I try to do is do 'sameness', but make it a little bit special rather than try to be different. I think 'different' is a dangerous thing, especially for young people who all try to be different to the point where they become irrelevant. What I like to do is make ordinary things a little bit extraordinary. I like to take something that is ordinary and the same, and just make it a little bit special."

"We will do whatever we think is right for the job." If Brown and Fishlock believe a technique is relevant and will help reinforce the message, they would not be against using it despite the fact it appeared in other commercials. Everyone is open to the same influences from movies and TV shows, they point out. They believe the issue is bigger. "We pride ourselves in having no style," quips Brown. "If you have to ask *why* a technique was used, it shouldn't be there. Technique should actually just be part of the fabric of your message. As soon as it comes to the fore and has its own personality within the commercial, it's an add-on." Very few technique-driven commercials are genuinely breakthrough.

Bob Giraldi addresses the use of techniques and the need to be different. "People are desperately, desperately trying to stand out; desperately trying to be unique. The music is the same now, we're in a hip-hop world. Commercials are pretty much the same now, funny mockumentaries. Techniques go up and down. Because what are we, after all? We're a follow-the-leader nation. We're a flavour-of-the-month country. We're not very original — yet we're the most original country in the world. We're not very inventive — yet we're always at the forefront and lead everything in terms of the arts. We're very artistic — yet we're also the best bottom line country in the world. It's unbelievably contradictory."

Matt McGrath points to the dichotomy between huge execution and minimal execution. "The ground in the middle is, you didn't have enough money to do something amazing or different. People are so critical." At the very least, he argues, *doing something fresh compensates for a low budget.*

Cohen is also wary of *under*production. He argues for a different kind of idea because people are used to seeing beautifully executed television. "If you try and do something inexpensive or low budget, your client comes across as cheap. So you have to think of ideas that are so simple that people don't look at them that way. For example, you could do a commercial and put one compelling word on the screen for 20 seconds. People aren't going to say, oh, that word wasn't very well-produced, *they're going to look at the idea for the idea's sake*. It's not possible to do that idea in an expensive way." Cohen believes that a lot of clients won't do television because production costs are prohibitive. "With cable television you can now literally buy a very specialised target on niche programming. If you can find inexpensive ways to put something onto videotape in a 30-second format, it makes a lot more sense to spend a client's money that way. There's no wastage. We're now creating commercials, in the agency, on a Mac for a cost of around $500."

At his agency, Cohen says budgets range from $500 to $500,000. "If the production gets in the way of the idea, you've either spent too much money, or too little."

How Should You Choose A Director?

"It's like a dog at a fire hydrant," maintains Grace. "When some directors look at anything, they want to make it *theirs*. Their contribution isn't necessarily always good for the end result. I've had directors talk to me about ideas of mine and what they wanted to do would have totally destroyed the idea, but it would definitely have made it *theirs*."

Grace addresses two questions when choosing a director. "Does somebody truly understand what you're trying to do? Is somebody mature enough, and talented enough, to surrender to the logic of your idea and try to enhance it — rather than *supersede* it — with an idea of their own?" You have to manipulate and control your own ideas as well as manipulate and control people, Grace says. "It's an art, a craft, a skill, that not many people have. Once you get the great idea, that's when the hard work really starts. Making your idea come to life. That's where many, many people fall down. I can't tell you how many things, how many wonderful ideas, that I've approved through my life as a creative director. And the people went away and came back with garbage. Absolute, useless garbage." Grace prefers to work with directors he knows; in earlier days, with Howard Zieff, and later Henry Sandbank, @radical.media. "I know what they can do. I know what to expect. There's nothing more anxiety-provoking than being on a set, fighting the light, and somebody is strapping a lens from Mars on the camera. And then you have discussions about halation or polarising or some idea that's just occurred to somebody that they think they should try. I've been through that. It's not like a print ad; if you make a mistake in a print ad, most times you can say it's not quite working, let's try this. But in television, you can't. You really want to know whom you're going in with. But then there are times when the person you want to work with is not available, or the people you like to work with are not the right choice, and there is somebody new who can add a dimension to what you're doing. In truth, your favourites, your standbys, were new people at one time."

Grace also worked with the same editor for twenty-five years. "I don't like tricky things. I like the idea to come through as strongly as possible and not to be conscious of cutting. The ideal commercial is like the ideal movie, you're not aware it's edited, it's invisible, it's seamless." As he reminds us, the real task of this business is coming up with something that has never existed before.

Nunnally Johnson spent four decades writing dozens of Hollywood's best movies. Among his credits: *The Dirty Dozen*, *The Three Faces of Eve*, *My Cousin Rachel* and *The Grapes of Wrath*. He once said that the director's contribution was highly exaggerated. A director, he rationalised, deserved little more credit than a railroad engineer. The engineer didn't create the railroad track; all he has to do is stay on it and get to where he's supposed to go. The film director, likewise.

Hunt reflects on how directors can add to an idea. "Quite often, we are avoiding people trying to add to the idea, in the hope that they will actually just get the idea right. I suppose that's because we've had difficulties over the years in Australia getting really world class production. That's changed, to some extent, over the last ten years, but before we were just quite happy to get what we wanted on film. Now, assuming we have the luxury of better, more experienced directors and better production standards, we do trust directors who have a good track record. I'm a little bit conservative about using unknown, up-and-coming directors in the hope it will work and I would tend to use not only directors, but also art directors and writers who had already proven many times that they can do it. It's a conservative view, but it seems to work." Hunt loves working with really good producers. "Normally, though, I find it's best not to take any notice of what they say creatively, or indeed to do the opposite."

"At the least, I want directors to deliver what we want," says Mather. "And that's at the *least*. It's hard enough doing great ideas, you don't want them messed up. If they can add to it so we get a better product, that's great. If they can say, you don't need that last shot, it'd be much more powerful with so-and-so ... if they give you *another 20% on top*, that's what you're looking for. The good directors will do that. The danger is when you see it mutate, when it starts to go in the wrong direction. At least if you've got an idea you can pull them back to it, it's like a bar. But if there's no idea, you don't know what will take you there..."

Godfrey agrees. "You want the director to put in a few ounces of his own thing. The best contribution they can make is to like the idea that you've written, agree with you that there's a way of doing it, and then to surprise you because it's come out *at least 20% better* than you thought it might do."

"Work with the good advertising-based directors," Whybin recommends. "People who understand strategy, people who actually understand what communication is about, rather than just what execution is about." However, he is not averse to taking a risk on young, unknown talent.

Gray says you have to understand your own script. "You have to know what you want from your script. If you're not sure in your own mind, you can never be sure you've got the right director. I don't know how you learn that, but I know, and all the art directors I've worked with know. When we go to meet directors, we already have a very clear idea of what we want. That *doesn't* mean that we want them to give us exactly what we're thinking; but if you sit down with a director and he doesn't sound the same kind of notes, you have a choice. Either you can walk away and say, well, he's much better at this than we are, so let's let him do it. Or you can say, no, he's not right. A lot of people, especially people who haven't done much telly, think that because the director has a big name that he is right for the job." Gray believes in having a lot of dialogue with the director prior to the shoot. "There are lots of boxes you have to tick; nobody knows more about the brief, the script, the client than you do. I want to know I can talk to the director on the shoot as well. I'm not prepared to be shut out on the day."

"The first thing production companies should do is to get ads on their reels that have great ideas." Too many showreels concentrate on techniques, says Redman. That's a mistake because creatives look for ads with great ideas. "If a director doesn't screw up an idea and if he can make a great core idea look fantastic technique-wise, creatives will tend to choose that guy over someone who might be more technically competent. When you're dealing with an idea, you want someone who is adept at taking that idea on board, making it better and enhancing it. If creatives have great ideas, they're not going to give the job to someone who just makes weak ads look pretty. They'd much rather go with someone who's not so technically proficient but who can take an idea and do it justice."

HOW does David Blackley choose directors? "Very carefully. We have a bit of a rule that if we can't get the director we want — and it's not always the most expensive or most famous director — if we can't get someone who we think can do an absolutely top job, we tend to do it ourselves. If you drop down to the second and third rung directors, often they don't add anything to it that you can't do yourself." The agency has its own film production company. "We direct about half of our stuff ourselves, without any outside directors." Its output includes Blackley's Mercedes-Benz spot.

"Trust, fear and trepidation." Kash Sree describes the process of selecting a director for another Mercedes-Benz production, this time in Asia. His E-Class launch commercial was going to screen in markets as diverse as Taiwan and Singapore. "Often you think the idea is perfect when it leaves your room. You try and protect it from being taken apart. But at the same time there's that organic growth and you don't quite know which way it's going to go. Sometimes the organic growth makes it better. You've got to let go and wait and see where it goes, and at the same time try to hold onto it in case it gets ruined." Sree admits that he and art director Andy Fackrell started with references like *Natural Born Killers*, just for a juxtaposition of types of film. "We didn't use it, but it was a good thought process. The director had to bring a lot to it obviously. We had very specific subject matter and that subject matter didn't have to be moving greatly. So we wanted someone who could emphasise the drama of each object, almost like a stills photographer. Some directors are just purely abstract in their beauty, but there was enough of a story in our commercial that they might lose it. However, if we'd gone to someone who was just a great storyteller, we mightn't have got that richness of film and those aesthetic qualities. Often when you choose a director, lots of people will have different ideas. But when Jeff Darling's name came up, there wasn't any argument. He just seemed right." As Sree admits, Darling is a selective director. "I was very nervous of Jeff not liking the ad. But when we told him the concept and said these are some of the modules that could fit into that concept — the pregnant woman, the nautilus shell and the clockwork — Jeff liked that flexibility and he tends to rewrite things anyhow. There were little disagreements, your visions will always be slightly different, and that's when you've got to make sure you're not being defensive and you're not holding on too tight. Jeff brought out the beauty in things and seeing that the whole ad was about beauty, it was a perfect match. Jeff communicated that the external beauty was surpassed by the internal beauty." The commercial won high recognition, including a Silver Nomination for cinematography and acceptance into the direction category at Britain's D&AD Awards.

MOST creatives appear to favour a select stable of proven directors, people they can trust, people they can relate to. Or, they might choose someone who has directed a similar style of job.

"I'm afraid I would always go for somebody who's done something similar, which is probably why I'm better doing it myself," admits French. "Thankfully, I'm not very adventurous and I don't have a lot of faith in directors. I've seen so many so-called good directors screw up a film completely."

The greatest commercial director in the world has no tricks up his sleeve, states Jim Riswold. "Joe Pytka. Never. He doesn't need tricks. It's in the idea and it's in a human exposition of the idea. That's all it is. Very simple. You don't have to get so wrapped up in the execution."

"I've been in the fortunate position, for most of my creative life, of having to use very few directors," confesses Riney. "Most of my work has been directed by only two people: a fellow named Dick Snider, who died young, and after that, Joe Pytka. The reason I like to use the same people is that, from the outset, we're all on the same page. We don't have to spend half the time in production arguing about what we're doing or where we're going. Yes, we sometimes take a risk on unknowns, but that's almost always a result of budget restrictions." If the job requires some special effects, Riney adds, he would go to a company providing that expertise.

Michael Patti talks about his trust in Joe Pytka. "It comes from history. The first time I ever worked with Joe, ten years ago, he didn't talk to me for the first week I was working with him. He knew another person on the team and he talked to him. I would have an idea and he wouldn't even look at me. If I said something halfway intelligent, I'd see him doing it on the shoot even though he never acknowledged me. Over the course of time, that changed. He's famous for being difficult to work with. He can say things to your face that are unbelievably harsh. One day when we were having a tremendous fight on the set, I turned to him very passionately and said, Joe, let me tell you something, if my father had said half of the things to me that you said, I would never speak to him again as long as I lived. And I meant it. And Joe waited one beat and he looked at me and said, yeah, but your father can't shoot film." Pytka, says Patti, is not afraid to come to him and Don Schneider halfway through a shoot and recommend a casting change. "A commercial is a very collaborative effort, the work of a lot of people, like Joe, like Don Schneider, like Ted Sann. It's never just one person."

"We have people we trust, people who understand us," says David Lubars, "but it's always good to try new people, too."

Is it a gamble? Wee believes the risk isn't all that great. "It depends on the commercial and the budget. It's a risk, but on the other hand, if you're there supervising, it can't go that wrong."

"As a producer, you have to devil's advocate the situation." Sitley says you can always find a "raft", someone who has done something similar before and done it really well. "The convention in the business is that 99% of the time you go to see if that person's available to do your work, because that's what they're expert at. This is a very stupid American way of approaching things. It's certainly not the way it's done in England or Europe. There, insofar as somebody is good, they're good in their *versatility*, in their journeyman qualities, they're good in *whatever* they do. Here, there's niche marketing, and people tend to rely on the same old people to do the same things in a certain genre, or even on a certain brand. Aside from anything else, that only helps to *further* homogenise stuff. In other words, how does stuff have any impact if you haven't figured out a way of giving it some impact? You should give it to an *unexpected* director who will up the ante in what they bring to it." Sitley is a firm believer in choosing directors against type. For that reason, he does not think that in-house agency directors provide enough diversity. Once he chose a premier fashion director to shoot financial commercials. "We used his eyes and taste for quirkiness. That genre had *never* been dealt with in that way." The same theory applies if you're working in a more glamorous domain, says Sitley. "Don't use the same old people for the same old look. Bring in people who will break their back to show you their breadth and give your clients a certain kind of presence."

Bildsten agrees. "There are directors like Frank Budgen who can do virtually everything. I also love discovering someone, getting someone on the cusp as opposed to getting someone at the back of the curve, or someone when they're so famous they don't really have time for you."

Jan van Meel also advocates choosing a young or "unexpected" director, rather than make the easy choice for someone famous and proven. "Look at tons of reels. Find a director who can give you what the idea needs."

McGrath prefers to take risks. Clients need to be surprised, pleasantly surprised by the outcome, that it was even better than they thought it could be. He wants a director who can contribute something that he can't do, but not at the expense of the idea. "We won't work with people who won't be completely open about what they are intending to do before the shoot. We like to explore everything beforehand. We talk to the director every day. We get them to do a really detailed shooting board and discuss every frame. They have to get all the visual reference on anything they're thinking about doing. Everything has to be worked out beforehand with the actors, so that on the day we know exactly what we're doing." Once everything is bolted down, McGrath contends, it allows a little extra time to occasionally experiment with something on the shoot. "Something great might happen that's completely different from what we'd planned..."

Linus Karlsson would definitely assign work to a new director. "For me, that's everything. You meet the person; you sit down and talk to him, not necessarily about advertising, but about other things. What's important for him? After a while you find out if this is a person you want to spend time with." Karlsson says "looks" can be created; what can't be created is a personal connection. "As long as you connect on some kind of level, the rest is details."

Cummins works with modest budgets in Melbourne; established directors are unaffordable. "Ninety percent of my commercials have been shot by first-time or fairly new directors. Coming from student films, my budgets must look like paradise. They can even afford catering..." Cummins challenges a director's need to be filmically esoteric. "I'll remind them in as pleasant a way as possible that we have only got thirty seconds. No one wants to emasculate the director, but the best directors fundamentally *know* the tempo of any advertising message."

Bildsten on budgets: "I've seen people pull off some amazing things, but as a creative director I have my teams think of ideas in terms of the resources they have at their disposal. Where you get trouble is when someone has what appears to be a pretty decent budget, but they come up with a huge, mega idea and they still try to execute it within that budget. Some hungry director or production company will try to do that for them and they're usually the worst disasters of all."

"There's the director, and then there's the direct*OR*," quips Cohen. "Sometimes the director is a director, but sometimes he will be a direct*OR*. On every shoot, the director is going to want to have his little direct*ORIAL* moment where he tries some stupid shot that will never make it into the commercial, but you have to humour him. Dave Cook, who does all our work, lets that happen but will know why it's happening, whereas less experienced people might say, yeah, let's do it that way."

"Ninety-nine times out of a hundred, the director's cut is a complete overkill; an indulgence. Put a director and an editor in a room and there's a loss of perspective." Bill Oberlander is always looking for the next up-and-coming director.

ONE man who arguably knows more about selecting talented directors is David Perry, director of broadcast production at Saatchi & Saatchi New York. His turf includes the agency's New Directors Showcase, an annual event at the International Advertising Festival at Cannes. Only twenty to twenty-five new directors will make it into the Showcase each year. "The Head of Television in London Mark Hanrahan and I cut the world in half. We cull our own regions, and we have help from offices in other regions. We narrow it down, then Bob Isherwood's worldwide creative board has a look and makes the final decisions with a little fine-tuning from Bob."

To qualify for the reel, Perry explains: "You need to have been directing commercials for only two years or less. You could have been directing in another area like music videos or documentaries or photography, so you don't need to be a complete neophyte." What does Perry look for? "It's always hard when you judge a director's reel to separate out his or her contribution. We're looking for the classic director's contributions, the primary production values: the casting of the people, the way it's staged and lit, edited and scored. Except in the States, directors have control over the whole process; here, it's pretty much a fragmented process where the director turns the dailies over to the agency and never sees it again until they send him a U-matic for his reel." As Perry admits, "When you look at a great commercial, it seems that everybody did their jobs right and it's very hard to draw a line and say we're only going to look at these elements."

The Showcase has become an international barometer of directing talent. "Primarily the entries come from production companies. By the time someone is ready to be a finalist, they've got a good reel with a solid company behind them or representation. Very few are freelance directors." The Showcase is a way to help people cut through, says Perry. "It helps accelerate them getting onto the world stage. It can get a talented young director in Sydney in front of the people in Los Angeles, or somebody really good in Warsaw gets shown to the folks in Bangkok. I've had calls from them to say, I'm now three years ahead of where I was going to be because my work was up there in front of the elite of the worldwide advertising community in Cannes. All we're saying in the Showcase is that these guys are great. Here's this year's crop of bright young kids you ought to pay attention to. We're shown a couple of hundred of them over the years and not all of them went on to become Tarsems. But we don't need two hundred Tarsems; we only need three or four."

How Do Directors Choose *You*?

Perry demolishes the myth that great directors can be hired to save weak ideas. "Great directors aren't susceptible to money. The only way to hook them in is to challenge them with something they really want to do. They can't be bought."

"The idea is always the most important trigger that sparks my imagination — but not necessarily the only one." Director David Denneen looks for scripts that challenge him as a film maker. "A script that lets me get my teeth into talent direction, into designing and building sets, into lighting them so that every shot can be a piece of art. So if I'm given a great idea that only involves one or two shots and my involvement or contribution would be minimal, I'd probably pass on it. The bottom line is, I like to tell stories and I like to be challenged by the scope and scale of a job, and if there is a great idea involved, that's even better."

"I can tell a good script from a bad one; whether it's funny or whether it's hackneyed." Frank Todaro was an agency creative director for twelve years. "I can help with ideas. I've never had anybody say, please don't touch my script, just go point the camera. At the early stage, when I'm on the phone with the agency I might say, do you know what might be funny? And if they respond positively, you know you might be on to something. It's not my style to jam anything down anyone's throat. I like to work with people on the same page. Let's figure out the voice of this thing and make it as funny as possible." Todaro refuses to do commercials for violent video games, despite the very funny scripts that come along. He remains in awe of the old DDB days. "It was clever, smart stuff that gave people a little credit. How fantastic it was that they did the old Volkswagen *Funeral* ad. Now people get laughs by way of being crass; they're willing to be completely tasteless or offensive. I'd like to go back to being *cerebrally* funny, than funny because some guy got killed."

When Bob Giraldi, a 30-year veteran, picks up a script he likes to get "something in the pit of the stomach. Whether I laugh or cry or if I say, wow, that's something I haven't seen before, something's *got* to happen. Most scripts that we get, all of us directors, we take and we look at it and say, how can we make it better? And then we attempt to improve it, collaborating with the agency, fighting and arguing, and sometimes not ending up friendly ever again, but most times coming out all right. It's few scripts that come across your desk that you say, wow, that's going to happen, it's written that well. The weakness of our business is the writing. It is the toughest. It is humbling. People can become directors left and right, actors can become directors, producers can become directors, editors and photographers can become directors, *but not one of them can become a writer*." Giraldi vividly remembers a script that came in advertising WLS-TV in Chicago. "It was something that was true, it had happened, and I was just to re-enact it. It was the story of two old people in a Chicago neighbourhood who were left alone when most of the block moved out because of the minority influx. As the minorities came in, these two old white people didn't move. Because they were *blind*. And together they threw a block party for the neighbourhood kids who were black and Hispanic. And I re-enacted that day of waking up and throwing that humble, modest block party. And I cried on the camera, one of the few times I ever did. It was a piece that will be in my heart for as long as I live. Both actors, who weren't blind, played blind. They aren't alive today. It was a long time ago. But I knew when I saw it on paper, I knew there was something there. It reached me, and it evidently reached other people, too. Coincidentally, it was the piece that Michael Jackson saw of mine that said to him that he must work with me." Too often, scripts are not crafted. "Let's go on a set now and see what happens, let's go for a happy accident..."

AT Sydney's Window Productions, ranked among the top ten production companies of the world at Cannes in 1998, Ray Lawrence looks for some sort of conflict or dilemma, be it in the genre of comedy or drama. One of Lawrence's most celebrated commercials was *Retired Milkman*. "If it is purely somebody talking about a product, then I'm not interested. I've just shot a commercial where a young man leaves home in his car to go for a job interview. It starts to rain. He drives past a woman with three kids whose car has broken down in the middle of the road, so he stops his car, gets out and helps her, gets totally wet, sprayed with oil, but gets her back on the road. Eventually he gets to his interview and gets the job. It's only then that you see he was hired as a roadside serviceman by the NRMA, an emergency breakdown organisation." The Saatchi & Saatchi Sydney commercial was written by Jane Caro and Jason Mendes, and art directed by Gill Bull.

The problem with commercials, says Lawrence, is that creatives like to think their work is cutting edge. "But you can't cut any edges, because you have to be just *behind* all the trends. You actually can't create trends. I'm not talking about visually, but in terms of *content*. To me, content is everything, and then light is second. Everything pyramids down. I don't like glossy things. It's a piece of film; I want to see how close I can get to the truth within the parameters I'm given, within the idea." These days, Lawrence points out, television commercials go from the sublime to the ridiculous. "They either give you all the information in thirty seconds, or none at all. People do these colour and movement ads and you think, what was all that about?" Lawrence believes nothing is more interesting or more involving than mystery. If you can interest somebody but not give them all the information immediately, so they work it out themselves — *that* involvement is the crucial part. "Television commercials are basically dead in the water. I remember quoting on a script for a bank; in one scene a farmer reaches across the desk and shakes the bank manager's hand and I said, you've got to be joking. Who are you kidding?" Clients have agendas, states Lawrence. "Clients are just working in a company; they don't want to rock the boat, so they won't challenge anything. The agency is trying to make the commercials interesting, but in the end everyone just gets worn down."

"Ask any of our directors and they'll say, bring me a great script, that's all I want to see," says Steve Orent at Hungry Man. "It starts with a great idea and a great client. There's usually a certain smartness in the writing, that's what you're first taken by. We like to do stuff that's unique, not campaigns that have been done already. We like to blaze new trails. Can we take a mediocre board and make it better? Yes, if the agency is willing. There are a lot of former writers here, but we're *not* an agency. We're first and foremost a production company." There is no house style, says Orent, even though the directors share the same sensibilities. "When we started the company we didn't say we're just going to be a comedy shop. We're a company of humorous directors and the people we're associated with are all humorous writers. But if you put the same board in front of each of our twelve directors you'd get twelve different commercials."

Terry Bunton looks for an idea and debates whether it has been exploited to its fullest. "How do you recognise one? Well, you just do, don't you?" As an ex-agency copywriter, Bunton believes his greatest contribution as a director is being true to the idea. "Keeping the idea and throwing away any extraneous stuff. If it involves a bit of dialogue, getting the line said the right way." Bunton does his own shooting board, frame by frame. "While we quote I work out the scenes, sometimes trying to get rid of scenes that the agency had in there that don't contribute to the idea. Usually though, if the script has been through research, every scene has to stay." Some agencies have fixed ideas. "I prefer to have more latitude. When I was in an agency I wouldn't tell the production company the way I thought it should be directed. The production company can bring another eye to it. When agencies come with really fixed ideas, they miss an opportunity to expand the horizons for the spot."

Jeff Darling, @radical.media Sydney, looks firstly for emotion. "Inevitably it's about emotion, whether it's a story-based thing with a narrative thread or purely image-based. You're trying to find emotions or combinations of emotions that you necessarily haven't seen before. Conflicts, juxtapositions of things, maybe shooting people in a differing way." Darling's decision to accept a project is often a personal reaction to his previous assignment. "I divide things into two palettes. One is image-based; the other is an esoteric sense of narrative. I define them as two strings to my bow and I'm trying to develop both, one as a reaction to the other. If I've experimented enough with a certain sort of imagery, the next thing I might be looking for could have a narrative base, so I can explore film language within narrative. I'm not so keen to just tell a simple narrative that I feel I've experienced before. I'm not that excited about the A-B-C-D sense of simple storytelling. Being of a visual background with a history of photography and cinematography, the visual has always been my angle into it. The visual medium has produced for me the idea of metaphor, the idea of juxtapositions, the opportunities to exploit film language. It takes a lot to digest those things before you just go to the next level. It's never about, well, here's something I can do, and we'll turn it over. It's trying to find something that will take you somewhere else."

At Great Southern Films Melbourne, Helene Nicol looks for commercials that move audiences to *do* something. The hundreds of international awards won by the company include the original Transport Accident Commission campaign directed by John Lyons. "We've always done commercials with some sort of emotional value, but we've never been particularly driven by visuals alone. We want to be true to the idea and not bury it in production values. We've done commercials here on the smell of an oil rag and sometimes they're the best ones." While Nicol believes in idea-driven work, she acknowledges that sometimes visuals can be *such* an experience that they are in themselves enough. Her main concern is the quality and durability of an idea. "We get a lot of things that we call ideas which are good on paper, particularly spots that end with a joke. You read them on paper and they're funny, they're cute. But then you realise that when it's been translated into a commercial and people have seen it more than once, it's already worn out. So you have to beware of them. They're very tempting when you first see them." Nicol stresses the need for structure and storytelling. "We're film makers and quite often we see ideas which are essentially good, but the creatives might want you to give away something at the beginning of the commercial or they want to put a big gag at the end. Some people listen, some don't. Some people are so anxious about their relationship with their clients that once a script is approved they're really worried about touching it." A lot of work comes in just as a storyline, not a script, reports Nicol. "The agency will say, make this into something that will work."

Nicol's advice to young creatives: "Try not to be superficial. Understand what it is that engages people and build that into your work."

Stone The Cast First

"When I think of all the commercials we've done that haven't worked that well, I think it was usually casting that let them down," reflects Hunt. "The more experienced I get at this, the more casting is critical, just as it would be in a Hollywood movie."

"I always felt that casting was the dirty little secret that all the great performance dialogue directors had," says Perry. "The one thing that Pytka and Dektor and Giraldi and Sedelmaier have in common is that they put a ton of money and their own personal time into seeing the actors and really pushing them hard. Some directors like Leslie Dektor won't even show the actor the script. He'll give them something else to read first, a play or a poem or a letter, just so he can get *a sense of the person*." Once many actors are exposed to a script, explains Perry, they will try to make it into an ad too quickly. "He can't then tell the actor to forget the script. It's too ingrained in their heads and they can't be fresh."

Film, says Giraldi, has turned out to be an actor's medium. "Actors totally call the shots today in movies. With a few exceptions, directors mean nothing, control nothing." Giraldi discusses his casting methodology for a campaign about parenting. "I liked the subject, I loved the four scripts, and I talked to the agency; I said, I want to do these, if you'll have me, but if I do them, I'd like to approach them in a more theatrical, cinematic way. Now what does that mean? That means I don't want to go to the usual suspects. I don't want to go to the usual casting people who do commercials. I said, I want to be able to cast theatrical people, movie people, not because they're supposedly stars, but because that will bring in different actors from different agents, especially kids. Kid actors are different to *commercial* kid actors. Commercial kid actors are cute, they've got Buster Brown haircuts, their mommies bring them in, they can react. But kid '*actor*' actors are kids who take home blinds, pages of the script, memorise them and deliver a performance. There aren't a lot of them, but they're around, and I convinced the agency that we were going to go that way. Now the agency was a little nervous this morning when they walked in and saw the first day of casting. There were actors standing against a brick wall, with sides, pages of the script, in their hands. They weren't acting, they weren't playing it out, they weren't doing scenes. They were reading aloud, one person at a time, so the director could look and say, I like his voice, I like his look, I like the way he approaches a little bit of dialogue; now let's call him back to sit with a kid and do a scene together. That's a very subtle difference..." Giraldi, in fact, was conducting a typical *theatrical audition*. "The agency got very nervous. They were used to seeing forty to fifty people for each role. Instead they saw twelve people for each role, because the casting director went to some good actors and good agents and made her choices, and it was my turn to see whether I could go on from there."

Redman references Tony Kaye. "I think he was absolutely right when he said the first priority was casting. If you've got a script and it's a great idea, just put that aside for the moment. What is going to be the *first* thing that is going to catch people when they're watching an ad? If you haven't got talent, it's going to be the location or the type of location you choose, which is in effect casting for the location. If you've got talent, then you need to find people who have got some character in their faces, if that enhances the idea. I think it's important to find people who have something special, whether it's their eyes or just the interesting way their face is constructed. If the point is to be normal, you'd be surprised how difficult it is to find really 'normal' looking people."

"I don't want to say casting is the third most important thing, or the second most important thing," says Grace. "*Everything* is the most important thing and casting is totally critical."

How critical?

"I think casting is 90% of the commercial," asserts French. "The only times I've screwed up is when I've tried to save money on casting."

Bildsten still invests time to personally view casting tapes. "When it's something with characters in it, I really know what I want. I want to see every one of them."

"Paul Arden said you should always cast *against* the kind of character you're looking for," recalls McGrath. "Get a guy who looks like a garbage man to play a doctor."

Sitley agrees. "Cast against type. I have a bias towards using theatrically trained actors in commercials, not commercially trained actors."

Riney argues the case for real people. "Early on, I found that working with real people, as opposed to actors, offers a better chance to reflect credibility and honesty. Personally, I've always been distressed by the tendency of most advertisers to idealise their intended consumer, with slick actors who — perhaps as a result of the narcissistic qualities that led them to the acting profession in the first place — radiate phoniness and superficiality."

The Little Caesars campaign was often cast on the street during lunch breaks, recalls Arthur Bijur. "We used to always send casting people out to malls and old folks homes and trailer parks and street corners. They would find these interesting characters for us. We'd write these scripts and we'd have people try them. Sometimes we found the non-actors brought the most interesting qualities to the performances. That was the great thing. So many of these people were just being themselves. They weren't acting. You could feel that, you could really sense it." For one unknown, plucked from obscurity by Cliff Freeman's, fame flickered briefly. "He was a real person," says Bijur, discussing the young man for whom things kept getting better and better. "He was a bank teller. He had never acted in his life. He did the commercial. He became very recognisable very quickly. He quit his bank teller's job, got himself an agent, and I don't think he ever worked again."

"A lot of people would say that I don't like people," admits Lawrence, "but I like what people can do. There's nothing better than a good performance. For me to get to the truth of your performance if you're an actor, I have to put you in a truthful environment. And I have to trust you." When Lawrence accepts a project, the first thing he does is ring his casting person. "I might just say I need twelve old-age people, four males, eight females, *and that's it*. She knows to get me good actors. I'm not interested in saying things like, oh, he has to be sort of like Steve McQueen, because then they go away and concentrate on what Steve McQueen looked like, and not what Steve McQueen *was*. I might say, I want a 35-year-old male and he's going to be a postman. That's it. If you have to intellectualise what a postman is, you will limit yourself. So by not being specific, I'm not limiting myself. A long time ago, if Hitchcock had the part of an accountant to cast, he'd go and photograph twelve accountants and there'd be a commonality there that he'd use; the stereotype was the truthful one."

Casting, Oberlander suggests, is a mechanism that can push the brand. It did, in a new campaign for a major investment firm. "We wanted to portray the firm as an Internet-user investment bank, so it had to look contemporary and modernistic. At the same time, it had to look traditional, conventional, reliable, credible, a company that's been around for fifty years. So we cast a guy who looked like De Niro, only with a shaved head. He looks around-the-block-a-couple-of-times, and he's bald, so we happen to have the convenience of bald equals older, but also now bald is actually trendy. It goes both ways. He looks like a hard-arse with a shaved head in a kind of conventional, older man kind of way, but at the same time he looks really chic."

"We're known for our casting." Orent says it's the most important thing. "We dig and dig and dig until it's the night before the shoot. We turn up every stone and we push the casting agents for new faces. Our directors often start their mornings at the casting sessions. We like improvs; sometimes the actors will say funny stuff, come up with lines. We also have our own stable of go-to guys, great guys we've shot with before."

"The secret is, it's all about casting, casting, casting." Nicol says advertising is not movies. "There's not enough time to establish character. You've got to *be* character. People are always interested in other people." One caution: "At times clients will say, I don't think I like their teeth and you have to say, their teeth are really not so important, it's their whole character we're using."

Darling believes the atmosphere on set can dictate performance. "It's important to have an atmosphere that lets the actors be quite free and gives an energy to the whole environment. You can set an atmosphere just with the kind of music you play to the crew. Or you may want to have a little bit more conflict, tension or confusion, depending on the performances you're after. That might influence the duration of takes. You may not actually say 'cut'; you may just say, go back and do it again."

It helps to understand something of the craft of acting. The celebrated British director Sir Carol Reed, whose classic films include *The Third Man*, started work as an actor. He began as a spear carrier and progressed to a dope fiend. "You just shiver and shake and people think, well, isn't that good." Reed maintained that his experience helped him understand actors' problems. "Having been an actor, I can tell those signs by which an actor shows he's been made awkward by the movement I've asked from him."

Lee Strasberg's Method acting was intended to provide a method of working that would achieve reality in performance; at its core was recreating or reliving an intense emotional experience *at will*. Stanislavsky's theory was reformulated: if the circumstances of a scene indicate your character must behave in a particular way, what would *motivate* you, the actor, to behave in that particular way? The actor seeks a substitute reality that will help him behave truthfully. Actors must create their characters without imitating previous performances. In the French cinema, one director achieved this by making his casts rehearse their lines without expression, as though they were reading the telephone directory. Once their formulae were shed, he believed, miracles could happen.

If the script doesn't "play", perhaps you shouldn't change the cast; you should change the copy. "You don't always appreciate whether a line or an idea will work," Bunton says, "until you have your first casting session. Assuming, of course, that they're reasonable actors, they'll show you how it should be, whether the lines aren't working, whether a line should be dropped. They should get the creative director's fee. Sometimes when they look bewildered at the script, you *know* it needs fixing."

Casting is critical in comedy. "The way I approach casting is that everything has to come out of the idea," says Rowan Dean. "The moment you can't directly relate wardrobe or casting or set design back to the idea, you've lost your way. Why is the character doing this? What sort of person would be doing this? So that tells you the sort of person, and that tells you the way to go with the wardrobe. What sort of room is he in? That should come out of his personality, too."

Chuck McBride actually sees the faces of his characters as he writes scripts. "Erich Joiner and I worked really hard to create that mould for *got milk?* The director and a lot of other people weren't necessarily sure if they wanted to go with the guy we used on *Aaron Burr*. I said that guy is the weirdest looking guy I've ever seen in my life and if we don't put him into this commercial it won't be half as interesting. If I see him, an eccentric guy, living in this world and knowing so much and then being so wrong, he's the perfect foil. We needed to create a visual style that was all ours, a die for a lot of the other guys to follow. It became much more about creating a world where the people are *just a little left of centre* than your everyday world." McBride reveals his style has changed. "Now I'm completely the other way round. I'm trying to figure out ways to hide the comedy within scenes of normalcy, disguising it within normal life. You know it's going to be funny, but you just don't know when it's going to happen, or where it's going to come from, and then all hell breaks loose."

CREATING THE LOOK

How do you go about creating a unique look for a commercial? What factors determine the style of cinematography and lighting? How is the visual texture determined?

"My first choice for a look is backlight and reflective light," explains Denneen. "This gives the shot a strong, graphic look, whether shooting a set or exteriors. Most of the look of the film comes from the grading session at the post stage, and of course the art direction contributes as well. Lens selection has a big influence on the look, and I usually opt for wide-angle lenses and long lenses, but rarely do I use mid-range lenses because they don't give the film an attitude, except for 'normal'." Denneen keeps up with current styles. "Unless the trend is for the raw look, with no real lighting or lensing style. There is nothing wrong with the raw look; there's quite a bit of film with that look around, but it's just not for me."

Rick Dublin discusses the hidden pressure on directors. "There are a lot of influences. Your reps are out there saying everyone's doing this recolourisation of their films so you'd better do it, too. Also, you can't help but be attracted to some techniques. Some are valid. Others get used for the wrong reasons. Some people want techniques even when they have nothing to do with the script. I've seen mockumentaries done poorly so often; they look like *Blair Witch Project*, bad quality film and bad light. Frankly for me, bottom line is storytelling. Whatever works best to tell the story correctly."

In Melbourne, Nicol identifies another pressure. "There's a demand to cram more and more information into commercials. One commercial we did recently had three layers of images on the screen at the same time."

How does Darling determine the way he will shoot something so it looks fresh? "Inevitably you are looking at other images, and looking at references, but it's understanding how to interpret those things. In the back of your mind you've got an overall feeling that you're trying to get through the film. You're not just putting a collage of images together. I'd like something that puts a big question mark on me. I want something to take me to some exotic place, but to do it in a different way. And I don't just want to be there and see a beautiful landscape, but I want an emotion to come with it. It's not going to happen in any new way if I just show a beautiful landscape. It's going to have to have *another* element in there. I did a spot for Boeing; there was one scene set in Tibet. There was a little kid playing with a cardboard box. On top of the box was a little model of the Eiffel Tower. The commercial was all about globalness and journeying. I was trying to find a very naïve way to show a global perspective from his point of view as opposed to just photographing a kid playing in Tibet. It's being credible with that kid in that environment."

Darling starts by putting quite intangible thoughts down on paper. He has filled masses of journals with notes of visual ideas. "It's almost impossible for me to re-read some of them because of the way that I think. Bits of imagery. Just seeing a little model of the Eiffel Tower; that sat there for weeks until it got integrated into something. It's about making connections from a point of view of understanding what the commercial is trying to say and applying the language of metaphor. You're sitting down with a backstop of knowing what emotion you want out of the film. You're writing things down based on that emotion. And that may be very different from the images you end up with."

Darling then considers structure and form. "Maybe, if I just put all these images together, I'm going to end up with a very vacuous thing. Maybe I need a device or an element, a filmic idea to really piece the thing together and put a difference on it. When you get that, originality will start to come into the imagery. Once you get to the storyboard, it's probably close to the end of the process. Then it's about being able to craft the whole thing in perspective, craft the timing of things; you're understanding why you're repeating things just for an edit room, why some things may have three or four more shots than they need. Maybe there are two scenarios you're shooting that may be very equal and you might realise in an edit room there's a good chance you're going to drop one but you want that choice. There are always the other possibilities once you get on location and you don't quite know what is going to fit together..."

Perry talks about the phases that the industry goes through. "Some of them are very short-lived, they're almost all imitative, and they're almost all, in one way or another, production-related. They aren't conceptual-related phases, because except for a couple of bright moments, most advertising is heavily executional." Perry suspects the industry never permanently moves anywhere. "I think we stand still in a sense and we try things out for a few months, for a year or two."

"Unless you're a film buff, you shouldn't notice the 'look' any more than you'd notice good typography in a print ad." Vaughan says the only concern should be the viewer's net out-take. "You don't want people to say, oh, the eating shot was fabulous, oh, the lighting on that pack was superb."

"If I'm working with a really great script, my job is to make it as clear as possible and not muddy it with technique." Making it work, says Lawrence, will be his single greatest contribution as a director. Charm and humour are triggers that should be inherent in the script. "There's a place for technique, but if I've got this actor and his performance has been realistic, *why* put black bars at the top and bottom? *Why* desaturate it? What am I doing? Am I putting something in the way of the idea and me?" Lawrence says he has never been interested in special effects. "Light comes all the way from the sun. The test is, a lot of people don't use daylight because they can't work with it. They're not competent enough; they can't work fast enough. A lot of the time I work with a zoom lens." He is equally scathing about other film making conventions. "They have this thing on films called 'final checks'. The makeup and wardrobe people rush in and do their stuff, then you shoot the wide shot, and then they rush in again — why? Nothing's happened. The men in my commercials don't have makeup; you don't need any makeup, you're going to look like what you look like. The women have street makeup and they generally do that themselves. We have a makeup artist on the shoot, just to fuss and make people feel good — but *NOT* to change their looks. It comes back to trust and getting closer to the truth in any given situation."

Location, too, should be inspired by the truth of the situation. "We'd get a location that *doesn't* need art direction. Art direction to me is simply, wouldn't it be nice if we had a couch over there; we haven't got a couch? So get one..." Lawrence says there is no such thing as being original; it's all been done before. "When I talk about the truth, I don't want it to sound pretentious. I'm only talking about commercials. That's all they are. When I talk about truth, I'm talking about what I try to bring to a commercial and which is reflected in a totally abstract way. You could call it Method directing. For me to function as a storyteller as clearly as possible, I have to find what I think the truth is. I have to develop a point of view for anything I shoot, a film or a commercial. It's all based on trusting the idea.

When you make a decision to do a particular spot, the first thing is to form an opinion about the script, then everything is based on getting those performances. Nothing should be seen; camera shouldn't be seen, art direction shouldn't be seen, wardrobe shouldn't be seen. *It should be just the idea and the performances.*"

DIRECTORS AT WORK

Bryan Buckley, Hank Perlman and Steve Orent. Hungry Man is the hottest new production company in the States. Bryan Buckley, teamed with Frank Todaro, had won major awards with the original ESPN SportsCenter campaign. Hank Perlman was a writer at Wieden & Kennedy. Executive producer Steve Orent was Henry Sandbank's assistant director, @radical.media New York. "We all had this great relationship," recalls Orent. "Out of a whim we felt it was the right time. We said, hey, what do we have to lose? We can always go back to what we were doing…" Was success anticipated? "We've got a long way to go yet. The idea was to form an entertainment company and not just do commercials. We'd all had success in what we'd been doing. We're all very ambitious, otherwise we wouldn't be in this business, and we all just wanted to do the best possible work that was out there. We're all very driven, but not to step over people or drive into concrete walls to get there." Orent stresses that Hungry Man is not just a vehicle for Buckley and Perlman; it has nurtured the talent of other directors like John O'Hagan whose credits include Outpost.com.

Orent believes there is a trend for writers like Perlman and Todaro to become directors. "A lot of people have had success doing it. It's a natural progression. But there are two sides; sometimes, strong creatives don't want to hire directors who have a creative writing background, they just want someone to execute their boards. But if you hire someone like Hank, you get more than a film maker; you hire someone who's going to bring that much more to the table. Especially when you're doing comedy and dialogue, things change by the second. If you have someone who can think on a dime and give you three lines in a matter of seconds, it's so valuable. Bryan and Hank collaborate with agencies and listen. That's our philosophy, we're all in this together, so why not draw on Bryan and Hank as great creatives?" The greatest contribution Hungry Man can make to a commercial, Orent says, is knowing not only what's funny but what works for the client. "Our directors have been down that road so many times. Getting the point across for the client, but still staying within the context of the creative."

Why Hungry Man? "We agonised over what to call the company. Then at two o'clock in the morning when we were talking about how we were going to structure the company, Bryan Buckley said, I'm hungry, man. We put that into a hat with some other names and it was plucked out. We still struggle with the name a little bit; we never wanted people to presume that we'd do anything to get a job."

Significantly, Orent eschews the usual industry hype. "I live in my own bubble, maybe to a fault. I'm not familiar with the competition. I look at *Shots* reels, but a lot of times it's been on my desk a month before I get to see it. We do what we do, as best we can. Hank Perlman still sees his mockumentary style of ESPN work; it comes in on boards with a cover letter from the agency as if they've just invented it. They're five years behind the trends. It's scary. We still get a ton of boards with guys in costumes..."

Orent's advice for young creatives and aspiring directors is to *conquer one thing at a time*. "Don't put the cart before the horse. Get great at what you do first. Everybody wants to get ahead so fast that they're always one step ahead of themselves. There are young guys in agencies sending me their director's reels after only a year. You have to concentrate 150% on what you're doing at the time, then move on from there. You'll be a better director once you understand how every facet of an agency works." Orent, in his late thirties, says he spent a long time in the trenches. "Young directors all want to do what Bryan is doing. They all want to be Tarsem. But if we put a young director in a position where he's completely over his head, we all lose. Know your craft inside out, learn something new every day. And if you do make the same mistake twice, it won't be as bad as the first time. *Your time will come when it's ready*."

Jeff Darling. Still shooting much of his own work, Darling admits he is now less technically interested in that process. "I light by eye and move forward. I'm not reading things all the time, which can become a bar." Darling combines pragmatism with poetry. He started as a stills photographer, then a DOP for two of Australia's foremost directors, David Denneen and Peter Cherry. "The benefit of shooting your own things is that I'll know what I can do with an image. I can turn around and grab an image in two minutes, as opposed to having to brief somebody first and take fifteen minutes. And I'll know what it is I'm shooting, and how I'll piece it together. I'll know what's worth bringing production value to, what's worth bringing filtration to, and also what to discard."

Darling is a firm advocate of pre-production. "Some directors use the set as the exploratory element." He prefers to understand the advertiser's objectives. "I'm trying to direct towards a certain outcome. It's not just a personal indulgence. *If there is a difference in the image to start with, people start to look at the content in a different way as well.*" He ascribes the reliance on filmic metaphor in advertising to the advent of the computer age in business. "Every corporation is trying to do something metaphoric because there are so many intangibles in what they are about." Telecoms providers are a prime example, suggests Darling. "Poetic metaphors became the means of communication."

He resists genre conventions. "I've never walked into a genre and seen what has been done before. You're not really trying to go into that genre at all. You want to bring a different language to it. I look at films and stills, but not commercials as such. I want to see where contemporary thought is. If you're playing with the more strange and esoteric juxtapositions, you want to see how far you can push things with audiences."

How does Darling approach commercials? "It's like any film making; when you really get down to it, you're trying to understand *yourself*. Yes, we've got this script, it's a commercial entity, I understand the parameters of the client, but inevitably you're trying to put yourself into it in a poetic way, or to create more conflict within things, designing something aesthetically opposed. It's about having more confidence in the process of designing, storyboarding and shooting it, then going through the post stage. The process does have a way of getting to its own end; the big thing is to start the process. *You've got to really believe in your own personal search.* That's the one thing that's going to keep you more inspired. It gets more complex as you journey into it. It doesn't get easier." The search is self-sustaining. "There are always more things to discover. You feel you can always do better. Each script that comes through the fax machine, you feel there are new items to be explored. It's a discovery process and each time you move forward into it, forgetting about conflicts and politics, it lets you see more of yourself; you get to understand who you are, how you communicate. Other people use writing or painting. This is my device. And because of the personal exploration, I have never felt I have to do it as a mercenary thing."

David Denneen. His *CEO Jordan* spot for Nike was organised like a military exercise. Sydney-based Denneen flew into Chicago, Michael Jordan's hometown, from a shoot in Argentina. "Michael could only give us two 6-hour days to shoot a 90-second commercial to launch his own clothing brand. We only had five days pre-production time to organise the shoot and the days Michael was available were right after a long weekend. I had a 64-frame shoot board, with Michael in every shot, and four days total shooting time. It meant shooting *sixteen* setups a day. We also had to shoot Michael against green screen to matt him into background plates. We wanted to give the film a classic 30s look, so fortunately the architecture and style of Chicago were perfect."

Denneen chose locations in close proximity to each other to maximise shooting time and minimise travelling. He built extra sets to cover as many shots as possible at the Opera House. Two additional sets were located at a nearby television studio, twenty feet of a corridor set actually protruding from the studio door. Two excellent Michael Jordan doubles were also hired.

"I wanted every shot to be an art piece. The first assistant director worked out exactly how much time we had on every shot. From memory, the longest was forty-five minutes. On the tech scout, we decided it would be necessary to have two lighting crews, one pre-lighting ahead of us. That meant I had to work out every shot, including which lens to use, so the DOP knew where to put his lights."

One of the highlights for Denneen was the shot of Michael Jordan making his exit through a side door of the Opera House. "Word had got around that he was there. When he and I exited the door, there were about five thousand cheering fans, police, barricades, the full thing. That moment was the closest I've come to feeling like I was shooting some big Hollywood feature film."

Denneen's reality check: "In this business you are only as good as your last job. The Nike spot with Michael Jordan had a great deal of prestige and publicity attached to it. I wanted it to be great and I believe with everyone's hard efforts, that's exactly how it turned out."

Denneen originally founded his company, Film Graphics, as a Sydney animation house in 1964. Denneen has long been recognised as a major international talent. A team of highly awarded directors and successes at D&AD and Cannes are opening doors for Film Graphics to expand further into foreign markets.

Rick Dublin. Dublin's first TV job won Gold at Cannes. Suddenly, the unassuming stills photographer found himself in demand far beyond downtown Minneapolis and clients like Fallon. "It was a sideline campaign for Hush Puppies. I'd shot a whole series of print ads with the dog for Bob Barrie at Fallon's. So when they said, hey, do you want to do some TV, I said, okay, yes, sure… So I scrambled a rag tag crew together. Being a stills guy, I pre-lit everything the night before with my assistant, Joe Lampi, because I didn't trust those film guys."

After Cannes, Dublin Productions became the hot name to call. "I didn't have a producer on staff and I'd panic every time somebody called because I didn't know how to bid the jobs. We just put some numbers on a piece of paper and sent them back." Today the bulk of his broadcast work is shot in Hollywood for clients from as far afield as New York and Atlanta. One downside of Cannes was the perception that Dublin only shoots with a static camera. "It was hard to break out of locked-down photography. You get pigeonholed. Even after ten years people still think that's what I do. I don't think there's one thing on my reel that represents that particular look." A short film by Dublin recently got into Sundance.

The director's role is to make the writer's and art director's vision come to life, says Dublin. "At the very least, their vision should be fulfilled and hopefully plussed. You don't just do your little piece and go home." Directors should understand what the creatives are trying to do and immerse themselves in the whole creative process.

Dublin advocates that creatives should keep open-minded. "Expose yourself to past work. And to life in general. The more you experience life, the more you see in life, the better you'll be because you'll have so much more to draw on. It's very important not to get yourself so sucked into advertising that you get stagnant."

Bob Giraldi. Some thirty years ago, Giraldi and Phil Suarez threw punches at each other in the midst of an advertising league basketball game, became best friends and started Giraldi Suarez Productions, America's longest running commercial film production partnership. Giraldi had been to New York's premier art school, the Pratt Institute, on a sports scholarship to play basketball and baseball. After four years of studying, art won. Just as well, Giraldi observes. "I'd probably have ended up spending two years in minor leagues or in a gas station, married a blonde who'd have got very heavy and then my life would have been over early."

It was the late 60s. The commercial art world had a revolution going on, Bill Bernbach was at the height of his powers, and Giraldi's classmate Ron Travisano called him over to Young & Rubicam. "The face of advertising became whimsical and conceptual and exciting. It was about selling products *and* about creativity. How to create interesting dilemmas and situations, great lines and witticisms. Yes, it was mostly New York. Yes, it was mostly Jewish, mostly New York writing, sardonic, sarcastic, the art of the great one-liner." It was Suarez who convinced Giraldi he had the talent to move from art direction to film direction, but not before he had absorbed the culture of idea-led advertising.

"Where is the idea?" asks Giraldi of much contemporary work. "The idea is not in telecine. The technique of stuff today has almost become the idea because kids have grown up on technique. I have enormous respect for technique. The idea and the execution have both been very good to me for thirty years. But at the end of the day I'd rather have an idea on my reel than something beautifully photographed because I'm not a photographer. I would rather have something beautifully written and poignantly acted than I would the latest technique from the video world. It's hard to reach somebody in an emotional way with technique. You can reach them in a visceral way, in a 'wow, that's beautiful' way."

Giraldi no longer works with shooting boards or production boards. "They're worthless. They're rubbish. Sometimes people call me and say, Bob, you're going to have to do a shooting board. And I say, sorry, I don't do shooting boards. Shooting boards are for clients. In movies, you can script a shooting board and follow the game plan pretty well. In a commercial it's almost impossible to follow a game plan unless the weather is exactly right, nobody makes a mistake, everybody is on time. Our medium is the kind of medium where you have to be very, very agile, on your feet. I like to build things organically. Some guys like Ridley Scott build things differently, they come from a different place. But I like it very organic. So why do a shooting board? It's going to change. Sometimes they say, do a shooting board before we see the location. How would I do a shooting board before I see the location? If I drew a wall over here, the wall might be over there. I may not want the wall anyway. The joy of this business for me, as an artist, is that I show up with my palette and my paints and my brushes — my crew and my actors — and I invent. I want to work with someone who wants to play from the beginning but play with a purpose." Giraldi is uncompromising. "Whenever Suarez and I were down, we'd look at each other and say, *if you do quality, you'll do quantity,* but it never works the other way round."

What's the *single* greatest contribution he can make to a commercial? "I don't know if there is just one, but I guess for Bob Giraldi he can make it honest, he can make it somewhat believable, somewhat palatable. One of the things I've always been ashamed of in our business is when people see a commercial and they roll their eyes, or they look away. I hope that people will say in the years from now that Bob's stuff had an integrity, had a specialness, had a quality that you could watch and like and believe. I try hard every day not to make my stuff too slick, too commercial. My work is not totally edgy, I don't go there. I don't try and make my stuff dark, I'm not a dark person. I am very eclectic. I don't go for one technique. I'm not one of those technique maven guys. I'm an art director by craft so I like to solve each problem as it comes along. I try to make my work whimsical and, above all, *likeable.* Commercially, I understand the business of selling through film."

Giraldi talks about the influences on creativity. "America is the most indulgent, excessive country in the world. And if you think about it, it's difficult for artists. Because creating is really not about excessiveness. Creating is really more about necessity, more about something in your mind that you have to scratch and claw for. Lionel Richie once said to me, Bob, it's hard to write love songs in the backseat of a limo…"

Ray Lawrence. "The problem with advertising and making commercials in general is that things get complicated when there's no need." Lawrence does not do storyboards. He attends pre-production meetings, but believes they are of no use to the shoot. "The pre-pro should encourage trust. I'm not being paid to destroy the commercial."

Lawrence was ranked fifth most-awarded director in the world by the 1999 *Gunn Report*. His minimalist style is legendary. "It's not that intense. The difficulty of it is accepting the simplicity of it," he quips. He is dedicated to simplicity. "If I get a script that's very complicated, I simplify it. How simple can I make this, right down to the basics? What's it about? What are the important scenes? It's simplifying it, and then *keeping it simple all the time*…" Does he shoot only the bare minimum of takes? "I just stop when I've got it. If it's a wide shot of a room in two seconds, what do I need twelve takes for? It's experience. And trusting what you do. *You have to trust what you do.* There are lots of gifts along the way on a shoot. Ninety percent are totally unexpected. There's not a lot of stress on our shoots."

Lawrence recalls an episode from a shoot in America. "I'm not at all interested in cars. They're easy things to photograph. There is a set of rules; if you stick to them, the car will always look beautiful. You learn those rules a long time ago. After that, cars are really boring and predictable. I had a car ad to do in the States, mostly dialogue, so I did all the dialogue and said to the DOP, you can go and photograph the car because I'm just going to be bored. The agency heard me. And I was kidding around, but I wasn't that interested, and I knew the DOP was going to do a great job and I trusted him. They got really upset that I was being flippant and not worrying about the car. They thought I didn't care."

How can young directors develop a voice? "When I was starting out, I was really influenced by directors like Sidney Lumet and Roman Polanski. You also want to try everything. And slowly, because it wears you down, you have to decide on some specifics. *You have to find out who you are and specialise.*" He references the top echelon of American commercial directors. "They work three hundred days a year. To do that, no matter who you are, you have to have a formula. You're really repeating yourself every day of the year. As much as I have a particular style, it's more abstract than visual."

How Important Is The Audio?

Someone once said a television commercial should work with the sound turned off. The implication was clear: television is a purely visual medium and it would be unwise to rely on the audio track to contribute much to the presentation. In reality though, isn't it like trying to play tennis with one hand?

"That's one of those stupid things that gets said," counters Hegarty, "and people pick it up and say, wow, that's right, yes, of course, you should be able to turn the sound down and it should still work. It's applying a formula to something. Music is incredibly powerful, as we discovered. I used to say that 70% of a Levi's commercial was music, not that we started there, but we realised that music could enhance the power of a piece of visual communication. Music appeals on an absolutely emotional level. It enhances the emotional value of the film that you've shot. Therefore, I can make my film *more powerful* with the right piece of music."

"That was said back in the days when advertising was a logical profession," concurs Steve Henry. "Even back then, actually, it was an emotional profession. Advertising is about emotion, it's about gut instinct, it's about laughter, tears, it's the same thing the movies are all about."

"I'm very suspicious of things like that," says Adrian Holmes. "It's a bit like saying a print ad should still work if you cover the headline."

"It's absolute drivel." French says movies rely on sound and music. "It's like saying you shouldn't use reverse type. Union Bank of Switzerland without the sound? It's nonsense! *Perfect Day* without

Familiar children's icons cover their eyes.

They are the mute witnesses of child abuse unfolding around them.

Nothing is shown.

Everything is conveyed through the sounds of outrage.

End graphic: *NSPCC. Cruelty to children must stop. Full Stop.*

How a single-minded visual idea and appropriately crafted sound communicate a harrowing appeal against child abuse. While the visuals alone communicate on one level, Raja Sehgal's sound design intensifies the emotional impact. Written by Kes Gray and art directed by Dennis Willison, Saatchi & Saatchi London.

the sound? I'm sorry…" When French uses music, he uses it "to death, and with absolute cynicism. The mood in which you want somebody to listen to your words can be completely changed with music. In the cortex of somebody's brain, when they hear Elgar or Greig, it says this is important and they listen to it in a completely different way." French talks about the contradiction between the sound and the pictures. "*Sometimes the wrong piece of music is the right piece of music*. There was a scene in Carl Foreman's film, *The Victors*, where they dragged a deserter out into the snow to be shot. The silence is quieter than you can think. No silence is quite like snow. You just have the noise of the feet crunching in the snow as they tie the poor kid to a pole and out come the guys with the guns. The moment the guns go off, you're expecting something tragic and on comes Frank Sinatra singing *Have yourself a merry little Christmas*, and that just blows you away. It makes the picture far more horrific than you ever thought it could be. It's one of the arts of film. There was a movie a long time ago called *The Green Machine*, about American football. It was the first time I'd ever seen huge footballers thumping into each other to the sounds of Mozart."

ACCORDING to the cynics, music "bullies" the audience. It's the equivalent of canned laughter in a sitcom.

"Music can be an incredibly important branding device, a mnemonic," Whybin says. "As long as you're not using it in a stupid way — grand scale sound design just for the sake of having it."

"There is a point where you *should* be able to turn off the sound and still be able to experience something," suggests Darling. "Especially on a narrative, you should be able to turn off the sound and still be entertained and understand the thread of it and be emotionally drawn to it. What the music will do, on a lot of levels, is *reconfirm* things. Music can put you in a state of mind. Music can position and enhance things quite incredibly. You can play with opposites in music or with things that create suspense or pre-empt." He describes music as a last frontier. "A lot is underexplored. There are so many other levels. You may start off with a certain idea of what the music will be, but then you get to the edit room and the piece changes and you've got to let it become itself — *you've got to listen to what the film is telling you.* Maybe there should be conflict between the sound and the picture. Maybe it should be a sound you haven't heard before, or a sound you feel comfortable with that lets you experience the images from a more comfortable point of view." Darling adds a caution. "There's only so much of a certain tone you can do. Like the number of times someone will try to force an Enigma style of track on you…"

Marco agrees you should be able to communicate with the visuals alone. "I saw an interview with Steven Spielberg, addressing young directors. He said, watch your favourite movie without the sound on; it should still work. I had a film teacher at Art Center. He made us watch a film without the sound, and go back and write down what the story was."

Some commercials can work without sound, says Marcello Serpa. Others need a track to make sense. "I have clients who complain to me, if I turn off the sound, can I understand the commercial? But some commercials need the sound. Other clients say, I want people to understand the commercial without seeing it; they want people to relate the commercial to the client because they remember the sound. It's not a rule."

"Everyone loves music," confirms Hunt. "It can be a very important part of a commercial. Jingles gave music a bad name in Australian television, and I hated them, too, because I never thought that they actually got the words across very well. But there's nothing wrong with music. I've seen some research somewhere that says the most popular commercials are, in order of appeal, humour, then second, music. And I guess a good humorous commercial that had great music would be the best of all worlds. If you think of the wonderful Hamlet commercials, they were very funny with great music. There have been lots of great commercials with music, and lots of great ones without it. It depends." As Hunt says, "I'd like to do more with music in commercials, but not *in lieu* of an idea…"

"Music is a very small part of the equation for me." Dean believes it only really works in reaffirming a cliché. "If you've got somebody running in slow motion, something familiar like *Chariots of Fire* always kicks in. It's a short cut to an emotion. It should serve the idea like lighting does, like a set design does. Hamlet was the best use ever of music in advertising. It started at the moment of poignancy and reprised every Hamlet commercial they'd ever seen. And that idea has been copied endlessly."

"Music is secondary." Wee says it should complement the idea. "If I can just use the visuals to communicate, it will be far more powerful than relying on a piece of music or a famous song."

"I like music to instruct the audience that they're watching the film the right way." Lawrence calls music an affirmation of what is happening.

Michael Prieve and Stacy Wall regard music in terms of "choices". Wall says: "Music can be used offensively and in a pedestrian manner. You want to sell orange juice so you buy a song that has the word 'orange' in it…" Prieve adds: "I'm insulted when I see the orange juice commercial and they colour-correct it so it's all orange. That's just as offensive…"

"Music doesn't rescue a commercial." Delaney says it plays a fundamental part in how you feel about something. The no-go areas, however, include mundane library tracks. "Music can turn a spot from being one thing to being something entirely different. But the way we do it is very haphazard." Delaney's agency has even bought a track that will be released at about the same time as the commercial. "We had a Pepe Jeans spot; we tried every-which-way to get it right, all kinds of things. We even turned the music off at one point, but ultimately you use a composer you trust, you give them a good brief, and you hope they'll come out with something appropriate. Sometimes you have to go again. Other times you can hit it once."

Music can not only change the character and mood of a spot, Bildsten says, the music itself can be the most memorable thing about a commercial.

"Music is a paintbrush," says Schuldman. "You can paint different emotions with it. You can change tonality without changing an idea. People are expecting to hear something different as well as see something different. Whether we like it or not, the way our industry is going we are making little movies."

"You have no control over how the soundtrack affects you, it just does," argues Todaro, "the same way a great movie score can choke you up."

Bijur discusses the correlation between doing great radio and crafting great television soundtracks. "That sensibility fine-tunes you to lots of little craft-related things that help you with television. It's all about tight performances, it's all about timing, it's all about working with a much more limited variety of sensory input than television. Those same things are very useful. I've always been particularly pro-radio. I used to love going off to the studio and doing my own thing. It's one of the only opportunities in this business where you can just do something yourself, especially for a junior person. Radio teaches you to really think visually as a writer."

SOUND, especially the sounds of machines, provided comic focus for the richly detailed visual anarchy of Jacques Tati. His films subverted the rules of film comedy. The sounds of gadgets, traffic, production lines, even garden fountains, assaulted the humanity of his *alter ego*, Monsieur Hulot.

"Sometimes, hearing something and not seeing it can make your imagination fill in the pictures which can be three times more powerful than what you are actually seeing," says David Droga.

It would be hard to imagine some of the great classic movies without music. For example, would *Casablanca* have endured so well without its music?

"Paul Arden once said that music is 50% of everything," confirms Les Gock, chairman and creative director of Song Zu, the biggest music recording organisation for movies, television and radio in Asia and Australia. "In fact, some film academics have said that the soundtrack represents as much as 70% of a film's narrative meaning and perhaps 100% of its emotion."

Governments and churches throughout history have known about the political power of music, attests Gock. "Even Aristotle and Plato said that music had the power to change a society. Confucius believed that music could either make people live in harmony or it could divide the country." Harness some of this power, Gock says, and fewer words will need to be spoken in the track. "Hire the movie *Jaws* and have a look at the opening scene where we first encounter the shark. What are we seeing? A girl having a pleasant midnight swim. She's laughing, teasing, playing around in the water. What are we not seeing? The shark! *But what are we hearing...?* A two-note motif that gets faster and faster, and more and more intense, as the camera approaches the girl. What do we feel? Unbridled fear!" The young Spielberg was not reinventing the wheel when he used this technique, contends Gock. "He was just being *economical in his narrative delivery*. He could say more with two notes than he could with a voice-over or any amount of animatronics. Perhaps more commercials could use music in this way."

Significantly, the most Oscars so far won by any individual in film history were awarded to Alfred Newman, the General Music Director of Twentieth Century Fox. A gifted composer, conductor and administrator, and the man who wrote the famous Fox fanfare, Newman received forty-six nominations resulting in nine Oscars.

How Should You Choose The Music?

Music is probably the most subjective call in television. Young teams bring in their favourite CDs. "I hear a lot of music in advertising that seems nothing more than somebody's current passion," Perry observes. "It has nothing to do with the ad. Your new CD and your new ad somehow find each other."

Music has always polarised opinions. Two of the world's greatest musical treasures, Tchaikovsky's Violin Concerto in D Major and his Piano Concerto No. 1 were originally pronounced unplayable, trivial and vulgar. Never trust the critics.

"The best way to brief music is to talk less about what you want to hear, and more about how you want the viewer to feel," says Gock. "Love, hate, sad, happy ... these are the words that should be used in a music brief."

A specific musical style can flag down your audience. However, the use of an unusual style against a particular demographic can be equally relevant, urges Gock. "Use bagpipes instead of guitars for a skateboard commercial; a little extreme, perhaps, but you get the idea..." Gock was once assigned a Pepsi spot where the main character spoke ridiculously fast. "There didn't seem to be any musical style that was hip enough and yet didn't fight with the voice track. Finally, we came up with the idea of *fighting fire with fire.*

We decided to create a track that was as fast as the dialogue track. So we thought of the fastest song that we knew, which was *Flight of the Bumble Bee*. Then we got a grungy band to come in and trash it. The spot worked incredibly well, not only because it sounded hip, but we could even understand some of the lyrics."

When Nike licensed the Beatles song *Why Don't We Do It In The Road*, the intention was to run the original track. "The idea was simple," Gock explains. "Show real weekend warriors going through their strides. People playing basketball in back lanes, joggers sweating through inner city back streets, people shadow boxing in a park. The song was perfect, except there was a proviso in the licence. The licensee could not use the Beatles version; nor could he re-record the song to sound like the Beatles. To say that the client was a little uncomfortable about paying what was the equivalent to the GDP of a small country in order *not* to sound like the Beatles is an understatement." Gock was called in. "The solution is always to put the idea on a pedestal, to go back to the original thought. Which was, real people doing it in the street. So I decided to re-record the song, literally, out in the road. We gathered a couple of people around the studio, went out the back to the car park with a DAT recorder, and recorded the song. The result was a soundtrack that matched the idea in a way that the original version could not have done."

ARE there any rules for selecting music?

"There is no formula," says Hegarty. "We coined a phrase, *film vibration*. A film has vibrations in it, and what you've got to do is find those vibrations and find the piece of music that works with them. It's not that you've made a film on mermaids, so let's look up music on mermaids. You've got to find the film vibration, and it's not logical at all. It can be quite *illogical*. Sometimes you can see a piece of logic, like *Mad About the Boy* for Levi's *Swimmer*, and you can say, yes, I can see why that's working. But I could equally show you commercials where there isn't logic. We did a Levi's commercial, *Refrigerator*, where a guy leaves his jeans in a refrigerator and the original music for that was James Brown's *It's A Man's World*. When you think about it, it's quite logical. We shot it, put the music on it, and it was the most depressing 60 seconds of my life. It just didn't work. The bloke's acting was appalling. It was just terrible. It was awful. Nothing worked in it. I was really depressed and I thought, this is it, we're going to have to scrap this commercial and start again. And then we changed the music. And we found Muddy Waters' *Mannish Boy*, off his *Electric Mud* album. We didn't change the cut at all, we just literally laid the music over it, and all of a sudden, everything was transformed. The bloke's acting, the music, it all made sense. So that's the power of music."

"You have to be careful because a lot of music can overpower the idea, especially famous songs." Patti uses songs that work with his storylines; the further you get into the spot, the better the song gets. "I never think about music as the main concern. Someone once said, *people don't know what they like, but they like what they know.* That's why familiar songs that bring up images from their youth are good to use; they give people an overall feeling that they can relate to."

"You have to be aware of your own subjectivity." The favourite track that you may personally want to hear in your ad could sometimes take you to the wrong place, cautions Fishlock. "The post-production process is often so compressed that we don't give ourselves the time and mental space to get it *wrong*. There are fabulous examples of people who have had the same piece of film and put two different music tracks up against it and the experience was at opposite ends of the scale. You've got to live with it for a couple of days, and then go off in a completely different direction. Is it a bit of polka, is it a bit of country and western, is it a bit of opera?"

"You should never start with the music and then find an idea," warns Gray. Sometimes, he says, the music choice is obvious. "*Dambusters* had to use the old movie theme. *Squirrel* had to use *Mission Impossible*." At other times, he suggests being ironic. "We once shot a film secretly in the toilets of a club in Essex. It was all about clubbers. We put cameras behind the vanity mirrors. The thought was, *If you want him and he wants you, you both want a condom.* Instead of putting a club track on it, we put Perry Como singing *Hot-diggity-dog-ziggity-boom-what-you-do-to-me.* My dad used to like Perry Como, so I grew up with Perry Como music. I knew the track." Everything is out there, Gray says. He recommends never closing your mind. "Certain things that you do will open little boxes in your mind. I wouldn't profess to be in the slightest bit trendy, but I do try to have an awareness of music that I don't like. I'll buy CDs in areas that frighten me, because I know that one of those tracks will be right for something I work on and I always want to be in a position where I am at least aware of other forms of music." Gray questions the criteria for the Best Use of Music category in advertising award shows. "I don't believe that putting a track on a film is actually 'use of music'. To me, a great use of music is an ad like Maxell."

McGrath also advocates trying something unexpected. "Instead of putting a contemporary track on a commercial, put on an Irving Berlin track from the 20s or 30s and see how the character of the commercial changes. That's one way of making it terribly distinctive. Music can be as important as the filmic technique. It's something we think about very early on."

"Contrast is what it's all about," stresses Redman, citing *Miami Vice* where a beautiful romantic ballad will play during a murder scene. Redman prefers to craft his own music. "An original score is yours."

"Integrity," says Paul Malmström who plays bass and guitar. The music must be true to the idea. "Sometimes you see commercials where you can really feel that they were going towards young people so they used some hard core grunge music. The young guys will be just turned off by it because they can see that you're pandering to them. You should show your integrity; this is what *we* feel is cool for this spot, like it or not. And that's how you get liked."

It depends on how complicated you want to be, McBride advises. "How many *other* messages do you want to bury within the message? They should all still signal where you're going." Referencing his own work: "When we were working on *Aaron Burr*, we brought on these ticking sounds. And the sound of steam hissing. It was all in his head; it wasn't coming from anywhere. The music we used, *Vienna Woods Dance in D*, which was a made-up music title; the public radio kind of announcer; they were all a big part of it, they all played into it. Sometimes it can be overdone. But done with restraint, you can do so much with the sound and music," says McBride. "I've probably made B commercials that became A commercials because of some of the sound behind them."

Like Arden, Fink believes music is 50% of the commercial. If you can get great music you are "halfway around the dog track", he says. "You can argue about an idea with some kind of logic. You can argue about the cut with some kind of logic — it doesn't tell the story, or I didn't understand it, you must recut it. The thing about music is, I can really like a piece of music and you can hate that piece of music, it's totally emotional, it's totally subjective. And I don't know how you get round that, apart from just having to fight." Another problem is the pressure placed on creatives to play the client something before they're ready, and often before the commercial is even shot. *"Don't ever play your client any piece of music until you've tried it with the edit.* Everybody makes this mistake. The commercial hasn't been made, and you may shoot it differently to how you think you're going to do it. You may *not* even want music when it's finished. But some music is needed 'just for research', so you put something on it 'just for now'. And of course what happens is that everyone gets so used to listening to this piece of music for the next three months that when you find a better piece of music everyone still loves that first piece of music. They've got it in their heads and you cannot shake them." Fink prefers to use music that already exists. "The chance that someone is going to write something great is very minimal. Even the Beatles didn't write great stuff every time. Nor does anybody. That's why they have those *'Best of'* albums. Occasionally someone will write something great, or they'll write 'in the style of', but it's never really as good."

Mike Cozens also resists making the final music choice until he's seen the final cut. "We're always pushed to come up with music. I can come up with something that may be suitable, but I always reserve the decision till afterwards. Sometimes the commercial is researched with a particular piece of music and it doesn't work as well in the final cut. There was a Levi's commercials we did a while back at BBH where we towed the truck with a pair of Levi's. It had a track called *The Joker*, and it worked okay. Then I tried a different track, *Be My Baby*, and it worked so much better." Fortunately for Cozens, the marketing manager agreed. "Usually, a client is too scared of changing music that has already been researched."

SHOULD you cut the vision first or should the music be the driver?

Darling believes the vision should take precedence. "Cut the image first to really get the structure of things. It's a process of not trying to confuse yourself. It's very easy to sit on a bit of music and feel that it's doing everything, giving you all the emotional answers. You're better off forgetting it. When you really understand and feel more comfortable with the film, *then* throw a bit of music on and say, well, it does that and that, and then get rid of the music again for a while. Inevitably the last quarter of the edit is about adjusting to the music." Darling advocates a collaboration between the editor and composer. "If you're doing a sound design for the piece, it's better if it's a two-way street, and not just for a beat thing."

"Music can dictate the cut and sometimes you get the wrong cut," warns Bunton. "Sometimes you'll cut to a piece of music that you're not going to use, but it always ends up with everyone falling in love with it." Bunton's advice is cut first and get the communication right. "You should be able to turn off the sound and still get something out of the cut. But you will eventually need the sound to get people into the idea quickly." With a lot of dialogue commercials, Bunton considers that music doesn't help at all. "If there's no dialogue, then music is fairly important to the idea."

Gibbs reverses the usual procedure and *cuts the music to the picture*. "I get the music house involved very early, sending them storyboards and talking to them about the script. Then, instead of the music guy rigidly post-scoring to the edit, he writes 4- to 5-minute pieces of music. He sends those to us at the edit house. We can take that music and cut it up any way we want."

Cummins adopts a very pragmatic approach. "A lot of my work will be either all music with no words, or all words and no music." He argues that music and words will sometimes fight each other; rather than the music becoming the junior partner, with the audio levels ridden so low it can't be heard, he advocates leaving it out of the equation totally.

"It'll Be Right On The Night": Adventures In Post-production

If the computer enslaves art directors in print creativity, how much more seductive is the technology of post-production?

McGrath says: "Post-production is a problem when you can see the post-production. If you watch a commercial and you're conscious of all the visual effects, it's probably a commercial that's lacking in a solid idea. Visual effects are not an idea. They should be a way of communicating the idea. There should be a seamlessness about them."

McBride believes in putting forward the foundation of the story first. "I'll look at a gross edit where we're just taking scenes that tell the story. And it will run as long as we need it to, up to two minutes if it has to, so we can understand what we've got. Then it's combing from there. What are ways we can combine action?" Hopefully, says McBride, a lot of the story decisions will have been made prior to production. He recalls one such case: working on his Isuzu script with director Michael Bay at Goodby, Silverstein. "We had a crow come in and grab a turtle and fly away. Then it drops the turtle and hits a rock. The rock falls down the mountain and crashes into the Isuzu. And that was about, *Now, dual airbags*."

Unfortunately post-production technology encourages people to concentrate on techniques rather than ideas, Hunt reminds us.

As Holmes puts it: "The only computer you should work with is the one that resides between your ears. John Hegarty once said, the only thing a creative person should switch on in the morning is the person sitting opposite him." Holmes recounts a story from America. "There was a creative director who went around putting stickers on all the computers that said, *Warning, this machine does not have ideas*."

"Those things are just tools to me. I don't design things for certain techniques." Grace always has an end goal in mind. He lets the experts tell him what is the best way of getting there. "I've always made it a point to be ignorant about these things. I have studied very hard to be ignorant. Obviously I know what Flame and Harry and the latest 'it' are. But just as I knew nothing about film or lenses, all I ever want to know is: *what am I trying to achieve? Can it be done?*

I don't care *how* they do it, or *what* kind of machine they do it on; I always ask the question, *can* we do this? And if you do an idea that pushes the envelope, you've got to be absolutely sure that you can make it come out superbly."

"I know of commercials where people spend six to eight weeks in post." What they are doing is crafting the beauty, which Redman believes is dangerous. "You can spend a week on a shot that is only going to exist for two seconds in a 30-second commercial. You're sitting in a darkened room, most of the time falling asleep, while someone tinkers around on a machine and you can forget why you're having that shot in the ad, and is all that time you're spending on it really worth it?" On the shoot itself, Redman says you know that if something doesn't work you can shoot a background plate or strip in a sky. "You're always thinking that way only because you're thinking of what will make it a better product at the end. But that should be tempered by a little bit of sobriety as to what the *idea* is and how you're going to make that the best possible idea."

"The great thing about being Australian," says Brown, "is that everyone expects you to be blunt. You don't have to waste any time being nice to people. Everyone involved in the process should have a very clear understanding of your vision." Everyone will bring something new to the party, he warns; everyone will have their own idea of what the special effects should be. "So you have to be very forceful. You don't have time these days to get people in a nice frame of mind and slowly work them around to your point of view."

Cummins loathes being told, "we'll fix it in post." He finds sitting in post-production suites intensely boring. "I haven't seen any great leaps of communication strength through all the development of this technology." He observes that vast amounts of time and money are invested in shot-by-shot enhancement, while illegible supers are added with old technology and no design skills in evidence whatsoever. In fact, he has invented his own technology that transmits a signal through normal television speakers. It allows brand building to coexist with direct response. "If the viewer wants to respond to a commercial, all they have to do is pick up their telephone receiver. They don't even have to dial." The idea, which is patented worldwide, has been launched in Australia.

"Some commercials do need incredible executional values," Blackley concedes, "but the kind of people we have here are the kind of people who write things like the *Retired Milkman* commercial. They tell a story in a fairly simple way. They don't have to go into the Flame for twenty hours." The Just Jeans retail chain is the agency's busiest television production client with over fifty commercials a year to make. "They're only on air for a week. So it's a good discipline for our young creative teams. They learn they have to have a very strong idea. They have to pull it off themselves in production without a director, and they have to do all the post-production themselves without the luxury of going into Flame. They are as exposed as if they had done a radio spot or a print ad because they don't have all the helpers around them."

"Anything you can imagine you can do," cautions Bildsten. "Therefore it is incumbent on people to try to think of things you *couldn't* do on a computer, that have to be *real*, even if ultimately you execute them that way. The first thing every good director talks about is doing it in the camera, while everyone is acutely aware of doing things in the computer. It's too easy."

"Great classical directors used to do it all in the camera." Whybin debates the over-obsession with post-production; even grading, he believes, can become counter-productive. "Sometimes you should just let the neg ride. Often someone goes away and grades all day, and I get a sanitised version of what was a luscious neg."

Famed French director Jean Renoir claimed that technical developments had not improved film. "The camera should capture exactly the colours of the world in front of it. You mustn't make colours for the sake of making beautiful pictures." As for special effects, "as I grew older, I became more fascinated in discovering reality."

Sree agrees. "Our work should look honest. If it looks retouched, if it looks like it's been messed with, people's guard goes up again. Sometimes it's better if your work looks less polished. It just feels more real. You can cut slightly off the beat so it feels a little bit more jarring and naïve and honest."

"If you get into Tech Land, not many normal people are interested in that," argues Malmström. "They don't get touched by it as much as they do a good story told well *in the camera*."

Hitchcock was perhaps the greatest *technical* director the world has ever seen. Everything happened in the camera. He knew the capabilities of every lens. According to film legend, he could make complex calculations in his head. He once instructed a propman about a wineglass that would contain poison: "Make me up a glass six and a half inches high and four inches wide and shoot it with a fifty lens, the glass being three feet from the camera and the actors five feet beyond that."

DIRECTORS today have different perspectives on post-pro.

Weak ideas can rely on slick visuals to dress them up with the aid of Henry and Flame, agrees Denneen. "But this is a new and exciting era in film making. Directors are allowed more visual tools, with more control, to create looks at ever-decreasing prices." The weak idea, Denneen believes, has to be traded off against the creation of very good visual directors and a more creative art form. "Weak ideas do serve a purpose on our side of the advertising fence. They push our standards of film making higher. Also, with smaller budgets, directors now have to shoot faster, not allowing the DOP the time to refine the lighting or adding grads and filters to enhance the shot. All this can be done in post with a computer."

Should the director be involved in the edit? In America, he isn't. In fact, the term "director's cut" is mostly a disparagement. Carol Reed, speaking of movies, admitted he was once locked out of editing sessions. "A director *must* work with his editor," he protested.

"We probably cut 30% of the work that we do." Hungry Man has its own editing suite. Orent calls editing the most frustrating part of the process; directors are totally excluded. "In America, the director is kept shooting. We like to stay involved, but you don't want to always be doing director's cuts. *Our first priority is to get the agency cut to be the greatest cut possible.*" Orent describes himself as a purist. "Anytime you can do something in the camera it's that much better. Or shoot it in camera and enhance it. Viewers are so sophisticated now."

"Too many things are added, too many fingers are in the pie," observes Bunton. "Effects-driven stuff has taken the ideas out of the business. However, that's not to say that ideas would necessarily work against the market of today. Multilayering and pop music videos have changed the way people look at things, although kids still love movies like *Notting Hill* and there are no special effects in there…" Bunton condemns the over-reliance on post-pro. "But then I don't do those kinds of commercials so I'm allowed to say that. Even on story commercials, people still feel a need to produce them more than they need them to be the truth."

"I've never been a big technique fan, even in my still work," admits Dublin. "I usually try to stay away from it. I don't think straight motion picture photography will ever go away. I don't think we're ever going to remove ourselves from reality that much that we'll have to surround everything with technique."

"All the techniques are there to be used," argues Darling. "You can throw technique at it to supply content, or take the place of content. But you've got to understand what you're doing, what tangential things you're doing. With technology now, things do get more polished. There are stereotypical devices in the way things are airbrushed. And that's something you start to fight against so it's not a perfectly commercially packaged visual. A lot of my work is poetic, beauty-based, emotional; more and more I'm trying to bring a *rawness* back into it, to try and get another kind of tangent on it." Darling believes that when you enter the edit room, you should leave your preconceptions outside. "Conceptualisation and pre-production are 90% of the creative process and the anxiety. When you get to the shoot, a lot of times it's a means to an end. You're trying to get as much done as you possibly can; recently I did 150 set-ups in three days. Then you'll get to the edit room and you say to yourself, now I'm going to go into a different process; *now it's going to have its own life*."

D.I.Y.

Directing-it-yourself is *not* an option for many creatives. Some of the world's most accomplished creative men have actually stepped behind the camera, but only briefly.

"I tried it; I didn't really like it," admits Grace. "For me, the real joy of the business is still thinking of the ideas, and making sure nobody screws them up after you've thought of them. There was a time at Doyle Dane Bernbach when being an art director was almost like being in prep school for being a director. Everybody wanted to direct. I didn't. A lot of people just become art directors as a stepping-stone for becoming a director, and they also begin to do ideas that look good on a director's reel but not necessarily good on an art director's reel."

Delaney recalls his D.I.Y. experiences. "I directed a Citizen watch spot with Steve Dunn. It was more Steve's project than mine, and I enjoyed it a lot. I don't think it's difficult to direct commercials because you have a lot of help. But I think it's like everything in life. You can always do a couple relatively well, but whether you continue and do them well, and then good, and then excellent, and then top end, is more a matter of whether you have an attitude about it; whether you believe you can bring something new to it. There's no point in just saying, okay, I can point a camera and do the same as sixty other people. There are a lot of directors who don't work a lot because they're *not different...*"

Directing your own work with the safety net of an agency job is one thing. Hanging out your shingle as a full-time film director is another matter entirely. Some famous creatives have taken the ultimate plunge, adopting what David Perry calls "the bad boy philosophy".

Terry Bunton. Bunton started off as an art director in Sydney, went to London and became a copywriter at DDB in 1965. After nine years working with creatives like David Abbott, he returned to Australia. Creative directorships at Young & Rubicam, Grey Advertising and The Campaign Palace led to the start of his own agency, which he later sold. In 1985, he astounded the industry by leaving Saatchi & Saatchi Sydney, where he was a partner. Closing the door on his award-winning advertising career, he announced he was going to direct. "I'd been wanting to do that for fifteen years." Easier said than done. No jobs came in for the writer-turned-director with an empty reel. "I didn't direct any spots while I was still writing at Saatchi's, which was really dumb I suppose, but I personally felt it was unethical." Eventually two agencies took leaps of faith and Bunton hasn't looked back since.

An ordinary saucepan is placed inside a Crown Corning Vision saucepan.

MVO: *A new Vision saucepan has many advantages over an ordinary saucepan.*

The ordinary saucepan is now being cooked inside the Vision saucepan. Super: *Laboratory test at 850° C.*

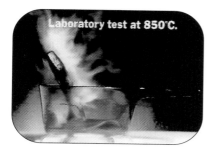

MVO: *It will never stain and is easy to clean. Its handle can't work loose...*

Flames are now leaping from the ordinary saucepan.

MVO: *...and as you can see it's not a bit perturbed on a heat that can turn an aluminium saucepan into sauce. Vision. Designed in France from a remarkable new material with a ten-year warranty from Crown Corning. The future in saucepans is absolutely clear...*

The charred, twisted ordinary saucepan is tipped out.

Vision Melting Saucepan *was named Australia's Best of 25 Years. Written by Phil Gough and art directed by Vic Waterhouse at Saatchi & Saatchi Sydney over twenty years ago, it is a classic tabletop commercial — simple, convincing and compelling in a category often overlooked for dramatic work.*

"I hate to say it, it goes against the grain, but execution can replace ideas," he concedes. "Ideas should come out of the product. Now everything is me-too, and it's harder to find an emotional selling proposition than a unique selling proposition." When he was writing commercials, he worked on storylines rather than taglines. "Lines don't work by themselves. You have an idea that might end up as a tagline, but you must first express it as television idea. I wouldn't just think of it as a series of pictures."

Bunton never directed his own commercials while he worked for agencies. "I think you compromise yourself. You might make the commercials more complicated so you'd look better as a director." There are very few breakthroughs; nobody goes for simple ideas. "It's all execution-based. Everyone sees *Shots* reels. Things tend to mirror each other." He loathes the trend whereby pretentious reverse titles separate a series of black-and-white images. "I can't see why they do it. If you want to do a print ad, why not do a print ad?" He also loves black-and-white cinematography, but doesn't have a black-and-white commercial on his reel. "If you're aware of what's happening in the product category and if you're going to use a technique, it should be one that stands out from the others."

Bunton quite happily considers himself typecast as a director. "Dialogue stuff and very simple commercials where nothing gets in the way of the idea. Anyone would love to shoot a Vision Saucepan commercial." His greatest satisfaction, however, was shooting the *Aircraft Carrier* commercial for Dunlop Tyres. "We had to do it all in the camera. It was done before the special effects era. We had to build an aircraft carrier to scale and shoot it off Coogee Beach in Sydney. Then I had to weld together two separate shoots. Today you'd just shoot four different scenes and put them together by computer. You wouldn't get the same satisfaction..." Bunton admits he is sustained by a love of ideas and production of any sort. "I loved cutting up type in print ads. There are certain frustrations in the business, but there's still the satisfaction at the end of each job."

For aspiring creatives who want to do great television, he has only one word of advice: "*Bloody-mindedness.* Be bloody-minded. Get solid, simple ideas and never let *anybody* get in the way of them."

Rowan Dean. "The best commercials are based on ideas," says

Dean, opposing style for style's sake. He maintains style and technique must serve the idea. The moment they submerge or subvert it, the commercial will be forgotten. "No one remembers those commercials. Commercials that have strong ideas are remembered years later. People can't remember what a 'look' was, or what the lighting was, but they can remember ideas. So long as all your tools are serving the idea, you can't go wrong." Because the best writers and art directors are steeped in the notion of the idea, Dean believes the best directors come from advertising agency backgrounds.

"For me it's always comedy, even if it's not overtly funny, just a smile and the enjoyment of the moment. I can't help going into comedy. Humour is universal. Something like *Photo Booth* just works anywhere, any time." Dean is concerned with the current obsession with techniques. "I've been in meetings with teams and we've discussed the script and they'll say, now what about the look? And I'll say, what do you mean, the look? And they'll say, what about the look, shouldn't we give it a special look? There was that thing we saw on air last night that had this funny out-of-focus thing, and they stretch the image…" Dean argues that the idea has to have integrity. "Why slap some gimmick on it? We shot *Photo Booth* with the lighting that looked right for a photo booth, in a set that looked right for a photo booth. We didn't then add some other element. And that's for me the most detrimental thing about what has happened with the whole *Shots* ethos that's grown up. It's the constant craving for a new look, a new visual gimmick." Once, he says, the idea was at the core of advertising. "I think advertising went hugely off the rails when the central position of the concept came under attack in two ways. From people who couldn't have an idea and therefore substituted a technique. And from planning, in the mid- to late 80s. Unless we return to the idea as the central proposition, advertising will flounder."

Graham Fink. "It was very exciting, but it was very scary. I suddenly went from earning bucketfuls of money in an agency to absolute zero salary." Fink was on the verge of starting a radical new advertising agency when renowned British director Paul Weiland offered Fink the chance to direct for his company. "Most of the

For his Pretty Polly Space Hopper *commercial, director Graham Fink created a monochromatic set with grey padded walls and black-and-white targets on the floor. The girls bounced on space hoppers proving that Pretty Polly tights stayed up all day. "I wanted it to look like a scientific experiment," Fink says. Agency: TBWA London.*

Director Graham Fink of Paul Weiland Films used a small rig that "bounced" up and down with the girls. Fink achieved the effect of a moving background which he says gave it "a weird kind of look".

STILLS PHOTOGRAPHY BY PAUL MYATT, LONDON.

directors at Weiland's are ex-advertising writers and art directors, so it's very idea-strong, like a mini-agency. So I bit the bullet and jumped at it." Fink calls it a career change with a new learning curve. "I'm arguing about different things now. I'm not in an agency arguing about the size of the logo."

Fink bins 90% of the scripts he receives. "I look for the work that allows me to experiment with something. If the script is even half-decent, I'll talk to the creative team. Either they'll think it's fantastic you're coming in and helping to make their script better, or else they'll get very protective. I might ask them what they think it should look like, and they'll say, don't know really, it's up to you, you're the director. They haven't thought it through. Half the creative people don't time out their scripts; I get so many scripts that are sixty seconds long and they say they're thirty seconds at the top of the page. If a team isn't open to anything, if you can't change anything, then I'll let the job go." In the event the team becomes three people, Fink sees his contribution as bringing a particular look to the idea. "It could be a photographic look, or the way it's edited, or something interesting with the sound to give it a completely new, original feel when you're watching it."

Fink revisits his Pretty Polly *Space Hopper* commercial for Trevor Beattie at TBWA London. The proposition was that Pretty Polly tights stay up all day. "Putting the girls on space hoppers so they bounce up and down was a great idea. We all remember those things as kids. I immediately saw these girls all in black, black tights, black high heels. I made the set very monochromatic. I wanted it to look like it was a scientific experiment so I put them on these black-and-white targets. The background was grey, like a padded cell, because if it were a scientific test they'd have to have something to fall back against rather than hurt themselves. I knew that when I put the orange space hoppers in they would really zing out. I wanted it to look very sexy but classy. I didn't want it to be tacky." Originally, Fink imagined them bouncing around bollards in a car park. "But I couldn't really light it beautifully so it had to be in a studio." He also wanted to put the camera on a space hopper as well and bounce up and down with the girls. "We couldn't physically do it so we had a little rig that bounced up and down with the girls. It looked like the background is moving which gives it a weird kind of look."

There are two types of commercials director, he says. "Those that go to film school and learn their directing craft properly; and those that come from an advertising background, like myself, who haven't been trained to direct but can look at a commercial script and judge an idea very easily. I'm just so used to reading scripts, working with scripts, and I always go for the idea, whereas a director from a film school background isn't necessarily interested so much in the idea, he's much more interested in the film craft, the geography." Fink says a line that he discovered inscribed in a temple inspired him: *In beginners' minds there are many possibilities, in experts' minds there are few.*

Neil French. French began directing his own work because of what he calls the Disappointment Gap. "Very early in my career I became disappointed, then frustrated, then infuriated, by the fact that when a film was finished it bore little resemblance to the film I saw in my head when I wrote it. I used to rate work by the size of the Disappointment Gap." Eventually, French took matters into his own hands. As he recalls: "You've just explained everything in intricate detail to the director and you think that you have it absolutely down. You've bought him because of everything he's done before, and you know he's going to do what you want him to do with bells on. And then you get it back and you think, what went wrong? How could he possibly have misunderstood what you'd said? What happened was, at some point he wanted to put his own personality on it. But I just want his expertise, I don't want his personality or his thinking. If he was smarter than me he'd be doing my job. As it is, he's just a glorified cameraman; keep it in focus, keep the timing right, thank you very much. I'll be there to help him cast, I'll be there to do all the hard work. Then it occurred to me, after having done all this several times, that I might as well direct it myself. Directing is only a series of decisions. It's like being a computer, they're all yes/no decisions."

French always directed his own work at The Ball Partnership, now Euro RSCG Partnership, and Ogilvy & Mather.

"If I'd sold it well enough, the client would say, Neil, carry on, I trust you." French's television work is invariably driven by deceptively simple ideas, shot so that the idea is brought to the fore.

His impatience with "personality directors" is legendary. "Other people want that kind of director. They've heard of a name. They're hoping that a Tarsem will get them out of their pit. And maybe he will. But at the end of it, can they look at that commercial and say, that's my ad? No, they can't, it's Tarsem's ad." French went out on his own as an independent director before returning to Ogilvy & Mather and becoming worldwide creative director. He directed some of the world's greatest actors for the Union Bank of Switzerland through Advico Young & Rubicam Zurich. "The problem with well-known actors like Sir John Gielgud, Paul Scofield, Alan Bates, Maggie Smith, Harvey Keitel and all that lot," French recalls, "is that they walk in, they've never heard of you, they don't know you from a hole in the wall. You've only got a day to shoot them. Within an hour you've got to have their trust, so it's a huge con job. It's about being The Man Who Knows, being forceful and friendly, all those things that you know will work. There's more acting in that than there is in the rest of the day. So long as they know that *you* know what you want, they will give you a great job."

One of French's most controversial successes was "directed by necessity" for The Ball Partnership, Singapore. The original intention was to film a futuristic Mitsubishi concept car that would lift the marque's profile in the Singapore market. "We couldn't have shown the *real* cars..." Then disaster struck. "We were told, no, you can't shoot it, it's in Spain. So we said, we'll fly to Barcelona and shoot it there. And then they said, no, it's gone to Finland, so we said we'd fly to Finland. In the end, they said no, it's gone back to Japan, so we said okay, we'd go to Japan. And they came back and said, no, the Japanese film crew is psychologically incapable of working with you." Meanwhile, the Singapore distributor who was paying for the commercial had booked his airtime and insisted it went ahead. "So we decided to make a fake car. We made bits of it. Willie Tang, the cinematographer, shot the bits, and we put in other bits, like a body in plastic having paint poured over it, and worms being poured into a machine, because we had nothing else to fill thirty seconds." But what was intended to convey bizarre, forward-looking technology was perceived in the market as some hallucinatory vision of rape or childbirth, or both. "Whereas, of course," protests French, "it was just a series of disconnected images that didn't have an idea."

French eschews a particular directing style. "I want a commercial to make a point. If you look at my reel, nothing looks like anything else. I have a vision of every second in a commercial before it goes to air. That's what I want it to look like and I'm not prepared to let anything get in the way." French acknowledges the industry's obsession with certain star directors and the self-perpetuation of individual styles. "Tony Kaye tends to shoot Tony Kaye-type films. And that's fair enough, people choose him to do those, if they can afford him." But generally speaking, says French, the director's individuality should serve the commercial, and not the reverse.

Ron Mather. From the creative directorship of Saatchi & Saatchi Sydney, to independent commercials director, then back into the business as national creative director of The Campaign Palace, Mather's transitions provided a unique learning curve. "There were too many directors in the business who weren't advertising directors. They just liked to make things look nice, rather than make an idea come out. I thought there was a really good position for a director who understands advertising ideas and could actually make the ads work. So I set up with my producer, Kare Godsell, and we were Mather Godsell. We did a lot of work for The Palace, won a few things. I'd still be directing if The Palace hadn't come along and talked to me."

The prospect of a creative giant like Mather critiquing one's script cut both ways. Some teams relished it; others refused. "We used to get scripts through from agencies and we'd say to each other, we must be missing a page, this can't be the end of it. On the positive side though, I did meet some very good people, people who really wanted to do good work. Sometimes they were in agencies that didn't allow them to. They had great ideas that will never see the light of day. There are so few good agencies, it's frightening. And the only difference between The Campaign Palace and an ordinary agency is that we have less stuff lying up against the wall." The value of the idea was reaffirmed. "If you've got an idea, at least it's like a safety rope. You can keep referring back to it. Are we drifting away from the idea? Is this getting in the way of the idea?"

Mather believes great commercials should be fresh and able to

We observe the desperate death throes of a fish out of water.

The fish thrashes about wildly, flipping over and over in grainy slow motion.

There is absolutely no sound.

A typeset message that the world's water supply has halved slowly rolls up the screen.

End super: *Treat water with respect.*

Director Antony Redman and photographer Charles Liddall shot the dying fish on the roof of Batey Ads Singapore. Redman resisted all advice to add sound effects, so that the mute commercial played its own track in the head of the viewer. The commercial was awarded a Bronze at the One Show.

sustain repeated viewing. "A great idea, possibly even on an old brief, but done so well you've seen nothing like it before. It's something that breaks new ground. Most important, it's got to be something you'd *want* to watch."

Antony Redman. When Redman switched from being an agency creative director to an independent film director, his work was selected for the Saatchi & Saatchi New Directors Showcase at Cannes.

The young Australian began directing commercials while still on the payrolls of Batey Ads and Euro RSCG Partnership (The Ball Partnership), Singapore. "I was getting frustrated with directors who always wanted to show how clever they were in their directing technique, rather than simplifying their technique to suit an idea. Also, on a lot of our jobs we didn't have money to afford really good directors so I just put my hand up." When Redman stepped out from the creative leadership of Batey Ads to become a commercials and indie movie director, the agency was ranked in the trade press as the region's most creative agency. He admits to a certain disillusionment with advertising. "It was getting too easy. I found directing commercials was a fantastic medium; you're dealing with so many different products and techniques, you're always learning. I still love the business of making these 30- and 60-second pieces of madness."

Is there a risk that commercial directors become typecast? "Film companies who are keen to represent you will see your work and say, well, he's the weird guy, or he's the beautifully photographic guy, or he's the dialogue guy. It's a dangerous thing. It's something I'm trying to avoid. I guess when people are looking for a type of feel or a type of treatment it makes them feel comfortable to deal with someone who's done it before."

Redman recalls one of his favourite commercials that won a Bronze at the One Show. "Graham Fink had come down to Batey Ads to work on Singapore Airlines and we were sitting having a few white wines. We spent an hour talking about our Save Water campaign, *Treat water with respect,* and doing some press ads. Then I discussed the idea of a dying fish, a fish out of water, which came from the fact that in the last thirty years the world's water supply has halved. Everyone's seen a fish flapping around on a jetty or in the bottom of their boat. The idea was to shoot a dying fish for forty-five seconds, in slow motion, flopping, twisting, turning, and landing on its head. It's a painful thing to see. I recruited Charles Liddall, who is a British stills photographer based in Kuala Lumpur who wanted to move into commercials. We got a 16mm Arri and built a set on the rooftop of Batey Ads for a couple of thousand bucks. We had a bench and we put some rocks in behind it to make it look like a dried-up riverbed. Then we sprinkled fuller's earth on it so the fish would kick up a lot of dust. We shot in natural light, cut off with scrims a bit. We got what we needed in the first take; it was one shot, shot at 75 frames a second, and then slowed down again to 150, so it would become even more harrowing and grainy. But we were both still a little unfamiliar with film at that stage so the negative wasn't exposed properly. When we went to telecine there was no picture. The colour grader had to work for about five minutes just to pull out an image. Finally when it came out it was quite grainy and nasty, which wasn't exactly what I wanted. I'd wanted it pristine, so you could see the shimmers on the fish's skin." Then came Redman's toughest decision; everyone, it seemed, had lots of ideas for the soundtrack. "I didn't want to use any sound. It made it more painful. I thought a 'boom' sound or a thud every time the fish hit the ground would be distracting." While Redman was happy to let people imagine their own sound, the reality was that TV stations baulked at running mute commercials; viewers would think there was some technical fault. "Somehow we managed to convince CNN to run it. I wanted to prove that forty-five seconds of silence is more powerful. But when the commercial was entered for awards, we got an urgent fax saying we had sent a mute tape by error and could we please send the correct version with audio."

"Patience" is Redman's advice to other young creatives. "Build up your visual side. Hire a camera, shoot some test commercials, just little ideas, and experiment. Go out and take stills. Watch movies. Be pro-active. Get focused on craft. The *Shots* reels are a fantastic reference point, but the first thing you've got to do is don't make anything you do look like anything on *Shots*."

Frank Todaro. Former agency colleagues Frank Todaro, Bryan Buckley and Hank Perlman have become icons for young American creatives. Buckley and Perlman are directors at Hungry Man.

Todaro, @radical.media New York, recalls: "I was guilty of both writing and art direction. My first job was art direction, but I quickly started taking all the radio assignments from my writing partner who hated doing radio. I loved directing the actors and putting it together the way I wanted." After stints at Cliff Freeman's and Scali McCabe Sloves, he hooked up with school buddy Bryan Buckley to run an agency which they later sold. Meanwhile, one of their former employees, Hank Perlman, had joined Wieden & Kennedy. "Wieden's were doing the advertising for ESPN, but they couldn't handle the volume of on-air promos for upcoming games. They were 15-second things, very disposable, so Hank called us and they put them into our hands to shoot and edit. Bryan and I ended up doing hundreds of these things, running out to ice rinks and arenas, shooting all sorts of weird things, sometimes getting thrown out."

Todaro did not start directing out of a sense of frustration. It was something he had always wanted to do since college. He attended film school at NYU. Deciding that his original choice, journalism, wasn't going to work for him, Todaro discovered advertising, "which incorporated music, film, writing and art". When Hugh Hudson and Ridley Scott started coming up with movies, his own career path crystallised.

Today, he believes, young creatives have more tools available to break through in their careers. "You can shoot an ad and edit it on your laptop. The software is there. If you think you would really like to do it, then just try to do it. Even if it doesn't succeed, you'll have learned something from it. The first time out, if you wait, it's not going to happen. You have to do a couple on your own first. Even if it's not broadcast quality, you can show what it is you can do."

Todaro practised what he now preaches. The first commercial he ever did was for Hertz at Scali McCabe Sloves. "It was a very simple ad for a weekend offer. I had a director lined up. Then the client didn't want to do it. I said, it's too good a spot not to do. So I got a 16mm camera and some friends, went to this guy's roof, and filmed it in one take. When I showed it to Sam Scali he said, you're right, the agency will pay to finish this and we'll show it to Hertz. And it ran."

In the *Gunn Report* for 2000, Todaro was ranked the world's third most-awarded director.

9

THE GLOBAL PICTURE

I s there such a thing as an international creative standard? And if there isn't, should there be one?

"When the words 'Global Campaign' were printed on a brief in the old days, a collective groan went up," reflects Adrian Holmes. "It was then thought that to have a piece of work that would appeal all around the world would, out of necessity, result in the lowest common denominator creativity." Today, says Holmes, possibly because more brands have become global, requests for global campaigns are being made increasingly on creative departments — and not just on ordinary creative departments. "Once, the best work was done at a national level by local agencies. Now those same agencies have grown and have taken on global clients and so cannot sidestep the creation of global ideas. So for the first time, global briefs are being given to really talented people, whereas before it was often the less-inspired international agencies that were doing that kind of work. Now it's the hotshops that have got big — like Wieden & Kennedy with Nike, and like ourselves with Smirnoff, which was an advertising idea that worked in forty or fifty countries." Obviously, Holmes says, certain product categories such as jeans, alcoholic beverages, airlines and soft drinks are more susceptible to global solutions, where perhaps the emotions are universal from culture to culture. "Writing for a global market shouldn't really change your basic behaviour. The same principles apply. You find the one single thing and make that as impactful as possible. You should write the ad first, without any feeling of constraint." One crutch, however, is removed. *"You can't rely on tricks of language and puns, which we so often do. That support is taken away from you."* Prominent features of the global landscape are two equally pernicious phenomena, Holmes warns: the not-briefed-here and not-written-here syndromes. "You have to use your political wiles to get around them and work out whether a genuine difference or problem exists or whether it is just local client or agency politics."

Before Adidas, Leagas Delaney was a "local" British hotshop. Then came the plunge into global creative work. Tim Delaney recalls: "It was a formative thing for the agency. We started out in late '92 with Adidas, and we soon realised that the things which we liked in television — the sense of daring, bravery and trusting the consumer to fill in the gaps, to logic-chop, knowing that they could follow the logic — weren't confined just to the UK market. *They were universal things.* We didn't have to say, well, because it has to go to everybody let's have an idea that somehow goes to the *lowest* common denominator. That, Wieden & Kennedy taught us."

Michael Lynch publishes two editions of trade magazine *Campaign Brief*, one for Australia, one for Asia, and reports on Cannes every year. He observes that the region's best work shares the same qualities that all Cannes winners have in common. "Cannes winners are *universally understood* commercials with powerful, single-minded big ideas. *Sometimes* they also have cutting edge production values."

"A good ad is a universal thing." Ron Mather served on an international award jury representing fifteen different countries. "A good ad came along and fifteen different countries put their hands up. It's quite amazing." Mather chaired the 2001 Clio TV jury.

Great ads, like great films and books, will always be universally applauded. The problem is that great work seems to flow from West to East, from North to South. Is it a case of setting one standard which all must follow?

"I'm always intrigued when commercial television first comes to a country," observes David Perry. "I remember when it happened in one of the Scandinavian countries, and the commercials they did their first couple of years were absolutely wonderful. Everybody was a neophyte. Nobody had been exposed to adverts on television before, so it was a wide-open field. They didn't know any of the rules, there were no restrictions, there were no 30-, 60- and 90-second lengths so it would be 47 seconds, it would be 1 minute and 2 seconds, whatever they wanted it to be." The more evolved the market becomes, says Perry, the more sophisticated, knowledgeable and advanced it gets, the more the restrictions are tightened.

Linus Karlsson remembers starting in advertising at the Paradiset agency in Stockholm. Commercial television had just arrived in Sweden. He and his art director Paul Malmström, fresh out of advertising school, cut their creative teeth on Diesel. "Diesel broke all the rules not only in Sweden, but in Europe and the rest of the world. The ads said, this is something you've never seen before. Levi's had been such a dominant player, what they did became the truth, so we said, let's just go as far away from Levi's as we can. This was the time at the beginning of the 90s when all the guys had tank tops; they were out on motorcycles in black-and-white in the desert. So we said, let's not go there. Let's go colourful. Let's add humour. Fashion was so serious, almost pretentious. We said, let's give it a break; can't fashion be fun?" Six and a half years later, Karlsson and Malmström moved to what he describes as "the frontier", Fallon in Minneapolis. "For me, the frontier is daring to go into the unknown, daring to go into the things you are not sure if you are going to like, or handle, or control. Starting at Paradiset at the beginning of the 90s, an agency that no one had heard about, that had no track record, that was very exciting, that was the frontier for me at that point."

Where are today's new frontiers? Sadly, most new markets resemble intellectual colonies. They have a low opinion of themselves and their own creativity. Denying their own existence and culture, they pay homage to DDB in the 60s or CDP in the 70s. Remote from the main stage of advertising, the better locals dream of one day working at Wieden & Kennedy or Leagas Delaney. The whole process fundamentally reinforces advertising creativity as it was, not as it could be. For creative people, the choice is well-defined: either you do advertising "properly" and win awards, or you buck the system and risk oblivion.

SHOULD YOU BE LOCAL OR GLOBAL?

"No question. Local." Neil French shares his perspective as a global creative director. "Travelling as I do, to every continent and all the major cities in the world, the main thing that strikes me is how much *more* parochial we're becoming. Contradictorily, a lot of it has to do with the explosion of worldwide media and the Net. As satellites and cables bring us more worldwide culture, our need to 'belong' to a clan increases. And clans tend to be clans within tribes, and tribes within nations. The more specific you can be to your audience, the better your chances of being heard and noticed."

The other side to this coin, argues French, is that larger countries are becoming more insular, more scared of the barbarians at the gate. "The US in particular has become a huge pocket of frightened folk. It's as if all the maps have been redrawn, with everything beyond their Atlantic and Pacific shores marked '*Here be dragons!*' It's why so little of their advertising travels well and what does, does so for its curiosity value. Everyone talks about how wonderful the Outpost.com ads were. And they were *very* funny. Can anyone outside the US tell you what Outpost.com actually does? But contradictorily, they're right. They're advertising to themselves. Why *should* they care what the rest of the world thinks? It's only when they try to impose their culture and their peculiarities on the poor benighted foreigners that they become irritating."

He believes that the British, too, have become insular. "Obsessed with themselves. It's a more healthy obsession than colonialism, it has to be said, but it makes a lot of their work gnomic to the rest of us."

Overall, says French, it is a good thing. "It allows countries to formulate their own 'looks', attitudes, mores and symbols. The days are over, thank Confucius, when some expatriate thought that the only answer, when producing an ad for China, was Jackie Chan or an hilarious out-of-sync *kung fu* parody. It's cultural differences that make the world interesting. The next few decades will see *more* of

Japanese advertising is always true to itself. In 1993, Japan's Hakuhodo agency won the Cannes Grand Prix for its brilliant Nissin Cup Noodles Hungry *campaign, proving that the international standard is not exclusively set by the West.*

this, and we'll all be better for it."

Marcello Serpa, fiercely independent and Brazilian, is an international creative icon. He won the Grand Prix at Cannes when he was twenty-eight. His perspective is sobering: "*I am never really concerned about making work that looks international. I am very concerned with making work that I like.* I'm very lucky that I live in a country that allows me to do good advertising. The clients like good advertising. The people on the street like good advertising. They talk about it. I like the way I work; I like simple stories, simple ideas. I am an art director, so I like to see a story being told in pictures, without speaking too much. We are always looking for something that's really bold, really different, and somehow it also works on an international basis…"

Serpa believes those countries like India, Thailand and China can do local work that will win international recognition. They don't have to slavishly follow America or Britain. "I really think that the more Indian an Indian guy is, he can bring something out of India that is relevant for all over the world. People know India; people know what India is all about. They know all about the gods, they know about Ganesh, they know about the culture. If you can use this, and add some relevance, some cleverness, some intelligence, some

CHAPTER 9

How can a man who lives in a little shack afford a black-label whisky? That's what the local Godfather wanted to know.

The Thai equivalent of the Mob descends on our hero, complete with choppers. He is totally surrounded. Accusations are hurled. The *kung fu* team and kick boxers close in.

Unperturbed, he reveals his secret — economical but excellent Black Cat Whisky. All is forgiven.

Proving that great humour travels, the Black Cat Whisky commercial has won
accolades far from its native Thailand. Marcello Serpa described it as
"absolutely different from everything that had been done before".
Results Advertising (Ogilvy & Mather) Thailand.

difference, this would be really appealing to *everybody*." Serpa advocates the use of humour, which has propelled Thailand's work to prominence. "If you take yourself seriously, you're going to fail. You've got to put some twists in your work. The Black Cat Whisky commercial has become a cult commercial for Brazilians. It's Thai. It's absolutely different from everything that had been done before. It's the kind of Asian movie you always see, but the Thais made a joke out of it, and used it for a product, and people all over the world can enjoy it because they know *kung fu*, they know kickboxing. So you should use it, rather than copy the Americans or the British, which is ridiculous…"

After recent visits to Bombay and Johannesburg, Indra Sinha articulates a similar sentiment. "I kept being shown ads by people which looked as if they'd been done in London, or looked as if they'd wanted people to think they'd been done in London. I advised them, and so did Trevor Beattie who was with me in Johannesburg, to stop doing ads like people do in London. London agencies are already full of people trying to do ads like they do in London. Just start doing ads like you do in the inspiration of your mind wherever you happen to be, and do something that no one's ever seen before, *including London*." As Sinha explains, he could not see any connection between the world the ads depicted and the world he was seeing outside his hotel room. "The contrast was stark in both countries, but much starker in India, because the sea of poverty laps right at the doors of these luxury five-star hotels and leaves that sludge of human misery on their marble doorsteps, and you have to step over it, and leave footprints in it, as you come and go. None of the ads reflected the huge problems that they had around them. None of the advertisers seemed to think that keying their products into the situation as it actually existed, rather than some idealistic situation where they all lived in Manhattan, would work. There was a big poster campaign in Bombay for a paint company called Jensen & Nicholson that said *When you see colour think of us*, which had surrealist images like fried eggs with blue yolks. When I saw their hoarding up over this filthy building I began wondering, why not take half the budget of that campaign and use it to subsidise up to 50% off the paint, in order to get building owners to paint their buildings, thus demonstrating the cleansing and monsoon-proof qualities of the paint, and then run a television campaign that said *Whenever you see a bright new building think of us*. You would achieve the client's aim and sell more paint, the campaign becomes a demonstration of the paint's quality, and some social good is done from which the client benefits as well. I want people now to hijack their clients' budgets and look for synergies like that, where the product can be demonstrated and work in the real world in a way that improves things in some aspect. It can't work for everything all the time, but there's a vast, vast, vast pool of advertising money out there, and if even a fraction of it is diverted into things like that, it would do something."

According to Gee Thomson, the creative playing field has become more level and the turbo lag has ceased to exist. "Because of the process of new ideas working their way through the system, certain tactics used in Europe or America might once have taken two or three years to get through to creative teams in South Africa or South America. *Now there is a more balanced ability worldwide*. Ideas are not being borrowed as much anymore; they are being invented in their own territories." However, Thomson warns, while creative teams may not need to play catch-me-up anymore in terms of creative thinking, local audiences may still need time to understand and appreciate new forms of advertising expression. "Stuff which works in one region may still not work in others. Audiences in the UK and the US are well-versed in sophisticated humour like satire and irony. Such tactics might not work in, say, the Eastern bloc of Europe where people haven't been exposed to those sorts of commercials for all that long."

Based on work coming in to *Shots*, Thomson says the markets that are challenging the dominance of America and Britain are Australia, Asia, South Africa and Scandinavia. "Scandinavian work is refreshing. It has a strange northern European flavour in humour; it's very quirky and it's travelled extremely well worldwide. It's influenced a lot of UK and American commercials, specifically the work of Traktor and Jhoan Camitz." Thai humour is incredibly quirky. There is a definite flavour from Australia and New Zealand, one of hardened cynicism and irreverence that works very well.

"Information technology, websites, web-thinking, global TV — all those areas of thinking, imagery and culture are now reaching a level playing field, too. It is now the same game people are playing, worldwide."

Malaysian-born Jonathan Teo has worked in Malaysia, Singapore and Australia. "I never really think I'm in Malaysia, or I'm in Singapore, or I'm in Sydney. I just do it."

David Droga has also worked in three countries — Australia, Singapore and the UK, where he is now executive creative director at Saatchi & Saatchi London. He talks about the advantage of *naivety* and coming from cultures outside of Britain. "Australia is such a young country and at the agency where I worked, OMON, we were young and irresponsible. We didn't really know the rules of the industry and what was required of us. We were just there to make an impact and to hell with the consequences, compared to what the other agencies were doing. Then I moved to Saatchi & Saatchi Singapore, which is a very competitive country. I was blessed with a creative department that was almost like the United Nations; Chinese, Indians, Americans, English, Australians. It's not often you get to mix that many cultures in a department. Everybody was there with something to prove. But because it was a peripheral advertising country, everybody was very competitive. We weren't used to having so many layers of hierarchy and things taking so long and so much formality as there is in the UK and the US. So we were quite naïve about everything. We just assumed things *can* be done. We wanted to change the world and compete against everybody. The market moves at such a rapid pace that you don't have time to understand how things are done formally, so we just dove head first into everything. In markets where the ramifications are so big, people spend time discussing what is going to prevent something, whereas in Asia you just have to get to the solution so quickly. You don't have time to think, well, we wouldn't normally do it this way, or that's not the way it's been done in the past, or can we really pull this off? We were just naïve to the whole industry which was very successful for us because we ended up achieving a lot for a little agency in Singapore, more than most big agencies around the world." The 1999 *Gunn Report* listed Saatchi & Saatchi Singapore in the top twelve most awarded agencies in the world, ahead of such famous names as BBH London, Goodby Silverstein, Fallon, and Saatchi & Saatchi London. "We made a massive impact because we did it our way, at a speed that we wanted to work at, not someone else's speed, not an industry speed."

The major advertising capitals of the world, Droga says, may well be exciting but they are also myopic. "People rarely look beyond the shores of where they are. There was no need for them to do so. The UK has been such a dominant force in advertising, and to a large degree still is, so the interest of the people in the industry was very much what is happening down the road, not what is happening across the globe. People were content to compete against their neighbour, as opposed to someone who is doing something more exciting at the other end of the earth. What I want to do is make people realise that great thinking doesn't just happen in Britain. British advertising emulates itself; it's very incestuous and lacks any fresh perspectives. The same criticism would apply in America. People *have* to be exposed to a lot more. They should feel *inspired and threatened* by creative thinking from around the globe."

One such market is New Zealand, he says. "New Zealand realised that if it just tried to compete with Australia, it would be the poor cousin. So why not try and rock the world?" It's not a question of breaking the rules, says Droga. There are no rules in the first place.

EXPORTING AGENCY CULTURES

The world is dominated by Western agency brands with Western agency cultures. Or is it? The truth is, very often, it is a case of putting the same name on different doors, minus the sense of mission and creativity.

Building an agency's international creative reputation, says Holmes, is like trying to eat Chinese food with billiard cues. "You can't run a worldwide group of creative people in the way that you ran a creative department in one agency. In any case, we have very good creative directors for each office. We haven't opened Lowe offices and put people from London there to clone headquarters. Some agency groups have grown that way, but with Lowe it's been a case of us going into partnerships with like-minded entrepreneurial

A series of beautifully crafted shots of women passing by on the street…

In a store…

On a train…

On an escalator.

Men turn to look at them, furtively directing their gaze towards their breasts, ogling their cleavage… while the classical strains of Pachelbel's *Canon* create an almost hypnotic mood… causing us ultimately to wonder what we are watching and what it will be all about…

Male VO: *If only women examined their breasts as often as men do…*

Super: *Consult your physician for advice on breast examination.*

Creating discomfort in a conservative society, the Singapore Cancer Society broke through the apathy barrier with help from Leo Burnett Singapore. Written by Curt Detweiler and co-art directed by agency creative director Linda Locke, it was stills photographer Russel Wong's debut as a director. Awards included Silver at Kinsale.

agency people who believe in the same things that we do. That's how the Lowe network grew, so that has established a principle of creative autonomy among our partner agencies. We've achieved creative direction in other ways." Holmes operates an annual creative seminar in partnership with Andy Langer, vice chairman of Lowe Lintas & Partners in America, a week-long course addressing the lack of basic training for young creatives. The seminar is conducted in London and New York by turns. "All our agencies are invited to send a team. We usually have fifteen teams, thirty people, so suddenly a guy from Singapore is sitting next to a guy from Brazil. We spend the whole week talking about ideas, how to get them, how to improve them…" Holmes says the creative seminar has spawned a parallel programme for account handlers and planners on how to write great briefs and sell work.

Fallon McElligott, now Fallon Minneapolis, is a world-respected advertising icon. But how can a Minneapolis-based agency export its Midwest values to markets beyond America? Its first leap to a foreign culture was New York. London followed. The global arm, Fallon Worldwide, is stretching further to Singapore.

"A lot of networks are formed, and they're just a whole bunch of offices all over the place, some have got 120 offices," says David Lubars. "A few of them are good, a lot of them are terrible. We're trying to figure out a new way to do it, a way to do it that's not acrimonious, everybody's become part of the same family. It's a newer construct." Lubars points to fewer offices, each great in its own right, as a likely scenario. His brief is strengthening and innovating the agency's brand of creativity so it can reach out across the world. "You can't live off the fumes of the past, you have to continue to inject new juice into it."

Being inspired by your own geography is one thing; being part of a global agency network, working on global brands with global campaigns, is another. But no matter how many offices there are in an agency network, and no matter how small the world gets, each market is different — or different enough — to defy sameness and fuel freshness, if we wish it to be so.

CHINA

"There are two thousand to six thousand advertising agencies in each major provincial city, depending on the city's size." Peter Soh, an award-winning Singaporean creative director, is now chief executive officer and executive creative director of Saatchi & Saatchi Shanghai. He lectures on advertising at Beijing University and has judged China's national awards for years. "Most commercials are basic. Ninety percent just tell you what the product is, or create a situation where the product is needed and demonstrate how it works. But I am beginning to see around 5% of the work with very good ideas. Execution is still influenced very strongly by Hong Kong and Taiwan. They haven't shaken loose of that."

Daniel Lim, a fellow Singaporean, was formerly creative director at Saatchi & Saatchi Shanghai. "The standard is very basic by Western standards, but slowly becoming more sophisticated. A typical spot consists of one or more of the following: cheap special effects; outer space theme, popular with electronics clients; happy family; scenic shot of mist-shrouded mountains; scenic shot of mist-shrouded valleys; a romantic storyline with exaggerated acting; a growing up storyline with exaggerated acting..." Lim says many commercials will end with rhyming taglines. The music will be traditional Chinese, or library music, or composed music that sounds like library music, or outer space music. "Product names are often repeated three times or more by a stern male voice-over, in the space of ten seconds, with supers. Revolving metallic logos are commonplace." However, says Lim, commercials with analogies, storytelling and lateral ideas do exist in China "just as they exist anywhere else in the world".

Cheryl Chong, formerly Motorola's Beijing-based group marketing communications manager for China and now heading eDongcity, a dot.com venture, believes Chinese consumers want aspirational imagery. "People are into upgrading their lives. It's a stage that consumers are going through. There are too few creative ads in China, just like anywhere else in the world. Very often clients are unwilling to go for what we call 'creative' advertising because it means an element of risk. Because there is so little creative work going on, people don't realise what it *could* do." Even marketing executives do not fully understand the concept of branding, she says. "I gave a presentation on brand equity to a group of ten Chinese distributors who basically knew nothing about advertising. Their mean age was 35-40. I put two bananas on the table. I asked them, would you ever think about which one to pick? They said, no. So I took a marker pen and drew the Motorola logo on one of them. I said, now which one are you going to pick? And they stopped, because once there was a brand on it they had to think."

China opened its doors to advertising only twenty years ago. The Western advertising model is being imposed. Given all the differences, should we expect Western ideas to be relevant in China?

Nike and Budweiser are just some of the Western commercials that go down well with Chinese audiences, Lim advises. "Budweiser's *Ants* commercial was the country's favourite beer commercial, although market research cannot accurately tell us why."

Chong agrees. Nike works. "Anyone up to 35 years old would be able to tell you about Nike imagery." She says the commercials that work best have visual ideas that are relevant to the viewer. "Because of the dynamic economic growth, the socio-economic mix is crazy. You get extremes. There are so many layers. There are regional differences, and within regions there are further differences. Getting from one place to another is still difficult. People's exposure is limited. Only a very small percentage has travelled. If you're speaking to a farmer, don't get fancy. Just get to the point."

Things tend to work differently in China. For instance, the Chinese don't eat cereal, and a large percentage of the population is lactose-intolerant. Instead, says Soh, some drink beer with their breakfast. A cab driver in Beijing, he reports, earns 500 renminbi a month, around US$60. A family living in a 2-room apartment might have a household income of 1,000 renminbi a month, or US$120. On a household income of 180 renminbi, about US$18 a month, buying a bottle of Coca-Cola would be out of the question.

Audiences can be very literal. "One local told me that all ad men are conmen," relates Soh. "I asked him why. He said he saw an ad on TV that said you would smile and laugh after you ate the product. He ate it and didn't smile or laugh." However, as Soh reminds us, certain human factors are universal. "When I show overseas reels, they laugh as much as we do, but they aren't able to *reproduce* that humour yet in China." Soh believes that the Apple *1984* commercial and Goodby's *got milk?* campaign would be understood in China. "Key cities recognise Western landmarks and icons like the Statue of Liberty. Only in the last twenty years were they allowed to see these things and read about them. They wouldn't mean as much to Chinese viewers as they would to us in Singapore or the West. I knew all about the Great Wall of China and how it could be seen from the moon, but until I stood on it myself it meant nothing to me." China, he argues, is too big and too complex for Caucasians to understand. "Even for me, I would never be able to think like a Shanghainese." In some parts of China, he says, people are still reading brochures to understand product functions. "In the back of their minds they might believe that a foreign product is better designed, but it doesn't mean they will shy away from the local product." He identifies the key developing cities: Shanghai, Beijing, Guangzhou, Nanjing and Xiamen. "The younger cities with universities are catching up fast. Shanghai will push ahead fastest. The return of Hong Kong and Macao has increased the confidence of the Chinese. China has a very good business sense."

One problem with bringing global campaigns to China is the lost-in-translation factor. Leading Chinese-language creative director and copywriter Paul Tan talks about untranslatable slogans. "Some English slogans are virtually impossible to translate and still keep their original Western spirit."

There is no past, present or future tense in Chinese. The verb resides at the end of a sentence. A word-for-word translation from English is usually meaningless in Chinese; individual words often have a dozen different meanings and only by placing them in combination with another word will a particular meaning emerge. The single word *sheng* (生) means grow; existence and life; living and livelihood; to get or have; to light a fire; unripe; raw, uncooked; unrefined, crude; strange or unfamiliar; stiff or mechanical; a student; a suffix for certain occupations like a doctor; the male character type in Beijing opera; and to give birth to. Much Chinese advertising draws on *cheng yu*, idioms and set phrases that are loaded with innuendo.

As Tan explains, abstract English words like "it" have no direct equivalents in Chinese. "JWT Shanghai did a good Mainland Chinese version of *Just do it*. It simply says, *I dream*, or *I dreamed*, because there is no past or present tense. It is beautiful in Chinese because it has implications of making your dream come true, which is a less aggressive, very Chinese way of saying *Just do it*." Other examples of difficult-to-translate slogans Tan quotes are Citibank's *Where money lives* and Microsoft's *Where do you want to go today?* The Pepsi slogan, *The Choice of a New Generation*, is relatively easier to translate, he says, because there are Chinese equivalents of the key words *Choice* and *New Generation*.

While it is not difficult to translate an English-language commercial into Chinese, Tan says that nine out of ten times the impact found in the original language will be lost. "It is best to create commercials using original Chinese concepts. Then there will be no cultural baggage to carry during the conceptualisation and execution processes." Tan recalls a Nike soccer commercial that won Gold at the 7th China Times Chinese Creative Awards. "Familiar local scenes of soccer being played in the street were contrasted with serious training on the field. The passion of the young players showed their desire to excel and win. It ended with a well-practised banana kick being saved by the opposite team's goalkeeper, and an end line that is totally Chinese, *A hero is not determined by his success or failure*. It is wonderfully, powerfully Chinese."

Can simple English words be understood? "If talking overall, in all the provinces like Mongolia, the answer is no," maintains Soh. "I would risk it in Beijing or Shanghai, especially in Shanghai, to create a new sort of culture. And if it's just one word. But if it were English like Dickens, it would be a tall order. The younger generation is more than willing to learn, even though their English may not be great now."

The most highly acclaimed Chinese television campaign in recent years was a collaboration of East and West. It was directed by Zhang Yimou whose award-winning movie credits include *Raise the Red Lantern*. Mike Fromowitz, then chairman and executive creative director of Batey Ads Hong Kong, created the campaign for Ericsson. "Ericsson, as a company, wanted to be seen as an integral part of the

A businessman brings his elderly father a remote control TV and a microwave.

Duty done, he tells the old man he has to hurry off and meet his friends.

As the old man prepares himself for another lonely night, his son makes an unexpected return. He has had second thoughts and spends the evening with his father.

Ericsson helps bridge the people of China. Batey Ads Hong Kong creative director Mike Fromowitz and famed Chinese director Zhang Yimou created a campaign with social value, examining such issues as the breakdown of filial piety and the fact that children no longer communicated as much with their parents.

CHAPTER 9

Mainland China telecommunications industry," explains Batey Ads group chief executive officer Rod Pullen. "They believed that in time domestic Chinese telecoms companies would emerge and the number of foreign companies might one day be restricted. They wanted to be seen as a company that truly understands China. When we looked at what other people were running in China, a lot of the local work was about 'technology', which dates easily. Most of the foreign multinationals were showing case histories." The creative breakthrough came when Pullen and Fromowitz found a statement from Ericsson's chief executive officer that said, *It is all about communication between people, the rest is technology...* "That seemed to sum it up," says Pullen.

Fromowitz developed a campaign that focused on the consumer, not the company. "What happens when you can't communicate with each other?" he asked. "Everything breaks down." He explored key social themes. Filial piety, for example, was under strain. With rapid urbanisation and changes in the economy, people were spending less time in traditional ways with their parents. Likewise, modern parents were paying less attention to their children. These aspects of human nature became brushstroke themes for commercials. "The pitfalls are that you try to be real and touch people, but the work is actually unreal and hackneyed," observes Pullen. "It ends up clearly as advertising. But Mike Fromowitz had a passion for dramatising advertising, and making commercials that were more like movies."

There are no product shots in the commercials, no overt sales messages of any kind. "Ericsson stands for more than mobile phones," says Fromowitz. "It's about bridging the people of China." Fromowitz needed a director whose strength was in presenting real Chinese life, with people facing real problems, speaking the way real people speak. Zhang, China's most famous director, was initially reluctant until he saw the scripts. "Zhang Yimou believed in the social value of the commercials," Fromowitz recalls. Zhang also attracted a different kind of actor. "He brought them all to my office, to act their parts in front of me." The two men communicated through interpreters. "Yimou spent two weeks on the casting, going over each of the scripts to ensure every word and nuance was just right." In *Generation Gap*, a businessman gives his elderly father a remote control TV and a microwave; duty done, he hurries off to meet his friends. As the lonely old man peers out the window, his son makes an unexpected return. He has had second thoughts and spends the evening with his father. In another view of family relationships, *Father and Son*, an angry father screams at his son's bedroom door; finally the conflict is resolved by a mother's words. *Coalminer* is a charming tale of a man who journeys to the city to meet the girl with whom he has been corresponding. He has never even seen a photograph of her. She promises to wear red so he will recognise her. When *three* women in red are there to greet him, he knows immediately which is the love of his life.

Zhang Yimou cut the commercials on a Steinbeck in his Beijing home before they were taken to Hong Kong for finishing. The unconventional campaign swept the Hong Kong 4As Awards including Best of Show. Such was its impact with consumers and the media that a special feature on the making of the commercials ran on cable TV across China. Fromowitz is now at BBDO New York.

EARLY days still. The question remains, however: should China evolve its own unique creative style, like Japan and Thailand have done in Asia, and arguably like France has done in Europe? Or should it follow the West?

According to Soh, China looks to Hong Kong and Taiwan for ideas, but is also exposed to American and British award books and reels. "To a certain extent China hasn't fully understood Western culture. One of the obstacles is not understanding the language. They may not fully 'get' the idea and not understand *why* something was done. Whether we like it or not, China and the West are fifty years apart." Soh is adamant that Chinese advertising creativity should take root in Chinese culture. "I still love Western creativity, but when I give talks at the Beijing University, I encourage them to use their own culture. I wish I could learn a bit more about Chinese culture myself; I feel more like a student than a lecturer. Whenever I give seminars, I am swamped with questions. They are so eager to learn, so eager to do a good piece of work, and I caution them that they can't hurry that situation." At a workshop for young creatives from all over China, Soh discovered a lack of conceptualising skills. "On day one they would present their ideas, half of which were brilliant. But on the second day when they presented their executions, I saw no trace of the ideas. It was all execution." Soh has not seen a "China" style emerging yet. "At present it looks too Hong Kong or there's a big pinch of salt from Taiwan. I have judged Hong Kong work now three times in the last six years. Hong Kong has nice production values, but no breakthrough ideas. A foreign judge seeing Hong Kong work for the first time would think, oh, this is *so* Chinese, but the trouble is I have seen the same executions done years ago." Editing is a big issue in China. "Former movie directors make a lot of commercials; they all seem a couple of frames too long. There's a lot of sepia in use to depict the old days; one of the frequently used scenarios is, I was like that before, but now I'm in a big city." Soh believes China could learn from the way the Japanese create advertising. "Japanese ads are not American. When you look at their Nissin Cup Noodles ads with the dinosaurs, that campaign has got nothing to do with any culture, nothing to do with any language."

Soh predicts that China's advertising industry will develop like America's. "America has Madison Avenue, but then you have great agencies in Chicago, San Francisco and Minneapolis. I think each area of China will have its own style." Today, the best work is being done in Shanghai and Beijing; however, Soh recalls seeing great ideas created in Guilin, Nanjing, Wuxi and Guangzhou. "As Chinese manufacturers extend to the West, their agencies will follow like Dentsu followed its Japanese clients. A good number of local agencies are facing a big issue. They don't know what to do next. They are two or three years old, they have made good money by being 'the agency next door'. I think these local shops are the agencies that *can* produce work that is 100% made-in-China. There's nothing wrong with the learning process, you can pick up skills; but in the end, the ideas have to be *yours*, not just translations of something that was conceptualised in New York or London, Hong Kong or Taiwan." Soh is optimistic. "Having judged the China awards six years in a row, I think the time is coming for Chinese creativity."

Chong shares a similar perspective. "My understanding of being 'creative' is when you make people think differently about something; I don't have to spend a lot of money running it over and over again to get a result. China has a long way to go. Marketing and advertising are very new, they're importing talent from overseas, and there's not enough maturity yet. A lot of creative people leave the country, come back and do some stuff, but there still isn't enough depth." Chong says local agencies will emerge to rival multinational agency networks. She predicts the day when more Chinese brands will go to the world. "People are in a hurry to do their own thing."

"Advertising is pretty much a product of the West," says Tan. "The progression for the Chinese and the West must be according to the advancement of their respective economic development and personal lifestyles. What is relevant and effective to Westerners may not be the same for Chinese across the board. What works for the Chinese in Hong Kong or Taiwan might not be appropriate for the Mainlanders or the Singaporeans. That applies to the local cities of China as well; Shanghai is more advanced in many ways than Beijing. So the clever commercial, compared with the more traditional, conservative, straightforward commercial could be appreciated in Shanghai, but may not be suitable for the consumers of Beijing." Generally, Tan says cleverness is not an issue. The key consideration is comprehension. "Will they understand it? Will it be relevant to their daily life at work or at home? Is it negative or offensive? This last point is more important to the Chinese than the Westerners. Mainlanders have not quite learned how to laugh at themselves yet, so don't use negative platforms to sell."

After twenty years in Asia with Ogilvy & Mather and Batey Ads, Pullen identifies problems common to China and other Asian markets. He revisits the fundamentals of the advertising briefing process. "Very often clients in Asia *assume* that they only need to give you what you need to know. Agencies need everything. It's like mining diamonds. You can't have enough information. Now what that *isn't*, however, is someone opening a pantechnicon and throwing five hundred books at you; that's just lazy." Clients must learn to trust agencies and tell them their secrets. It's like someone confessing to you, Pullen says; first, agencies must bring about that trust. "There has to be an equal responsibility on the part of agencies to ask intelligent questions. Asking intelligent questions is a skill. Some people are born with it; others have to learn how to do it. And not to score points but to get answers." Pullen discusses the abdication of responsibility by agency account people. "Account people need to direct. Experienced account directors, who understand the client and his business, need to *direct* where the advertising is going. There's no doubt that great account people of the ilk of Frank Lowe are, by definition, creative thinkers." Pullen maintains that the creative process has to begin in the brief. "Briefs should have ideas. They should give creative people a thought, a direction. And briefing *has* to be face-to-face." Pullen's advice to Asian creatives is to simplify their work. Not enough effort is made to distil, craft and edit. "Most advertising ideas are *too complicated*. Consumers have become very wary of them. Too many ads are blunt, insensitive, unrealistic, badly put together, not interesting and not engaging. A lot of it just hasn't been thought through." Asian advertising lacks Big Ideas, he says. "Big Ideas are ideas that lodge in the target's brain and are not easily forgotten. If you're a big brand, you keep showing that idea to people with consistency as often as you can afford. I actually don't believe Big Ideas are born big. I think they're born, and then grow big over time."

Lim believes the future can only get better. "Right now the breaks are flooded with Hong Kong-Chinese, Taiwanese-Chinese, Japanese-Chinese, Malaysian-Chinese, Singaporean-Chinese and even Western-Chinese ideas. The Chinese viewer hasn't seen all that much, so it's not too difficult to impress him. There are a couple of Chinese commercial directors with potential, but they need to be nurtured. The market could do with some world class production houses." Lim recalls his own experience in China. "I'd been in China two years, not a very long time, but on a recent trip to London, New York and San Francisco I discovered that so much of the world had slipped by me. The movies, the art scenes, the music, the books, the street culture, the advertising, all seem to be of another place and time. All of a sudden, I find that I don't know much about the world anymore." It's hard to measure China's advertising in terms of Western values, he says. You couldn't, for example, tell a vampire joke in a commercial because the government has forbidden horror films to be aired on TV; then there's the bigger argument of what the public's impression of a vampire might be, given the lack of shared information. "But things are changing rapidly. The Internet is spreading like an electronic bushfire across the country. More and more Chinese nationals can afford to travel abroad, and are allowed to do so, and they're even coming back. For once in their 5,000-year history, the Chinese are beginning to take an interest in the rest of the world. I hope to see another poetic and artistic era rise, like the Tang and Ming dynasties of the past, something more in tune to the world this time. There's already a healthy film industry going. Installation art could be a fertile ground for exploration next. Even the just-woken-up hairstyle sported by men all over China may one day become fashionable elsewhere. And why not? Once we can define the true China-Chinese culture, not the Hong Kong-Chinese, Taiwanese-Chinese, Japanese-Chinese, Malaysian-Chinese, Singaporean-Chinese or Western-Chinese culture, the advertising here will naturally take shape. Maybe, too, somebody can start by doing something about the current lot of Chinese typefaces! For our industry, it's just a matter of time before we're picking creatives from a quarter of the world's population. There won't be enough Pencils to go around when the time comes."

INDIA

The world's biggest advertising club is not based in New York or London. The Ad Club, Bombay (now Mumbai) boasts well over three thousand members with a fair share of clients on its board. Consistently, India's top three creative agencies are O&M, Enterprise Nexus led by the legendary Mohammed Khan, and Contract Advertising (J. Walter Thompson). Experts point to an industry in a state of creative flux.

"Most stuff done in India still hasn't been able to break the mould of jingles, collages, happy people, happy families," observes Ravi Deshpande, Contract's executive vice president and national creative director. The agency's creative product is regularly awarded at international shows; Cannes Lions and acceptance into D&AD are recent achievements. "Indian commercials also tend to be very noisy, probably because they are still done keeping in mind the lowest common denominator."

Deshpande likens much of the work to *khichadi*, an Indian rice

A bald-headed man is staring straight at camera. A rueful jazz track plays throughout, spiced with actual sound effects.

Suddenly a coffee mug is slammed down onto the man's head. *Clonk!*

Then someone's feet plonk down onto it.

A fly circles it and lands. Suddenly a rolled newspaper slams down on the fly. *Thwack!*

A bowl of noodles is next. Noodles slop everywhere as someone starts helping themselves.

Then a scalding hot teapot is dumped down.

Male VO: *Just a reminder of what your furniture goes through every day.*

Cut to product. VO concludes: *Touchwood Polish with polyurethane. Protects your furniture from scratches and stains and just about anything...*

Suddenly a mobile circular saw enters frame and gets closer and closer to the man's head...

End logo: *Asian Paints.*

A "tabletop" commercial with a difference. In this single-minded idea, a bald head becomes a metaphor for furniture. Contract Advertising India.

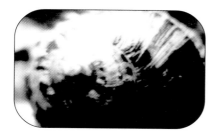

The following images are in black-and-white.

An intriguing shell fills the screen…

Bizarre music begins…

We follow the elegant progress of a snail down a piece of wood.

Even the super takes its own time. It begins: *SHOP at your own…*

Then, after a pause, another word is added…

Super: …*pace.*

End logo and super: *Shoppers' Stop. Feel the experience. While you shop.*

Contract Advertising India demonstrating how you can shop at your own pace.

porridge. "There's a large chunk of work that relies on slapstick, desperately trying to make the audience laugh. Another trap is the tendency to use common stereotypes and clichés like the 'traditional' Indian family to Indianise the communication. In the bargain, they are missing out on the *finer* nuances of Indian life and culture."

What works best in India? "All those techniques like storytelling, rational demonstrations and purely executional work have been followed at some point of time, but there are no guarantees that they will definitely cut across all the complexities of our diverse cultures," Deshpande explains. "What unifies Indians, what touches their soul most, is music. Music is how Indians absorb messages. Music is the thing, thanks to the huge addiction to Indian cinema where no movie is complete without at least five songs. And these songs can be heard everywhere; at roadside food stalls, in barber shops and cabs, on music channels like MTV and [V] and even in elite discos."

Anil Thakraney, publisher of India's advertising trade magazine *The Brief*, agrees. "When David Ogilvy visited India in the late 80s, he insisted on watching all the TV commercials created out of O&M India. Sometime during the screening, he suddenly clutched his ears tightly, exclaiming 'Why do you Indians love to make such noisy commercials?' He was, of course, referring to the fact that every second commercial produced out of India was, and still is, jingle-based." Thakraney says the singsong style of jingle typifies Indian advertising. "We love to do them. Their roots can easily be traced to the rich Hindi film song culture most of us Indians grew up with and adore."

The massive Bombay film industry, better known as Bollywood, is the world's most prolific. Indian movies and music are the drivers of pop culture. However, before Indian commercials can catch up with their international counterparts, Deshpande believes they must become *more idea driven and their portrayal of Indianness needs to be more insightful*. Thanks to the diversity of India's cultures and languages, he says there is a huge bank of nuances to draw upon. Executional standards will need to rise, too. More committed and professional commercials directors are needed. "Currently I can count them on one finger." Deshpande categorises his agency's culture as product-centric and open-minded. There are no rules, he says, but admits that creative people have to be natural planners. "I don't think you can be a good creative person in advertising if you don't have a strong planning mind. You must be strong on creative, strong on strategy, and have a strong creative voice on the top management."

A young man is persuading his girlfriend to learn how to ride his Bajaj Sunny.

One of those typical boy band songs underscores the innocence of it all.

First you say you're always with me,

You say you'll go the whole distance...

Reluctantly she mounts the monster, overcoming her nerves. As she gets more confidence, she ventures further afield.

But at a bend in the road, a handsome hitchhiker is thumbing a lift.

She stops and he climbs on behind her. To her boyfriend's horror, they're off.

End super: *Bajaj Sunny. Easy come. Easy go.*

Boys meets girl, boy loses girl, thanks to Contract Advertising. Like many Asian commercials that have to communicate with multi-lingual audiences, a music track replaces dialogue. Simple visual narratives eliminate language barriers.

DO Indian consumers resist commercials? Over the years, have they become less trusting?

"Anyone who is anyone in India has a very clear opinion on advertisements, even more than cricket," muses Thakraney. "The Indian audience is totally involved and freely criticises and cheers the ads they read or view." Nevertheless, he points to a rising level of cynicism in recent years. "More irate consumers write to the ASCI, India's advertising morality watchdog than ever before, complaining of misleading and untruthful ads. Consumer involvement in the ad world is well and truly reflected in our media. Very often advertising stories are broken more regularly by our morning dailies than the advertising magazine I edit!"

But as the world gets smaller, Indian creatives are more exposed to Western advertising influences. Indians are quick learners, says Deshpande. *Shots, Archive* and award annuals are on every desk. "Unlike the Japanese and Thais, we haven't been able to evolve a style that can be called truly Indian. In Contract's work, we admit to a British influence. As far as the industry is concerned, there is an overall Western influence." Deshpande contends that it is possible to create commercials for the Indian market which work across urban and rural areas, all cultures, and all education levels. "We've done it and we know it works with ideas that are universal and simple. If Spielberg's *Jurassic Park* can cut across the entire globe, if he can appeal to the Americans and the Japanese at the same time, so can we. But it's a huge task, because ideas that are universal and simple are hard to come by, especially before the deadline expires."

Expatriate Indian copywriters have cut a swathe through Asia. They are the writers-of-choice for agencies in Singapore. After bagging enough awards, America is the next stop.

Thakraney shares their optimism. "India is slowly coming into its own in terms of world class standards of advertising. Clients are increasingly waking up to the need for powerful advertising and that's definitely a good sign. Television is the most 'happening' medium at the moment and is likely to be so for many more decades. Technologically and in terms of production values, Indian film makers can match anyone in the West. However we are still evolving in terms of single-mindedness of ideas. I think this millennium will see India roar louder at Cannes. Watch out, the Third World is coming!"

MALAYSIA

Malaysia is a multicultural market of 22 million. Advertising messages are mainly delivered in Malay, Mandarin and English. Long ago, Malaysia banned the import of foreign commercials in favour of a "Made in Malaysia" policy. Thanks to the MIM rule, all work that runs in Malaysia has to be shot in Malaysia.

At Leo Burnett in Kuala Lumpur, Yasmin Ahmad is co-creative director with Ali Mohamed. She believes that television programmes have gone ahead of television commercials. "There are more intelligent dramas and comedies in Malay and Chinese than there are commercials. The commercials are better produced, but the programmes are far more intelligent, funnier, more moving." Yasmin argues that consumers are capable of understanding better work. "Thirteen years ago, they used to say things like the consumer will not understand it, but that isn't true anymore. It hasn't been the case for a long, long time." The fault, she says, does not lie with *orang puteh* (Caucasian) clients. "They are completely trusting of local insights. In fact, they ask if a concept is deep enough."

"The usual criticism is that we do poor imitations of Western advertising," attests S. P. Lee, executive creative director, FCB and chairman of the advertising industry's creative council. "There was probably more uniqueness about the 60s ads. The 80s were terrible. It was a desperate attempt to be modern. We have to become comfortable with ourselves, using the way we talk, the way we dress, the way we smell, to actually sell a product." Lee questions whether there is a distinctly Malaysian advertising voice. "Language is a prison. Once you learn a language you are trapped. A lot of Asians in advertising are in a bit of a dilemma. It's not an unhappy dilemma, but it's an interesting one. I'm not sure we know who we are. We're Asians, but we're very universal. We know more about the West than we know about ourselves. I've never read a single Chinese book in my life because I can't read Chinese. And I've read maybe five Malay books. So all the software, all the information in my head, comes

We are listening to one of the most dramatic moments from opera — the aria *One Fine Day* from *Madame Butterfly*. The music continues throughout. There is no VO.

A VU meter is registering the level of the music. The needle moves in response to each note.

As the aria swells to its tragic climax, the needle enters the red level and blood begins to trickle from it.

Super: *Pure drama in your living room.*

End super: *Opus Channel 303. The World's Greatest Operas.*

Opus Channel 303 is one of thirteen radio and twenty-eight TV stations available on ASTRO, Malaysia's satellite home entertainment system. At Dentsu Young & Rubicam Kuala Lumpur, writer-art director Cary Rueda employed a single-minded visual idea to demonstrate that grand opera is anything but boring. The commercial won Gold at the International Broadcasting Awards, Hollywood.

from the West, but I live in an Asian environment. We're constantly challenged by local culture, so our sensibilities I guess are confused. You see that sometimes when you take what you think is a really great and funny ad and present it to a client who is very Malay or very Chinese or very Indian and his background is different. I can't say, oh, he is stupid. But how do you explain understatements to him?" Thailand, Lee affirms, is an easier market to understand. "You can go in there for three days, you can figure what's going on. They're homogeneous, they're all Buddhist, they all speak the same language, they all love the King, they are lovely people, and I think you can slip into their skin much faster than you can do here. I love its diversity, but I find my own country the hardest to understand."

Ted Lim, creative director of Naga DDB Kuala Lumpur, reviews local work. "If you switch on the television at any point of time, you'll find a lot of stuff that is, at best, mundane, photo-executional. Simple ideas seem to have been lost. Good ideas are over-executed. We're far behind London or the United States." Lim's print work has appeared in the One Show, London International and other award shows. Television remains the challenge. Yet if Malaysian audiences watch the same movies as the West watches, surely commercials could become more sophisticated? "That's a very strong argument for better, more intelligent commercials. Unfortunately it is an argument that isn't heeded. Clients think audiences are morons who can't understand a monosyllabic word so you have to speak slowly and bulldoze them with images." Local authorities, says Lim, have a code called VHSC — violence, horror, sex and counter-culture. "Anything that has a hint of violence or horror or sex or anything that is contrary to our culture, would be automatically rejected. We would love to do something like the Diesel jeans *Showdown* ad where the fat, bad guy kills the slim, wholesome hero. The bad guy wakes up with an ugly woman next to him. He digs his nose, he kicks a dog on the way out, he spits, he kills the hero, and he laughs and lives at the end. He does everything that is politically incorrect; he breaks every rule in the Malaysian advertising book. There's no way you could get even a *tenth* of that commercial to run here." Rules also prohibit showing armpits. In deodorant ads, the product is sprayed into sleeves.

The commercial presents a powerful study of contrasts.

An engaging little boy stands outside his peaceful Malaysian home and tries to tell us why he likes it.

As he chatters on about his mum's cooking and his nice bed, we see harrowing scenes of war, disaster and children dying of starvation…all the things that little boys in Malaysia don't have to worry about.

End super: *Happy National Day.*

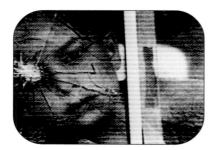

The national Malaysian oil company Petronas raising national consciousness. The familiar security of home life is contrasted with the world's most horrific events.
Leo Burnett Kuala Lumpur.

At Bozell Worldwide, creative director Dharma Somasundram says the commercials that work best are the ones that make you laugh or cry. "Also, big budget commercials whether idea or non-idea driven. Malaysia is largely semi-rural and rural, and the 'wow' factor cannot be discounted as would happen in a more cynical cosmopolitan market."

EXECUTIONALLY-driven work dominates.

"When you fail to sell a good idea, you create a bimbo," observes Lee. "If it's not smart, at least it looks good."

"We've seen in the fashion world where the execution *is* the idea," challenges Yasmin. "I don't think that's such a bad thing. Who knows what an idea is anyway?"

Kamal Mustafa of Cinequip Kuala Lumpur, is famed as a "people" director and storyteller. "Stories can be beautiful, moving, or funny, but most clients and agencies want 'look-good-feel-good' stories that don't rock the boat. Frankly, I hate formal slickness in art, literature, photography, and especially so in advertising. Most times, slickness becomes an end in itself. Things in life are never slick. I like people. I'd like to think that I am a keen observer of their idiosyncrasies, the way they pick their teeth after a meal, or the way they clear their throats and spit when no one is looking." Kamal believes a lot of work in Malaysia and Singapore is executionally driven. "We don't have the courage to look into ourselves to say that the idea is good as it is. We look at reels from London and New York, and imagine our work to be included on them. But the minute we look inwards, we lose our bearings. I think the problem is not just in commercials. It's in the whole machinery of the advertising industry. In the minds of many agency and film people that I've worked with, *execution is a measure of competence.*"

"All visual acuity is a matter of exposure, of educating the eye," affirms Paul Loosley of Axis Films. "Malaysian audiences are a lot more sophisticated than people give them credit for. People are getting exposed to the same things as the West. People are learning to decipher the clues, even the subtle ones. People are reading more into it than was ever intended. I've always believed advertising and film are about reward." Loosley believes the advertisers themselves have yet to catch up with their audience. "They think it's best to be

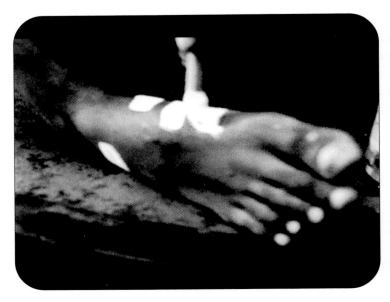

Director Paul Loosley draws a connection between bandage strips and Adidas stripes as he unfolds the story of Village Boys *aspiring to be famous footballers. Agency: BBDO Kuala Kumpur.*

obvious. As Ronnie Kirkwood said, you have a responsibility to take a risk. If you don't take a risk, then you're talking down to them and you never advance anything." Loosley, with a 20-year track record in the market, concedes that in some parts of Malaysia, people live very simple, rustic lives. In contrast, the capital city Kuala Lumpur is sophisticated. "In terms of ideas, the advertisers mostly end up compromising. You end up with a poor average. But even in the UK and the US, there are only a few gems; the rest is mainly rubbish. There are real peaks and real troughs. That's what we don't get enough of here — real peaks and real troughs. It's all a very comfortable and acceptable level." A former agency creative director, Loosley still looks for strong central ideas in scripts. He wishes that copywriters would take more time to craft them better. "People are borrowing from bunches of unoriginal images. But that happens everywhere." His advice: "Don't go anywhere near storyboards, animatics or ripamatics until you can stand in front of a client and present the idea off a piece of paper."

But is it relevant to compare Malaysian work with Western

commercials? For instance, would a great Malaysian commercial be great because it looked "international", or because it worked in its own local context, or *both*?

"Malaysians should not be embarrassed about looking to America for film making techniques," considers Yasmin, "because America got its film making techniques from Germany, and Germany got its from Russia. Film making belongs to the world. I've always admired John Ford. He knew America, he talked to America and by doing that, he talked to the world. I've always admired John Webster's work. The film making in Webster's commercials is not uniquely British; it is international and simple, but the content is peculiarly British. *The deeper you go into local insights the more universal your appeal will be, but if you try to be universal, you'll end up not turning anyone on.*" Like many other creatives, Yasmin says she feeds off what is going on around her. "I take my stories from the streets, not from the ether. I feed on people's idiosyncrasies. I look for stories. Stories have words, stories have pictures, they have it all." And you won't find them in advertising watering holes, she adds.

PERHAPS humour offers the best option for the future?

"Clients feel insecure," argues Lim. "If people laugh at the commercial, they must be laughing at the product or service, too. Which, of course, isn't true. People in the West are more relaxed; they have no hang-ups, or fewer hang-ups, about buying humour. Very few people are secure enough here to have a good laugh. Laughter suggests weakness. However, there are little, interesting ideas starting to get across. It's going to be a slow and painful process before we can even hope to catch up with Thailand. But if everyone continues to try, more and more clients can see that humour sells and that you *can* afford to laugh at yourself."

"All these hurdles are put there by product managers," says Lee. "What gives a 29-year-old product manager a better idea of how people react? You present a board to ten people, they laugh and say *we* get it, but the guys out there won't. Why *can't* Malaysians understand a 30-second spot? They aren't stupid. Humour here is heavy-handed, slapstick and in your face. However, Mr. Bean is very popular. It's British, but it's also Malaysian."

We are looking at some kids talking and having fun among themselves.

Suddenly, they are interrupted by the VO: *All those who believe beauty pageants are immoral, please stand up...*

The kids react with shock. We understand why when the camera pulls back and reveals they are all seated in wheelchairs.

End graphics inform us: *The Miss Malaysia/World Pageant has helped raise over two million* ringgit *for handicapped children.*

With your support, more children can benefit from this event.

Unless, of course, you think it's immoral.

Miss Malaysia/World Pageant. Beauty with a purpose.

Naga DDB Malaysia communicates that beauty has a purpose. Creative director Ted Lim says the strategy was to show the unfortunate children who would lose out if the public refused to support the beauty pageant.

Humour, Kamal argues, is always the best platform, but there are problems. "In Malaysia, we cannot offend people, so we try to look for humour in characters, situations and simple one-liners. The kind of humour we find safe and acceptable is very character or situation driven that cuts across all racial groups. As much as I enjoy the subtexts in a Traktor spot, I have to be careful about my attitude when I am shooting here; you will be told that iconoclasm, individualism, etcetera, are Western concepts alien to Asian values." The situation is different in Thailand or the Philippines, he says. "The Thais and Filipinos, in contrast, are very liberal in this respect. They can laugh and take no offence. As a nation, we are very sensitive. This, I think, is the biggest stumbling block towards the development of a particular Malaysian humour."

Language is another, says Loosley. Scripts have to be funny in English, Malay and Chinese. Dialogue commercials have to be overdubbed, usually unconvincingly. By law, all supers have to be in Malay. As a result, irony — the staple of many Western commercials — is an alien form of humour rendered even more difficult when it can only be done in pantomime. "Maybe that's why there's been a victory of form over content," Loosley concludes. "People have historically said it in pictures. A picture is worth a thousand words."

The talent pool is also limited.

"In nine out of ten commercials, I'll be working with amateur, off-the-street talent; housewives, clerks, security guards, college students, guest relations officers," explains Kamal. "I try to get underneath all the amateurism and self-consciousness and slowly coax characters out of them and pray that when the camera rolls, they will remain consistent and sustain the mood." Some clients, he says, inevitably want an "aspirational" look.

Loosley uses a code with his camera operator. "I call 'Cut', but he keeps the camera rolling. When they all start relaxing and become normal people again, we get what we want."

ACCORDING to Lim, the Malaysian market is less cynical, less developed, more trusting. "DDB did some global research that showed in the West, direct mail is junk mail. In Asia, every piece of junk mail gets read to see if there's a discount, if there's a promotion on. The mentality is different."

Lee agrees Malaysians aren't cynical about advertising. "A lot of it isn't good enough to even be noticed. The average Malaysian can name you seventy-three great spots for lunch. But you'd be lucky if he can name you one good spot on telly." Lee believes there are only ten great ideas in the world. "What I'm always looking for is the eleventh idea. It's the British Airways ad in the cinema where someone got up and talked to the people on the screen; it was a new medium. It's putting messages on the floor about landmines that stick to your feet when you walk on them."

"Malaysian audiences can appreciate very modern film language," Kamal points out. "But to most Malaysians, film is André Bazin's *Truth 24 Times a Second*. They don't want to do any more thinking over a film, much less a commercial. An ad is an ad. It occupies an even lower position in the hierarchy of things creative."

Yasmin points to the emergence of consumer associations. "They've been quite fierce. A few years ago, they wrote something nasty in the papers about a particular advertisement and some consumers replied and said there was nothing wrong with it." She believes people are much too busy to bother with complaining about commercials. "You'd have to have a lot of leisure time to sit down and write letters about commercials, don't you think?"

Somasundram talks about new media. "Delivery channels are exploding. Creative ideas formerly and perfunctorily developed for TV, radio and print will now have to extend themselves to other channels, working as a totally integrated communication."

LOOKING further ahead, the publisher of Malaysia's advertising trade magazine *ADOI*, Harmandar Singh, calls for an end to the industry's "fortress mentality". He predicts that Malaysia will drop its MIM policy within the next three years. "We have been a 'closed' market for too long to allow any quantum leap in creativity. Without doubt, the MIM policy has developed the local film and audio industry, but I believe it has also become a ready excuse for shoddy work. There's too much style and little substance. Cloaking one's thinking with a protected frame of mind breeds lethargy. We need to open our minds and borders to compete, instead of looking inwards."

But can great ads be made in Malaysia, despite all the restrictions and problems?

"They're just an excuse," states Loosley. Virtually all the latest technology is available, he says. And as for the rules: "The rules are rules. If you play soccer, you can't pick up the ball and run down the field with it; it's against the rules." Rules can frustrate you, he says. But they can also inspire brilliant solutions. Hitchcock, for example. "Remember his movie *Notorious*? The American censors, called the Hays Office at the time, wouldn't allow a single kiss to be longer than so-many seconds. So in their love scene, Cary Grant and Ingrid Bergman just started giving each other lots of short kisses, small, half-second kisses." Another cinematic masterpiece inspired by adversity: "When Orson Welles was making *Othello*, he ran out of money and the costume suppliers cabled him from Rome to say no money, no costumes. So he set the whole conspiracy scene in a Turkish bath. It was so mysterious with the swirling steam, it was magical, much better than if he'd had the costumes!"

Lee sums it up. "Advertising problems are universal. The issues are different, the fears are the same."

THAILAND

"Thai advertising is like *tom yam goong*," says Bhanu Inkawat, the legendary chairman and executive creative director of Leo Burnett Thailand. The analogy with his country's famous fiery soup is appropriate. "It's full of flavour. It's not just in our advertising; it's in everything we do. We're never really one way or another. To enjoy *tom yam goong*, it has to be salty as well as sour as well as hot. That's our life, we like everything to be rounded, so to talk about things too seriously might be boring for the Thai consumer. So we try to put all the flavours into our work as well as make sure the message gets across."

After Japan, Thailand's television work is Asia's most distinctive and internationally recognised. Both Leo Burnett's TelecomASIA and O&M's Counterpain commercials won Silver Lions at Cannes. Results Advertising's Black Cat Whisky scored a Bronze.

"Japanese commercials are very Zen," Inkawat considers. "The closest in spirit to Thai advertising are the French, maybe. French

It is late at night in an almost deserted airport lounge. An unassuming business traveller with glasses and a rather unfashionable haircut is hunched over a public phone having an animated conversation. He is performing odd gestures and pulling strange faces.

Man: ...*And the witch flew through the window, landing in the princess's bedroom. The princess was terrified. She yelled out for help. "Help me, help me!" And before she knew what was happening, the sky was illuminated with brilliant sparkling stardust. In a flash the fairy godmother appeared, waving her magic wand. The wicked witch cried out in agony, "Aahhhhh", and the handsome prince came galloping along and swept the princess away...*

VO: *TelecomASIA believes that one picture can say more than a million words.*

Only then do we realise that the man has been using a video phone to tell his daughter a bedtime story. We can see her on the screen, sleeping soundly.

TelecomASIA demonstrates what the future will mean to Asians, employing emotional appeals that would work universally. Leo Burnett Thailand.

commercials in a way are unpredictable, whereas English work is always very disciplined copywriting. But our work is a little bit unpredictable because we are still young; we're still learning and finding our way. We're still fresh because nobody knows what we have to do next."

Inkawat credits the rise of Thai creativity to an Australian. "Barry Owen is the guru of Thai advertising. He is an Australian but yet he saw Thai advertising in a totally different way." Owen is the long-time creative director of Ogilvy & Mather Thailand. Inkawat believes Owen's work opened up a lot of things in Thai advertising and inspired an entire generation of Thai creatives. "People started to look at advertising as an art form, rather than just a tool to sell products. My generation came back from studying abroad and we looked at advertising from America and England and Japan. We started to see different characteristics from these countries and we started to ask, *what is Thai?* What would make Thai consumers enjoy watching advertising? And that's when the new era of advertising started in Thailand, in the early 80s." According to one theory, Thai advertising is unique because Thailand itself has always been independent. While Malaysia, Singapore and India were once controlled by Britain, the Thais and Japanese preserved their own language and culture intact. "We had no knowledge of how to do great advertising," Inkawat explains. "So, at that time, we followed what American advertising was doing. We tried to learn from the way that they produced advertising. We formed a Bangkok Art Directors Club so we could meet each other often and define what was Thai."

Inkawat, who originally graduated as a graphic designer, became the first Thai creative director at Leo Burnett. "Burnett's philosophy is similar to Thai. They're not 'New York'; they're not very flashy. Burnett is very human, and that to me is similar to the Thai way of thinking. Thai people are very human and down-to-earth. We're not very posh and modern and high tech. The way that Leo Burnett thought, the way he used to dig deeper for human insights, is similar to the way we like to work."

That said, when Mr. Burnett extolled the virtues of inventing characters like *Snap, Crackle & Pop* and *The Jolly Green Giant*, he never dreamed that one day his agency in Thailand would invent a

A hand covers the lens. A bizarre, high-pitched voice asks: *Guess who?*

The hand is removed. We are in a car with "Lead", which is symbolised by a band of silver-painted transvestites. Outside, we see other cars inflicted with them, too.

Male VO: *You cannot avoid the Lead Devil if you still use leaded gasoline.*

A Lead Devil asks: *Why doesn't he switch to unleaded then?*

The other Lead Devils slap him around. Suddenly, the car pulls into a PTT station and fills up with Super 97.

Male VO: *PTT Super 97 substitutes lead with two additives — super protection and super power for your car's maximum performance.*

When the car drives off, the Lead Devils are battling to hang on. An operatic aria plays as they are flung from the car, one by one.

Eventually only one survives, sitting coyly next to the driver. They exchange a final glance before the last Devil goes sailing through the air.

VO and end super: *Super 97 PTT.*

Leo Burnett Thailand gave leaded petrol a human form. The Lead Devils *were the unwelcome travelling companions of every motorist who didn't switch to PTT's unleaded Super 97. By using Thai humour, client Petroleum Authority of Thailand cleverly underscored its local origins vis-à-vis foreign oil brands.*

440

car full of silver-clad transvestites called the *Lead Devils*. "PTT, the Petroleum Authority of Thailand, has been our client for a long time," recounts Inkawat. "Their brand essence is about being Thai, the brand that is very close to Thai people compared to Shell and Esso. When they briefed us that they would be first to get rid of lead in their petrol, we wanted to make the brand become even more important for Thai people. We learned about how people are really fed up with pollution, especially in a city like Bangkok. So we thought of a way to show them how we've been living our lives with these pollutants all around us, and how it's very difficult for us to get rid of them, how they hang on to you. That's why we visualised lead pollutants as a person, as a being." The commercial is outrageous. The silver transvestites cling to the driver and his car, but thanks to a tank of new unleaded gas, he's rid of them.

Inkawat believes that the concept idea is always in the brief somewhere, usually in the information that comes with the brief. He traces how a National Energy Policy Office commercial evolved. "The brief was not to waste energy. At that time, before the economic crisis, Thailand was booming. Nobody cared about saving energy. *The more energy you wasted, the more you told people how rich you were.* So we had to come up with a story that reflected how that thinking was wrong. In the brief it said that if you waste half a plate of rice, it's just five *baht*. What people didn't realise was how much energy has been wasted along the way; getting the rice from the paddy field, transporting it to the mill, then bringing it from there to the city, then cooking it in the restaurant. So that was news I learned from the brief, and I remembered how our grandparents had taught us to be sensible. So I thought, why don't we show this businessman wasting food in a restaurant to show off how rich he is, then suddenly his old mother is there to tell him off and make him remember what she told him when he was young." Inkawat ensures that clients share the agency's strategy before scripts are presented. "Get them to understand your thinking, your direction. They must buy into the idea first. Once I thought I should present very polished work, but now I involve them early instead. Reading the script is much better than showing a storyboard."

Sharing an idea with colleagues helps make it grow, says Inkawat,

Our camera is locked off on a suburban house. A little old lady hurries inside from a taxi. Her voice is heard throughout as she moves from one room of the house to the next.

Angry woman's voice: *What is this? It's broad daylight and nobody has the brains to turn lights off. I've told you a thousand times and I'll tell you again and again, turn them off! And who are we entertaining here? The ghost? Air conditioner is on, TV is on, and not a soul in sight. What are they thinking? Please tell me. And my gosh, now I know why Bangkok is flooded... because my son has left the water running.*

As she sweeps water from the balcony, she is startled to hear her son's voice. We pan to the identical house next door from which her son frantically calls.

Son: *Ma, what are you doing over there?*

End VO: *Forget anything, but always remember to help Thailand save energy.*

An old lady shouts some spicy abuse at her family for wasting energy. The problem is, she went into the wrong house. Leo Burnett Thailand for the National Energy Policy Office.

A rich businessman has left his fish untouched in a restaurant. He calls for the bill.

Waiter: *Would you like to take the fish home?*

Businessman: *Poor fish. Why don't you put it back in the river?*

The businessman roars with laughter at his own joke. His colleagues all join in. Suddenly he freezes. His old mother is calling his name.

Businessman: *Mama, what are you doing here?*

Mother: *You promised to be a good boy. Why are you wasting your food? Don't you remember the rhyme I taught you?*

Businessman: (Thoroughly shamed...) *Jack and Jill set out to sea, To bring me fishes for my tea; They used up fuel, they used up ice, and cooked with gas to make it nice; They even have to work by night and use up the electric light; Just think of all the energy, I mustn't waste a single bite...*

End VO and super: *Wasting food wastes energy. Think before you order.*

Once, the amount of food you wasted indicated your wealth — until Leo Burnett Thailand made it unfashionable. Client: National Energy Policy Office.

A weight lifting competition is reaching its climax. One of the contestants has just finished his lift and looks to the judges for their verdict. They are trying to press their buttons and record their votes, but nothing seems to be happening.

The strain of holding the weights aloft is beginning to show.

Judge: *Technical problem. Just a moment, please.*

Now he is really sweating. His whole body is in agony. But he can't let go of the weights until the vote has been recorded.

Meanwhile, the system is still down. A judge gives him a sad, what-to-do shrug.

Dissolve to Counterpain product shot and tagline.

You don't have to copy the West to make the world laugh. The Counterpain Weightlifter *commercial is a typically Thai bitter-sweet observation of life that appeals universally. Creative director: Barry Owen, Ogilvy & Mather Thailand.*

but in the end you still have to sit alone, filter all the comments and come up with the actual script yourself. "Advertising is not like a feature film. You don't see it once; you see it a hundred times so you get bored pretty easily. Funny commercials that have a punchline at the end always work once or twice, *but that's all*. A commercial should have a lot of magic along the way, so you see more and more things as you see it again and again. With our commercials we try to treat them like a storyline, so as you follow the story there's a joke here, another joke there, there's something you like and something you learn, there's maybe a reaction by one of the talent. TV has to draw attention, but in an involving way so people stay on to find out how the story develops; there should be enough magic in it to draw them to the end. Our Thai directors understand what advertising is all about. They're not just directors from a production point of view. They know how to enhance the idea, not just add things for the craft's sake." A lot happens on the set, says Inkawat. Unlike the US or the UK, there is no professional talent pool. Casting happens off the street, by luck.

Looking at the region, Inkawat says Asian advertising lacks great enduring campaigns. "Asian advertising is a great one-off idea here, a great one-off idea there. We should be building brands with long-term enduring ideas. It doesn't mean you have to keep doing the same thing; that's boring. But you should grow your idea from one commercial to another so at the end, when you step back, it is all one brand, one essence, one continuing format."

BRAVE NEW WORLD?

"In a slightly smug and paternalistic way, the established advertising nations like to kid themselves that advertising crosses borders simply because we see the developing world copying the formulae we invented and feel comfortable with." Paul Fishlock is one of the world's most celebrated copywriters included in the D&AD *Copy Book*. He is a partner in the Sydney agency, Brown Melhuish Fishlock.

"For a brief period in the 80s," he reflects, "Australia produced ads that were proudly Australian — brash, confident, and rarely to the tastes of the creative elite, but beyond doubt the product of a country that really believed in its own identity. Many Australian agencies today seem unhealthily hung up on doing work they think will impress people in the UK or the States. Not only does this introduce an agenda to creating advertising that is contrary to the one you're being paid to do, it invariably fails to produce even half-decent work; just poor copies of what got up at the One Show or D&AD last year or the year before."

Fishlock believes international awards have perpetuated a certain type of advertising. "The international shows have a lot to answer for in terms of stifling a regional identity for advertising that the rest of the world may not and *should not* always understand. Whilst the international shows occasionally unearth a wonderful unchanging human truth that knows no borders, they also *encourage and reward global ubiquity*, potentially at the expense of genuine insights in the local market. A certain type of ad always does well at Cannes and much as I enjoy it, I don't believe it's the benchmark every campaign everywhere in the world should try to emulate. How much more interesting would world advertising be if a country new to commercial television started with a blank canvas rather than a box of old CDP reels!"

10

CREATIVITY PROVED

I s there a connection between effectiveness and creativity? James Best has seen the evidence.

"If you correlate the winning papers in the IPA Effectiveness Awards with the winners of British creative awards such as D&AD, you will find a much *higher* correlation than you would expect."

The IPA Effectiveness Awards are judged purely on the merits of the job done, says Best. Did the work achieve its commercial objectives? Did the campaign ultimately make money for the client?

Britain's collective advertising agency body, the Institute of Practitioners in Advertising, conducts the awards every two years, Best reports.

"Long papers are submitted, much more detailed and deeper than the Effies™ in the States, for instance, with a lot of statistical backup. We use a lot of econometric modelling to prove the cases. They are judged by panels of clients after various academics and researchers have pored over them, short-listed them, and tested them, and they're published in extremely heavy, dense books which send you to sleep but contain a lot of wisdom."

Do Creative Ads Sell?

"Just because a commercial wins awards doesn't make it more likely to sell; in fact, award-winning commercials are less likely to sell, and most probably won't sell anything at all." Donald Gunn had heard it all before.

After four years of research and four hundred case histories, he concluded in 1996 that award-winning commercials are *over two-and-a-half times more likely to sell* than those that aren't creative.

Gunn proved that 346 (86.5%) of the 400 most awarded commercials in the world in 1992, 1993, 1994 and 1995 had worked in the marketplace.

Gunn's research began in 1993, when he was Leo Burnett's Chicago-based worldwide director of creative resources. Persuaded by the Cannes advertising festival president to do a seminar the following year, Gunn chose to "nail the myth" that creative ads are just done for creative people. He wanted to challenge the widely held belief that stuff that works never wins awards, and vice versa. "Leo believed advertising should sell goods in the short term *and* build the advertiser's reputation for the long haul. And the way to do that was to create advertising that was so fresh, so engaging, so interruptive, so intelligent, so human, so believable, so well-focused as to themes and ideas that it delivered on *both* these goals. Leo told us those qualities led to success." Gunn concedes that he had expected a 70% success rate. But what if he had proved that award-winning commercials *didn't* sell? "I knew in my heart that that wouldn't happen. If it had, then we'd have had to close down the agency because we had totally the wrong philosophy and beliefs."

Gunn proved that creativity works on two occasions.

1992–1993. His first survey investigated the two hundred most awarded commercials in the world from 1992 to 1993. The universe comprised forty-five award shows in total, including international competitions of the calibre of Cannes and D&AD, and respected national shows such as the British Television Advertising Awards.

The survey showed that 86% achieved a significant result for the brand, succeeding against pre-determined objectives,

while 14% had failed to arrest the brand's decline or increase its market share.

Addressing the sceptics, Gunn said that of the 172 successful commercials, 117 case histories were backed by hard data showing sales results; the others were substantiated by reputable tracking studies on attitudinal or image-related goals. "Virtually everyone used independently audited figures to make their cases." Gunn's methodology was straightforward enough. He called the chief executives and executive creative directors of the 103 agencies involved and the clients they represented to secure their co-operation. They were asked to complete questionnaires stating the original objectives, whether they had been achieved, and if not, why not. Only one agency declined to take part. "Several UK agencies even supplied us with their IPA Effectiveness papers, while shops like Goodby, Silverstein & Partners submitted their Effie™ files."

Included in the case histories was Howell Henry Chaldecott Lury's first Orange Tango commercial. The big orange man pushed up sales by 26%. Brand awareness rose from 42% to 72%. Agreement that there was "no mistaking the orangey taste of Tango" increased by 65%. Agreement that the advertising was good went up by 450%. Another impressive case study: Bartle Bogle Hegarty's award-winning work for Levi's saw European sales jump by 27% in 1992 and a further 29% in 1993.

Gunn's parameters were tough: a commercial was deemed to have failed if it had merely held market share rather than increased it. Of the twenty-eight failures, three were Best of Show winners. Gunn estimates that at least three of the other winners had been made as "award show entries" and therefore had no real sales objectives in the first place. Two other winners were not actually commercials in the traditional sense: one was a segment from a TV show and the other was a non-broadcast event opener.

1994–1995. In 1996, Leo Burnett and 120 other agencies evaluated the two hundred most highly awarded commercials of 1994 and 1995 from a mix of international, regional and local shows. The two hundred winners were the work of 129 different agencies in twenty-six different countries. The US led with forty-eight winners; Britain was second with thirty-seven.

**Of the world's most awarded commercials, 174 (87%) had
been successful; 26 had failed in the marketplace.**

Of the 174 successful cases, 119 had worked against hard data
objectives such as specified increases in sales value, sales volume or
market share. In each case, these objectives had been either
achieved or surpassed. The other 55 cases were successful against
attitudinal, awareness or image-related goals.

The case histories included some of the world's most famous
commercials. The Campaign Palace's work for the Australian Meat &
Livestock Corporation had increased beef consumption for the first
time since 1988, reversing the trend away from red meat in western
societies; the value of increased sales totalled US$196 million from a
media investment of US$4 million. Diesel jeans, whose highly
controversial ads were created in Sweden, tripled sales in the first
four years of the campaign, 1991–1994; 1995 sales were up 43% over
1994, with the brand extending to 54 markets and the campaign
running in most of them. Tag Heuer's campaign broke in 1995 and
won many awards; turnover in Europe was up 14.5% for the year to
February 1996, versus a 4.4% decline in the global watch industry's
turnover. And the New York State Lotto saw 1995–1996 sales up by
28.5%; awareness of the tagline *Hey, you never know* hit an all-time
high, as did profits to the State Lottery Education Fund: US$1.26
billion.

**More than fifty campaigns — 25% of the total — had
actually *over*achieved.**

AS Gunn admits, the studies were not 100% scientific; he doubts if
any study into the subject could ever be 100% scientific, given the
difficulty of breaking out the effect of advertising from other
elements in the mix. However, he believes that the hard data and
independently audited results, as well as the numerical depth of the
study involving four hundred commercials, make the conclusions
compelling.

The Leo Burnett Great Commercials Library is another Gunn
invention. Over 5,700 commercials are exclusively available to every
Burnett office in the world from a secure website. "Over 2,000
commercials a year are chosen internationally in Cannes or Clio, in
regional shows or in their own countries, as being great," explains

Gunn. "But only 300 of each year's crop of award winners will get into the library." The selection includes fresh new work as well as what Gunn calls "a classic story like lots of others that have been done before, but it's just a great new one." The GCL is classified under 23 product groups and 260 product sub-categories, and cross-referenced under 35 basic selling ideas, 41 dramatic formats, 42 different advertising features and 29 production features as well as by brand, agency, production company, region, market and length. "The best commercials ever made can be called up for any of these criteria, or any combination thereof," says Gunn. It allows such precise search options as "Car commercials from Australia with a selling idea of safety featuring a dog". Each commercial comes complete with a photopage: five key frames in colour, a 100-word description and a transcript of voice-over, dialogue and sound effects.

Retired from Burnetts, Gunn served as president of the Cannes festivals in 1998 and 1999. His current project is compiling the annual *Gunn Report*, which tabulates the most highly awarded agencies, agency networks, advertisers, brands, commercials directors, production companies and countries of the world as well as the one hundred most awarded commercials, print ads and campaigns of the year. Launched in 1999, the *Gunn Report* became an instant global brand in its own right for the advertising industry. Several of the biggest agency networks already use it as a yardstick for setting annual goals and even as a factor affecting performance bonuses.

Scottish-born Dunn started as a print and TV copywriter in the UK and worked in South Africa where he twice won local Grand Prix awards. Not surprisingly, Gunn says he has the radar to know what will win an award. He did the Cannes predictions reel, which was shared with the press, from 1989 to 1998 and tipped the Grand Prix winner eight years out of ten.

ADVERTISING: AN EXCHANGE OF ATTENTION FOR A REWARD

The fundamental truth of how television advertising has worked remains the same. There has to be some transaction. And in the harsh light of the coming new media, Andy Berlin believes the entertainment value of advertising will become more and more germane. "Advertising is a combination of entertainment and information transfer. So often the entertainment value was pooh-poohed by the anti-creative people. Today, without it, where would we be? There's a machine now that puts PC technology and hard drives together with a zapper. You can now pause a 'live' television programme so that you can eat dinner, or make love, or go to the bathroom. You can fast forward thirty seconds and skip the commercial. Unless that commercial is so good that people want to watch it, *it simply won't be watched*. Advertising that is interesting and engaging and fun and valuable will always have a place."

If that is the kind of advertising that you wish to create or approve, then this book has been worthwhile. No matter who you are, you only work for one person. Yourself. And the cutting edge is within you.

APPENDIX

ADVERTISING'S ALL TIME FAVOURITE MOVIES

Alien   *Mike Gibbs, Tracy Wong*
American Beauty   *Arthur Bijur,*
 David Denneen
Animal House   *Michael Lynch*
Apocalypse Now   *Graham Fink, Steve Henry,*
 Bhanu Inkawat, Jim Riswold
The Bad News Bears   *Stacy Wall*
Battleship Potemkin   *Andy Bridge*
Ben Hur   *Nigel Dawson*
The Big Chill   *Scott Whybin*
Blue Velvet   *Tim Delaney*
Bob le Flambeur   *Mark Sitley*
Breaking the Waves   *Sue Carey*
Bringing up Baby   *Richard Butterworth*
Caddyshack   *Scott Vincent*
Casablanca   *Ted Lim, Antony Redman,*
 Peter Soh
The Castle   *David Blackley*
Un Chien Andalou   *Linus Karlsson*
Chinatown   *Kamal Mustafa*
Cinema Paradiso   *Ted Horton, Ian Macdonald,*
 Hugh Mackay
Citizen Kane   *Jeff Goodby, Paul Loosley*
The City of Lost Children   *Jonathan Teo*
Conan the Barbarian   *Andy Berlin*
The Conformist   *Bill Oberlander*

Delicatessen   *Rick Dublin*
Dr. Strangelove   *Hal Curtis*
Doctor Zhivago   *Rowan Dean*
Les Enfants du Paradis   *Terry Bunton*
The English Patient   *Ravi Deshpande, Eddie Wong*
The Enigma of Kaspar Hauser   *Michael Newman*
Fatal Attraction   *Francis Wee*
The Game   *Siimon Reynolds*
The Godfather Part 1   *Warren Berger, Mike Cozens, Donald Gunn,*
   Steve Orent, Paul Tan
The Gold Rush   *Michael Patti*
Goldfinger   *Les Gock*
The Graduate   *Michael Prieve, Naresh Ramchandani*
La Grande Bouffe   *Rod Pullen*
La Haine   *Jeff Darling*
Happiness   *Kirk Souder*
A Hard Day's Night   *David Lubars*
Harold and Maude   *Ron Mather*
I'm All Right Jack   *Adrian Holmes*
The Iron Monkey   *David Droga*
It's a Wonderful Life   *Kes Gray*
Justice at Nuremburg   *Dharma Somasundram*
Kuchh Kuchh Hota Hai   *Anil Thakraney*
The Lady Eve   *Frank Todaro*
The Letter   *John Kingsmill*
Life and Nothing But   *Gee Thomson*
Life Is Beautiful   *S. P. Lee*
Love Letter   *Yasmin Ahmad*
El Mariachi   *Chuck McBride*
Mon Oncle   *Neil French*
Monty Python and the Holy Grail   *Bruce Bildsten*
The Night of the Hunter   *David Perry*
On the Waterfront   *Paul Fishlock, Bob Giraldi*
One Flew Over the Cuckoo's Nest   *Nick Cohen, Lee Garfinkel,*
   Steve Gray, John Hegarty, Lionel Hunt, Ray Lawrence,
   Chris O'Shea
Planet of the Apes   *Sean Cummins*

Powder   *Ian Batey*
The Producers   *Mike Fromowitz, Professor John Philip Jones*
Pulp Fiction   *Indra Sinha*
Raging Bull   *Ron Lawner*
Rashomon   *Roy Grace*
The Red Balloon   *David Holmes*
Rumble Fish   *Kash Sree*
Salò   *Daniel Lim*
Scent of a Woman   *Jack Vaughan*
Schindler's List   *Harvey Marco*
Secrets and Lies   *Dion Hughes*
Seven Samurai   *Andrew Bell, John Webster*
The Silence of the Lambs   *Cheryl Chong*
The Sting   *James Best*
Taxi Driver   *Warren Brown*
Top Gun   *Jan van Meel*
Trading Places   *Rob Gibralter*
Trainspotting   *Paul Malmström*
Tu Vas Bien   *Matt McGrath*
Twelve Angry Men   *Neil Godfrey, Jon Steel*
2001: A Space Odyssey   *Marcello Serpa*
Unforgiven   *Harmandar Singh*
The Wages of Fear   *Anthony Simonds-Gooding*
The Wizard of Oz   *Peter Carter, Ken Schuldman*

BIBLIOGRAPHY

Jones, John Philip. *When Ads Work: New Proof that Advertising Triggers Sales*. Lexington Books, 1992.

Jones, John Philip. *How Advertising Works: The Role of Research*. Sage Publications, 1998.

Jones, Professor John Philip. *What's in a Name? Advertising and the Concept of Brands*. Lexington Books, 1986. Special Indian edition, Tata McGraw Hill, 1998.

Levenson, Bob. *Bill Bernbach's Book: A History of the Advertising that Changed the History of Advertising*. Villard Books, New York, 1987.

Mackay, Hugh. *The Good Listener*. Pan Macmillan Australia, 1998.

Mackay, Hugh. *The Mackay Report: Media Roles*. Mackay Research Australia, 1992.

Mackay, Hugh. *The Mackay Report: Media Credibility*. Mackay Research Australia, 1995.

Manning, Jeff. *got milk? the book*. Prima Publishing, 1999.

Steel, Jon. *Truth, Lies, and Advertising: The Art of Account Planning*. John Wiley & Sons, 1998.

INDEX

INDEX

ABOUT THE AUTHOR

PHOTOGRAPH BY RUSSEL WONG

Jim Aitchison, an Australian, was former creative director of Singapore's legendary Ball Partnership and Batey Ads. He has won hundreds of awards (many for Chinese ads which he wrote), and judged some of the world's top shows. After twenty years in advertising, he is now an author and divides his time between Singapore and New York.